Thoughts on Preaching and Pastoral Ministry

THOUGHTS ON PREACHING AND PASTORAL MINISTRY

Lessons from the Life and Writings of James W. Alexander

JAMES M. GARRETSON

Reformation Heritage Books
Grand Rapids, Michigan

Thoughts on Preaching and Pastoral Ministry:
Lessons from the Life and Writings of James W. Alexander
© 2015 by James M. Garretson

All rights reserved. No part of this book may be used or reproduced in any manner whatsoever without written permission except in the case of brief quotations embodied in critical articles and reviews. Direct your requests to the publisher at the following address:

Reformation Heritage Books
2965 Leonard St. NE
Grand Rapids, MI 49525
616-977-0889 / Fax 616-285-3246
orders@heritagebooks.org
www.heritagebooks.org

Printed in the United States of America
15 16 17 18 19 20/10 9 8 7 6 5 4 3 2 1

Library of Congress Cataloging-in-Publication Data

Garretson, James M.
 Thoughts on preaching and pastoral ministry : lessons from the life and writings of James W. Alexander / James M. Garretson.
   pages cm
 Includes bibliographical references and index.
 ISBN 978-1-60178-413-1 (hardcover : alk. paper) 1. Alexander, James W. (James Waddel), 1804-1859. 2. Presbyterian Church—Biography. 3. Preaching. 4. Pastoral theology. I. Title.
 BX9225.A524G37 2015
 285'.1092—dc23
 [B]
                            2015027894

For additional Reformed literature, request a free book list from Reformation Heritage Books at the above regular or e-mail address.

Contents

Foreword vii
Preface xi

Introduction 1
1. Early Years: 1804–1821 7
2. Seminary Student: 1822–1824 17
3. Tutor at the College of New Jersey: 1824–1825 39
4. Licentiate: 1825–1827 63
5. Charlotte Court-House Church: 1827–1828 73
6. Trenton: 1829–1832 85
7. Editor: 1833 133
8. Professor of Rhetoric and Belles Lettres: 1833–1844 139
9. Duane Street Church: 1844–1849 205
10. Seminary Professor: 1849–1851 243
11. European Voyage: May–October 1851 267
12. Fifth Avenue Presbyterian Church: 1851–1857 279
13. Europe Again: May–October 1857 325
14. The Final Years: 1857–1859 333
15. God, My Exceeding Joy 363

Appendix 1 Presbyterial Charge: 1841 409
Appendix 2 "O Haupt boll Blut und Wunden" 413
Index 417

Foreword

James Waddell Alexander (1804–1859) is little known today, but he was a vibrant believer and faithful servant of God who received a great Christian legacy and passed it along to future generations. He was the son of Archibald Alexander (1772–1851), the mighty Presbyterian preacher and scholar who founded Princeton Theological Seminary. He was also the grandson (through his mother) of the physically handicapped preacher James Waddel (1739–1805), under whose preaching listeners were moved "as the trees of the wood are shaken by the winds."[1]

James W. Alexander took up his forebears' mantle and carried it well both in the pulpit and at the professor's desk. This book traces his extensive labors in both the spoken and the written word. He served God faithfully despite bouts of severe depression, which he called "that deep and horrible over-clouding of the soul."[2] His death at age fifty-five was a grievous loss to the church.

Charles Hodge summed up Alexander's ministry with three words: "He preached Christ" (Acts 9:20).[3] In one of his sermons, Alexander said that "God is love in such wise, that when we sinners look up to him through Christ we see nothing but love, as he who looks up to the

---

1. James W. Alexander, *Memoir of the Rev. James Waddel* (n.p., 1880), 31. Waddel's left hand was rendered nearly useless in a childhood accident, and he went blind later in life.
2. James W. Alexander, *Forty Years' Familiar Letters of James W. Alexander*, ed. John Hall (New York: C. Scribner, 1860), 1:43.
3. Charles Hodge, *Sermons Preached before the Congregation of the Presbyterian Church…1859* (New York: Anson D. F. Randolph, 1859), 3–22, quoted in *Pastor-Teachers of Old Princeton: Memorial Addresses for the Faculty of Princeton Theological Seminary, 1812–1921*, ed. James M. Garretson (Edinburgh: Banner of Truth, 2012), 135.

sun's flaming disk in mid-heaven sees nothing but a blaze of light."[4] Yet Alexander preached God's love together with God's justice as a gospel of propitiation. When "we were objects of punitive justice," God did not save us "at the expense of infinite right," but through the sacrifice of His Son; so that we learn to exclaim, "God is justice!" and "God is love!"[5]

The evangelical truth of the cross empowers worship, as Alexander recognized when he translated the German hymn of Paul Gerhardt (1607–1676)—which in turn was a translation of Bernard of Clairvaux (1090–1153)—into "O Sacred Head, Now Wounded." The doctrines of penal substitution and vicarious atonement were never better encapsulated than in these words from stanza 3:

> What Thou, my Lord, hast suffered, was all for sinner's gain:
> Mine, mine was the transgression, but Thine the deadly pain.
> Lo! here I fall, my Saviour! 'Tis I deserve Thy place;
> Look on me with Thy favor, vouchsafe to me Thy grace.

I also treasure Alexander's ministry because of his book *Thoughts on Family Worship*.[6] In a culture where so many Christian fathers are abdicating their responsibility to nurture their children in the teaching and discipline of God's Word (Eph. 6:4), such a book is a clarion call to return to the ancient practice of family devotions. One modern reviewer observes, "Alexander's book is solid food, yet it is easy to read."[7]

These examples are, as you will see when you read this biography, just some of the graces and gifts that God gave to this godly man. He was a scholar and the pastor of a large congregation in the bustling city of New York. He loved music. He preached regularly in the African-American church. He wrote a wide array of books, including many books for children.

Alexander was greatly talented in many ways and honed those skills through rigorous study. Yet the core of his personal greatness lies

---

4. James W. Alexander, *God Is Love* (1860; repr., Edinburgh: Banner of Truth, 1985), 18.

5. Alexander, *God Is Love*, 21.

6. James W. Alexander, *Thoughts on Family Worship* (Grand Rapids: Soli Deo Gloria, 2012).

7. David Wegener, "A Father's Role in Family Worship: A Review of James W. Alexander's Classic Work, *Thoughts on Family Worship*," *Journal for Biblical Manhood and Womanhood* 3, no. 4 (Winter 1998): 13.

not in ability or education, but in his holy submission to Jesus Christ. Alexander's friend, Theodore L. Cuyler (1822–1909), said of him after his death: "All his splendid attainments, all his many-sided and multiform life-work, he laid as an humble offering before the throne."[8] May this biography be used by the Holy Spirit to move us to do likewise.

—Joel R. Beeke
Puritan Reformed Theological
Seminary
Grand Rapids, Michigan

---

8. Theodore L. Cuyler, "James Waddel Alexander D. D. Address," in The Alexander Memorial, by *Archibald Alexander*, quoted in *Pastor-Teachers of Old Princeton*, 174.

Preface

My introduction to James W. Alexander occurred while a student at Covenant College in the late 1970s. I had recently become acquainted with the ministry of the Banner of Truth Trust and was eagerly reading everything I could find that they had published.

One sunny spring day I found myself immersed (better, *mesmerized*!) in reading a collection of bound articles from the early years of their monthly magazine. It was on that occasion that I first came across observations from Alexander on the pastoral ministry that would forever change my understanding of the role and responsibilities of the ministerial office.

Alexander argued eloquently for an educated ministry and for one that would be totally devoted to the preparation necessary to effectively fulfill the obligations which the office entails. His arguments were both convincing and convicting. At the time, I knew little about his life, ministry, or publications, but I determined that I would learn more about him in the coming days.

In the intervening years, Alexander's writings, as well as those of his father, Archibald Alexander, have pointed me back to a time and place when the pulpit ministries of our land were undergirded by a biblically informed theology of pastoral ministry that was faithful to the Scriptures and the high calling of the ministerial office. While culture-bound in the sense that all ministerial activity is exercised at a particular time and place, the bulk of their writings on the Christian life and pastoral ministry transcend the period in which they were produced inasmuch as any literature does that remains faithful to the timeless teaching of God's Word as revealed in the pages of the Old and New Testaments. With a number of J. W. Alexander's books currently in print, it seemed fitting to provide a digest of his life while highlighting some of his writings in order for today's reader of his works to better appreciate how God prepared and used his pastoral ministry to the benefit of the church and advance of His kingdom during the first half of the nineteenth century.

As always, I would like to thank my wife, Susan, and children (Asha, Trace, Michaela, Rebekah, and Isaiah, as well as my new son-in-law Gregory Johnsen) for their prayers, support, and interest in this project.

Mr. Ken Henke, Curator of Special Collections and Archivist, Princeton Theological Seminary, has again provided me with much-needed bibliographical assistance.

Thanks are also due to Mr. Gary Steward for his gracious willingness to finish writing a book he knew little about when first asked if he might complete the project in the case of my premature death. Alexander died at the age of fifty-five, the very age at which I began writing this book. But this year was different for me: Heart surgery and a separate surgery to remove a cancerous tumor left in question my ability (or possible availability!) to complete what was a nearly finished work but one that still needed some final touches. Gary agreed to complete the manuscript in case I could not. I assured him that one way or the other his name would end up in the preface—either by writing it in my place or by me mentioning his name in gratitude for his gracious willingness to assist if necessary!

The friendship and prayers of one of my former students Mr. William J. Nader remain a source of encouragement to the author which I trust has been reciprocated in equal measure throughout the years.

As with previous works, Mr. Jay Collier and the staff of Reformation Heritage Books have provided invaluable assistance in the birthing of a manuscript into a published text.

Special thanks are also due Dr. Joel R. Beeke for his kind foreword and interest in the writings of the men of Old Princeton. Happily, the experiential piety and preaching represented by men such as Alexander in the nineteenth century live on in the work of institutions such as Puritan Reformed Theological Seminary in Grand Rapids, Michigan, where Dr. Beeke serves as president.

It is the prayer of the author that Alexander's life will continue to be a source of inspiration and instruction for a new generation of ministers equally in love with Christ and passionate for the work of the pastoral ministry.

—James M. Garretson
Cambridge, Massachusetts

J. W. Alexander

I fear none of us apprehend as we ought to do the value of the preacher's office. Our young men do not gird themselves for it with the spirit of those who are on the eve of a great conflict; nor do they prepare as those who are to lay their hands upon the springs of the mightiest passions, and stir up to their depths the ocean of human feelings. Where this estimate of the work prevails, men even of inferior training accomplish much.... The pulpit will still remain the grand means of effecting the mass of men. It is God's own method, and he will honour it. The work done by Wesley and by Whitefield, and by Christmas Evans in Wales, could not have been accomplished by any other human agency—the press, for instance. In every age, great reformers have been great preachers; and even in the corrupt Roman Church, the most wonderful effects have been produced by preaching.... To be a great preacher a man must be nothing else.... The channel must be narrowed, that the stream may flow in a rapid current, and fall with mighty impression. Even the learning of the schools must undergo a great process of transmutation and assimilation, before it is suitable to be produced in the pulpit. Great is the difference, though little apprehended, between a theological dissertation and a sermon, on the same subject. The crude matter falls heavily upon the popular ear. Only the last exquisite results of mental action are proper for public address. Not that the truth of doctrine is to be neglected; this is the very substance of all good sermons, and of every sentence of them, even in their most impassioned parts; but it must have undergone a great change in the mind of the preacher, and present itself in a more popular form, with more of colour of imagination and warmth of passion, before it can reach the deep places of the heart with due effect.

—JAMES W. ALEXANDER

Introduction

Among nineteenth-century American Presbyterian pastors, few were held in as high esteem as James W. Alexander. Although he would die prematurely at the age of fifty-five, Alexander left a lasting influence on his generation and ones that followed.

Born in 1804, Alexander's lifetime witnessed the westward expansion of the United States, impacted by the industrial revolution on American commerce, expanding immigrant population, massive social problems associated with mushrooming growth in cities, and ever-sharpening sectional tensions within his country over the institution of slavery. He lived during a time when the United States was at war with England and later Mexico, dying just a few short years before his beloved country went to war with itself.

The firstborn son of well-known pastor, preacher, educator, and theologian Archibald Alexander, James W. Alexander would as a young man embrace the same Savior that his father had done many years earlier. Coming to faith in Christ at seventeen, few could have anticipated the impact that his life would leave on the American Presbyterian Church and the country at large. Educated at the College of New Jersey and the school which his father helped to found, Princeton Theological Seminary, Alexander's educational background served well to prepare him for the varied labors in which his life would be spent.

As a young man, Alexander sensed a call to the gospel ministry and devoted the remainder of his life to the living out of that divine commission. Early experience in pastoral ministry gained in Virginia would later be augmented by urban settings at Trenton, New Jersey, and New York City. While the majority of his life was spent in some form of pastoral ministry, intermittent years would see service as a tutor, editor of a denominational news magazine, and appointment as Professor of Rhetoric and Belles Lettres at the College of New Jersey. From 1849 to 1851, Alexander served as Professor of Ecclesiastical History and Church Government at Princeton Theological Seminary. Honorary doctor of divinity degrees were conferred from Lafayette College in 1843 and Harvard University in 1854.

Alexander had a multifaceted personality, capable of extreme emotional highs and lows. Early bouts of melancholy would remain a lifelong oppression with which he continually had to struggle. While his affliction with a melancholic disposition was never as severe as that of the well-known poet and hymn writer William Cowper, Alexander identified with Cowper's writings on the topic and found encouragement from them to press forward in the triumph of God's grace through the salvation he enjoyed in union with Christ. In Alexander's life, affliction became a means of redemptive grace that served to strengthen his spiritual fortitude even as it enlarged his sympathy for the suffering and sorrows of the people among whom he lived and served. A brilliant student, scholarly educator, master of multiple languages, polymath in learning, humorist, musicologist, prolific author, astute theologian, loving father, popular preacher, and caring pastor, Alexander was beloved by his generation and remembered long afterward by those whose lives he had touched.

While Alexander would surely have had a successful academic career before him had he chosen to pursue this professional path, his calling as a Christian led him to devote his talents to the work of the pastorate and related positions of editor and educator. Marked by quick wit and a deepening spirit of humility, Alexander died, as it were, to his earlier dreams of academic recognition and prestige which he longed for as a young man. Instead, he dedicated his talents, energy, resources, and ultimately his life to addressing the spiritual and physical needs confronting his generation. What began as a self-focused temperament while a teenager was transformed, by God's grace, into a life of unrelenting sacrificial service on behalf of others.

In this respect, Alexander's zeal for the spiritual welfare of his contemporaries knew no sectional boundaries between North and South, nor was it restricted by race, creed, or color. In his pastoral ministry, he sought to minister to people from every level of social strata. His regard for the rich was no higher than that of the poor. Men, women, and children from all classes of life—immigrants, citizens, and slaves—found themselves the objects of his pastoral affection. Whether it was in the incessant rounds of pastoral visits, catechetical instruction of the youth in his church and community, countless publications intended for the young and the working class, or the various organizations, agencies, and strategies to which he gave his undiminished support for alleviating the poverty and deteriorating social conditions of the cities in which he ministered, Alexander was unrelenting in his desire to "do good unto all men, especially unto them who are of the household of faith" (Gal. 6:10).

As a preacher, he was one of the greatest of his generation. Rich and poor, educated and ignorant, black and white alike—all found his preaching of spiritual benefit to their souls. While an extemporaneous preacher in style and preference, his published sermons were widely read and disseminated.

The most valuable legacy that Alexander offers for those interested in learning about his ministry is the vast library of material which he has left behind in the form of letters, occasional observations, novels, articles, essays, historical studies, sermons, and posthumously published material on preaching and the pastoral ministry. The scope and breadth of his interests is breathtaking. His literary output is enormous and beyond accurate assessment since his smaller writings and contributions were often published anonymously. Church historians, theologians, specialists in the classics, instructors in rhetoric, researchers of evangelical social activism in the nineteenth century, lovers of all things cultural, and students of ministerial biography and a biblical theology of pastoral ministry will find something of interest in Alexander. Specialized studies in any of these areas is certainly possible, and even warranted, as we seek to better understand the impact of Christian ministerial influence on church and society in the United States during the nineteenth century.

Despite the enormity of Alexander's influence, no biography of his life has ever appeared. To date, researchers have had to rely primarily upon the extensive correspondence in which Alexander engaged over a forty-year period with his lifelong childhood friend and later fellow minister of the gospel Dr. John Hall for piecing together the narrative of his life. Apart from a few funeral eulogies and mention in extant biographies on individuals from the period in which he lived, Alexander's letters provide the most extensive primary source material available for an understanding of his life and ministry.

Readers of Alexander's correspondence quickly realize that the letters contain (as letters do) a random series of observations, reflections, and commentary on any number of subjects—often totally unrelated to the sentence that preceded it or that follows. For obvious reasons, researchers of his life have had to burrow through extraneous material relevant for the information it provides on all kinds of matters though not always germane to the specific purposes of more focused topics of interest. The present study is intended to provide a condensed narrative of Alexander's life for understanding his approach to preaching and pastoral ministry. While numerous areas of his life and ministry merit further attention, it is the formation and development of his convictions on the role and responsibilities of the Christian ministry that is the focus of this study.

The biography of a minister's life is inseparable from the theology of ministry that his life embodies. The answer to the question about the way a man preaches is directly related to the reasons why he preaches. In this respect, we can learn as much about how God prepares a man for the work of the ministry through the challenges, doubts, struggles, and victories of the life of God in the maturing piety of his soul as we can from the public record of his preaching, writing, or pastoral activity.

Because all piety is personal in nature and development, I have attempted to allow Alexander opportunity to "speak for himself" at as many points as possible in order that the reader may enter into the spiritual pulsebeat that animated his life and actions. As Alexander would later highlight in his inaugural address as Professor of Ecclesiastical History and Church Government at Princeton Theological Seminary, this inner pulsebeat, or animated piety, is what gives rise to the principled convictions whose personal and public effects become the facts of which church history is the written record.

For these reasons, the massive correspondence in which Alexander engaged is invaluable for tracking the spiritual development of his life and the way in which it shaped his practice of pastoral ministry. In addition, his sermons, books, and especially his reviews also contain valuable personal statements that shed light on his character and convictions.

Readers will find themselves at times laughing alongside Alexander's humor or otherwise feeling sullen as they journey with him through periods of melancholy, physical illness, and bereavement. Alexander's frank and often temperamental remarks betray the integrity of spiritual transparency missing in the façades behind which many ministers hide.

His sense of the brevity of life and the future day of judgment informed his understanding of the kingdom horizons in which he exercised his ministry.

Bracing, heartening, and at times frustrating, the story of Alexander's growth as a Christian and development as a minister is the story of a man subdued by God's grace and a life marked by a growing conformity of character and outlook into the likeness of Christ. Alexander knew the love of Christ in his life and offered his love in return for all that Christ had become to him. For those whose privilege it is to serve as ministers of the gospel, his life and instruction provide much inspiration and wisdom for how to do pastoral ministry well and with all of one's heart.

His education in the College of New Jersey, in the close association of his family with the Theological school, and the comparatively few students of its first years, is to be regarded among the preliminary steps of the youth in the course of divine designation. That designation was as yet concealed; for whilst everything in the literary and religious life around him, in his own dwelling and in the public institutions and men which give fame to the village, was as favourable as outward circumstances could be to the highest intellectual excitement and the earliest religious impressions, it was not until his college course was closing, that he became thoroughly awakened to his great advantages and responsibilities in either respect. But even then, he was only in his seventeenth year. At that period, having been graciously brought to a clear apprehension of his spiritual condition, he made his first public profession of faith (April, 1821).

—JOHN HALL
October 9, 1859

Chapter 1

EARLY YEARS: 1804–1821

James Waddell Alexander was born March 13, 1804, in Louisa County, Virginia. The eldest son of Archibald and Janetta Waddell Alexander, James was privileged to belong to a home marked by Christian piety and strong affection for the work of the pastoral ministry.[1] Both his mother and his father came from families in Virginia with a legacy of piety extending back several generations.[2] Married in 1802, Archibald and Janetta enjoyed a happy marriage that provided an ideal environment for the upbringing of their children.[3]

---

1. For a biography of Archibald Alexander's life and ministry see James W. Alexander, *The Life of Archibald Alexander* (New York: Charles Scribner, 1854; repr., Harrisonburg, Va.: Sprinkle Publications, 1991).

2. The rich spiritual heritage of Christianity in Virginia has been well documented in nineteenth-century works published by William Henry Foote. For appreciative reviews of Foote's volumes see James W. Alexander, "Sketches of Virginia, Historical and Biographical," *The Biblical Repertory and Princeton Review* 22, no. 2 (April, 1850): 208–34, "Sketches of Virginia, Historical and Biographical," *The Biblical Repertory and Princeton Review* 28, no. 2 (April, 1850): 244–55. For a review on Virginia's history see James W. Alexander, "A History of Virginia, from Its Discovery and Settlement by Europeans, to the Present Time," *The Biblical Repertory and Princeton Review* 19, no. 2 (April, 1847): 224–35.

3. Janetta Waddell Alexander is eulogized in a biography by her son J. A. Alexander: "She had dark liquid eyes, and her face wore a look of repose, benevolence, good sense, and sometimes, when animated in conversation, of gentle raillery and humour. Her sensibility was extreme and tremulous. She had a sweet gayety of spirits, shaded at times by a pensive melancholy. She was, in every acceptation of the word, devotedly pious. Her laborious reading to her aged and sightless father had injured her own vision. She loved her Saviour, and the house, people, works, and word of her God. She was fond of religious books. No one could take a more unaffected pleasure in the writings of Flavel, Bates, and other non-conformists. It was her study to do good, and to make her home and the home of her husband and children cheerful and happy; nor did any one ever succeed better in such an attempt. Though naturally diffident and very sensitive, she loved company and when she pleased was one of the most entertaining persons in the world. Her children were all proudly attached to her." See Henry Carrington Alexander, *The Life of Joseph*

At the time of James's birth, his father was serving as the president of Hampden Sidney College in Prince Edward County, Virginia. By the time James was two years old, the family relocated to Philadelphia where his father had accepted a call to pastor the Third Presbyterian Church.

Having served as an itinerant evangelist, rural pastor, and most recently as a college president, Archibald Alexander's background was well suited for the work that he had undertaken in the growing metropolis of Philadelphia. A renowned preacher and talented theologian, Archibald Alexander's congregation prospered under his leadership. Gifted with a pastor's heart, he was intimately involved in the life of his congregation and the emerging needs of the urban environment in which he ministered. Pastoral visitation, catechetical instruction, Sunday-school programs, ministry to the poor, and innovative services on Sunday evenings marked the new pastor's philosophy of ministry.

It would not be long, however, before the General Assembly of the Presbyterian Church elected Archibald Alexander to serve as the first Professor of Didactic and Polemical Theology at the denomination's newly established seminary in Princeton, New Jersey. Founded in 1812, Alexander had played a major role in establishing the school and was an obvious candidate to serve as its first full-time faculty. Eager to preserve the Presbyterian Church's ministerial heritage and prepare for its denominational future, the founders of the seminary intended the school to be a nursery of piety and learning that would prepare coming generations of young men for the work of the gospel ministry as Presbyterian pastors, teachers, and missionaries.[4]

Addison Alexander, D.D., Professor in the Theological Seminary at Princeton, New Jersey (New York: Charles Scribner & Company, 1870; repr., Laurel, Mass.: Audubon Press, 2008), 1:1–2.

4. For a brief study of the issues that precipitated the founding of the seminary see Mark A. Noll, "The Founding of Princeton Seminary," *Westminster Theological Journal* 42 (Fall 1979): 72–110. For an introductory study of the seminary's history see William K. Selden, *Princeton Theological Seminary: A Narrative History 1812–1992* (Princeton: Princeton University Press, 1992). For an institutional history published in conjunction with the seminary's bicentennial see James H. Moorhead, *Princeton Seminary in American Religion and Culture* (Grand Rapids: Eerdmans, 2012). For a sympathetic analysis of the spiritual emphases that characterized the institutional atmosphere of the seminary training from its founding in 1812 until its reorganization in 1929 see David B. Calhoun, *Princeton Seminary, Volume 1: Faith and Learning, 1812–1868* (Edinburgh: Banner of Truth, 1994) and David B. Calhoun, *Princeton Seminary, Volume 2: The Majestic Testimony, 1869–1929* (Edinburgh: Banner of Truth, 1996). For a recent introduction to the men and theology that marked the institutional identity of "Old Princeton," see the fine study by Gary Steward, *Princeton Seminary (1812–1929): Its Leaders' Lives and Works* (Phillipsburg: P & R Publishing, 2014).

Although but a young lad when his family moved to Princeton, J. W. Alexander retained fond memories of his early childhood years in Philadelphia. In addition to the boyhood friendships that he formed, it was here that he first began "the study of Latin in the school of James Ross." A respected educator and "author of the best Greek and Latin grammars of his day," Ross was known for "the rigid accuracy with which he grounded his pupils in the rudiments of the classical languages."[5]

Upon arriving in Princeton, J. W. Alexander continued his study of the classical languages under leading educators in the community.[6] His instructors included the Rev. Jared D. Fyler, the Rev. James Carnahan (afterward the president of the College of New Jersey from 1823 to 1853), and the Rev. Daniel Comfort. Alexander also studied "in the school of Mr. James Hamilton, subsequently a Professor in the University of Nashville." Additional tutoring was received from students enrolled at the seminary. At age thirteen, Alexander "was admitted to the Freshman class in the College of New Jersey at the spring term of 1817."[7] The College of New Jersey was the premier educational training center for Presbyterian youth in the middle colonies from its founding in the 1740s and the school of choice for many Presbyterian families.

By the year of Alexander's matriculation, the school had undergone significant educational reform under the leadership of then President Ashbel Green.[8] In the years prior to Green's arrival, student campus behavior had deteriorated and the curriculum adjusted toward a more scientific focus, but this was at the expense of the training in ministerial development intended by the school's founders. The need for a change in presidency became obvious. Following the resignation of his predecessor the Rev. Dr. Samuel Stanhope Smith, Ashbel Green was elected as successor. Green became president of the college in 1812 and acted

---

5. *The Biblical Repertory and Princeton Review*, "James Waddell Alexander," Index Volume no. 1 (January 1870): 68.

6. J. W. Alexander would later write: "In the month of July 1812, Dr. Alexander arrived in Princeton, with his wife, then in the bloom and freshness of a health which endured to old age, and with four children, of whom the oldest was not nine years old." *Life of Archibald Alexander*, 357.

7. "James Waddell Alexander," 68.

8. For a detailed study on the college's history and institutional changes under Green's leadership see Mark A. Noll, *Princeton and the Republic 1768–1822: The Search for a Christian Enlightenment in the Era of Samuel Stanhope Smith* (Princeton: Princeton University Press, 1989).

quickly to reform the campus environment and revise the curriculum emphases. Besides his work at the college, Green also served as president of the seminary's board of directors. A towering figure in nineteenth-century American Presbyterianism, Green combined a strong passion for education with an equally strong commitment to the cultivation of piety among the student body.[9]

In addition to the faculty under whom he studied at the college, Alexander was also surrounded by an exceptional group of fellow students who would go on to establish their own distinguished careers.

> Among his classmates were several whose names have, like his own, become conspicuous in public life—such as Governor George W. Crawford, of Georgia; President Finley, of the College of South Carolina; Chief Justice and Chancellor Green, of New Jersey; Governor and Judge Haines, of New Jersey; Rev. Dr. Kirk, of Albany and Boston; Professor Lindsley, of the Medical College, District of Columbia; President Talmage, of Oglethorpe University; Messrs. Gholson, Iverson, and Rodney, members of Congress; President Z. Butler, of Mississippi College.[10]

It was during his second year at college that Alexander began a near lifelong correspondence with John Hall, a young friend from Philadelphia, "somewhat his junior, and still a schoolboy," which would continue for the next four decades.[11] During these years, some eight hundred letters were exchanged between the two correspondents—a selection of which was later published by Hall following Alexander's death in two volumes under the title *Forty Years' Familiar Letters of James W. Alexander, D. D.*[12] The collected letters provide not only a remarkable narrative of Alexander's

---

9. For a biography on Green see Joseph H. Jones, ed., *The Life of Ashbel Green, V.D.M.* (New York: Robert Carter & Bros., 1849). A review of Green's biography by Alexander appeared in the same year: James W. Alexander, "The Life of Ashbel Green, V.D.M., begun to be written by himself in his eighty-second year, and continued till his eighty-fourth; prepared for the press, at the Author's request, by Joseph H. Jones, Pastor of the Sixth Presbyterian Church, Philadelphia," *The Biblical Repertory and Princeton Review* 21, no. 4 (October 1849): 563–82.

10. "James Waddell Alexander," 68–69.

11. In the early years, Alexander's letters are as much newsy reports as they are spiritual missives intended to help secure Hall's salvation. The same applicatory focus may be found in later years, only now spoken in the context of the common salvation which they both shared.

12. John Hall, *Forty Years' Familiar Letters of James W. Alexander*, 2 vols. (New York: Charles Scribner, 1860; repr., Laurel, Miss.: Audubon Press, 2008).

spiritual development, but also a running commentary on current events and characteristics of nineteenth century culture.[13] One of Alexander's biographers notes:

> In such a series of letters is to be found, besides the greatest accuracy of the facts which belong to a memoir, the best exhibition that is possible, of the development of the writer's mind and character. It not only makes the writer the best biographer of himself, but *undesignedly* the best, and therefore the most unreserved, guileless, and complete. In this feature the Alexander "Familiar Letters" have scarcely a parallel in literature.[14]

The correspondence between the two friends began in May 1819 and continued until June 1859. Apart from a two-year hiatus between April 1820 and August 1822, the communications increased in frequency and volume.[15] Hall notes that the decrease in correspondence from 1820 to 1822 paralleled a period of soul-searching in Alexander's life. "It was in this interval that Alexander's mind became engrossed with the subject of his personal religion."[16] Although raised in a Christian home, Alexander had not yet come to embrace the faith of his parents. At this point in his life, his knowledge of Christ was intellectual and not personal. In the words of one writer, "He had been living without the Christian principle. He had not honoured his church birthright. For a time, 'he found no place of repentance, though he sought it carefully with tears.' But at length he discovered that it was not to be found by tears."[17]

Happily, the Spirit was active in Alexander's heart and would soon bring the young college boy to a place of genuine faith in the promises of

---

13. Alexander's letters also provide a window into the broader engagement with antebellum culture that marked faculty associated with the College of New Jersey and Princeton Theological Seminary during the early nineteenth century. See Gary Steward, "Old Princeton and American Culture: Insights from J. W. Alexander," *The Confessional Presbyterian* 8 (2012): 55–64.
14. "James Waddell Alexander," 69.
15. Alexander's letters embody the purposes for which he felt such personal correspondence should be written: "A letter, as the thought just now strikes me, should be as nearly as possible the transcript of one's common-talk; or perhaps a better description of a good, that is an acceptable letter, would be that it is a soliloquy in black and white, penned with the freedom of a private meditation, yet written for the eye of another, with whom the disclosures it contains, are just as safe as in their native bosom." Hall, *Letters*, 1:43.
16. Hall, *Letters*, 1:4.
17. "James Waddell Alexander," 69.

God's Word. Hall includes Alexander's reflections on the spiritual transition that took place at this time in his life:

> On September 3, 1820, walking across the field, hardly daring to ask for faith or repentance, these words burst upon my mind—"*Waiting for the moving of the waters.*" I saw myself the impotent man in a moment, and I thought that Christ had been saying to me, "Wilt thou be made whole?" hundreds of times in my hearing, but now it seemed to be addressed particularly to me. From that moment I felt able to trust my whole hope and life upon the Lord.[18]

Once a stranger to grace, Alexander had passed from a state of spiritual death and become a recipient of the eternal life that Jesus promises to all who put their trust in Him to be their Savior. Hall continues the narrative of Alexander's life following his conversion:

> At the end of this September he finished his college course, but delayed a public profession of faith until the next year; then the return of his birthday, and the death of a young friend, combined to make him feel the risk of further postponement. He was received to full communion by the session of the Princeton Church, March 30, 1821, and sat at the Lord's table for the first time on the following Sabbath, April 1st.[19]

A private entry in his journal made two weeks later on April 13 records Alexander's developing interest in the work of the pastorate. Although he felt called to the gospel ministry, he was conflicted as to whether he had the gifts necessary for public utterance. He writes, "When I look forward to future life, a dreary darkness presents itself. What am I qualified for? I never can, in conscience, embrace any other profession but the 'gospel of Christ;' but alas, where are my qualifications? I never, never can be a speaker."[20]

As time passed, Alexander came to realize that his assessment of his gifts was misguided. Apparently, Alexander compared himself to the great pulpit orators of his time and mistakenly concluded that he would not be successful as a preacher apart from similar gifts of eloquence. Hall records that "in a note written some time afterwards," Alexander's perspective had changed: "I thank God for having shown me that this

---

18. Hall, *Letters*, 1:4.
19. Hall, *Letters*, 1:4.
20. Hall, *Letters*, 1:4.

conviction was in some measure unfounded and hasty. Though I never can be eloquent, yet God's spirit may make me a useful preacher."[21]

In the months that followed, Alexander came under conviction for not having applied himself to his studies while a student at the college. He recognized the educational opportunities that were wasted and sought to make up for his delinquency in personal study.[22] An extended entry from August 23, 1822, describes his deepening sense of accountability:

> Since I last saw you, many strange and unexpected things have no doubt befallen each of us, and I have had a goodly share of vicissitudes, painful and pleasant, during the three years just elapsed, but whether any of them could give you any pleasure, I cannot say. I presume I need not tell you that my time spent in college ran sadly to waste; indeed, I cannot look back upon the opportunities of acquiring useful knowledge which I then abused without shame and regret. Like most brainless and self-conceited boys, I undertook to determine that such and such studies were of no importance, and made this an excuse for neglecting them, although the wise of every age have united in declaring their utility. I was foolish enough to suffer almost all my previous knowledge of classical literature to leak out *e cerebro* [from the brain], and consequently I found myself a much greater dolt when I was invested with the title and immunities of an A. B., than when I entered as an humble Freshman. I had acquired, not a vast amount of erudition, but an insufferable budget of silly opinions, self-conceited views of my own abilities, and innumerable vicious habits, which alone are sufficient to neutralize all the good which a college course can give in the way of knowledge. The labour of the two last years has but slightly repaired these injuries, and I have hardly reached the point which I ought to have attained, at the term of my collegiate race.[23]

Alexander's renewed interest in academic study coincided with plans to enroll as a student at Princeton Theological Seminary.[24] He viewed his

---

21. Hall, *Letters*, 1:4.
22. "He immediately applied himself with the greatest diligence to the branches of study he had neglected in college, and found it an easy task to recover the lost ground, under the excitement of what now seemed to him newly-discovered treasures." "James Waddell Alexander," 69–70.
23. Hall, *Letters*, 1:4–5.
24. "As to his future life he felt as if there were no alternative to the ministry of the gospel, because he saw no other occupation in which he could so fully devote himself to his redeeming Lord, and use his influence for good." "James Waddell Alexander," 70.

reading of the classics and metaphysics as preparatory for his program of theological study at the seminary:

> To proceed with my egotistical harangue, (for I have nothing better to give you,) I have devoted most of my time since to classical reading, and my eyes I think are opened in some measure to those beauties, which, blinded with ignorant self-sufficiency, I was unable to perceive formerly. It is the fashion of this superficial age to decry the study of ancients, and more so in America than in Europe, more among the idle and ignorant coxcombs of this day, than the men of science and taste. I had caught this song at college, and like other *graduated* fools I presumed to laugh at those authors who have been the models of taste, and fountains of polite learning, for more ages than we have lived years. Homer was a favourite butt for my ridicule. I have read the old fellow's Iliad twice through of late, with new pleasure at every opening, and it is my intention if my life be spared, to spend one hour *per diem* for the rest of my life in reading the classics. No doubt, this prosing must be offensive to you; my next letter shall be more taken up about present concerns, as I hope to receive something from you to serve as a cue for my response. If you are curious to know what I am now studying—I have been for some weeks upon metaphysics, another of my old despicables; I now am much enamoured with it. You know, doubtless, that I expect to enter the theological seminary this fall. I anticipate the course of theology with a great deal of pleasure; many of my best friends expect to enter with me, and the studies are such as suit my taste. Theology is certainly a noble science, inasmuch as its subjects are the most exalted in nature, i.e. the relations subsisting between man and his Maker. "This is that science," says *Locke*, "which would truly enlarge men's minds, were it studied, or permitted to be studied everywhere, with that freedom, love of truth and charity which it teaches, and were not made, contrary to its nature, the occasion of strife, faction, malignity, and narrow impositions."[25]

The "labour of the two last years" to which Alexander refers included not only personal study, but time spent with the young assistant instructor at the seminary Charles Hodge.[26] Alexander admits that when he began

---

25. Hall, *Letters*, 1:5–6.
26. Charles Hodge was a close friend of the Alexander family. Archibald Alexander functioned as a kind of surrogate father for Charles upon his father's death and was instrumental at a later time in encouraging Hodge to serve as an instructor at the seminary. Hodge would become one of the most influential theologians of the nineteenth

his study of the classics it was done "merely from a sense of their importance, and not from any love to them." As he engaged in a fresh reading of the classics and contemporary English poets, his appreciation for their writings deepened. A letter written on September 10 explains the new value that he attached to their works:

> Mr. Hodge and I devoted an hour each day to the study of the Latin and Greek writers, and continued this practice for eighteen months, during which time we had read several authors; and the effect has been a thorough revolution of my taste. I could now obey Horace's exhortation, and spend my days and nights in perusing these authors, but I do not think the time would be profitably spent. Of late, I have been engaged in reading our English poets, for whom I have a GREAT esteem. Cowper is my favorite among them all. He resembles very closely my other favorite Horace. As it regards pungency of satire, and close and powerful argument, I think these poets are unequalled by any of their own nations. If I except the odes of Horace, and a few blots in the satires, I think they are also parallel as to morals: I mean, of course, to measure each by the standard of the age in which he lived. Their faults are somewhat alike also; an apparent contempt of harmony of verse, where an idea would lose one morsel of strength by gaining in elegance. I hope you will determine not to forswear the reading of these authors as I did when I left college.[27]

Alexander enrolled as a student at Princeton Theological Seminary in November 1822. At the time he began his studies, the full-time faculty consisted of two professors, Drs. Archibald Alexander and Samuel Miller, and the assistant instructor, Mr. Charles Hodge.

Although small in number, the three men formed the core of what was to become one of the finest ministerial training centers on the North American continent during the nineteenth century. It was here that Alexander would be prepared for his future work as a gospel minister, educator, and author of important works of theology that would be kept in print long after he completed his earthly sojourn.

---

century and the principal purveyor of the seminary's philosophy of ministerial training for generations of theological students. For a contemporary biography of Hodge see Archibald Alexander Hodge, *The Life of Charles Hodge, D.D., LL.D., Professor in the Theological Seminary, Princeton, N.J.* (New York: Charles Scribner's Sons, 1880). For recent treatments of Hodge's life and ministry see Paul Gutjahr, *Charles Hodge: Guardian of American Orthodoxy* (New York: Oxford University Press, 2011); Andrew A. Hoeffecker, *Charles Hodge: The Pride of Princeton* (Phillipsburg: P & R, 2011).

27. Hall, *Letters*, 1:11.

Without being guilty of the enormity of eaves-dropping, I have by various chances heard the opinions of divers persons respecting myself, and if I am to judge of myself by these, I am truly an odd compound of qualities. "He's a tolerably clever fellow," say some; "but very eccentric." I acknowledge that I am a clever fellow, and also eccentric. As to the last attribute, I heartily wish I had none of it, and that my orbit was less elliptical. Like a comet, I am sometimes heated, and extravagant, indulging in untimely mirth; and soon, as you might prophesy, chilled with melancholy. Sometimes I am accused of unseasonable levity, and oftener of moroseness and obstinacy; so that, if I take all the advice which my kind friends so liberally bestow, I shall soon find myself in the predicament of the old man, who with his son carried the ass to market; you remember the fable. I have long since determined to shape my own course, without reference to the opinions of every counselor; if I can discover the path of duty, I hope I shall muster up courage to tread it. The advice of my parents, and those who have a right to counsel, I shall always deem invaluable. As to my habits, there are some which I cannot but deplore, but which I fear will cleave to me usque ad canitiem; among these I rank first, an unconquerable spirit of trifling, and levity; my natural temperament makes me ready at all times, upon all occasions, for any silly jest—(verbal jokes, I mean, I have no taste for "practical jokes"). Habits of idleness appeared deep-rooted in me when I left college; I have, however, happily acquired a taste for study; so that, as it is my greatest pleasure, I wish I could say that my improvement has been proportional to my labour; I seem to have been very laboriously doing nothing.

—JAMES W. ALEXANDER
September 27, 1822

Chapter 2

SEMINARY STUDENT: 1822-1824

The seminary had just completed its first decade when Alexander enrolled in the fall of 1822. Like many young men of his time who came from homes that valued a strong educational foundation, Alexander had benefited from a superior upbringing. Having completed studies at various academies and the College of New Jersey, Alexander was familiar with the rudiments of a classical training. Along with the personal mentoring which he had received from his father and Charles Hodge, he was uniquely prepared for the courses the seminary curriculum prescribed.

Although his preparatory training had been thorough, Alexander found his program of study demanding.[1] "My studies are overwhelming," he told Hall, "and as we study subjects rather than books, they are unlimited. I feel disposed to read all that I can on each subject, and when I have spent all my time thus, I find that I have only stepped upon the thresholds of these various apartments of science."[2]

Alexander enjoyed his life as a seminary student.[3] The institution had been a part of his family's prayers long before it was established. He found particular satisfaction in knowing the role that his father had

---

1. "My habits have changed considerably since I entered the Seminary. I have bidden farewell to ennui, spleen, hyp., and all that class of old hangers on: also to the flute, to romantic air-castles, and walks in groves, to the company of ladies—item to poetry, magazines, novel, &c., &c., too tedious to mention." Hall, *Letters*, 1:16.
2. Hall, *Letters*, 1:14.
3. "I said I was happy,—never more so in my life. I enjoy good health, good spirits, and I have a most comfortable room, and most delightful room mate. I never had so great a variety of excellent company before: Metaphysicians, Wits, Theologians, &c., &c. I have here dearly prized friends, who endear Princeton to me. Our studies are not burdensome, and far from being irksome." Hall, *Letters*, 1:14–15.

played in the school's founding and in his work as its first professor. "I love our institution so much," he remarked, "and am so happily situated in every respect, that I shall not be soon weary of my subject."[4]

In order to make the most of campus life, he took residency in seminary housing rather than living at home with his family.[5] New friendships were quickly formed.[6] He described the benefit of this:

> The greatest advantage which I experience from being in the Seminary, and this is increased by my being an inhabitant of the house is...that we live in a kind of literary atmosphere; all the conversation carried on here is of a literary kind; at table, in our walks, and wherever a cluster of us assemble, some lively discussion takes place which causes our time to fly very rapidly and pleasantly away. All our opinions are brought into the arena of free discussion, and we must defend them or relinquish them. Opinions founded upon ignorance, or prejudice, habits and manners which are unpleasant, and almost every eccentricity which is fostered during the course of a private education, is here likely to be rubbed off.[7]

---

4. Hall, *Letters*, 1:14.

5. A brief note following the departure of his roommate, Jared B. Waterbury, describes his campus housing: "I am now sole proprietor of this my little chamber. View me in imagination, seated in my chum's immense elbow chair, writing by the light of a shaded lamp, heated by a funereal looking stove just before me. Beginning at the south corner of my domicile, you observe first a row of shelves, containing all my little store of books, and many not my own, modestly covered by a gingham veil. In the same corner you may discern my spacious literary throne with all its appendages of drawers, &c. I need not direct your eyes to my scanty stock of chairs. A red desk standing in solemn guise among the sticks of fuel which lie in a capacious box, ready to feed the aforesaid stove. A high stool. A table. A mirror large enough to reflect my haggard features. An assortment of trunks, my own and Waterbury's. Three maps. A wash stand and appurtenances. A solitary picture to decorate my naked walls. A cluster of pantaloons in suspense. An axe and saw wherewithal our wood is cut. And finally, (though not least precious,) near to my room mate's couch is placed my lowly cot, into which wearied nature bids me presently creep." Hall, *Letters*, 1:17.

6. "In his own class, numbering about forty, and in the two other more advanced classes, making nearly one hundred in all, and in the still larger accessions of the two following years, he found in the Seminary circle all that could be desired of fellowship and stimulus in preparation for the sacred calling. The catalogues of those years present many names that were then preparing for the distinction that has since surrounded them. Bush, Barnes, Woolsey, Pressley, Kirk, Waterbury (his roommate), Peers, Brinsmade, Bethune, Proudfit, and Nevin, are among them, and scores of others who, if less known in church and college, in authorship and leadership, were among the most laborious and useful of pastors and missionaries." "James Waddell Alexander," 70.

7. Hall, *Letters*, 1:16.

A letter written to Hall on the "last day of 1822" highlights Alexander's daily schedule. His letter provides a valuable record of campus life at the seminary during the 1820s.

> I rise at half after six. Public prayers in the Oratory at 7. Breakfast at 8. From 9 to 9½, I devote to bodily exercise. From 9½ until 12, Study. 12–1, Exercise. Dine at one. 2–3, I usually devote to works of taste, and to composing. 3–4½ at Lecture. 4½ Prayers. Until tea, at Exercise. After tea, until 12 (at which time I close my eyes) Societies, study, &c.[8]

His letter also includes a listing of his weekly activities. Besides the formal instruction he received at the seminary, prayer meetings, sermons, and lectures at the college were a regular feature of campus life.[9]

> We recite twice in the week on Hebrew, once on Greek, once on the Confession of Faith, once on Biblical History. Hear Lectures once on Theology, (preparatory to the full and regular theological Lectures,) twice on Biblical history, once on the Criticism of the Original Scriptures, once on Jewish Antiquities. On Monday night, I attend a society for improvement in the criticism of the Bible; President, Mr. Hodge. On Tuesday night, I am at liberty to attend an evening lecture at the college. On Friday night, Theological Society, where questions in ethics and divinity are discussed. On Saturday night, a weekly prayer meeting. On Sunday we have sermons from our three professors, and Prof. Lindsly, in rotation.[10]

The training at the seminary was a unique combination of academic learning suffused with a strong interest in the practical application of biblical teaching for cultivating a life of piety. Students learned that growth in godliness was as much a matter of doctrinal conviction as it was a lifestyle marked by personal devotion toward Christ in all that He is and represents to His people. Personal and corporate worship were central to the students' experience in the preparation in which they were engaged in order to become leaders in Christ's church. Academic accomplishments

---

8. Hall, *Letters*, 1:16.
9. The college curriculum placed special emphasis on the interrelationship between piety and learning. For a representative message examining how piety and education were related in the college instruction during the 1820s, see Samuel Miller, *The Literary Fountains Healed: A Sermon, Preached in the Chapel of the College of New-Jersey, March 9th, 1823* (Trenton: George Sherman, 1823).
10. Hall, *Letters*, 1:15.

were to be conjoined to a life of sacrificial service in fulfilling the calling of the pastoral ministry.[11]

Founding faculty members Archibald Alexander and Samuel Miller brought to their classroom instruction a strong pastoral focus that enabled the students to learn the relevance of formal studies for the work of the gospel ministry.[12] Of particular importance was the example of Reformed experiential preaching which they modeled and taught to their students.[13] Their example as preachers and instruction in an experiential theology of preaching helped shape the students' understanding of the pulpit responsibilities they would one day assume.[14] Archibald Alexander was renowned as one of the great extemporaneous preachers of his time and became a powerful influence in shaping the preaching style students at the seminary would emulate.

---

11. For a primary source collection of sermons, lectures, articles, and essays on the theology of pastoral ministry which was taught at Princeton Seminary during its first century, see James M. Garretson, *Princeton and the Work of the Christian Ministry*, 2 vols. (Edinburgh: Banner of Truth, 2012). For a history of the teaching of practical theology at the seminary during the past two hundred years, see Gordon S. Mikoski and Richard R. Osmer, *With Piety and Learning: The History of Practical Theology at Princeton Theological Seminary* (Zurich: Lit Verlag, 2011).

12. For a biography of Miller's life, see Samuel Miller Jr., *The Life of Samuel Miller, D.D., LL.D., Second Professor in the Theological Seminary of the Presbyterian Church, at Princeton, New Jersey*, 2 vols. (1869; repr., Stole-on-Trent, Staffordshire, UK: Tentmaker, 2002).

13. Joel Beeke's observations on Calvin's preaching provide backdrop to the "experimental" theology of preaching taught at Princeton Theological Seminary: "Experimental or experiential preaching addresses how a Christian experiences the truth of Christian doctrine in his life. The term experimental comes from *experimentum*, meaning trial, and is derived from the verb, *experior*, to know by experience, which in turn leads to 'experiential,' meaning knowledge gained by experiment. Calvin used experimental and experiential interchangeably, since both words indicate the need for measuring experienced knowledge against the touchstone of Scripture. Experimental preaching seeks to explain in terms of biblical truth how matters ought to go, how they do go, and what is the goal of the Christian life. It aims to apply divine truth to the whole range of the believer's personal experience as well as in his relationships with family, the church, and the world around him." Joel R. Beeke, "William Perkins on Predestination, Preaching, and Conversion," in *The Practical Calvinist*, ed. Peter A. Lillback (Fearn, Ross-shire: Christian Focus, 2002), 207. For a recent treatment of Perkins's model of ministry and theology of preaching, see W. B. Patterson, *William Perkins & the Making of a Protestant England* (Oxford: Oxford University Press, 2014).

14. For a study on Archibald Alexander's theology of preaching, see James M. Garretson, *Princeton and Preaching: Archibald Alexander and the Christian Ministry* (Edinburgh: Banner of Truth, 2005). For a related study examining Miller's instruction on preaching and the work of the pastoral ministry, see James M. Garretson, *An Able and Faithful Ministry: Samuel Miller and the Pastoral Office* (Grand Rapids: Reformation Heritage Books, 2014).

In conjunction with the example that the faculty provided, students were introduced to major figures in church history who modeled the kind of preaching most valued. Among the many preachers identified—men such as Luther, Calvin, the Puritans, Whitefield, Wesley, and influential colonial preachers such as Edwards—the Tennents, Davies, and others were presented as exemplary of the model of preaching Archibald Alexander and Miller recommended. While their styles varied, a number of these individuals practiced an extemporaneous approach to preaching often delivered with great benefit to their hearers.

Alexander's appreciation for an extemporaneous preaching style also developed while he was a student at the seminary. Of the three primary models in vogue—the reading of a manuscript, a memorized recitation, or an extemporaneous delivery that was preceded by a careful study of the text and consideration for the words to be used in the act of preaching—Alexander preferred the latter. It is perhaps not unexpected that having sat under his father's preaching for so many years and having observed the power of his extemporaneous delivery that Alexander would have embraced this approach.

His enthusiasm for this style of preaching is highlighted in his correspondence to Hall. Alexander informed Hall that he was gratified to learn of the growth in extemporaneous preaching taking place in the areas in which they lived. "I am happy to observe by the public prints as well as by private information, that extemporary preaching is becoming more and more common, even in the frozen East and North, and that the opposition to the cold, unnatural, modern way of pleading with dying sinners, is increasing."

In addition to the formal instruction which the seminary provided, Alexander found the debate societies in which he participated valuable training for learning the art of public speech. At one point he writes:

> Lawyers are not often heard to complain of an inability to extemporize, nor should a clergyman; and he who does is unfit for the pulpit. This change is peculiarly consolatory to me. I never expect to be able to read a sermon with any life; and as to committing to memory, I would rather write ten sermons than get one by heart. Upon this ground, I reckon our debating societies among the most interesting and important institutions about our Seminary.[15]

---

15. Hall, *Letters*, 1:37–38.

While Alexander appreciated the academic atmosphere at the seminary, his letters also demonstrate the strong emphasis that he placed on the cultivation of personal piety in preparation for ministerial service. "But amid all my comforts," he said, "I am miserable unless when I am enabled to found my satisfaction and contentment upon a broader basis than any thing temporal. I find no substantial unmingled pleasure except in a conscience void of offence; which that I may always possess is my earnest and reigning desire." Alexander hoped Hall would not be offended by his frequent references to the benefits of a religious life with respect to his desire to see Hall's conversion. "I know very well how repugnant it is to any one of nice feeling to have religion drummed into his ears, but I feel assured that a *word* in its favour will not offend you. I should be unworthy of the title of friend, if I did not endeavour in some feeble measure to make my friends partakers of the greatest happiness I can conceive of."[16]

Testimony to God's Grace

In the exchange of letters that took place between himself and Hall, Alexander often expressed concern over his friend's spiritual condition. During the early years of their correspondence, Hall was not a Christian but still open to conversation about the topic. Eager to respond to Hall's inquiries, Alexander took every opportunity to talk with him on the subject of salvation.

Writing to Hall at the end of January 1823, Alexander provided a detailed and thoughtful analysis on the subject of religious inquiry and why it is that men often refrain from coming to Christ for the salvation that they may receive through Him. It is a marvelous summary of biblical teaching, and Alexander was but eighteen years old when he penned the following words to his friend:

> I rejoice at the hint you have given me, that you do not feel that unmanly and dastardly antipathy to the contemplation of the noblest of all objects,—the Great First Cause, and of the relations subsisting between Him and us. Why is it that the most sublime of all sciences, the science of man considered as an immortal being, and of God as the author of that immortality, be shoved aside on all occasions from the mind's view, and thrust, whenever practicable,

---

16. Hall, *Letters*, 1:16.

into oblivion? Is it because our interest in this subject is small—our personal interest? because these truths are merely speculative, and have no bearing upon our future and present happiness? because the importance of the subject is small? because life is so long as to warrant the hope that a better occasion for considering it will occur? because the addition of years is likely to take away our reluctance to consider it candidly? because we are not at all criminal in neglecting it? because our criminality is lessened by delay? I think that none of these are the arguments which keep us from its investigation. A real though hidden hatred of those truths which condemn us, and curtail our pleasures; a feeling that the gate to heaven is a strait, a narrow gate, and that few enter it on account of various encumbrances, these things keep our minds from viewing the truth aright. Till we are willing to sacrifice pride, vanity, love of fame and pleasure, and all love of created things to the pure unalloyed love of God himself, we must remain without the gate; an agony is requisite to enter it. This is a hard doctrine; but the kingdom of God suffereth violence, and so we are informed from the source whence all our knowledge of these things flows. The Scriptures represent man as a rebel, a lover of himself rather than of God; they command him instantly to repent, and all means are provided to enable him to know God's will. But it is useless to speak of means to attain any end when that end itself is hateful. The man of the world desires to be happy, but he does not desire to be happy in the way of God's commandment, in the way of self-denial, humility, and godly sorrow and fear. I am not at liberty to say that it is an easy thing to become a Christian. It may be easy to a being, if such there be, who has no sins to forsake, no pride to vanquish; who can, without any reluctance, crucify every evil affection and unruly desire, and live agreeably to the gospel. Some one may say, "Who does this? no man is sinless" granted, but none was ever a Christian who did not *desire* to do it.[17]

Perhaps most interesting is the connection Alexander makes between belief and behavior. He recognized that there is a moral dimension to knowledge, but also that sinful propensities will prevent men from coming to knowledge of the truth as it is revealed in the pages of the Bible and person of Jesus Christ because of the moral change that will be required in how they conduct their lives. Alexander continues:

---

17. Hall, *Letters*, 1:18–19.

Many are prejudiced against the Gospel without knowing what it teaches. No man ever CANDIDLY and PERSEVERINGLY studied the system of truths represented in the Old and New Testaments without finding his belief in them follow. Where there is belief, *real, firm belief,* that belief will result in corresponding *affections;* these affections necessarily lead to a holy life.[18]

In an effort to personalize his conversations with Hall, Alexander would illustrate from his own experience the profound changes that had taken place in his life since he became a Christian. His correspondence is quite candid about his former manner of life, and while descriptive in nature, his letters were clearly intended to assure Hall that although he had been intellectually and spiritually in the same place, all he once lived for was now surpassed in the relationship he enjoyed with God through Christ.

A letter written on March 1, 1823, provides a descriptive account of Alexander's student days and how God providentially intersected his life during his time at college. Alexander's testimony also serves as an evangelistic invitation to Hall to join him in his new life in Christ. "I often recall," Alexander mused, "a merry circle of careless college blades seated about 'the witching time of night' around a Nassau fire, by the way a pre-eminently good one, enveloped in fragrant clouds, enjoying all that flow of youthful hilarity and good humour, which a release from irksome duty engenders." "Perhaps I feel too much pleasure in contemplating these old scenes," he remarked, "but in my hours of twilight musing, and castle-building, I often read in a bed of glowing coals, the almost faded story of these old times, and pictured to myself the future various destinies of my old friends and classmates. But these joys, though they were sweet when I was in the midst of them, vanish in comparison with others which I experienced within those same walls." He continues:

> It was there that, I humbly trust, my eyes were first opened to see the true value of eternal things; there I first saw with clearness, the awful nature of the rebellion which I was waging against my best friend and sovereign; and I there first determined to give up all hopes of happiness from the world, and to seek it in religion. I need not tell you that my determinations and resolutions have been broken, and unfulfilled, and that I find every day the truth of that

---

18. Hall, *Letters,* 1:19.

solemn declaration, that the carnal mind is enmity against God, and is not, nor can it be, subject to his law. At the time of which I speak, I enjoyed happiness which I can find no words to express, and which has been lost only because I have so often returned to seek my consolation from mere earthly enjoyment. There cannot certainly be on earth any greater pleasure than to see without doubt, oneself condemned justly by God's law, and at the same time saved *freely* by the sovereign mercy of God in Christ. The satisfaction which I then felt in committing all my cares and concerns, my soul and body, into the hands of a Saviour whose infinitely lovely character I then saw, I never expect to receive from any other source. I remember that at that time, I looked back with unspeakable astonishment at the carelessness and indifference with which I had viewed the realities of another world; with what calmness I could contemplate all the particulars of my unfeeling ingratitude to God, and I remember that I then thought, that if at any time I had seriously and soberly considered these things for one hour, I could not have viewed them any longer with apathy. The friendships which I formed under these circumstances, are the closest and most tender I have ever known; and I feel attached to these friends in a way which I never knew any thing about before. Perhaps you may ask, "Does religion make you happy?" Alas! If I possessed religion in its purity, unalloyed, I should be perfectly happy; but I do not; my soul is still attached to the beggarly elements of this world, and I fear most deeply the force of divine truth, that is, when I feel myself most deeply a lost sinner, when I see the hellish blackness of sin, and the infinite loveliness of the divine character, then I feel most happy. I have known seasons when I could willingly have given up my life, and departed to enjoy the most unspeakable raptures of the heavenly state; when I could so unreservedly devote myself to God as to be willing to live or die, to go to the ends of the earth, or dwell in obscurity just as he pleased, to say *ex animo*, Thy will be done, and at such times, I have felt more unmixed bliss in one half hour than in a month as I commonly spend it.[19]

As if to make certain Hall had grasped the implications of all that he had just said, Alexander's letter concludes with a series of implied hortatory applications. Without wishing to overstep the literary proprieties appropriate to such exchanges, Alexander pleaded Hall's indulgence for his extended observations:

---

19. Hall, *Letters*, 1:19–21.

No reasonable excuse can be given by any man for not loving supremely the most adorable perfect being in the universe. God calls upon all men now to repent, and has sanctioned his command by most terrific threats, and alluring promises. But I need not tell you these things. You have doubtless heard them urged powerfully and repeatedly, and I am but trespassing upon your patience.[20]

Glimpses of Early Melancholy

While Alexander was eager to evangelize his young friend, he was not hesitant to speak openly about some of the personal struggles he faced. Like many young people his age, Alexander wrestled with matters of identity and the problem of depression. In his case, the turbulent emotional highs and lows he experienced would not be outgrown with increasing age and maturity. Correspondence from early April 1823 mentions the incipient melancholy that had begun to afflict Alexander.[21] The carefree innocence of youth was also beginning to give way to the ordinary routine of daily life and anticipation of the responsibilities that he would one day undertake as an ordained minister. He writes:

> When I walk for exercise, I usually plunge into the thick woods to the east and south-east; I am fond of such roaming, especially at this season, when nature is beginning to resume her verdant drapery. I have indeed lost much of the *romance* which formerly entered so deeply into my character; but I still like to indulge sometimes in moonlight reveries, and ramble through dark and melancholy groves, or to catch the sweet breath of rising morn upon some gentle hill; but I soon ejected from any such elevations of fancy by the sober realities of *life as it is*. The great pressure of studies, and the solemn prospect of the responsible duties which I expect before long to assume, dispel those airy visions which will sometimes rise before me in the shape of multiform delightful scenes of "fairy-land." A

---

20. Hall, *Letters*, 1:21.
21. An earlier allusion can be found in correspondence at the end of January 1823: "I can assure you that I am in no humour for joking this morning. My old complaint the *blues* has come upon me like a strong man armed. Misanthropy is a sin which threatens at times to destroy not my own comfort only, but that of my friends around me. I despise it, and I loathe it, and yet, paradoxical and inconsistent creature, I hug it to my heart. I cannot say in truth that I hate many things just now; but truly I am depressed; devoured by spleen, and fostering a crabbed, morose, churlish, silly, girl-like, sinful despondency." Hall, *Letters*, 1:17–18.

dark cloud of melancholy sometimes casts a shade over my horizon, but it is only for a moment; my greatest struggles are with a childish levity, and love of joke, and quip, and jollity, which I would gladly leave behind me in the regions of boyhood.[22]

The first of many references to melancholy, Alexander's affliction would continue to be a source of consternation throughout the remainder of his life.

Exhortations to a Life of Piety

Writing to Hall on August 29, 1823, Alexander spoke about how to make the most profitable use of his time upon completion of college. Hall had devoted himself to his college studies in preparation for a legal career but had not yet made a profession of faith. Both correspondents had a common interest in literary acquirements, but only Alexander understood the potential threat that zeal for intellectual recognition was to the active pursuit of piety. An overemphasis on study could also be destructive to one's health.[23] Illustrating his points from personal experience, Alexander urged his friend to pursue a life of piety as a matter of first importance. Piety, Alexander assured his friend, is beneficial both for the present life and the age to come:

> Your feelings upon the occasion are natural, for the day of one's graduation is, so to speak, the day of initiation into the toils and mysteries of manhood. You speak as though your future pursuits were entirely undetermined. This is well; the danger in this age is of hurrying prematurely into the bustle and responsibility of public life. You appear to think of devoting a year or two to private study. If this is your plan let me exhort you to procure as many restraints and *stimuli* as you can; either by the superintendence of some literary friend, or by associating some companion in your studies. This I say upon the supposition that your character and feelings are like mine, and like most young men. It is difficult for one who feels himself entirely at leisure to exercise that decided resolution, and persevering self-denial without which it is impossible to make literary attainments. From

---

22. Hall, *Letters*, 1:22.
23. "An imprudent application to study during the first weeks of summer, and neglect of regular exercise, entirely unnerved me, rendered studying highly perilous, and drove me from my books to wander hither and thither in quest of health and spirits." Hall, *Letters*, 1:24.

experience which is now the subject of bitter regret, I know that the temptations to gratify imagination and taste and idle curiosity at the expense of mental discipline are almost irresistible.[24]

Alexander's letter concludes with an appeal to Hall to pursue a relationship with God. He knew from his reading of Scripture that "a friend loveth at all times" (Prov. 17:17), and that "there is a friend that sticketh closer than a brother" (Prov. 18:24). His correspondence with Hall exudes these qualities and bears testimony to how friendship is exercised in the context of evangelistic importunity.

> I shall not ask forgiveness for suggesting, what has no doubt suggested itself to you, the importance of forming moral as well as intellectual character at this critical point of time. Religion, that bugbear of the thoughtless and the voluptuary, and the laughing-stock of "the many" who know it only by name, is after all that can be said, the only safeguard to virtue, and the only source of real tranquility of mind. Aside from the peace occasioned by the quelling of an angry conscience, and the release from fears of future evil, the positive joys of religion are truly unspeakable. The lofty and sublime contemplations, the solid and rational hopes, the intimacy with Him who ruleth over all, the remedy for every care which piety professes to afford, and which its votaries say it does afford, surely are sufficient recommendations to one who looks beyond the outskirts of this limited world.[25]

A letter written the following month in late September 1823 describes the shock Alexander felt in learning about the death of one of his close friends from college Edward Thomas. Thomas was the sixth student to die from Alexander's graduating class, and it proved to be an unsettling moment in Alexander's life. His reflections on his friend's premature death shed light on his growing appreciation for the benefits of a renewed conscience and the hope that it provides in anticipation of one's own impending death.

> A call so loud to me to be ready to depart also, has roused my sluggish mind to look around me for a moment; but alas the return to slumber is so much more natural to wicked man, that I am led to think that in most cases, the repetition of such alarms, unless

---

24. Hall, *Letters*, 1:25.
25. Hall, *Letters*, 1:25–26.

effectual at first, seems only to deaden the feeling to all their influence. Death is not dreadful to me now, what new terrors may be disclosed by the dark and melancholy scenes of a sick chamber, and the more dark forebodings which are the harbingers of this imperial destroyer, I know not. My life and virtues and merits are so utterly destitute of having any value, intrinsic, or as purchasers of immortality, that, were my hopes based on them in any degree, I would be willing to take the shortest road out of this life. But I do daily see an increasing glory in that Saviour who was once to me an object, to say the least, of indifference, which declares him to be my ground of confidence, and my only source of joy. I confess that few, very few of my thoughts are fixed on him; I say few with reference to the degree in which I ought to fix my eye upon him, but joy, real and unequivocal joy, I never have, or expect or desire to have in any other.[26]

Alexander's observations continue by making note of how becoming a Christian results in a redirection of the affections in relation to the truth of the gospel message and the person of Christ. Building upon points made in an earlier letter relating to the religious "affections," Alexander wanted Hall to know how he had been delivered from his spiritual darkness and unbelief. He writes:

I know that there is not any exercise of those affections (which are ever seeking exercise somewhere) so truly social and endearing as the exercise of them upon the enlivening truths and realities of Jesus Christ's gospel. I know that there is an exquisite satisfaction in that kindly feeling which Christianity encourages and keeps alive. And I know that had this side of the picture met my eyes some years ago, instead of the harsh lines which are sometimes foolishly exhibited, that I should not have so long like a condemned criminal shrunk and retreated with such mental imbecility from all that bore the stamp of religion. Godliness is profitable for *all things*; having the promise of this as well as the coming life.[27]

Alexander's evangelistic testimony began to have an effect on Hall's conscience. In a letter written the following month, Alexander was elated to learn of Hall's continuing interest in conversation of a religious nature. Slowly, but deliberately, Alexander had "seeded" his friend's thoughts about the salvation that can be found in Christ. As their correspondence

---

26. Hall, Letters, 1:27.
27. Hall, Letters, 1:27–28.

shows, he was now in a position to speak more explicitly about the application of scriptural teaching to Hall's life. General statements about religion give way to more detailed instruction on the way of salvation and what it means to have one's life rooted in Christ. "The openness and candour with which you have met my proposals of a new set of topics for our correspondence, have gratified me very much," Alexander stated. "I rejoice to find that the important interests of religion have gained so much of your attention, and would beg you not to suffer this attention to decrease or to remain without increase." Writing in response to Hall's inquiry regarding the challenges one can encounter in seeking a relationship with God, Alexander directed his friend in the following manner:

> I entertain no shadow of a doubt that a patient and scriptural method of seeking God's favour was never yet fruitless. Indeed, while I profess to have faith in the word of God, no truth can be plainer; it rests on the immutable word of Jehovah. The pursuit may be a dark and tedious and discouraging one, and yet compared with the glory of that "αμαραντινον τῆς δοξης στεφανον," which is the prize held forth, how do all these labours dwindle to nothing. Among a host of Scripture passages, look at these: Ps. lxxxvi. 5. Joel. ii.32. Rom. x. 12, 13. The search must be indeed most sincere. Compare the petitions which you have offered to God for this great favour with what you may conceive to be the cries of one pleading for his life, and then compare the temporal and the eternal life. Deut. iv. 29. Jer. xxix. 13. For encouragement, for truths calculated to awaken as well as to sooth the conscience, for advice and direction infinitely more infallible than that of a fellow worm, fly to the precious volume of God's word. There, be assured, a prayerful, indefatigable, daily search will open to you supplies suited to all your necessities.[28]

An entry in Alexander's correspondence from a few months later urges the importance of approaching the study of the Scriptures with a simple childlike faith in order to benefit from its instruction.[29] Alexander's

---

28. Hall, *Letters*, 1:28–29.
29. An earlier correspondence recommends the counsel of Thomas Chalmers on this topic: "We must bring a free and unoccupied mind to the exercise. It must not be the pride or the obstinacy of self-formed opinions, or the haughty independence of him who thinks he has reached the manhood of his understanding. We must bring with us the docility of a child if we want to gain the kingdom of heaven. There must be no garbling of that which is entire, no darkening of that which is luminous, no softening down of that which is authoritative or severe. The Bible will allow of no compromise." Hall, *Letters*, 1:29.

reading of philosophers and biblical critics had shown him how "learned" men can obfuscate the simple teaching of the Bible's message when its content is repackaged into a skeptical philosophical framework. Mentally exhausted from a "day of close confinement" to metaphysical and ethical subjects, Alexander found satisfaction in remembering that Scripture has no need of "philosophical refinements" in order for its message to be grasped. His observations were intended to help Hall approach the study of Scripture with a proper spiritual disposition in order that he might experience the power of God's Word in his life:

> Clarke and Leibnitz, Hume and Brown, have led me an enchanting, but dangerous flight through the clouds of speculation by day, and have danced before my brain in the phantasms of the night. It is my satisfaction to know after all the mortification consequent upon a view of the inscrutable nature of many questions in morals, that the path to heaven and perfect unalloyed enjoyment of the truth is open to the humblest and simplest child of Adam. The New Testament, while it inculcates a system unparalleled for its sublimity and consistency, is obscured by no sophistical refinements, and defies the attempts of philosophy to complete or systematize it more fully. The general impression left by an hour's humble reading of God's word is unlike the effect of any other work. It is a feeling of calm submissive tranquility. I am inclined, therefore, to think that nothing tends so directly to the formation of a truly Christian character as the continual, prayerful, unquestioning perusal of the Scriptures. They do not present naked doctrines; they are addressed to the natural feelings, and they affect our hearts imperceptibly but powerfully. Let me pray you to be a diligent student of this holy book. He who takes delight in the Bible *must* imbibe its spirit; and its influence, I think, is all-powerful. After the learned prating of philosophers, the sweet and modest words of inspiration fall on my ear like melody.[30]

In a related context, Alexander urged his friend not to let speculative questions impede his interest in learning the Bible's message or to question the propriety of God's sovereignty in the manner in which He effectually calls sinners into fellowship with Himself through the propitiatory atonement of Christ's death. It may be that Hall was wondering the extent to which one had to embrace the entirety of the doctrinal system represented in the confession and catechisms of the Presbyterian

---

30. Hall, *Letters*, 1:30.

Church in order to be saved, or that he questioned certain of its formulations. Alexander wisely centered Hall's thoughts on the issues pertaining to a sinner's need as the matters of primary importance to which Hall should direct his study at this stage of his inquiry:

> "The purest churches under heaven," says our Confession, "are subject both to mixture and error," and therefore I should not feel secure in adopting every sentiment of our church, while I consider the system called Calvinistic, as the only system founded on the obvious meaning of the Bible, the only system reconcilable to a sound philosophy, and the most consoling system to one who feels himself a lost sinner. I say this after having once risen against the doctrine of Rom. ix. 15, with all the enmity of a rebellious heart. I trust that God has convinced me that no "foreknowledge of my conduct" was his motive for rescuing me from the slavery of sin; (alas, had this been the case, my conduct would have secured me eternal wrath,) and that "not according to our works, but according to his own purpose and grace, which was given us in Christ Jesus before the world began." I wish to impose my private sentiments on no man; as I have already said, go to the Bible, and believe not one word which is not there written. But I entreat of you, let not metaphysical speculations, or prepossessions antecedent to inquiry, forestall your judgment.[31]

Alexander revisited the topic of academic learning in a later correspondence with Hall. He wished to reaffirm his interest in literary culture, but his motivation for its acquisition was different than that of Hall. In Alexander's case, it was being pursued in preparation for the work of the Christian ministry. Alexander had surrendered his life and future to Christ and wanted his friend to know of the difference it could make for Hall if he would pursue the path upon which Alexander had embarked. Alexander wrote the following words for young men the same age as himself at the time, and his thoughts must have come with great force to Hall at a stage of life when ambition and worldly affluence were goals within reach to one of his background:

> I do desire to see learning prosper, to be learned myself; I desire to be happy in the good things of this world, so far as consistent with virtue; I desire to commend Christianity to the world by all that charm which courtesy and cheerfulness can give to as rude a

---

31. Hall, *Letters*, 1:32–33.

piece as I,—yet I could curse myself, (however unfaithful I may be now, or alas may be hereafter,) if I thought that I could ever consent to make merchandise of the cross, by bartering it for aught of earth. My wish is, in my humble measure, to make every effort tend to one point, the establishment of Christ's kingdom on earth, and in the hearts of men. And O that future devotedness might take the place of the worldly spirit that has, and does prey upon my peace. It would give me unfeigned joy, my dear friend, to see you brought to this noble stand which I wish we may both reach,—to renounce the joys, honours, cares of the present life, for the sake of living for God. Our only excuse, our only inability is our guilty, low, irrational love of the world and of self. God demands our hearts this moment. As a sovereign he thunders his requisition, as a father he whispers pardon, reconciliation, assistance. And what shall we mention to Him as the object of our preference to his service? Pleasure? gain? ease? glory? Life is a vapour, and we know it. Joy is fleeting. Let us determine, at least, to perish in search of God. I trust you suspect me of no wish to lead you to any system. Read God's word, without comment, without prepossession, without cavil.[32]

On the Brevity of Life and Making Plans for the Future

The seminary community continued to be visited with serious illnesses during Alexander's time of study. In a letter written during late winter, 1824, Alexander described the circumstances that had befallen two of his classmates. "One of our students has been very near death with the bilious colic, but has recovered. In the near prospect of death, he manifested great joy in the hope of soon meeting face to face the Saviour whom he had taken as his portion. Death, to him, seemed despoiled of all that is terrific," Alexander reported. "Bucknall, another of our students, is lying extremely ill with what appears a rapid consumption. Little hope is entertained of his recovery."[33]

The prospect of death made Alexander ponder his own future and query whether any of his plans to serve Christ in pastoral ministry would come to pass.

---

32. Hall, *Letters*, 1:34–35.
33. Hall, *Letters*, 1:35.

So many friends, companions, and classmates have sunk around me, that I seem most loudly called on to be ready also, as being ignorant of the day or hour when my soul shall be demanded. Would to God that I might be excited to do what is remaining to be done with all my might,—to become more holy, and to strive not to be taken from the earth without having done any thing for the benefit of my fellow-men. My qualifications for the ministry are so slight and defective that I shudder at the thought of being in eighteen months invested with that sacred office. So much ignorance, inexperience, and immaturity, seem ill to befit the character of a teacher and pastor. The truth is, I feel too young; and could I dispose of my time profitably, I should be glad to intermit my regular theological course for a year or two.[34]

In one of the final letters sent while a student at the seminary, Alexander congratulated Hall on completion of his college course and entrance into the practice of law. "Success to you, and all your future clients," he wrote. While he was proud of his friend's achievements, he remained concerned about the spiritual challenges Hall would face in the legal profession. His letter encourages Hall to be vigilant in these matters lest he succumb to the profession's allurements. "I am not one of those who suppose the profession of the law incompatible with the strictest integrity, although I think, what I believe no one denies, that its dangers and temptations are considerable."[35]

As Alexander reflected on their respective futures, he spoke of his intention to serve as an itinerant minister. "Wherever I may go, I trust that duty and a desire of usefulness will sway me. If my life is spared, it is not improbable that I shall spend two or three years in itinerating." "I feel daily my need of personal converse with the world," he said, "which is to be the theatre and the subject of my future operations. The clown, the mere student, the bookworm, though vastly learned, is no more fit to produce a moral than a political revolution; yet this is what we aim at."[36]

Knowing that eternity was but a heartbeat away for either of them on any given day, Alexander challenged Hall regarding the goals that he should set for his life ambitions as he moved into a new stage of professional obligation. The brevity of life and the uncertainty of what a

---

34. Hall, *Letters*, 1:35.
35. Hall, *Letters*, 1:37.
36. Hall, *Letters*, 1:37.

day may bring forth were matters of constant consideration for Alexander. The recent deaths of his fellow seminarians only served to reinforce Alexander's desire for Hall's salvation. Time was of the essence, and Alexander knew that the absence of a decision *for* Christ was a decision *against* Christ. Indifference to the claims of Christ would result in the same consequences as outright denial of His lordship. In a forceful exhortation, he warned Hall not to become hardened to the message of Scripture by living with indifference to its commands:

> Four years hence—and where shall we be? what manner of persons? how employed? If the impenetrable curtain which screens the future could be drawn aside, we might see some astonishing and unexpected change. It may be that the grave may then contain my mortal part, or the depths of the sea; or care and affliction may have eaten out all hopes of terrestrial peace, or a thousand other results, now unthought of. All things here suffer change, all things created are fleeting, God only remains. My dear friend, shall we not attach ourselves to this only support which can sustain the final shock? Is it not desirable, is it not wise, to "lay hold on the strength of God"? Small as our experience is, it ought to have informed us that the joys of this world are sweet and fascinating only in the pursuit, and that supposing and granting that they were exquisite in possession, they fade away like the tints of morning clouds. This you have heard, no doubt, until, perhaps, you are weary of it. And yet if these things do not affect us *now*, when the heart is susceptible, when its fibers are not entwined so closely as they shall be around the world, when we have not become intoxicated with pleasure and glory, is it to be hoped that they will affect us when the storm and hurricane of life is maddening us? Pardon me for saying that I consider the present moment of your life a most critical moment, pregnant perhaps with eternal consequences. You have made election of a profession, and expect that by becoming a lawyer you put yourself out of the reach of religious influence, or that the moral influence of your calling will be directly injurious to virtuous principles; but I say, with confidence, that in all probability, every successive step you now take will lead you further from a reasonable hope of salvation. I am speaking of human probabilities; we are not to take God's special dealing into our calculations. Do you find the love of honour leading you *now* from the consideration of the self-denying gospel? How will it be when ambition shall have received ten-fold strength from the continual fuel presented to it? Does multiplicity of business exclude prayer and devotion *now*? Look at the whirlpool of every lawyer's

cases. Do you find your heart becoming more insensible to religious motives? Believe me, it is but the presage of more dreadful indifference. In this matter there is no stationary point. Hearts do not amend by indulgence, sin loses no power by having the reins given to it, the world becomes no less fascinating, God is not appeased by continued defiance. Refer to the situation of any lawyer, one, for instance, whose circumstances you could wish your own, and say candidly, does that situation afford advantages for the cultivation of piety, such advantages as you *now* enjoy. This very hour is the best possible season which remains for you. I press this motive because it is one which struck terror once to my soul, and opened my eyes to the dangers of my situation.[37]

Alexander's passion for Hall's salvation would remain a dominant interest in his correspondence. Patient persistence in the bonds of Christian affection would bear its proper fruit in due time as the blessing of human friendship would be deepened in the spiritual unity shared by those whose hearts have been knit together in the fellowship of Christ's love. But for the moment, hope's desire remained deferred as Alexander waited on God's mercy in effecting the salvation in which he longed for his friend to share.

---

37. Hall, *Letters*, 1:38–39.

This is my first letter since I came into this house. I have indeed, time for nothing but the incipient duties and preparations of my new situation. I can promise you but few such voluminous reports as my last epistle. So fully am I occupied with little arrangements relative to my own accommodation and the admission of students, that I have not been at our house since yesterday morning. It requires all the effrontery which I can assume to fill my gown with any kind of effect, to sit in the focal point of vision before a hundred carping young gentlemen, on the scaffold yelep'd the stage, to march through the congregation at the foot of the refectory steps with manifold tokens of respect, and then to march at their head, and sit in state at the upper end of the long college table, &c., &c. However, in all such matters, when a thing must be done, I am fond of putting the best face upon it, and—"neck or nothing" going forward. I have never gained any thing by shrinking, although few have oftener made experiment of it, and shrink I will not, though my head should be the price of daring.

—J. W. ALEXANDER
Nassau Hall, No. 25
May 21, 1824

Chapter 3

TUTOR AT THE COLLEGE OF NEW JERSEY: 1824–1825

As Alexander contemplated the options that lay before him at the conclusion of his seminary studies, he had little interest in pursuing an academic career at his college alma mater. Although the trustees had already solicited his interest in serving as a tutor on two earlier occasions, Alexander had repeatedly declined their overtures. To his great surprise, however, he was informed in early April 1824 that the trustees had proceeded to elect him as a "mathematical tutor" and now requested his services! "When I heard it, late Wednesday, my feelings instantly revolted, and I said No with the most perfect determination and confidence," he informed Hall. But after further consideration, he reversed his decision and accepted the invitation.[1] "Upon weighing all circumstances, however, and finding upon consulting with my friends that they all, without exception, urged my acceptance, I have determined to enter upon the duties at the commencement of next session."[2]

While Alexander's heart was set upon the pastorate, he believed that his work as a tutor would give him additional time to prepare for the responsibilities of pastoral life.[3] Although it meant leaving the seminary program prematurely, Alexander felt it would not disadvantage his

---

1. "He was now prevailed upon to consent, as he saw the advantage it would afford him of improving his mind by general study, while it would only nominally separate him for a time from the Seminary. Accordingly, he transferred his residence to Nassau Hall in May 1824." "James Waddell Alexander," 70.
2. Hall, *Letters*, 1:42.
3. Alexander was equally concerned that life as a tutor might repress his social development: "My fears are not slight, that I shall, in these misanthropic walls, become 'the mere student,' and forget my duties to those without, as well as neglect to cultivate the society of the amiable and the tender. If I live until next Autumn, I shall probably, be even more a clown than I now am, and need an evolution of six weeks among softening scenes to bend and mollify me." Hall, *Letters*, 1:47.

future plans. A letter to Hall from this period jokingly speaks of his small stature and the boyish traits that had not yet matured into full manhood. "As for me I fancy that in the prominent traits both of the outer and the inner man, you will find me much the same boy as ever. I am no son of Anak, and have altered little in dimensions."[4] Alexander's assessment of his immaturity for any present pursuit of the pastoral office was as correct as the decision of the trustees to make him a tutor at the college. Although admittedly too immature for ordination, he was considered quite suitable by the college trustees for the work of a tutor. Both parties had made the right choice, and each would prove the beneficiary of the other in the course of the next few years.

Life as a Tutor

Alexander quickly settled into his new responsibilities as "mathematical tutor" at the College of New Jersey.[5] A burgeoning polymath, Alexander's natural curiosity, broad reading, and intellectual giftedness were a perfect match for his new position.[6] Although there were certain aspects of the job he did not relish, Alexander found himself well suited for the work.[7]

---

4. Hall, *Letters*, 1:42–43.

5. A descriptive account of Alexander's personality at the time of his tutorship can be found in reflections published in August 1859, by Dr. Samuel K. Talmage: "We were placed on terms of very intimate intercourse and communion as fellow-tutors during the year 1824. He had become pious since we had parted as students, and I now saw much of his inner life, as he disclosed it but to few. He had grown graver in manner, and somewhat prone to pensiveness of spirit. To the public eye he seemed retiring and apparently distant. But when with a friend in a retired walk or in the *abandon* and intimacy of private personal intercourse, he was the most cheerful of companions, abounding in playful remark and discriminating observation. He had a keen relish for the humorous, and a nice appreciation of the virtues and defects of his fellow-men. He had a perfect horror of cant, pretension, bigotry, exclusiveness, and was himself remarkably free from all these failings, thus imparting an irresistible charm to his intercourse with friends." Hall, *Letters*, 1:45.

6. "His father once said to Henry Boardman, 'My son James has always been a sort of walking Cyclopaedia.'" Cited in Calhoun, *Faith and Learning*, 1:286.

7. "This position involved him in many petty troubles annoying to one of his temperament, but as he wrote at the time: 'I need to be buffeted about a little, to call forth what little energy and firmness I may possess.'" John Hall, *Sermons Preached before the Congregation of the Presbyterian Church, Corner of Fifth Avenue and Nineteenth Street, at the Memorial Services October 9, 1859. Appointed in Reference to the Death of their Late Pastor, James Waddell Alexander, D.D. by Charles Hodge, D.D., and John Hall, D.D.* (New York: Anson D. F. Randolph, 1859), 37. Hall's funeral sermon for Alexander can also be found in James M. Garretson, *Pastor-Teachers of Old Princeton: Memorial Addresses for the Faculty of Princeton Theological Seminary 1812–1921* (Edinburgh: Banner of Truth, 2012): 145–71.

At the time he assumed his responsibilities as a residential tutor, college campus life was carefully regulated. Punctuality, cleanliness, a disciplined daily regimen, and participation in public prayers and private devotions were among the many regulations to which students were expected to adhere. College staff had responsibility for monitoring student behavior.[8] Besides the instruction provided in the classroom, staff were required to make several rounds each day throughout student living quarters in order to enforce compliance to the rules of conduct.[9]

While campus life could be rigid, students still found opportunity for pranks—often under the cover of darkness. One such incident is recorded in a letter from early June 1824:

> Had a cracker about two o'clock on the night before last; it was exploded at the prayer-hall door, which it burst open, about 25 yards from my head. I was not certain what it was that had awakened me, until my room was filled with powder-smoke, which came in through the glass ventilator above my door. No bones broken yet. Indeed the *physical* inconveniences of my station I do not regard one straw.[10]

At the end of his first year at the college, Alexander "exchanged the mathematical for the classical tutorship."[11] His new responsibilities provided opportunity for study on a variety of additional subjects which he had interest in learning.[12] During his time as a tutor, he found opportunity for the reading of poets, philosophers, theologians, and works of ancient and modern history. He enjoyed reading Jonathan Edwards's *The Freedom of the Will*, but thought his metaphysics questionable.[13] Works of

---

8. "My youth," he writes, "is likely to call forth the disrespect and presumption of some, and the exercise of that authority which I am called upon to assume must gain me the ill-will and ill offices of those who are its objects. Yet this is the tax which every man must pay, who is so happy as to aim at the welfare of his fellow-creatures " Alexander, *Life of Joseph Addison Alexander*, 1:58.

9. For an informative study on the Christian convictions that shaped the curriculum and campus life of colonial colleges and their institutional development into the nineteenth century, see William C. Ringenberg, *The Christian College: A History of Protestant Higher Education in America* (Grand Rapids: Baker, 2006).

10. Hall, *Letters*, 1:60.

11. "James Waddell Alexander," 70.

12. Alexander found inspiration in words from John Wesley: "Wesley's rule is a capital one: 'Have a time for every thing, and do every thing at its time.'" Hall, *Letters*, 1:72.

13. "Edwards on the Will, I have concluded, with great admiration of the author's profundity and acuteness, and yet with the opinion that he is unguarded in his use of language, and that his book is liable to great misrepresentation." Hall, *Letters*, 1:71.

apologetics were also perused. "As to my reading," he stated, "I have dispatched Butler's Analogy, an immortal work for its power of argument and depth of original thought; also Dr. Hartley's Evidences of Christianity, decidedly the best work on the subject which I have seen, and contained in the 5th volume of Watson's tracts."[14]

In another context, he wrote, "I keep myself alive by constant delving: four or five hours a day at languages; relieved by a little Biography, and a little Mineralogy, with which last study I have been amusing myself a little."[15] It was during these years that Alexander began contributing articles to newspapers such as *The National Gazette and Literary Register*. His contributions were so well received by its editor Mr. Robert Walsh that Alexander would also be invited to contribute articles to another influential journal Walsh would later found, the *American Quarterly Review*.[16]

Alexander placed special value on the reading of Christian biography. His heart was stirred by the lives of men and women who had faithfully served Christ in their generation whose example beckons others to follow in a life of service to His church.

> Biography has always been my favourite reading: in this I include all such developments of manners and mind as one finds in correspondence, in anecdotes, as well as formed characters. No kind of study so excites my enthusiasm. One example is more to me than discourses innumerable. This I find in the Scriptures forcibly exemplified. The history of wars and revolutions, and discoveries, are eminently dull to me, except so far as I find in them individual traits of character portrayed. The history of opinion, and of mind, is all that takes much hold of my feelings. For this reason, I never could join in the enthusiastic admiration, common to most learned men, of Gibbon, and Hume, and Robertson; while the histories of Roscoe, and Middleton, and even the Biographical dictionary, are delightful. I am sure that no works have had so much influence upon my religious feelings, as those which give the lives of pious men. The memoirs of Martyn and Brainerd are my continual advisers. I have this month read with high

---

14. Hall, *Letters*, 1:73.
15. Hall, *Letters*, 1:78.
16. "As his engagements in the College did not wholly intermit his theological reading; so he found time also for improving himself in German, French, mineralogy, geology, anatomy, music, and English literature, and began that practice of composition, in the shape of contributions to periodical works, which became the congenial habit of the remainder of his life." "James Waddell Alexander," 70.

satisfaction the Memoirs of Andrew Fuller, and Samuel Pearce, of the Baptist church. The latter of these had a soul of heavenly mould; and the man who can fail to love, when he reads his life, can have little sense of the beauty of holiness.[17]

During his time as a tutor, Alexander enjoyed remarkably good health apart from what appears to be a severe cold or flu that he experienced during October 1824. He found himself bedridden for a time, exhausted by the illness and "a head muddled with a week's debauch upon opium." Alexander's reflections on his illness shed light on the idiosyncrasies of his personality:

> I scarcely know why it is, but so contrary is my disposition, that the occurrences of life operate upon me in a manner seemingly opposite to their natural tendencies. I am never less solemn than when on a sick bed; perhaps, in this case, because I have been drunk with opium all the time. I know that I ought to feel the solemnity of the occasion, but it is all the reverse. On the contrary, in the crowd, and in the *fete*, in the merry circle, I am most ready to have a long face, to feel a great vacuity, and to be deeply impressed with the emptiness of the world.[18]

His letters during this period also include numerous observations on the weather and local scenery. Of all the seasons during the year, Alexander enjoyed winter the most. A letter written to Hall on December 6, 1824, paints a picturesque portrait of his collegiate lodging and related family life during the cold winter months.

> Spring may have its charms, but winter is the season in which I delight. It is not merely because I always enjoy much better health, but because of the numerous domestic and social enjoyments of this comfortable season. And whether sitting among the lively circle at our fireside at home, or as I now do, by my solitary but cheerful blaze, with my table spread, my candle lighted, my elbow chair adjusted, I feel nearer to contentment than in any other situation. When the nights are clear, I generally take a solitary walk about ten o'clock; this stirs up one's romantic feelings, braces the nerves, quickens the pulse, and prepares for a sweet sleep and pleasant dreams. As you may suppose, I am cast entirely upon my own resources for

---

17. Hall, *Letters*, 1:85.
18. Hall, *Letters*, 1:66.

entertainment; my visits at home are necessarily flying calls, and my books and pen furnish most of my amusement.[19]

The Art of Writing

As a young man, Alexander found personal pleasure in learning the art of writing. Besides the reading that he enjoyed during his years as a student and now as a tutor, he worked hard at mastering his writing skills. He was soon busy producing articles for magazines.

As he thought about his future prospects, he hoped that he might be given opportunity to bless people's lives through the use of his pen.[20] In order to make the best use of his time, he concluded that he should focus on projects of more permanent value than the passing interests of a weekly or monthly magazine. "I think I shall throw up *gazetteering*," he told Hall. Even as a young man, Alexander approached his plans for writing with thoughts of eternity in mind. He notes:

> It is my desire, I confess, to leave something behind me that may testify, after my death, that I have not been altogether a useless stock in this world; but ten years will not be too much to spend in secret meditation before thinking of such a thing. If I die within that time, God's will be done. If I live, I shall be able to have matured my crude and now only germinating notions, and to judge what may, or may not, do good.[21]

Although he would receive widespread acclaim for his publications, Alexander found it hard to begin writing if he were not in the proper mood. When asked by Hall to consider penning an article on a contemporary theological movement, Alexander told him it would not be possible for he felt "no motion that way at present." Like many of his fellow authors, he struggled to write on a topic if he had no passion for it. What is true of pulpit eloquence is also true of literary eloquence: The subject must have captured the imagination and emotions in order to flow naturally and fluently through a man's lips or his pen. Alexander understood this and did not try to force himself to do that which was not

---

19. Hall, *Letters*, 1:71.
20. Alexander's hope was fulfilled. As Calhoun notes: "There are 67 different titles by J. W. Alexander in the *National Union Catalogue*. The total number of entries under his name, including multiple editions, is 132." Cited in Calhoun, *Faith and Learning*, 1:476.
21. Hall, *Letters*, 1:61.

true to his nature. "I have not that enviable self-command which enables some men to decree that they will do this or that, and then sit down and effect it," he explained to Hall.

> I must take myself when I am in the notion of it. I must humour myself. Most of my scribbling is done at single sittings, and *currente calamo*. When I am full of a particular subject, and find that the ink will run, I usually drive the quill to its utmost, which is sometimes only ten lines. That I ever finished any thing, I dare not aver. I count those productions happy which have a beginning and an end, and of course are fit for the press.[22]

Melancholy

In one of his first letters sent to Hall while serving as a tutor, Alexander began to speak more frankly about his struggle with melancholy. A letter on April 21, 1824, acknowledges the problem and its dangerous effects. It had already impaired his health, although its extent was largely hidden from public view:

> There was indeed once some glow and bloom of health upon my face, which has departed. I confess, with the confidence of friendship, knowing that it is not exposing myself to ill-timed raillery, that melancholy has secretly and deeply preyed upon my spirits, more than my most intimate friends would judge from my demeanour.... My temperament is such that I am susceptible of the most deep emotions of pleasure as well as pain to a great degree, but the pleasure is generally succeeded by a proportionable depression.[23]

As Alexander's friendship with Hall grew, his correspondence began to detail aspects of the melancholy with which he wrestled. A number of the letters written during May 1824 address the topic. Alexander wanted to be open with Hall about his struggle. In a letter written on May 14, he requested that Hall not dismiss his statements as immature rants: "You must take me just as you find me; I don't ask you to pardon my failing; criticize them faithfully; but, prythee, bear with them," he said. Alexander's despair was real, and he wanted to assure Hall of its seriousness.

---

22. Hall, *Letters*, 1:65.
23. Hall, *Letters*, 1:42–43.

> When I speak of melancholy to *you*, I speak of it seriously, and of melancholy in its truest and most appalling shape; not the puling, pensive, pleasing reveries of a moon-struck lover, or a young, novel-reading, boarding-school Miss; but that deep and horrible over-clouding of the soul, which none can understand but those who suffer it, which can be described only by faint and insufficient similitudes, which, until my nervous system received a violent shock, I never knew, and which I do sincerely wish you may always be able, as I never shall,—to laugh at. Nervous irritability (I am not *com*- but *ex*-plaining) I have got in a very fair way by right of primogeniture, and have increased by neglect of proper recreation and exercise.[24]

His letter continues with a series of observations on the characteristics of his melancholy. His initial observations provide a thoughtful examination of the physiological symptoms associated with its development. Alexander recognized the interrelationship between the body and soul, and how the health or disease of one will affect the other in ways that, in his judgment, were not always preventable.

> You know how closely body and soul are united, and how mental and corporeal changes go hand in hand. But perhaps you do not know—and may you never—what it is to feel the *whole man* in a state of distressing disorder, without knowing whether the body has communicated the distemper to the mind, or the mind to the body; to feel the tremulous agitation of the whole material fabric of nerves, and the accompanying and more intolerable agitation of spirit, depression, blues, hypochondria, or what you will. Will you smile when I say that to shake off this state of soul—I call it so, for the suffering of body is trifling—is no less impossible than to shake off a fit of the stone? One is equally with the other a disease. Call it, if you please, a disorder of the imagination, and say that it is whim and folly. Granted; and yet it is no less dreadful, far more mortifying, equally beyond the influence of mere resolution. When a withered arm can stretch itself out for relief, then may a diseased mind heal itself. Could I once determine to be placid and cheerful, and so effect a change in the mental state, the cure would be already complete.[25]

Having addressed "the physiology of the case," Alexander proceeded to give Hall an account of how his spirit, or temperament, was affected

---

24. Hall, *Letters*, 1:43.
25. Hall, *Letters*, 1:43–44.

by the onslaught of melancholy. His letter vividly describes the effects of melancholy upon the human soul and the sense of helplessness it engenders in its victims. Speaking from personal experience, Alexander acknowledged his susceptibility to its debilitating effects:

> I am more easily excited to pleasure or pain than most persons. My joys are excessive; sometimes a little frantic. The same susceptibility makes me liable to depression from circumstances which would scarcely for a moment ruffle the feelings of some; and to depression, sometimes, which has no perceptible cause without. To compare levity and melancholy in a moral point of view, is comparing two sins equally repugnant to the mild placidity and cheerful calm which the truths of the gospel produce on a heart that is exercised aright. The latter afflicts *my* conscience least, because it is what I loathe, and what I would as joyfully shun as I would a delirium, and which it is just as much in my power to avoid. *Undue* mirth is a fault which brings with it, to me, its punishment, in the shape of the vapours which follow in its footsteps. Perhaps the words I may have used in a former letter convey to your mind an impression not exactly correct. Forebodings of future pain or misery are not often the subjects of my thoughts, but there comes over my soul, I can no otherwise describe it, a cloud, a blackness, a horror, which tinges every object without or within with a certain indefinable, vague, and terrific darkness; which absorbs the powers of the soul, and seems to concentrate all the faculties upon some hideous *something*, or *nothing*, and waste the mental energy in empty musing. I am sometimes months without such a visitation, and sometimes weeks with little else; and my condition has been somewhat this for a week past.[26]

In another letter, written not long afterward, Alexander speaks of the solace he found in William Cowper's writings on melancholy. A well-known hymn writer and respected English poet, Cowper (1731–1800) engaged in a lifelong battle with melancholy. At times the spiritual distemper incapacitated Cowper's ability to function. It would eventually compromise his health, resulting in his death. Cowper's writings and hymnody reflect the spiritual turbulence of his life and epitomize the feelings of those afflicted by melancholy. Alexander found his experience of melancholy virtually identical with that of Cowper:

---

26. Hall, *Letters*, 1:44.

> My melancholy...if I may compare great things with small, and pretend even to the blemishes of a great man, is described to a tittle by Cowper, in one of his letters cited in the "May Advocate." Like him, I find my bitterest ruminations so wrought up with fantastical thoughts and phantasies, that I am forced to laugh at my own creations, when I feel miserable enough to hang myself. Like him...I can be gloomy, yea wretched, without being sober, and the transition is often easier from hypochondria to levity, than to seriousness. Like him I find religion, and religious thoughts, not the causes or the concomitants of melancholy, but its surest remedy. When the promises of Scripture can be brought to bear, as I thank God they have sometimes been, upon my troubled mind, they have never, never failed to diffuse a calm and a sweet content which makes the Gospel more valuable, *as to this life*, to me, than it would be under different circumstances. Yet infatuated creatures that we are! that which we know, and have tasted to be the chief and only good, how ready are we to neglect and abandon![27]

Alexander worried that what he shared with Hall would be mistaken for a spirit of ingratitude from one who had enjoyed a privileged life. While his family was not wealthy, he enjoyed inestimable privileges growing up in the home into which he was born. He feared Hall would dismiss his musings as the temperamental reflections of an immature adolescent who refused to transition to the responsibilities that accompany adult life. What was not visible to the naked eye, however, was the internal struggle known only to Alexander himself. He writes:

> Does it amuse you to hear *me* talk of *sorrows*? I confess that to complain would be a heinous ingratitude in me. I have had perhaps more external favours and forbearance at the hand of Providence than most persons, and I do desire to thank God; but still, there is a world within, a world that seems as vast and wonderful, and inexplicable as that without, to one who has the habit or the disease of poring inward upon it. And here, whether from imaginary fears (though these are not my great tormentors) or conflicts between inclination and duty, between a restless, ambitious, proud and giddy soul, and a principle that strives to keep down its gigantic writhings, and labours to repress the upheavings and desperate agonies of effort, in the earthy spirit, which oftentimes gets the upper hand, and crowds under the poor weak element of piety, and triumphs in a mighty

---

27. Hall, *Letters*, 1:47–48.

rage—here in the inner man, when the gale of hilarity, and the bustle and hurricane of business is blown over, and when religion, through sinful neglect, is not at work to make this ocean smooth smooth,— "when," as Hurley says, "I am brought to face at night, or in solitude, that phantom self, which all day long I have labored to avoid; what can be conceived more horrible!"[28]

Subduing Pride

Whether rooted in his developing piety or exacerbated by his feelings of melancholy, Alexander's letters also describe his strong ego and the struggle in which he was engaged to devote his entire life to the calling which God had placed before him. "I have been ambitious to a high degree," he announced.

> What has been its fruit? Am I happier? Do I not still, and will I not forever be grasping after something yet to come? something which never can come? Will fame gratify me? Will universal honour give me peace? Will a conquered world make *me* more content than my insane name-sake of Macedon? No! my experience, and universal testimony, and the word of Jehovah thunder, *No!*[29]

As Alexander sought to prioritize his spiritual inclinations, he drew special encouragement from the life of Henry Martyn (1781–1812).[30] Having graduated with honors from Cambridge University in 1801, Martyn was elected as a fellow of his college the following year, appearing destined for an influential academic or legal career. But the fruits of an evangelical conversion which took place in 1800 began to mature under the spiritual influence of the Anglican evangelical leader Charles Simeon, as well as Martyn's subsequent reading of Jonathan Edwards's *The Life of David Brainerd*.[31] As a result, Martyn abandoned what had been a life in pursuit of worldly goals for one devoted to missionary service.[32] He would eventually travel to India, serving as a chaplain for the East India

---

28. Hall, *Letters*, 1:49.
29. Hall, *Letters*, 1:49–50.
30. For a recent reprinting of the classic nineteenth-century study of Martyn's life and ministry, see John Sargent, *The Life and Letters of Henry Martyn* (Edinburgh: Banner of Truth, 1985).
31. For a modern critical edition of Edwards's classic work, see Jonathan Edwards, *The Life of David Brainerd*, ed. Norman Petit (New Haven: Yale University Press, 1985).
32. "I have grasped this bubble *honour*, and it vanishes in my hand." Hall, *Letters*, 1:50.

Company and performing work as a missionary scholar in translation of the New Testament Scriptures into Persian and Arabic. He became an expert on Islam and engaged in what was at the time a pioneering outreach to Muslims.

Although Martyn died a premature death, his missionary zeal became an inspiration for Christians in Alexander's generation who pondered a life totally devoted to God's calling. "Did you ever read the life of Henry Martyn?" Alexander queried. "If you have not, upon the strength of our friendship, I charge and entreat you to do so. My present perusal of it is about the sixth, which for me, who seldom read any book through, is strong proof of esteem. If there is on earth or on record a character which I love more than that of Henry Martyn, I know not." "To meet *him* in heaven," Alexander wrote, "is a wish that burns intensely in my heart."[33]

Reflecting upon Martyn's life of devoted service caused Alexander to reexamine his own commitment to a lifestyle of wholehearted discipleship. Alexander recognized that self-denial is at the heart of genuine discipleship. He also noted how his pride often prevented him from pursuing his calling because he knew it would cost him his worldly ambitions if he were to devote himself without reservation to living out his Christian convictions:

> I have sometimes been inclined to murmur at the idea that we must *deny ourselves*, that we must give our *whole souls* to God, that it is impossible to "love the world" without being "the enemy of God,"—and to shrink from that yoke which, to my dim eye, seemed to bring no indemnity for the loss of good things; but the demands of the Scripture are inexorable, and it is not until we are willing to receive the whole truth and to obey it, that we can pretend to be willing to be saved. It is not because the gate of entrance is inaccessible, that I have felt my stubborn soul unwilling to strive to enter in. It is because it is too low for my pride, and too arduous for my indolence.[34]

Alexander was eager to maintain his spiritual vitality lest he become a minister who has the "form of godliness" but not its power. In reference to this topic, he agreed with criticisms Hall raised in one of his letters. "You speak with justice of the formality of ministers," he told Hall.

---

33. Hall, *Letters*, 1:50.
34. Hall, *Letters*, 1:50.

It is a woeful truth, and it is with shuddering that I anticipate adding myself to the venerable corps which contains already so many drones. Yet there are those who, bating the inevitable imperfections of nature, are what their Saviour directed them to be; and perhaps the reason why they seem to be so few is, that they do not seek the glare and bustle of publicity, and pompous anniversaries.

By contrast, Alexander thought the Moravians, known for their evangelistic fervor and missionary outreach, provided the proper example of ministerial zeal.[35] "My own favourite Moravians do seem to have caught some of the apostolic spirit."[36]

While Alexander might be criticized for an excessively introspective nature, his concern for a life of increasing godliness is evidence that he had experienced the new birth.[37] "In religion, in moral principle, in every branch of attainment and character, I see myself far, far below what I desire to be, and often can I enter into the spirit of the Apostle's remarks, Rom. vii. 14–25," he confided to Hall. But Alexander was also wise enough to recognize that any progress he would make in a life of radical holiness could only come about in the community of God's church. In this regard, his melancholic nature had not blinded him to the importance of Christian fellowship as the atmosphere in which piety is nourished. "I confess that I see very little in the selfish, secluded, torpid devotion of the monk, which savours of the glowing, expansive, ever *active* piety of the Apostles. I know too much of solitude to have very romantic ideas of the piety which is generated by it. Spleen and moroseness gain more rapid growth in the cell, than benevolence and humility."[38]

---

35. A letter on December 1846 comments on the lifelong esteem Alexander had for Moravian piety and hymnody: "Count Zinzendorf, on one occasion, (as I find by his Life,) extemporized six hymns, during one meeting; it was his frequent practice. Most of the Moravian hymns are by him, and these are very beautiful in German, however ludicrous in the wretched English version. The fine gold has become dim. If ever there was true religion, since primitive days, it was among the Bohemian and Moravian confessors." Hall, *Letters*, 2:61.

36. Hall, *Letters*, 1:57.

37. Alexander's commitment to a life of piety is noted in observations by Talmage: "His piety was, even at that period, deep toned, and remarkably advanced for one of his age. He was at times overwhelmed with a sense of sinfulness, and has told me that often he could scarcely refrain from crying out in the college chapel from an awful sense of guilt before God, under the pungent appeals of the beloved Professors of the College and Theological Seminary, although he was sitting on the stage before the assembled students as one of the Faculty." Hall, *Letters*, 1:45.

38. Hall, *Letters*, 1:58.

By midsummer, Alexander was able to report that his will had been broken in a manner such as he had not known before.[39] The months of struggle had passed; grace was operative in a new and powerful way in his life. Writing from Nassau Hall, July 10, 1824, Alexander was eager to share with Hall the breakthrough in spiritual life that he had experienced:

> I begin by informing you that I have finally been humbled by the *prostration* of my own will, which has been since birth free only to evil, to the point of entire submission to God. I have been a false and hypocritical professor, but God has in mercy, brought me to a view of my utter impotence, of the justice of the law which would condemn me to eternal wrath, and of my being helpless in the hands of an Almighty Avenger. Henceforward, my single aim is, to submit myself to God as an instrument in his hands to be used for what he chooses. Death would be a release, should it come this instant; and except to do God's work, I desire not to breathe another moment.[40]

Gospel Overtures

During his time as a tutor, Alexander's overtures to Hall regarding his need for salvation become more forceful and direct. In the same letter dated July 10, 1824, in which Alexander spoke of the new spiritual commitments which had come into his life, he also responded to the interaction which he had been having with Hall on the doctrine of election. Similar in focus to other correspondence that addressed the subjects of Calvinism and Arminianism, Alexander made application of the conversational talking points to Hall's conscience. Hall was placing too much trust in unaided reason to determine the credibility of biblical teaching. He warned Hall regarding the danger of this approach and his need for spiritual illumination by the Holy Spirit in order to properly understand and believe divine revelation.

> You talk of election, &c. Depend upon it you will ever sink into an abyss of perplexity and deeper and still deeper confusion, until you renounce a dependence upon your own powers of intellect. Spiritual

---

39. Hall draws particular attention to the profound change that took place at this time in Alexander's life: "It was just at this period, too, that his personal Christian experience passed through such a taste, as he said, of the terrors of the Lord, that it seemed to him, at the time, as if he had known nothing before of true conversion." Hall, *Sermons*, 38.
40. Hall, *Letters*, 1:64.

vision or faith is as different from intellectual vision or mere belief (in a human sense) as their objects are diverse. The one is conversant with naked speculations which might forever play about the head and communicate no spark of heat. The other is the gift of God. If any man will do the will of God he shall know of the doctrine whether it be of God. Believe in the Lord Jesus Christ, and you shall be saved, and a part of this salvation is a knowledge of the truth. Christ is "made unto us knowledge," when you have received power to be the son of God through him, then shall you see in him all that it is necessary for you to know. Read 1 Cor. i. 18–31. It is the Spirit that teacheth. 1 Cor. ii. 6, 7, and 10 and 14. If you wish to understand these things let me direct you to the Scriptures. Quere. How many days did you ever devote exclusively to the prayerful reading of the Bible? And how great is the probability of your understanding it until you dig in it as for choice treasure? And how great is your anxiety on the subject, if you have never given even a week to the book? Are you not more fond of reading human discussions on the subject, than of going to the fountainhead? Do you not often dispute in our own mind certain propositions before you have had them fairly defined? Are you not a little afraid of finding certain doctrines in the Bible if you should search it too closely or candidly? If this doctrine should stand out prominently as a declaration of the word of God, "God will damn all men;" would you believe it? If God should thunder it in your car would you believe it? If you would not, then you would be making God a liar; the very essence of that unbelief which keeps us from him. You wish to believe not as the word of God, but as the word of man: not because God says it, and you humbly credit whatever he says, but because it is demonstrated to you. At this rate you may become a grand skeptic, but never a Christian. If you do not come to the Scriptures with a mind equally willing to believe one thing as another, you come with a bias, you come without believing it to be the word of God, and you come in vain. Now observe, I assert nothing to be believed upon my *ipse dixit* [literally: "he himself said it"], or that of any human creature. Please to read over in connexion, without stopping for any difficulties, or quarrelling about any doctrine, the gospel by John; read it three or four times; and if you do not see that the Scripture is clear and consistent, and plain, too, if we were not blinded by the God of this world, then I forfeit my character.[41]

---

41. Hall, *Letters*, 1:64–65.

Hall's response to Alexander's admonitions is not recorded, but it is likely that he had not yet become convinced of Alexander's conviction on the work of the Spirit and the need for spiritual illumination in place of unaided human reason for understanding the message of the Bible.

As the months passed, Hall's interest in the Bible's teaching on Christ and salvation continued such that by late March 1825, Alexander was once again in a position to write another forceful letter to his friend impressing on him the urgency of his spiritual circumstances and need to act on what he had come to know as true through his study of the Scriptures. It appears that Hall's sensitivity to his spiritual condition had increased and that he was trying to determine how best to go forward in acting upon what he had come to understand. For various reasons, he was hesitant to repent, perhaps feeling it was an action premature to his state of preparation for receiving salvation. Alexander warned him that he had no grounds for delay—to hesitate is only to further the risk of increased judgment for the sin which daily accumulates in our lives. He encouraged Hall to repent today and not delay. The day of salvation is *now*, and Hall had no valid excuse for why he should delay his decision any longer:

> I preached another sermon last night, [a Seminary exercise,] with as little satisfaction to my self as ever I experienced. I do sincerely hope that I shall conjure up a little more life when I come to the real work. And now to say a little upon the very interesting topic which has often entered into our correspondence, I mean the matter of personal piety, permit me to say that you are mistaken if you suppose that I will under present circumstances exhort you to a mere use of means, however assiduous and sincere, as the mode of securing salvation. I will not say to you as a minister of your city once said, "Go on, persevere, be encouraged, I have known a woman seek Christ six and thirty years, and at last find him." No: this I consider at once unscriptural and cruel. I say, repent and believe. Do it now: delay not a moment; and instead of being encouraged, be alarmed at the awful truth, that every day you remain impenitent your burden of guilt, and your lot of wrath increases. Without *faith* it is *impossible* to please him; and whatever you do before repentance is odious in his sight. Though you should weep tears of blood, and macerate your body by prayer and fasting, nothing would rescue you from the curse until you submit to God. Compare this statement with Scripture, and "judge ye what is right." Do you say that you cannot pray aright, &c.? Let me quote from a work of the excellent Andrew Fuller a passage in point: "What shall we say then? Seeing he cannot repent, cannot

find it in his heart to *endeavour* to repent, cannot pray sincerely for a heart to make such an endeavour;—shall we deny his assertions, (viz. of inability,) and tell him he is not so wicked as he makes himself? This might be more than we should be able to maintain. Or shall we allow them, and acquit him of obligation? Rather, ought we not to return to the place where we set out, admonishing him as the Scriptures do, to *repent and believe the* gospel; declaring to him that what he calls his inability is his sin and shame; and warning him against the idea of its availing him another day." I can fancy you rising in revolt against such doctrine; I remember when my heart was stoutly and bitterly set against it; and yet no sooner had I gained any knowledge of the truth and of my own heart, than I was convinced that nothing prevented my submitting to the righteousness of God, but a willful, wicked, stubborn aversion to his most holy law, and to the humbling terms of salvation. I know that I can in no way evince the sincerity of my friendship more, than by dealing thus plainly with you. I do greatly fear that your present views will lead you to a kind of hardened indifference which naturally grows more and more hopeless, and is but the prelude to eternal death. The repentance I urge (μετανοια, a change of mind) is a solemn and cordial determination of soul, to renounce sin as a thing odious, loathsome, and damning, and to embrace the service of God as infinitely excellent and desirable. I entreat you to make this most reasonable of all determinations. Make it this very day. What but a willful enmity to God's holiness can induce you to delay? How can you venture, deliberately, to put off the solemn dedication of your heart to God even until to-morrow?[42]

As matters turned out, Hall did delay his response to repent but did not lose his interest in making further inquiry into the life of piety and what it would mean to live as a Christian. Whether at his own initiative or in response to the counsel of others, Hall had been reading various Christian authors on the Christian life. Accordingly, Alexander urged Hall to read some of the best "practical" authors for grasping the essence of what it would mean to live his life *coram Deo*, before the face of God.

In a letter written in early April 1825, Alexander makes recommendations for the kind of literature that Hall would most benefit from at this time in his inquiry about the nature of Christianity. Besides a classic volume on Christian spirituality by William Law titled *A Serious Call to a*

---

42. Hall, *Letters*, 1:75–76.

Devout and Holy Life, Alexander recommended select titles from influential Reformed preacher-theologians for Hall's perusal:

> Law's "Call" is a book read by vast numbers of people. It is a *sine qua non* among the Methodists; and while there is much in it to which I must except, I consider it a beautiful specimen of moderated asceticism. Gibbon says of the author, that he preached not a word more than he practiced. Since you are dipping into practical works, let me recommend the following to be put on your catalogue, all of which are excellent, though far inferior to *Law* in style. Baxter's "Call to the Unconverted;" Edwards' "Sermons," (Pres. Jonathan,) such as are addressed to the unconverted; Davies's *ibid.;* and "The Life of God in the Soul of Man," by Scougal, a book which was blessed to the conversion of Whitefield. Let me suggest, too, the propriety of allotting a certain portion of time for such reading, and adhering rigidly to your plan. We need every constraint to pin our minds down to a subject naturally unpleasant.[43]

Never wishing to lose opportunity of speaking to Hall's conscience, Alexander concluded his letter by sharing his hope that the two of them would one day be able to sit down together "at the table of the Lord." "Oh that you would cast in your lot with us, and taste and see that the Lord is gracious," he said to his friend. He urged Hall to give solemn thought to his sin, but even more importantly, to contemplate the mercy and love of Christ toward sinners as a means of pointing his affections in a God-honoring direction:

> To-morrow, if a cold the twin of that incubus I had last spring will permit me, I hope to sit down at the table of the Lord in commemoration of his death. We expect an addition of nine or ten new members. With proper sentiments and affections, such seasons cannot fail to be among the happiest and most sacred of a man's life. Such they have sometimes been to me, and oh that you would cast in your lot with us, and taste and see that the Lord is gracious. You are undoubtedly convinced that your defect is a defect of heart, and not of understanding; that you view divine truth in what Bacon calls "a dry light." Now to remedy this let me exhort you to force your mind to the solemn and daily contemplation of those subjects which seem most calculated to excite tender emotion, viz., your aggravated sins, the mercy and love of Christ, &c., &c. This contemplation is best of

---

43. Hall, *Letters,* 1:77.

all attained in prayer, therefore cry mightily unto God for a "new heart" and a "right spirit"; bearing in mind all the while that your solemn and tremendous obligation to keep the whole law is no whit diminished, and that you do nothing satisfactory to God until you believe in Him who has kept the whole law for you.[44]

Preparing for the Pastorate

By the end of 1824, there is a noticeable shift of emphasis in Alexander's letters toward the preparation he felt necessary for the work of pastoral ministry. He knew that his time at the college would soon give way to his primary calling as a gospel minister in the service of the church. A letter dated December 24, 1824, highlights his growing excitement for the work of the pastorate: "I am endeavouring as much as I can to concentrate my efforts towards a direct preparation for the active services of the pulpit and congregation, reading theology, and trying to write sermons," he said. His letter also records his early efforts at sermon composition. "I tried my abilities at preaching the other night at the preaching society of the Seminary, in presence of most of the ladies of Princeton. It was the first regular sermon I ever wrote."[45]

Like many young preachers, Alexander found sermon composition a difficult matter. In response to Hall's inquiry requesting a copy of one of his sermons, Alexander responded, "Nothing to which I put my hand ever dissatisfies me so much as sermon writing." He continues: "I am enough chagrined after every effort of this kind to throw the thing in the fire. Whatever complacency I may feel in any thing else, my sermons are truly mortifying to me. The ideas seem of the most unspeakably trite and shallow kind." Alexander felt that his friend would be better off reading sermons by established preachers rather than one of his feeble productions. "As a *sermon*, you could not be pleased with one of mine. Let me recommend you to one of Chalmers, or to good old Davies."[46]

While he found dissatisfaction in his early preaching efforts, Alexander was filled with spiritual delight in contemplating the privilege of serving God as an ordained minister. The thrill of the Christian ministry

---

44. Hall, *Letters*, 1:77.
45. Hall, *Letters*, 1:71.
46. Hall, *Letters*, 1:74.

was beginning to capture his affections more and more. He expounded on his thoughts in a communication on January 11, 1825:

> You may think it both affected and fanatical, but I certainly see very little in this world worth living for, except to be public benefactors. This is not the result of any peculiar exercises, but arises from my daily experience of this fact, that earthly enjoyments excite, but cannot gratify; that I am daily pursuing some expected good, of which I am daily disappointed. The labours of the ministry excite most of my wishes and desires; and I confess that to serve God in the Gospel of his Son, is the only desirable thing which I have in view.[47]

In his correspondence with Alexander, Hall expressed his belief that a call to the gospel ministry was the right match for his gifts and talents—even more so than the teaching profession. Alexander agreed. "You are right in your supposition that ministerial functions will suit me better than the tedious business of teaching," Alexander responded. "I say this with great pathos, as our semi-annual examination commences on Tuesday next. Waiving the considerations of duty and religion, the active labours of preaching, &c., will be to me peculiarly interesting; and I trust that while I live, I shall be enabled to give myself '*wholly* to these things,' according to the Apostolic injunction."[48]

As he contemplated where he might go for itinerant ministry, Alexander shared with Hall that he would be open to the Lord's leading but would prefer a location in a northern climate in deference to health considerations. The one place that he did not want to go, however, was to a large city! A letter written at the end of May 1825 relates his thoughts on the matter:

> For myself—as to situation, I am perfectly indifferent; always provided that I escape a large city. I am not averse to commencing with a Virginia Mission, though I have no idea of ever settling there. I should greatly prefer a high northern latitude; yet even there the summer (to me the trying season) might be intensely hot. I am too lazy ever to secure rigid mental discipline; too whimsical to be contented; too cool and sleepy to be popular; too cautious to be efficient.[49]

---

47. Hall, *Letters*, 1:72.
48. Hall, *Letters*, 1:76.
49. Hall, *Letters*, 1:79.

Alexander's call to the pastoral ministry was not without cost. He had come to enjoy his time as a tutor at the college and knew that it provided financial security that the pastorate may not.[50] A son of the manse, Alexander was familiar with the financial irregularities of the pastoral ministry. Princeton, with all its familial and collegiate associations, meant a great deal to him, but the call of God upon his life to serve as a gospel minister meant more.[51]

> I cannot ask more retirement, pleasanter company, greater literary and religious advantages, access to books, contiguity to the cities, competent support, good air—in fine, all externals that can make a man contented, than I have now, and have too, in the very bosom of our own family, and amid my most pleasing early recollections. As it respects the money matters, with my present $400, board, fuel, servants, library, &c., I am in a better situation than many ministers who have a wife and family to boot. In truth, nothing but a deep conviction of duty will take me from Princeton—my second birth-place—the birth-place of all within me that can distinguish me from a mere animal.[52]

Alexander's growing sense of call can also be seen in statements made in correspondence from early August 1825. Although he loved to read widely, Alexander was coming to recognize the importance of devoting his study to the subjects most directly related to the work of pastoral ministry. "I see many notices of new works," he told Hall, "but have seen and read none of them."

---

50. A letter on June 8, 1825, wistfully muses on his life as a tutor: "To see me mayhap upside down, or lounging among the silent walks of the vicinity, with my colleagues,—one would scarcely prognosticate much with regard to my future usefulness. I have so long acted on the delectable adage of Shakespeare's,—'No profit grows where is no pleasure taken,'—that I suffer my days and nights to flit away with scarce a memorial left in my memory or understanding." Hall, *Letters*, 1:79.

51. Alexander's mature reflections on ministerial support can be found in a later letter of 1853: "By-the-bye, I think the talk about supporting the ministry is good and indispensable; I can say so as suffering no personal need. Nothing seems more prominent or more plain to me in the New Testament; I often wonder, indeed, that it is alluded to so much, as it is plain that primitive Christians did not neglect that duty. I do not, however, agree with those who ascribe the fewness of candidates to this. Having lived much among such, I never knew a youth who seemed to me to be held back by this reason; and he who should be so had better stay out." Hall, *Letters*, 2:192.

52. Hall, *Letters*, 1:80.

> Indeed, the nearer I approach the actual labours of the ministry, the more deeply am I impressed with the importance of giving myself *wholly* to its great concerns. Life is so short, my knowledge of subjects strictly belonging to my calling so slender, the work so great, and opposition so varied and strenuous, that I can scarcely forgive myself for wandering among a thousand things interesting, indeed, and instructive, but then irrelative to the grand scope of my ministrations.[53]

New spiritual realities had gripped Alexander's heart. What his Scottish contemporary Thomas Chalmers spoke of as "the expulsive power of a new affection" had become a reality in Alexander's spiritual life. Worldly success, fame, and literary achievements had given way to a life devoted to the calling of the gospel ministry. He longed for the salvation of the lost and resolved to give his life in service to the spiritual needs of the generation in which he lived.

> I am willing deliberately to sacrifice the character of a man of science, of taste, of varied and elegant accomplishments, with all its ease, honours, and emoluments, for that of a "man of God thoroughly furnished unto all good works"—a character which is to be sought in the study of the sacred volume. In the recesses of the mountains I shall probably be immured, where ardent piety and sound theology will be the qualifications most in request. The old copy-book adage contains volumes of meaning, *Time is short, but Art is long*: and the one department of Art, which under God I intend to devote myself to, is the art of fishing for men.[54]

Alexander's letter is careful to note the recent changes that had taken place in his life. It also provides opportunity for him once again to implore his friend Hall to seek a relationship with Christ *now*, lest, with the passing of the years, his heart become hardened to gospel truths and he forever forfeit the day of salvation which was presently available to him:

> I suppose entering upon the cares of this world, and departing from your relatives and home, is a thing which you put far away. No man need desire it. It begins to assume a serious aspect to me. Yet the cause in which I go forth is one which ensures me every encouragement. Never for a moment have I regretted that religion has been my

---

53. Hall, *Letters*, 1:83.
54. Hall, *Letters*, 1:83–84.

choice, or that the ministry is to be my profession. My sole regret is that I have manifested so little devotion in the cause, and spent no more time and labour in forming a character suitable to the work. With regard to the whole matter, I can testify that the greatest happiness I have ever enjoyed has been in the exercise of religious feelings; and that all other sources of pleasure have in the end proved worse than nothing. I regret, therefore, that you have never made the serious and sincere resolution to renounce all worldly things—as a portion—and to devote yourself to God. I know, too, that difficulties must increase, and that five years hence, unless a callous and confirmed indifference shall preclude all such considerations, you will confess, if God has not renewed your heart, that you are tenfold more unable than now to obtain a proper spirit. I can say nothing new. But let me entreat you, as one not without some experience in these things, to have recourse to those means so often urged upon you; and above all, in view of your confessed alienation from God, to relinquish sin, and embrace the religion of the cross. You know that I speak what is reasonable; that your acts may be such, is my earnest prayer.[55]

---

55. Hall, *Letters*, 1:84.

I cannot…say enough of the freedom and cordiality with which the social intercourse here is conducted. You must come and see for yourself. The money which in the North is spent upon the houses and furniture, is here laid out upon the table. I presume that no people in the world "live higher" than the Low Virginians, or Tuckahoes, and by these terms I mean all who live on this side of the Blue Ridge. There is a suavity and grace in the manners of gentlemen of the first rank in this State, and a peculiar fascination in their elocution, which you will understand better if you have ever seen Tazewell, Clay, or John Randolph. The ladies have a frankness which surprises a Northern man at first, and leads him to think that he is receiving special condescensions, when nothing more than common civility is intended.

—JAMES W. ALEXANDER
Petersburg, Virginia
January 27, 1826

Chapter 4

LICENTIATE: 1825–1827

In the Presbyterian Church, men are first licensed to preach the gospel and only afterward receive ordination by the denomination. The intermediate step is intended to serve as an opportunity to gain ministerial experience alongside a seasoned minister and to test the budding gifts of young men who feel the call of God on their life to serve in pastoral ministry.

Hall notes, "Mr. Alexander was licensed as a probationer for the ministry, October 4, 1825, by the Presbytery of New Brunswick in session at the village of Cranbury." Alexander delivered a trial sermon on John 3:3 in partial fulfillment of the licensure process. Having sustained his licensure exams, Hall records that his "first discourse, under his license, was preached in the lecture room of the Cedar Street church, New York, on the 8th October, from Jeremiah ii. 19. On the next day, which was Sunday, he repeated the sermon in one of the churches of Brooklyn, and preached in the Cedar Street church from Galatians ii. 16."[1]

Writing from his home in Princeton on November 14, 1825, Alexander spoke of the affection he had for his surroundings and how busy he had become now that he was licensed. "I am so shortly to bid adieu to Princeton that I am more sensible than ever of the pleasures it has afforded me as a home. Since I saw you, I have been called to preach every Lord's day; and as this has always been out of Princeton, it has laid me under the necessity of riding up and down continually."[2]

Alexander informed Hall that he would soon be leaving for Virginia to begin his trial period. Providentially, Alexander was to be mentored

---
1. Hall, *Letters*, 1:88.
2. Hall, *Letters*, 1:89.

by his uncle, the Rev. Dr. John R. Rice, who served a congregation in the city of Petersburg. Alexander was both excited and a bit nervous about his move to the South.³

> My departure towards Virginia is fixed (Deo volente) at the 1st December. I feel not a little anxious with regard to my future course. Yet two things support me: 1st. I have devoted myself to a good work, and am willing to be spent in it. 2d. I am under the care of a merciful Providence, by which all things will be conducted aright. Something of my own insufficiency I feel—deeply feel—and sometimes am conscious of an ardent desire to live only for the work of Christ: but alas! My ordinary tempers and manners savour little of the cross. Yet I know the excellence of what I try to preach, and am ready at all hazards to proclaim it, and recommend it to others.⁴

While en route to Petersburg, Alexander visited Baltimore, Maryland, and Richmond, Virginia, for the first time. In a letter written from Baltimore on December 5, 1825, Alexander shared his impressions of the city: "Baltimore surpasses my highest expectations. I looked for much splendor in this great emporium and thoroughfare but so much elegance, and neatness, and commercial bustle, and public improvement, I was not prepared to find." He was impressed with the citizens whom he met and enamored at the peculiarities of the dialect he encountered. He writes:

> And the people whom I have as yet seen, are in manners and equally kind attention, superior to any *class* of persons I have ever known. There is something in the dialect of the Marylanders, especially as it flows from female lips, which is truly enchanting, being a golden mean between the curt and succinct enunciation (*ut ita dicam* [so to speak]) of the Yankee, and the full-mouthed rotundity and carelessness of the Virginian.⁵

---

3. In an earlier letter on March 17, 1824, Alexander had expressed reservations about a move to the South because of its position on slavery: "My constitution calls for a Northern climate. Lower Canada would suit me: my feelings and prepossessions would lead me southward, but slavery appals me: literary considerations make the Middle States alluring, though I can't say that this latitude fits my temperament. The wants of the church point out a large expanse of territory to the South and West, and I confess that (as the Quakers say) I *feel a drawing* to those three sister States north of the Ohio, where slavery has not set her foot." Hall, *Letters*, 1:37.
4. Hall, *Letters*, 1:89.
5. Hall, *Letters*, 1:90.

Hall notes that during his time in Baltimore, "Alexander was solicited to become the colleague of the aged Dr. Glendy in that city, and in Richmond he had the opportunity of receiving a call from the Shockoe-hill congregation; but he did not yield to either."[6] Alexander declined both invitations, preferring instead the rural area in Virginia where his father had first ministered as a young man.

Petersburg

Having arrived at Petersburg in mid-December, Alexander was surprised by the amount of work his position required. "When I came into Virginia, it was with little notion of the manner in which my time would be engrossed by necessary business, and constant avocations." The kind of pastoral visitation expected of him was also different from that which he had known in New Jersey:

> Scarcely had I reached this place, before I found myself under commands to hold forth at the rate of five or six times in the week; and in addition, there is hardly a day in which nine or ten hours are not taken up in giving and receiving visits; and these are not your short, formal city calls; but *bona fide* visitations, a houseful at a time, enlivened by the peculiarly abundant good cheer of this bountiful land, and the copious flowing of rum toddy, and the like reflections.[7]

He enjoyed the outdoor activities that a rural lifestyle provided—the confines of the Princeton community had given way to the picturesque scenery of the Virginia countryside. "Could you see me galloping in the neighbourhood upon a high-blooded horse, in company with fellow equestrians, and a carriage load of beauty and vivacity, you would declare that all the Virginian in me had been at once resuscitated and matured," he wrote Hall.[8]

While his workload was demanding, Alexander was pleased by the welcome he had received in his new place of residence. "As to society; I am free to declare, that I have never so enjoyed social and Christian intercourse in my life, as here. Without trying it, you can have no conception of what Southern hospitality means. After all my preparations

---

6. "James Waddell Alexander," 71.
7. Hall, *Letters*, 1:91.
8. Hall, *Letters*, 1:91.

and previous knowledge, I find myself daily surprised with the winning cordiality and kindness of the people. And this not merely in expression and words." "Every house seems at once a home," he said, "and every individual devotes himself heartily and with manifest satisfaction to your service."[9]

Because of the rural nature of the community in which he resided, most of Alexander's visitation took place on horseback. Riding skills were essential for the work in which he was engaged as he traveled the lonely footpaths and hilly terrain. "A man who comes here, must come with some equestrian skill, or expect to get his neck broken," he shared. "I have to ride through narrow passes in the hills, going to make visits in the country, where you would suppose a horse could scarcely balance himself, and on steeds which seem to be trained to curvet and run away. Let me assure you I have been more than once in 'bodily fear.'"[10]

Although Alexander may have found aspects of his workload burdensome, he acknowledged the satisfaction he discovered in giving himself wholeheartedly to his calling. Like his Lord before him, he found spiritual pleasure in the service of others even when it came at the expense of his personal time:

> Labour is growing upon me. I am engaged to assist my uncle for a month, and have as much regular duty as though I were actually settled. This is well: it fills my thoughts, and directs my attention to the work of my vocation; and my daily experience is, that the world has fewest cares, and my heart purest peace, when I can in some measure live among earthly things without expecting my pleasures from them. Never shall I regret having made religion my choice, though it is every day my lamentation, that it has through my willful inattention and unfaithfulness so little moderated my worldly affections, and lifted me above sublunary joys.[11]

Besides his work in pastoral visitation, Alexander was gaining valuable experience in learning how to preach extemporaneous sermons. While Northern congregations tended to prefer written compositions, churches in the South preferred an extemporaneous delivery style. "I find my time taken up altogether by my duties as a preacher. There is no

---

9. Hall, *Letters*, 1:91.
10. Hall, *Letters*, 1:92.
11. Hall, *Letters*, 1:92.

toleration here for reading sermons; so that my extemporary powers are called constantly into requisition."

The joy Alexander experienced in pastoral ministry was rooted in the life of piety which he often spoke about with Hall. In a letter on January 27, 1826, he invited Hall to join with him in tasting "the sweetness of piety" through embracing gospel promises. Alexander knew the spiritual satisfaction that salvation brings to one's soul and was eager for Hall to find the same spiritual repose in Christ in which he had come to delight in recent years. In the midst of the busyness of his new pastoral life, Alexander had not forgotten the spiritual needs of his closest friend:

> My business is one altogether delightful. In proportion to the zeal with which I devote myself to religion, I ever find my happiness increase; and I cannot but hope, that after having so long thought of religion theoretically, you will at length cast in your lot with us, and taste of the sweetness of piety, as a matter of experience and practice. I need not pretend to say with how much joy I would hail you as a Christian brother, if not a brother in the ministry of reconciliation. Will you not give [these] solemn claims a new hearing, and will you not seek [grace to] overcome those bonds which fasten you to the world. Of the guilt and danger of impenitence, it is needless for me to warn you; but let me say, Why will you not determine, immediately, and at all hazards, to beseech of God to grant you the influences of his Spirit?[12]

Slavery

Alexander's involvement in Virginian society caused him to reflect upon the plight of the slaves. He realized that the genteel culture at that time from which he benefited could not exist were it not for the institution of slavery. While he credited the way in which a small number of slaves had profited from their household associations, he acknowledged the abuse that many suffered under the "dread institution."[13] He wrestled with what could be done to correct the abuse and remove the institution now

---

12. Hall, *Letters*, 1:94.
13. A passing reference from a letter written November 14, 1825, highlights the inclusive educational environment of the seminary ministerial training program: "The Seminary has commenced with more than a hundred students; among the rest a coloured man from Schenectady—a very sensible, genteel personage." The contrast in African-American privileges in his present circumstances from that of life in Princeton could not have been more vivid. Hall, *Letters*, 1:89.

that the South had become so economically dependent on slave labor.[14] He did not think returning slaves to Liberia a suitable solution any more than the problems that would be created if the slaves were freed all at once.[15] His observations can be found in a letter penned to Hall on January 27, 1826:

> When I consider how much of the comfort, luxury, and style of Southern gentlemen would be retrenched by the removal of the slave population, I can no longer wonder at the tenacity with which they adhere to their pretended rights. The servants who wait upon genteel families, in consequence of having been bred among refined people all their lives, have often as great an air of gentility as their masters. The comfort of slaves in this country is greater, I am persuaded, than that of the free blacks, as a body, in any part of the United States. They are no doubt maltreated in many instances; so are children: but in general they are well clad, well fed, and kindly treated. Ignorance is their greatest curse, and this must ever follow in the train of slavery. The bad policy and destructive tendency of the system is increasingly felt: you hear daily complaints on the subject from those who have most servants. But what can they do? Slavery was not their choice. They cannot and ought not to turn them loose. They cannot afford to transport them; and generally the negroes would not consent to it. The probable result of this state of things is one which philanthropists scarcely dare to contemplate.[16]

Charlotte County

The remainder of Alexander's licensure period was spent in Charlotte County, Virginia. He arrived at his new post in May 1826. "The spring, with all its freshness, has opened upon us, and the early fruits are pouring in abundantly," he said. The terrain was far less hilly than that of Petersburg. "The face of the country exhibits no great variety; indeed, the forests of pine in many places obstruct the prospect altogether." But in ways similar to his work in Petersburg, large blocks of time were spent

---

14. The principal commerce in Petersburg was originally tobacco. By the time Alexander arrived, the tobacco commerce had largely shifted to Richmond with cotton now having replaced tobacco as Petersburg's primary cash crop.

15. During the 1820s and 1830s an effort was made by the churches to return and colonize slaves in Liberia. For an account of the efforts, see Archibald Alexander, *A History of Colonization on the Western Coast of Africa* (Philadelphia: William S. Martien, 1849; repr., Freeport, N.Y.: Books for Libraries Press, 1971).

16. Hall, *Letters*, 1:93.

traveling by horse to the families he visited. "All my moving from place to place is on horseback; and I ride from sixty to seventy miles in mere visits to the people whom I serve."[17]

The people in Charlotte County were also marked by a plantation subculture. Unlike today, farmers were among the wealthiest and most highly educated citizens of their communities—at least on the plantations. A letter written on May 19, 1826, records Alexander's initial impressions of his new community:

> The manners of the people are plain, frank, hospitable, and independent; proud of their Virginianism, and all its peculiarities. I suppose that no set of people in the world live more at their ease, or indeed more luxuriously, so far as eating and drinking are concerned. No farmer would think of sitting down to dinner with less than four dishes of meat, or to breakfast without several different kinds of warm bread. It is, moreover, (I speak of this county,) a moral country; no gambling, no dissipation or frolicking.[18]

Writing on February 16, 1827, from a plantation called "Retirement," Alexander updated Hall on his activities. He informed Hall that "preaching, riding, visiting my charge, and studying, principally Hebrew" were the primary ways in which he spent his days. Alexander also used the time to keep up on ancient and foreign languages. "I have read a good deal of French lately, and also twelve books of the Iliad in Greek." He would have enjoyed contributing articles to the *Biblical Repertory*—a new theological journal which had begun publication under the editorship of Charles Hodge—but he felt that his remote location kept him too academically isolated to review recent publications. He complained, "Every thing becomes stale before it reaches me."[19]

As he completed his licensure period, he looked forward to the day of his ordination. In God's providence, he would be installed to serve as pastor in the same congregation in Charlotte County to which his father Archibald Alexander had been called three decades earlier.[20] Thoughts of his personal inadequacy filled his mind as he considered the responsibilities he would soon be undertaking as an ordained minister.

---

17. Hall, *Letters*, 1:95.
18. Hall, *Letters*, 1:95.
19. Hall, *Letters*, 1:97.
20. One of Alexander's sons would later be called to serve the same congregation.

If nothing unforeseen occur to prevent, I shall be ordained on the 2d March. The solemnity of such an investiture is well calculated to excite some deep solicitude. Never did I feel more than at present my unfitness for the office. There is a frivolity and worldliness in my character, most remote from the sanctity of the Gospel. In my best moods, I feel great delight in its duties, and can with all my soul recommend its doctrines and spirit to all whom I love.[21]

---

21. Hall, *Letters*, 1:97.

Short as was the term of this engagement, the young minister learned valuable lessons in active parochial life, and in the practice of preaching sermons which there was not time to write. Here, too, he underwent the salutary discipline of a serious illness, which compelled him to return to the North, and finally to resign his charge. This made an interruption of a year to his capacity for active labour. But the time was not lost. His faith had a stern probation, and it came all the stronger prepared for future trials, for a more solemn, earnest treatment of the work of life, and for a more sympathetic intercourse with the afflicted. "Death" (this was his testimony at the time), "has been viewed by me as a precious entrance into eternal bliss."

—JOHN HALL
October 9, 1859

Chapter 5

CHARLOTTE COURT-HOUSE CHURCH: 1827–1828

Alexander was "ordained to the work of the gospel ministry by the Hanover presbytery" on March 3, 1827, at which time he was installed as pastor of the Charlotte Court-House Church. A large number of clergymen and laity attended the service. Alexander's uncle, the Rev. Dr Benjamin H. Rice, preached the ordination sermon from Col. 4:17—"And say to Archippus, Take heed to the ministry which thou hast received in the Lord, that thou fulfill it." "It was a solemn service," Alexander remarked, "one which I hope to remember with feelings of awe as well as gratitude."[1]

A letter written from Retirement on March 13, 1827, describes the beauty of Alexander's surroundings:

> We are now enjoying spring in all its sweetness. I am sitting with opened windows, into which the 'sweet south' is breathing. Our gardens are redolent with vernal fragrance. The time of the singing birds has come, and no country can boast of more charms in this respect than Virginia. The wood lark, and the mockingbird are songsters of the first order.[2]

Written on his birthday, Alexander's letter also records the emotions he felt about his spiritual progress as a Christian. Like many of his later letters to Hall, Alexander chastised himself for not having accomplished more by this time in his life.

> This day I am twenty-three years old; and the recurrence of a birth-day when properly viewed gives occasion for many solemn

---

1. Hall, *Letters*, 1:99.
2. Hall, *Letters*, 1:98.

reflections. How much of my life has passed fruitlessly! How little have I done in forming an elevated character! How many have been eminent public benefactors at this age! I feel as if my religious proficiency had been small indeed, compared with that of many whom I could name.[3]

Alexander's birthday reflections led naturally to concerns about his friend's spiritual welfare. Troubled by his personal spiritual failures and misuse of time, Alexander wanted to galvanize Hall to serious reflection on his own spiritual state. "Let me beg of you also, at this interesting period of our life, to ask seriously, what stand you intend to take with regard to the all-important matter of religion."[4]

Southern Life

A number of the letters written during this period are filled with anecdotal observations on Southern culture. Alexander took a genuine interest in community events. One of the more notable entries describes in detail the public "stump speeches" that took place on the day of a local election, the balloting process, and the fights that broke out at the end of the day among the losers! "After the election sundry petty squabbles took place among the persons who had been opposing one another in the contest. Towards night a scene of unspeakable riot took place; drinking and fighting drove away all thought of politics, and many a man was put to bed disabled by wounds and drunkenness."[5]

While his rural pastorate was far removed from the academic community in which he had grown up, Alexander still found opportunity for intellectual stimulation in his new home. Books were a mainstay in Alexander's life. Not only did they provide the cultural resources which he so enjoyed, but they also allowed him to keep company with the great minds in the history of the church and Western civilization.[6] Among Roman authors, Alexander cherished the writings of Cicero. "I have also read again such of Cicero's works as I own; greatly longing to possess them all, and in good truth might I tell thee my desire, I would fain have all

---

3. Hall, *Letters*, 1:98.
4. Hall, *Letters*, 1:98.
5. Hall, *Letters*, 1:101.
6. "What I have learned of Latin has been preserved not by classical reading, but the perusal of Latin works on Theology." Hall, *Letters*, 1:118.

the Roman writers, so rich are they in goodly matter, and adorned after so shining a manner with every device of wit and similitude." Alongside influential Roman writers, Alexander immersed himself in the works of "Owen, Baxter, Boston, Bates, [and] Cecil in English," "Mastricht, Mark, Witsius, in modern Latin," and "Calvin, Dwight, and McDowell, in modern English."[7]

The disciplined ministerial example that his father modeled is also to be found in Alexander's daily schedule. His notes provide an interesting glimpse of pastoral life in rural Virginia during the first half of the nineteenth century:

> Rise at 4; shower-bath; dress; shave; a walk or exercise in the garden; family prayers at 6; breakfast ¼ before 7; read Scriptures; a lesson in Hebrew; Greek Testament in course with commentaries; Old Testament with commentaries; cursory reading of Greek Testament; English bible; preparation for sermons; theology; German; I have luncheon at 11, dinner at 2 ½; after dinner I expatiate, read every thing, ride, walk, lie on the grass, &c.; tea at 7; family worship at 8; bed at 9.[8]

Alexander's letters also indicate the way in which he successfully adjusted to the extemporaneous pulpit expectations of the Southern churches. By the spring of 1827, Alexander had become more comfortable with his delivery style. "I have *not* written a single sermon since I have been in Charlotte," he informed Hall, "though I have composed more than a hundred."[9]

Although Alexander's experience in pastoral ministry may have been limited, his understanding of its responsibilities was quite mature. His family background, studies at Princeton Theological Seminary, and licensure experience under the tutelage of his uncle all contributed to a deepening appreciation for the work of the pastorate.

While he recognized the primacy of the pastoral office, he also respected the legal profession into which Hall had recently been inducted.[10] In a humorous note, he congratulates Hall upon his new profession while warning him of its "mental" liabilities:

---

7. Hall, *Letters*, 1:106.
8. Hall, *Letters*, 1:106–7.
9. Hall, *Letters*, 1:106.
10. "Pray inform me how you and the practice agree. Does the magnificence and awful grandeur of the divine science of law, as developed and exhibited within the walls of our courts, stupefy you with amazement? Or have you wrought yourself into the belief

Accept my congratulations upon your entrance into the practical arena of litigation. May you prove false the assertion of Burke, who while he acknowledges that legal science strengthens the mind, says, "but it is not apt, except in persons very happily born, to liberalize the mind exactly in the same proportion." Or rather, will I say may you prove that you are one thus happily born.[11]

By the end of summer, Alexander had fallen ill. A brief note written from Charlotte Court-House in late August 1827 describes his symptoms and the way in which Alexander sought to sanctify his affliction as preparation for eternity in case the illness proved fatal. "I have only strength enough to write a mere note," he told Hall. "My mind and body are racked with the lingering distresses of a bilious fever, shorter (as yet) but more violent in its immediate symptoms, than that of last summer. Through the mercy of God, I am spared again (I hope) to praise him more sincerely, and serve him more faithfully. Death has been viewed by me as a precious entrance into eternal bliss." As with many of his previous letters to Hall, Alexander urged his friend to devote his life to Christ in order that he might be prepared for the day when a disease became the appointed time for one's death. "My dear and early friend, I have only strength enough to say, devote your heart, your life, your all to the blessed Jesus."[12]

The illness incapacitated Alexander's ability to perform his pastoral duties, forcing him to return to his family home in Princeton. As the months passed, his letters began to take on a somber tone. His sense of pastoral inadequacy became more magnified. At times, it appears that his bouts of melancholy had gotten a strong grip on his outlook. The bright hues that mark earlier letters give way to shades of grey in the way he now looked out upon the world around him. Even his return to Princeton for recuperation of his health did little to nurse his sense of despair. A letter in March 1828 describes his feeling of hopelessness:

> Alack! The world looks barren to me. I am unable to face its calculating and censorious actors. I am too inert to be useful: too greedy of knowledge to digest any for use. Unworthy of the holy calling

---

that a cross-examination is the purest occasion of attic wit, and a feverish court room the arena for eloquence?" Hall, *Letters*, 1:108.
11. Hall, *Letters*, 1:107.
12. Hall, *Letters*, 1:107.

which has separated me nominally from the world, I have too much of worldly attachment to be bold and decided in my Master's cause. I am such a one as needs a task master through life: left to myself I am a mere butterfly, sipping at every flower. Divine mercy has again and again spared me; and I still wonder for what end, so useless do I appear to myself.[13]

During his time back in Princeton, Alexander began to contemplate a change in pastoral location. While he enjoyed the rural beauty of the Virginia countryside, he sorely missed the cultural variety and intellectual stimulation that a larger town or city could provide. He had strong attraction to a ministry in Philadelphia but did not feel competent to serve a city congregation.[14]

Writing from his family's home in Princeton on May 6, 1828, Alexander shared how his outlook had changed. A feeling of angst had overcome his youthful exuberance. The innocent pleasures of early manhood had given way to a more despondent outlook bereft of the joy he once had in life:

> The country is as lovely as the sweet and genial breath of spring can make it. From the window where I sit, I look upon fields covered with a rich and sudden verdue, and upon orchards in their fullest bloom. Something, however, has so chilled my nature, that I have none of those delightful emotions which I used to experience, when I carried Thomson's Seasons on my long walks, and found a pastoral scene in every grove.[15]

For a variety of reasons, Alexander's pastoral ministry in Virginia would soon end. While the Southern climate was more temperate, it appears that Alexander did not find it conducive to his health. Aspects of Southern society, especially slavery, were oppressive to his conscience. Likewise, the rural location was far too isolated for a man of his intellectual interests. His bachelorhood may also have contributed to his loneliness. By July, Alexander's letters from Princeton reveal a lack of direction in his future plans.

---

13. Hall, *Letters*, 1:108.
14. "I should relish highly a visit to Philadelphia.... There is no place where I would rather live, while I know my utter incompetency to fulfill the duties of a city pastor." Hall, *Letters*, 1:109.
15. Hall, *Letters*, 1:110.

My situation is superlatively *ennuyante*. Without a charge, without regular labour, or the stimulus of definite prospects, I suffer much from the increase of indolent and melancholy musings. As soon as summer is fairly over, I expect to revisit Virginia, with the view of winding up my concerns there, and then looking around me for some situation suitable to my talents and inclinations.[16]

As the weeks passed, the tension Alexander had about his future place of ministry becomes more exacerbated in the correspondence with Hall. A letter dated August 28, 1828, captures the ambivalence Alexander felt about his present circumstances:

My time at present hangs rather heavily upon my hands. Being in that amphibious state between actual labour and total idleness, without a settlement, and yet subject to the constant demands of persons who need preaching, I feel myself very much impaired in mind and spirits. Surely I am losing all that romantic sentimentalism which used to sweeten even my ordinary walks, and create a fairy world in moments of idleness. In the month of October I expect to revisit Virginia, to close my connexion with an affectionate and beloved people, and shall, with leave of Providence, return about the first of the year, with the hope of finding a resting place nearer home. I already feel that it is deeply injurious to a young man to be so long in forming permanent connexions. The habits acquired in this changeable sort of life are peculiarly adverse to mental improvement and maturity of character.[17]

By early October, a Presbyterian congregation in Trenton, New Jersey, had begun to solicit Alexander's interest in serving as their pastor. Given an alternative, Alexander would likely have chosen another location for pastoral ministry, but at the time, it was his only option. While it may not have been his preference, he saw it as a way out of the "slough of despond" in which he found himself.[18] "As to Trenton, the place has no charms for me; yet in my present circumstances I must do something,

---

16. Hall, *Letters*, 1:110.
17. Hall, *Letters*, 1:112.
18. "My time passes on in a very dull manner. I have had to preach every Sunday, without stimulus enough to lead me to the preparation which is my duty. I rise about seven, and spend most of my time in studying German; walk a little in the woods, and along the brooks, visit none, and have no company, no correspondent except yourself." Hall, *Letters*, 1:114.

and the unanimity and cordiality of the call to that place, in the absence of all other 'openings,' cause me to look with some favour upon the situation." "It would be no small satisfaction to me to be placed within a few hour's sail of Philadelphia," he assured Hall. Most importantly, the congregation was not in the South. Alexander's exposure to the slaveholding culture of the South had troubled his conscience such that he felt it would not be the best environment for a man of his convictions to do pastoral ministry. "As to my future course in life, I am able to speak only negatively; I shall never seek a settlement south of the Potomac unless driven to it by necessity."[19]

Alexander returned to Virginia during November in order to make arrangements for dissolving the pastoral relationship with his congregation. His emotions, understandably, were conflicted. He loved his congregation, and they loved him with an equal affection for all that he had done for them. Intimate and pleasing as the ties were, Alexander had come to realize that he would be better suited for a congregation "north of the Potomac." His months in Princeton had also reminded him how huge the cultural differences were between the Southern states and those in the North.[20]

A letter written to Hall shortly after his return to Virginia in November 1828 explains the contrast in lifestyle that he experienced:

> The dirty, gloomy ugly town of Petersburg presents the same appearance as it did three years ago, when I entered it for the first time. I now perceived that I was in Virginia by the gangs of negroes, some with burdens on their heads, others driving wagons of cotton and tobacco, women arrayed in men's hats, and children with scarcely any raiment at all. I preached five times in Petersburg, and came "up the country," by the mail route, in company with Mrs. Taylor of Petersburg, sister of Judge Marshall, a lady of genius and information. I expect never to see so many persons so rejoiced to meet with me, as appeared at the little church last Sunday. It is painful indeed to leave friends so cordial and sincere, but I believe I am pursuing the path of duty. I enjoy here a delightful retreat from the world, and suitable opportunities for study, if I had such books as

---

19. Hall, *Letters*, 1:112.
20. For a sophisticated study examining the culture of the antebellum South and growing evangelical criticism of its institutions and social values, see Robert M. Calhoun, *Evangelicals and Conservatives in the Early South, 1740–1861* (Columbia: University of South Carolina Press, 1988).

I desire. For my solitary walks, I have a boundless range, affording many varieties of rural prospect, and I indulge myself in many woodland rambles. In such a retirement, however, I feel the need of some extrinsic excitement which might urge to continued exertion: the total absence of this, and the stagnation of mind consequent upon this want, convince me that I shall not lose by going forward a few steps nearer to the busy world. I hope to be able to indulge my writing propensities, as I shall be nearer to the vehicles of thought and literature, and may perhaps stumble upon some department of knowledge, in which I may be useful.[21]

While Alexander sorrowed about the prospect of leaving his congregation, he was encouraged to learn about the revivals that had broken out among churches in the surrounding area while he was gone. The famous New England evangelist Asahel Nettleton had recently conducted a preaching tour in Virginia. His messages were convicting, and a number of people professed faith in Christ for the first time.[22]

> The noted Mr. Nettleton spent most of the last summer in an adjoining county, (Prince Edward,) and was made the instrument of a wonderful reformation. Multitudes of irreligious persons have been brought into the church, and among the rest some of the most respectable professional men in this region of country. In the church next to mine, 118 have professed religion during the last few months. This revival still continues, and is extending itself in the counties of Lunenburg, Cumberland, and Buckingham.[23]

The emotions Alexander felt about leaving his congregation were compounded by the news he received about a friend from his student days at the seminary. The sudden death of one of his former classmates reminded him afresh of the need to be prepared for his own demise. He was convinced that the possession *and* practice of genuine piety were both essential in order to be adequately prepared for the day when he too would die.

---

21. Hall, *Letters*, 1:114–15.
22. For informative treatments of Nettleton's life and ministry, see Bennet Tyler and Andrew A. Bonar, *The Life and Labours of Asahel Nettleton* (Edinburgh: Banner of Truth, 1975); J. F. Thornbury, *God Sent Revival: The Story of Asahel Nettleton and the Second Great Awakening* (Welwyn: Evangelical Press, 1977).
23. Hall, *Letters*, 1:115–16.

I have just heard of the death of Noel Robertson, a young preacher who was with me in the Seminary. He left North Carolina for the sake of his health, but has been cut off when he supposed that he had found a salubrious climate. How affecting a monition to myself! I see clearly that those men are the happiest who are most entirely devoted to a religious life, and who not only profess religion as I do, but exemplify it in their daily conduct.[24]

With his sights now set upon a pastoral call to Trenton, New Jersey, Alexander's December correspondence records a new confidence regarding his future usefulness in pastoral ministry.[25] His reading of John Newton's letters to William Cowper no doubt proved a spiritual tonic at this time in his life.[26] The happiness he now felt had been restored to his life was accompanied by a renewed interest in writing and translation of important articles.[27] It was through the use of his pen, perhaps more than anywhere else, that Alexander again thought he could make a lasting contribution to his generation and beyond.[28]

> The question *Cui bono?* [What or who is good?] is one appropriate to all our literary toils. Especially in composition I think it should be more my endeavour than it has theretofore been, to do something which may be profitable. The thought of benefiting our contemporaries is one which ought to excite the most sacred ambition, if such an expression may be tolerated. "For what am I living?" ought indeed to open our eyes to those practical duties which arise out of our social relations. This is undoubtedly very new to you, and perfectly

---

24. Hall, *Letters*, 1:116.
25. "But my duty as well as interest is to learn contentment with the exact situation in which I am likely to be placed." Hall, *Letters*, 1:118.
26. "I had just been reading [Rev. John] Newton when your letter came, and was pleased to find your opinion coincident with my own. The constant correspondent of Cowper could not be an ordinary man. His letters, though numerous, I think his best productions." Hall, *Letters*, 1:117.
27. "We may translate works truly great, useful, and popular; we can write originally little able mediocrity." Hall, *Letters*, 1:116–17.
28. Alexander believed that the ministry in Trenton would provide more opportunity for study and writing than he had experienced in Virginia: "Since I wrote I remember that Butler has published a life of Grotius, and just now I am so taken up with preaching and visits T.T.L., that I can scarcely find time to put pen to paper. If spared to reach Trenton, I may hope to have most of my mornings in my study, and this will be to me a sort of Paradise. When I preach in the week, it steals away a whole day, and a single visit is sometimes nearly as bad." Hall, *Letters*, 1:116.

original. I venture the thought because it has recently dwelt much upon my own mind.[29]

Having passed through months of emotional turbulence, Alexander thanked Hall for the friendship they shared:

> *Our* friendship has been made more secure in my opinion by its eminent sobriety; it has been free from romance and sentimentality. I know that you would be much overpowered if on meeting you I should give you an embrace, and tell you how greatly I loved you: yet such is the friendship of many. Some have thus caressed me, who do not at this moment care one straw for me, or my interests.[30]

Alexander preached his farewell sermon at the Charlotte church on December 28, 1828, from John 16:3. His pastoral experience in Virginia provided a valuable opportunity for him to learn firsthand the rigors of the ministerial office to which he had been called and would devote the remainder of his life. The friendships that were formed would also continue to be a source of encouragement and support to him and his family in the coming years.

---

29. Hall, *Letters*, 1:117–18.
30. Hall, *Letters*, 1:118.

If I am to be a pastor, and nothing but necessity could make me willing to be any thing else, I believe I have more openings to serve Christ here, than in any more laborious charge. I have counted up about fifty persons, with whom I have had religious conversation, and who are more or less tender. A great excitement would bring these to the anxious seat, and probably into the church; but without this I have an access to them which no other person could have, for a long time; and which I should not have to the same number elsewhere. The same kind of argument applies to a number of other topics. Still, I feel my constitution to be inadequate to the labours. I usually carry an aching head to a pillow of restlessness every Sunday, Wednesday, and Thursday night; and am truly incompetent for pastoral visitation. Yet, the life of a minister has great satisfactions and rewards, which I trust you may experience in a far higher degree than your unfaithful friend. Some of my most delightful hours have been spent in sick-rooms, by dying-beds, or among poor, unlettered believers, or especially in rejoicing with them that do rejoice for the first time in Christ.

—J. W. ALEXANDER
March 5, 1832

Chapter 6

TRENTON: 1829–1832

Alexander began his new pastoral charge in January 1829.[1] For the moment, doubts about his pastoral effectiveness seem to have subsided. He was excited to be back in New Jersey and close to family and friends. A letter written shortly after his arrival describes the satisfaction he felt with his new residence:

> My first business in my new lodgings is to write this epistle. I am peaceably inducted into my very pleasant little study facing a retired street, within five minutes' walk of my church, and convenient to the tavern, barber's shop, and post office. I have no shelves, desks, or any array of literary appointments as yet; and as to my ill-fated books, where are they?[2]

Alexander's personal library soon reached Trenton. "My books have arrived," he told Hall, "to my inexpressible joy." Alexander was thrilled to be reunited with his beloved books.[3] "No husband ever greeted his wife more gladly after a six months' absence," he remarked. "My books are indeed my treasure, and limited as their number is, they are dear to me, as being the source of my greatest enjoyment. My study is my

---

1. Alexander was formally installed as pastor of the First Presbyterian Church of Trenton by the presiding presbytery on February 11, 1829. "On that occasion his father presided, Dr. Miller delivered a discourse, the Rev. Mr. Colley gave the charge to the pastor, and the Rev. Mr. Perkins, of Allentown, the charge to the congregation." Hall, *Letters*, 1:119.
2. Hall, *Letters*, 1:119.
3. Alexander's reading interests while at Trenton included theology, languages, and the liberal arts: "Outside of his theological reading, including daily study of the original Scriptures, he read largely in the Greek and Roman classics; added Italian and Dutch to his foreign languages; translated from the German hymnology; dipped into chemistry, physiology, and civil law, and indulged in a wide scope of miscellaneous literature." "James Waddell Alexander," 72.

Paradise; and when evening has closed in upon me, and I find myself seated by a sparkling fire, with no threatening of interruption, and with a mind at ease, I envy not the autocrat of all the Russia."[4]

The church in Trenton numbered about two hundred fifty communicants, although Alexander thought "this is rather more than the number really attending with us." The congregation included noteworthy public officials, but not all were communicant members.[5] "The Chief Justice (Ewing) of the State, is one of my main supporters, and Mr. Southard will soon be a hearer."[6] The constituency of his new charge prompted Alexander to prepare messages that would minister to their educational level.[7] "Under the new circumstances I feel a greater stimulus to what may be called the external or literary part of preparation, than I ever experienced among my simple flock in Virginia."[8]

One of the first pastoral cases he reports on deals with the tragic illness of a young woman whose life had been spent on the vanities of high society and who was now facing an imminent and untimely death. Barely two weeks into his new pastorate, Alexander became intimately involved in ministering to her daily needs:

> In fulfilling my office as pastor, I am called every day to visit a young girl of seventeen in the last stage of consumption. You know the flush of uncommon beauty, and the brilliancy of eye which sometimes characterize the countenances of those who are the victims of this hopeless disorder. These are in an eminent manner exemplified in this interesting creature. She was a belle, and one of the most thoughtless, and it was her sin and folly to defer preparation for death until the last hours of her life. In consequence of this she had suffered unspeakable pangs of remorse and apprehension, and my sympathies have been awakened by the appeals of this lovely yet dying penitent to me a feeble instrument, for some ground of hope. After many struggles, I cannot but hope that she has found secure rest in an unconditional surrender of herself to the mercies of God

---

4. Hall, *Letters*, 1:121.

5. "Being the capital of the State, it was the residence of a number of prominent men of the bench and bar, and officers of the government and legislature." "James Waddell Alexander," 71.

6. Hall, *Letters*, 1:120.

7. "There is intelligence enough to afford me some stimulus, and as I generally observe a regular theological method in the succession of my morning discourses, I am enabled to make my reading in divinity a preparation for the pulpit." Hall, *Letters*, 1:121–22.

8. Hall, *Letters*, 1:120.

in Christ. No less than four young ladies within my limits are apparently dying with pulmonary complaints.[9]

The young woman died shortly after Alexander had penned his letter to Hall. In correspondence from the following week, he writes, "I mentioned to you in my last, the case of an interesting girl who seemed to be dying. She has now departed with great increase of hope in her last hours. I preached a discourse over her remains." The circumstances of her premature death reminded Alexander of the brevity of life. "Such scenes as these," he reflected, "make me sometimes feel the vanity of all things below, and the importance of being more wholly devoted to preparation for eternity; but alas! The impression is too often momentary."[10]

A letter written in mid-February indicates his satisfaction with the congregation's response to his ministry among them.[11] "So far as I can learn any thing of my people, they seem disposed to treat me well, and are very much such a flock as I like to serve." The congregation valued public worship and was committed to the practice of Sabbath keeping. "I am encouraged more and more every week," he reported, "and am peculiarly comfortable and happy in my private circumstances."[12]

Despair

By early May, Alexander was again bemoaning his work in pastoral ministry. Although he genuinely cared for his flock, Alexander was a loner who often preferred his solitude and books instead of human company. He recounts his frustrations to Hall in a letter on May 11, 1829:

> Yet I should be loth to have you suppose that I am discontented. In no place I think, except Princeton, could I be more at ease. There is no sort of liberty more precious in my eyes than the liberty of visiting only then and where you please. Now this is what a Pastor cannot enjoy. He must visit all his people; and if he does this faithfully, he is cut off from almost every other out of door's work. In Princeton I

---

9. Hall, *Letters*, 1:119–20.
10. Hall, *Letters*, 1:120.
11. Alexander maintained a rigorous daily schedule: "It is my plan, but I need not say that I vary more or less every day, in practice. Rise at 7; breakfast at 8; study Original Scriptures, Theology, and Sermons until dinner at 1; afternoon spent in visiting; tea at 6; and then meetings, visits, reading, writing, &c., &c., until 11 or 12, when I creep into my cold bed." Hall, *Letters*, 1:121.
12. Hall, *Letters*, 1:122.

scarcely ever went anywhere oftener than necessity drove me. You may conceive how little qualified I am for indiscriminate visits. I am averse to making new acquaintances, and fond of sitting at home, while I have an exquisite relish for the society of one or two whose pursuits are congenial, and with whom I can live without any mask of ceremony or dignity.[13]

His correspondence from late June records the presence of bile secretions—a problem that would prove a lifelong nemesis to his health. "Bile, bile, bile! thou chief of mysteries!" he wrote to Hall. "The old women tell of the stomach's being full of bile, and how it gets into the blood and eyes, and makes the face yellow. The doctors talk of secretions and excretions, of structural and functional derangement of the liver. I shall probably be forced to go to the springs before long."[14]

Whether related to his struggle with bile secretions or compounded by his ongoing battle with melancholy, correspondence from July 1829 reports Alexander's dissatisfaction with his achievements and growing disillusionment with life in Trenton. His letter details the developing signs of old age and the toll that time was now taking on his bodily abilities—issues that would become more pronounced in later years.

My feeling of good-for-nothingness is such that I would gladly spend my whole time for some weeks in riding about the country. It is an excuse for doing nothing, while it occupies the mind, and dissipates ennui.... The houses totter, and even our church-steeple has a paralytic tremor, whenever the bell is rung. The very river loses its animation as soon as it reaches Trenton, and in some lanes the grass contends with the pavement. Heigh ho! I sigh for the greenness and variety of Princeton. Perhaps the change is solely in myself, age creeping on, animal vigour decaying. Some gray hairs variegate my head, and I have a monitory decay of the teeth, and trembling of the hand.[15]

Keeping Focus

By the fall of 1829, Alexander's emotions were under control, allowing him the freedom to continue his pastoral ministry in an unencumbered manner. It was during this time that he considered taking on editorial

---

13. Hall, *Letters*, 1:128.
14. Hall, *Letters*, 1:129.
15. Hall, *Letters*, 1:131.

responsibility of the *Biblical Repertory*, a journal to which he would contribute a variety of articles over the course of his lifetime, second only to Charles Hodge in number.[16]

As the year came to an end, Alexander's mood had changed for the better.[17] In a letter dated December 4, 1829, he spoke appreciatively of his flock and the way in which he had been blessed during his first year of ministry in Trenton. He admitted that the occasional disillusionment that he experienced was of his own making and that he had no desire to repeat the painful pastoral separation that he had gone through when he left his congregation in Virginia:

> Yea: it is not to be dissembled that I feel a very lively satisfaction in finding myself in my own den, by my own fire, dipping into the accustomed inkstand, and listening (as I do this moment) to the clock of my own church. This pleasure is enhanced by finding a welcome, where I expected a scolding, and by renewed assurances of regard from my people; a regard which I reciprocate more cordially every day. In hours of discontent, I sometimes wish myself a thousand leagues away, and fancy that no one has so many perplexities; but the difficulties which afflict me arise, I am sure, from my own culpable indisposition to be faithful, and whither could I fly, where a slothful and evil heart would not make me unhappy? Once I have had experience of the wretchedness of leaving an affectionate people, and the experiment is one of which I crave no repetition.[18]

In correspondence written two months later, he commented further upon the temperamental mood swings to which he was prone and their impact upon his pastoral effectiveness. He writes:

---

16. Founded by Charles Hodge in 1825, the journal was initially titled *Biblical Repertory: A Collection of Tracts in Biblical Literature* (BR); in 1829 it was retitled *Biblical Repertory: A Journal of Biblical Literature and Theological Science* (BR). Between 1830 and 1836, the journal was titled *The Biblical Repertory and Theological Review* (BRTR); from 1837 to 1871 the journal was published as *The Biblical Repertory and Princeton Review* (BRPR). Established for the purpose of providing translations of important theological articles and representative publications of European authors to an American audience, the journal soon became a repository for original works of theology written by the faculty of Princeton Theological Seminary and others within the Reformed wing of the Protestant theological heritage.

17. A more playful spirit can be found in a letter written on Christmas, 1829: "Whatever the advantages of early rising may be, there is one gratification which it affords, viz., the delight of sitting in your chair, with fixed and staring eyes, perfectly content to indulge in meditation, as comatose as a cat, and even at times purring for very pleasure; in a word, asleep with your eyes open." Hall, *Letters*, 1:140.

18. Hall, *Letters*, 1:138.

I am very much discouraged as to my ever being of much use in the world, from a mortifying conviction of my very great fickleness of purpose, or rather perhaps I ought in justice to myself to say, variableness of feeling. A subject or an enterprise deeply interests and engages me for a month, and then before I am able to do any thing practically, I have come under the influence of a new passion which urges me in another direction.[19]

A Growing Social Consciousness

Despite his recurrent bouts of moodiness, Alexander maintained a strong sense of direction in his pastoral labors. His ministerial involvement in a city environment was influential in shaping his awareness of the peculiar needs of its population. As he was exposed to the destitution and disease endemic to city life, he became increasingly burdened to address both the spiritual and physical needs of the people among whom he ministered.[20] His exposure to these problems would remain a lifelong pastoral passion—especially in later years as he ministered to the population of New York City.[21]

One of the earliest indications of his developing social awareness can be found in correspondence on February 17, 1830. Although he was still

---

19. Hall, *Letters*, 1:142.
20. The time in which Alexander ministered was one of growing social consciousness, moral outrage over slavery, and developing interest in the effects of revivalism and New Measures evangelistic practice. Alexander's ministerial activity addresses these issues and is best understood when interpreted against this backdrop. For informative overviews of the period and the way in which the Christian churches engaged the surrounding culture, see Donald W. Dayton, *Discovering an Evangelical Heritage* (New York: Harper & Row, 1976); Timothy L. Smith, *Revivalism and Social Reform: American Protestantism on the Eve of the Civil War* (Gloucester: Peter Smith, 1976). For a valuable introduction to revivals in American history and the nineteenth century in particular, see Keith J. Hardman, *Seasons of Refreshing: Evangelism and Revivals in America* (Grand Rapids: Baker, 1994). For an older but still useful study filled with much primary source material, see Charles C. Cole Jr., *The Social Ideas of the Northern Evangelists: 1826–1860* (New York: Octagon Books, Inc., 1966). A complementary volume provides fascinating treatment of the development of American culture at the end of the eighteenth and beginning of the nineteenth century. See Fred J. Hood, *Reformed America: The Middle and Southern States, 1783–1837* (Tuscaloosa: University of Alabama Press, 1980). The classic modern treatment of the social transformation that occurred in the early decades of the American republic remains Nathan O. Hatch, *The Democratization of American Christianity* (New Haven: Yale University Press, 1989).
21. Alexander would later write a book encouraging ministry to the poor and downtrodden: James W. Alexander, *Good, Better, Best; or, the Three Ways of Making a Happy World* (London: T. Nelson and Sons, 1859; repr., Birmingham, Ala.: Solid Ground Christian Books, 2009).

a young man in experience, his remarks indicate his growing interest in pastoral ministry that addresses the needs of the whole man—both body and spirit. He writes:

> It is humbling to say so, but I really believe myself to be a visionary. Just at this moment, I am very much impressed with a sentiment which I cannot express otherwise than thus: "It is the duty of some men to devote their attention to the relief of the temporal miseries of mankind." Let me explain. I do not exclude spiritual beneficence; I do not mean that a man should become a knight errant; but I verily think that Christians are not touched as they should be with human suffering, bodily suffering, privation, &c., &c. Now, if a few men would concentrate their thoughts upon this, write upon it, paragraph upon it, influence the press, talk upon it, in a word Clarksonize, I believe great things must be done. In reading the N.T. I have recently been much struck with the fact that *all* the miracles of our Saviour were acts of benevolence, and usually in *relief of human bodily distresses.* Now, the thought has powerfully come over me, Am I, and are Christians, acting in any degree like their master? I have recently preached upon the subject from Heb. xiii. 3. I have an idea that the amount of effort now put forth in Christendom would produce a hundred times as much real good, if it were systematized and properly directed. Perhaps this crude thought will not be lost upon you. It may serve to gender cogitations of your own and to direct your scissors.[22]

Death, Marriage, and Eternal Life

The depth of Alexander's growing pastoral sensitivity can be gauged in a letter he wrote to Hall upon the death of Hall's wife. It is unclear from Alexander's statements whether Hall's wife was a Christian. It may help explain the general nature of his remarks as he focused Hall's mind on his personal spiritual condition. Alexander was careful not to promise what was not true for the deceased but concentrated his remarks on what could still come to pass for Hall if he would seek "the mercy of God in

---

22. Hall, *Letters*, 1:142. Alexander's counsel to "Clarksonize" is likely a reference to British abolitionist and author Thomas Clarkson (1760–1846), whose published essay on the African slave trade, first completed while a student at Cambridge University, catapulted him into a lifelong effort to abolish the Britsh slave trade. A friend and associate of fellow abolitionist William Wilberforce, Clarkson's writings, humanitarianism, and social activism were influential in shaping public awareness of the evils of slavery and proved formative in the eventual eradication of the practice in nineteenth-century British society.

Jesus Christ." Portions of Alexander's wise pastoral counsel can be found in a communication on June 7, 1830:

> I feel, I am sure, more tenderly than ever, the obligations of that friendship which has so long and so happily subsisted between us. My regret is, that your loss is such, that condolence and counsel are the most that the kindest friend can offer. Believing, as we both do, that all human affairs are under a most wise and holy ordering, our *judgment* may rest in firm assurance that all is right; we may be convinced that it ought not to be otherwise. To school the heart is more difficult, but I believe it to be possible through the application of the same truths. Let me earnestly beg of you, then, to seek by prayer and the reading of the Scriptures, that acquiescence in the will of God, which you will find nowhere else. And let me suggest that you strive to obtain, not merely the mitigation of natural sorrow, but that instruction which God so plainly means to convey by this dispensation. After all, "the heart knoweth its own bitterness," and to every adviser, you may perhaps be forced to say with Job, "miserable comforters are you all." For this reason, then, it is the dictate of wisdom to cease from man, and go directly to the fountain of all grace and consolation. There are many topics of worldly condolence which will occur to you—as the contrast with the heavier woes of others, the deliverance of your beloved partner from all sorrow and languishment—but the aching void will still remain, until you apply to the great origin of all good, and have the love of God shed abroad in your heart. O let your strongest efforts be put forth, at this seasonable time, to obtain the gift of God, and eternal life. Your mind labours under conviction of human inability, without a due apprehension of the correlative truth, that the grace of God is ready to supply your defect of power. In the January number of the Biblical Repertory, p. 113, you will find an article on the means of repentance, which I think would tend to remove some of your difficulties. When your mind will bear such exertion, give it a perusal. It is, I believe, usually found that when any person sets about this work, with a real desire to be reconciled to God, he does attain the object of his endeavours. This is what you need to make you happy under the adversities which you have so early begun to suffer. Now it is with you (strange as the expression may seem) a favoured time, and I do think that the door stands open through which you may enter to eternal joy. My dear friend, give yourself to these thoughts, bring your mind to dwell upon the presence of Jehovah, the selfishness and evils of your heart, the necessity of regeneration, and the

mercy of God in Jesus Christ. Only seek this as earnestly as we seek worldly satisfaction, and you shall assuredly find.[23]

At about the same time Hall's wife had died, Alexander announced he was going to Virginia in order to be married. At some point during his pastorate in Virginia, he had won the affection of Miss Elizabeth Cabell, "daughter of a Virginia physician."[24] The two were married on June 18, 1830, "at Ingleside in Charlotte County, Virginia, with the Reverend William Plumer—a Princeton graduate and now a pastor in Petersburg—conducting the service."[25] Unfortunately, there is very little discussion of his engagement in the published letters. Hall edited remarks of personal interest on this topic in order to respect the intimacy of the conjugal relationship Alexander was entering into.[26]

Following his wedding, Alexander shared with Hall how becoming a husband had helped him appreciate "the endearments of the marriage state." Alexander's thoughts on the benefits of marriage and his ongoing counsel to Hall for dealing with his personal bereavement are preserved in a letter penned on July 13, 1830:

> You will be disposed to excuse my delay in answering your last, if you will consider the great burden of calls and ceremonies which lies on me at this time. My mind often reverts to you and your bereavement. While I do not pretend to understand the bitterness of the cup which you are called to drink, I believe I can much more understandingly than before, speak of the endearments of the marriage state. With a dear friend by my side who can sympathize with me in all the varied feeling which I experience, I can form a better conception than formerly of what your loss is. Yet again I say, "the heart knoweth its own bitterness." It is not to renew your grief that I touch on this topic, for I would gladly, if I could, divert your mind from the remembrance of those painful scenes, but there is a profit

---

23. Hall, *Letters*, 1:142–43.
24. Elizabeth was likely one of the unnamed "ladies" mentioned in an earlier letter: "The number of agreeable and pious ladies is remarkable; and the easy access to everybody's [house] and heart, more free than I had ever expected in my fondest hopes." Hall, *Letters*, 1:92.
25. Calhoun, *Faith and Learning*, 1:286.
26. The same is true for the remainder of Alexander's married life—virtually all of which has been edited by Hall from the extant letters which were published. In the absence of such content, the narrative of Alexander's family life will lack the fulsome content found in other nineteenth-century biographies.

in affliction, which is to be obtained only by consideration of the cause of sorrow. My hope is that in this valley of humiliation, you will be instructed and led to surrender yourself to God. It would give my wife and me very great pleasure to see you in Trenton. We are living in the very humblest manner; some of my friends think too much so for my station, but it is absolutely necessary.[27]

While not wishing to dishearten Hall in the midst of his loneliness, Alexander was careful to balance the joys he now felt in the marital state with the ever-present uncertainty of the "evil that a day may bring forth." Ultimately, he observed, our lives need to be rooted in relationship with Christ, the one whose spiritual sustenance can enable us to endure the trials of this present world.

Under my present circumstances, it would be strange if I were unhappy; it will still be gratifying to you to know that I enjoy a degree of satisfaction far above my fondest expectations. Let me not forget, however, that all human joys are fleeting, and that before another year I may morn under a sad reverse, by loss of health, or a thousand possible occurrences. This is a truth which I am sure is deeply impressed upon your mind. May you not only find out the inadequacy of the "broken cisterns," but come to "the fountain of living water."[28]

In God's providence, the death of Hall's wife proved a "severe mercy." The tragedy brought Hall to trust in Christ for his salvation. The years of persistent prayer Alexander offered on behalf of his friend had found fruition in God's quickening grace. Alexander rejoiced in Hall's conversion and sought to encourage him in his newfound faith in a letter on October 1, 1830:

Nothwithstanding the criminal apathy of my heart in the concerns of immortal souls, I experience a lively pleasure in the comfortable assurance afforded by your latest letter, that you have joined yourself to the Lord in an everlasting covenant. It is not enough, according to the Scriptures, "to believe with the heart," unless also we "confess with the mouth the Lord Jesus." May the Lord ever be with you, enriching your soul with the graces and consolations of the Holy Spirit. I am convinced that many of us suffer exceedingly

---

27. Hall, *Letters*, 1:144.
28. Hall, *Letters*, 1:144.

from having very low views of the heights of religious joy which are attainable in this life. I have just been this morning to see my neighbour—, who has just been raised up from the jaws of death. I had scarcely supposed it possible for one so uniformly pious and exemplary to receive so great an accession of spiritual life and peace. His views of the Saviour's glory, the excellence of divine truth, ministerial responsibility and his personal vileness, seemed to be really unutterable. As a contrast to this, I called to see a man who cannot live, as we think, more than a day or two, who is almost in despair, on account of his long-neglect of religion.[29]

In ways that might have proved surprising to both men, Hall's conversion would begin a new chapter in his life—the effect of which would eventually lead him down the same path to pastoral ministry that his older friend had already embarked upon. Little could either man have realized at that moment in time that one day the Rev. Dr. John Hall would be invited to deliver a keynote message at the memorial service held on behalf of his lifelong childhood friend whose persistent witness was used by God in pointing him to the salvation that he came to find in Christ.

Invitation from the American Sunday-School Union

Alexander's reputation as an author and scholar often resulted in inquiries soliciting his interest in employment opportunities with churches, colleges, and parachurch organizations. While he would turn down an offer to the presidency of Danville College, he did entertain for a brief time an invitation from the American Sunday-School Union to serve as one of its secretaries. Founded in 1824, the organization would play a pivotal role in the education of America's youth through its many publications and active outreach across denominations. Originating in England during the 1780s through the efforts of Robert Raikes, the formation of Sunday schools to educate and train the nation's youth in biblical knowledge quickly became a transatlantic phenomenon. Part of one of a number of parachurch organizations founded in the United States at the beginning of the nineteenth century to advance knowledge of the Scriptures and minister to America's citizenry, Alexander was one of the

---

29. Hall, *Letters*, 1:148.

early supporters of the American Sunday-School Union and a lifelong contributor to their publishing house.[30]

Ultimately, Alexander determined that he lacked the talents necessary to perform the work of a secretary and that the pastorate was the ministry to which he was presently called. A letter to Hall in late December 1829 summarizes his reflections on the matter:

> My mind has been much harassed by the invitation of the A.S.S. Union. I gave their first offer a refusal, but received soon after a pressing letter from Mr. A. Henry, and an "ambassage" consisting of Messrs. Porter and Vinton, who held a colloquy with me of some hours. After all my meditation, I have pretty much determined to stay where I am. Upon making the trial, my feelings will not suffer me at present to give up the proper work of the ministry. This, however, should not be rumoured, until I have formally notified the gentlemen of the Board. You know that I would rather live in Philadelphia than anywhere else, and that I have peculiar difficulties in parochial duties, yet after seeking divine direction, and communing with my conscience, I cannot see my path clearly marked out in that direction, and I dare not follow an impulse or mere inclination. A year hence, circumstances might so change in my congregation as to alter my views, but at present I feel justified in declining; especially as I am conscious of no peculiar fitness for this special office.[31]

Books and Publications

In addition to his study of the Scriptures, Alexander read extensively in sixteenth- and seventeenth-century didactic theology during his time in Trenton.[32] He found the "controversial divinity of the 17th century" valuable for the careful precision of theological formulation. "Truly I

---

30. For a valuable treatment on the origins and development of the Sunday-school movement, see Anne M. Boylan, *Sunday School: The Formation of an American Institution 1790–1880* (New Haven: Yale University Press, 1988). An early publication on the American Sunday-School Union published anonymously in 1824 is attributed to Alexander. See *The Sunday-School Anniversary* (Philadelphia: American Sunday-School Union, 1824).

31. Hall, *Letters*, 1:154–55.

32. "With it all he never intermitted the daily study of the Scriptures in both the originals; and as he generally observed a methodical theological course in his morning discourses, he maintained through the week a continuous systematic study of divinity. His theological studies were at all times almost purely exegetical. To discover, by original research, the meaning of the Bible was his first aim; and human opinions in the shape of bodies of divinity, or commentaries, were only accepted by him as auxiliary to his independent research. The Greek Concordance was his great Commentary." Hall, *Sermons*, 42–43.

am astounded at the acumen and learning of the Reformed theologians; I mean those of whom a specimen appears at the Synod of Dort, A.D. 1618–'19. The scholastic studies of the age, while they perhaps confined the mind to a narrow channel, increased the vigorous impetuosity of the torrent." In his judgment, their analysis of the theological issues in which they were engaged addressed every topic that had recently agitated theological discussion among contemporary American theologians. "I perceive no important point in the controversy *actuellement* agitated in America, which was not apprehended and brought out in full proportion and relief by these ancients."[33]

Having studied theology under his father Archibald Alexander, J. W. Alexander came to appreciate the close theological reasoning found in the writings of Reformed scholastics such as Francis Turretin.[34] A successor to Calvin, Turretin's multivolume theology was used for the classes in systematic theology taught by Archibald Alexander and later Charles Hodge.[35] Alexander writes:

> The exegetical method of studying theology is certainly the right one. The simple view in which *systems* seem to me valuable, are as indexes to the subjects of Scripture. *Turretine* is in theology *instar omnium* [the example of all]; that is, so far forth as Blackstone is in law. I would not have you concur in all his scholastic distinctions; but the whole ground is traversed, every question mooted, and even where hairs are split, the mental energy and logical adroitness with which the feat is achieved present one with an exercise of reasoning equal to any thing in Chillingworth.[36]

The works of Puritan ministers Robert Leighton and John Owen he also commended to Hall.[37] "I am charmed with Leighton, and recom-

---

33. Hall, *Letters*, 1:169.
34. For a recent English translation of Turretin's monumental work in a modern critical edition, see Francis Turretin, *Institutes of Elenctic Theology*, 3 vols., trans. George M. Giger and ed. James T. Dennison Jr. (Phillipsburg: P & R, 1992–1996).
35. For an informative introduction on Turretin's life and influence, see James W. Alexander, "Institutio Theologiae Elencticae," *The Biblical Repertory and Princeton Review* 20, no. 3 (1848): 452–63.
36. Hall, *Letters*, 1:181.
37. For a valuable summary of Owen's life and collected works, see James W. Alexander, "The Works of John Owen," *The Biblical Repertory and Princeton Review* 24, no. 2 (April 1852): 165–90. Owen's works remain in print: John Owen, *The Works of John Owen*, ed. William H. Goold, 23 vols. (Edinburgh: Banner of Truth, 1965–1991).

mend to you immediately to read his Commentary on 1st Peter. All his writings are practical, and abound in the most lively and beautiful imagery. Doddridge appears, from his editorial preface, to rank him higher than any of his contemporaries."[38] Owen's writings were revered for their theological profundity and practical spirituality. Of the numerous publications by Owen, his studies on the work of the Holy Spirit were particularly prized. "Owen on the Spirit, I have read with much pleasure, and I hope to profit. The fourth book 'on the necessity of holiness,' seems to me eminently calculated to quicken the diligence of Christians; the third chapter is golden."[39]

Along with Leighton and Owen, the Puritan minister John Howe's writings also made a strong impression on Alexander.[40] "I have at last fallen in with *Howe's* works, and find myself possessed of a rich mine of truth and piety," he said. "He is profound, and (for the age) elegant, and his spiritual flights are the most sublime and sustained I have ever read. The latter part of his 'Living Temple,' is among the most original, striking, and impulsive works I have ever seen. Above all, I wonder at his singularly Catholic spirit, in an age when the 'mint, anise, and cumin' were deemed so weighty."[41] "No works," he remarked, "have ever given me happier impulses in my religious course than those of the English non-conformists of the 17th century."[42]

Alexander's readings also included the letters of Martin Luther and the works of John Wesley. While he found some of Luther's letters "gross to a degree," he continued to immerse himself in the Reformer's correspondence during the coming years.[43] He came to appreciate their historical

---

38. Alexander's review of the life and writings of Doddridge, an influential non-conformist, appeared in 1857: James W. Alexander, "Some Account of the Writings of the Reverend Philip Doddridge, D.D.," *The Biblical Repertory and Princeton Review* 29, no. 2 (April 1857): 234–58.
39. Hall, *Letters*, 1:150.
40. For a biographical treatment of his life and writings, see James W. Alexander, "Works of John Howe," *The Biblical Repertory and Theological Review* 3, no. 2 (July 1831): 177–96. Howe's works have recently been reprinted: John Howe, *The Works of John Howe* (London: William Tegg and Co., 1848; repr., Morgan, Pa.: Soli Deo Gloria, 1990).
41. Hall, *Letters*, 1:155.
42. Hall, *Letters*, 1:150.
43. Alexander contributed a review of Luther's letters to the *Biblical Repertory* in 1830: James W. Alexander, "Review of Luther's Letters, By De Wette," *The Biblical Repertory and Theological Review* 2, no. 4 (October 1830): 504–32. A review of Luther's life appeared in 1850: James W. Alexander, "The Life of Luther; with Special Reference to its Earlier

value for understanding the spiritual pulsebeat that precipitated the Reformation.[44] Wesley's writings fared better in Alexander's estimation. "I have read eight out of the ten volumes of Wesley's works, and esteem him one of the greatest and best men that ever lived."[45]

In addition to his pulpit ministry, Alexander pursued various writing interests.[46] His lifelong enthusiasm for the work of Sunday schools and the publishing ministry of the American Sunday-School Union resulted in a number of volumes contributed to their press.[47] One of the projects he considered for the Union was a commentary on the historical portions of the New Testament designed especially for use by Sunday-school teachers. "Introductions to the Scripture of a plain kind are very needful, and one to the New Testament, I think, I will endeavour to provide."[48] The manuscript was expanded to include both Testaments and published in 1838 as *The Scripture Guide: A Familiar Introduction to the Study of the Bible*.[49] He also began a volume on the Gospels that he later abandoned when he learned that Albert Barnes, a fellow Presbyterian minister, had written a similar work soon to be published.

Periods, and the Opening Scenes of the Reformation," *The Biblical Repertory and Princeton Review* 22, no. 3 (July 1850): 437–40.

44. A related review published twelve years later speaks of the spiritual insights Alexander had gained from the reading of Luther's letters: "It is now more than eleven years since we called the attention of our readers to the voluminous collection of Luther's letters, then recently set forth by De Wette. Ever since that day we have been diligent students of these volumes, and the consequence has been a continually increasing conviction that the key to the history of the early Reformation is to be sought in the private history of Martin Luther, and that this key is found in his own writing, and chiefly in his letters, prefaces, and autobiographical memoranda." James W. Alexander, "History of the Great Reformation of the sixteenth century, in Germany, Switzerland, &c.," *The Biblical Repertory and Princeton Review* 14, no. 1 (January 1842): 120.

45. Hall, *Letters*, 1:167. Wesley's works have been reprinted on multiple occasions. See *The Works of John Wesley* (London: Wesleyan Methodist Book Room; repr., Grand Rapids: Baker, 1998).

46. "His pen was never at rest. Its prose and poetry, in books, reviews, and fugitive pieces; in translations from the Latin and German; in copious notes on his reading, which was in all departments of knowledge; in sermons and letters, his manuscript work was already portending the vast bulk it attained." Hall, *Sermons*, 42.

47. "More than thirty volumes of the Catalogue of the American Sunday School Union are from his pen." Hall, *Sermons*, 16. Hodge's funeral sermon for Alexander can also be found in Garretson, *Pastor-Teachers of Old Princeton*, 135–44.

48. Hall, *Letters*, 1:190.

49. See James W. Alexander, *The Scripture Guide: A Familiar Introduction to the Study of the Bible* (Philadelphia: American Sunday-School Union, 1838; repr., Birmingham, Ala.: Solid Ground Christian Books, 2004).

A related project in biblical studies was one that Alexander completed on behalf of his brother, Joseph Addison Alexander.[50] The volume was a kind of miniature Bible dictionary listing of people and places recorded in Scripture. "Addison has consigned to me his papers and notes upon Sacred Geography, and I have been engaged in finishing the book, [for Am. Sunday School Union,] so that we shall have it between us," he said. "The labour has been very irksome. I spent twelve hours last week verifying the texts of Scripture referred to, by looking for all of them. The mere geographical part is interesting, although it is discouraging to find how little is really known of the site of many ancient places."[51]

Archibald Alexander had suggested that he and his son James co-author a "Biographical and Bibliographical Dictionary of Theology." Envisioned as a two-volume work, it would include biographical entries and a list of the books "of all writers on Theology."[52] Unfortunately, the work never materialized.

Among the contributions Alexander made to the *Biblical Repertory* during these years was a valuable article titled "On the Use and Abuse of Systematic Theology."[53] Troubled by the indifference that theological students could exhibit to the importance of a systematic arrangement of biblical doctrine, Alexander's article is a reasoned defense of the logical ordering of biblical truth.[54] Interestingly, Hall had reservations regarding Alexander's argumentation. Writing in response to Hall's concerns in a letter on May 23, 1832, he provided a succinct summary of why the

---

50. Joseph Addison Alexander was a gifted linguist and one of the nineteenth century's greatest biblical scholars. For an informative study of his life and ministry, see Alexander, *Life of Joseph Addison Alexander*.

51. Hall, *Letters*, 1:134. The completed work was published in 1830: J. W. Alexander and J. A. Alexander, *A Geography of the Bible: Compiled for the American Sunday School Union* (Philadelphia: American Sunday School Union, 1830).

52. Hall, *Letters*, 1:145.

53. See James W. Alexander, "The Use and Abuse of Systematic Theology," *The Biblical Repertory and Theological Review* 4, no. 2 (April 1832): 171–90.

54. Alexander was also sensitive to the developmental nature of confessional statements and their bearing upon preaching. A letter in February 1852 elaborates his perspective: "I can't help seeing that the apostolic preaching could never have been conformable to prophecies in John xiv.–xvii., unless greatly different from our Lord's. Progress and development mark all the teaching through his and theirs to the end. I look on a system as a mere *report of progress* in understanding Scripture, at a given point in history. Our *preached* system differs from the Confession of Faith, both by addition and subtraction." Hall, *Letters*, 2:170.

ordering of biblical teaching into systematic categories is useful for grasping the fullness of biblical revelation:

> It is difficult to speak of one's own practice without egotism, but I find it the shortest way here of expressing my sincere convictions, and you must bear with the fault. I have never read through any system of theology; I read as much in Wesley and Watson as in Turretine. My days are almost entirely spent in studies purely exegetical, in which it has been my principle for a long time, not to approach a commentary until, if possible, I had arrived at some rational exposition of the passage. Yet I wrote the article in question sincerely, and in opposition to the cant of multitudes, especially in our seminaries, who are far from going to hermeneutics in their flight from dogmatics, but pick up their objections, and their doctrines too, from the last influential patron with whom they have studied. And I have not fabricated one objection, but have had them all urged upon me in repeated conversations; some of them having been noted down in Princeton, long ago. I shall not say another word, however, upon this question, for I hate even the appearance of controversy, in letters as in conversation.[55]

Alexander's interest in the spiritual needs of the common man also bore fruit in a series of books dedicated to the working class.[56] Various articles began to be written during these years and would eventually find publication in book form in the late 1830s. The first, *The American Mechanic*, was published in 1838,[57] and a companion volume, *The Working Man*, was published the following year.[58] Both volumes were popular

---

55. Hall, *Letters*, 1:187. Hall notes that Alexander later completed the reading of Calvin's *Institutes* but had not done so at the time of this letter. Alexander contributed an article on Calvin's *Institutes* to the *Biblical Repertory* in 1845: James W. Alexander, "Calvin's Institutes," *The Biblical Repertory and Princeton Review* 17, no. 4 (October 1845): 572–90.

56. Alexander's literary efforts, sometimes published under the pseudonym "Charles Quill," earned him the affection of the working class: "His efforts to please and edify the working classes, under the style of 'Charles Quill,' were not unrewarded, and he was prouder of their good opinion than of the compliments received from the fastidious and learned. He was once presented by a Mechanics' Association with a handsome gold-headed cane, as a token of their good opinion." Alexander, *Life of Joseph Addison Alexander*, 2:492–93.

57. See Charles Quill (Alexander), *The American Mechanic* (Philadelphia: Henry Perkins, 1838).

58. See James W. Alexander, *The Working Man* (Philadelphia: Perkins & Purves, 1839).

treatments of biblical spirituality set in narrative form to whet the interest of average readers through a kind of popular storytelling.[59]

In addition to his more formal theological publications, it was during 1830 that Alexander began his first "humble attempt at a metrical version of Gerhardt's hymn: '*O Haupt voll Blut und Wunden.*'"[60] Subsequently published in later years, Alexander's translation of "O Sacred Head Now Wounded" resulted in the introduction of Lutheran hymn writer Paul Gerhardt's classic composition to English-speaking churches.[61] It continues in popular use at the present day. Alexander's passion for the translation of older German Protestant hymnody remained a lifelong interest, eventually culminating in the publication of a small collection of works published posthumously in 1861 as *The Breaking Crucible and Other Translations of German Hymns*.[62] As much as any believer who loves to sing praise to Christ, Alexander loved to sing the theology of the Christian church in private, family, and public worship as often as opportunity afforded.

Missions

The period in which Alexander lived was one of tremendous missionary expansion. A number of new organizations had been founded in the early nineteenth century for the purposes of domestic and international missionary outreach. Churches and parachurch organizations often worked together in pursuit of the evangelistic mandate inherent to the gospel message commanded by Christ. Millennial optimism was widespread,

---

59. The two books were published as a combined volume in 1847: James W. Alexander, *The American Mechanic and Working-Man* (Philadelphia: William S. Martin, 1847).

60. Hall notes, "His first translation of Gerhard's Passion hymn was incomplete; he rewrote it, besides making versions of several other hymns, for Dr. Schaff's monthly *Kirchenfreund*. A collection of those translations, together with two of Latin hymns, was published in the *Mercersburg Review* for 1859." Hall, *Letters*, 1:151.

61. Alexander found the work of translation a challenging feat as he sought to render Gerhardt's hymns into English: "Harris, the author of Hermes, once induced a friend to learn Spanish, solely that he might read Don Quixote in the original; we should think any man repaid for learning German, by reading Paul Gerhardt. The very excellencies of his verse forbid translation. The attempt to use English idioms as strong and familiar as his, results in coarseness and vulgarity; we cannot reproduce his felicitous jingle, nor the clink of his double endings." James W. Alexander, "German Hymnology," *The Biblical Repertory and Princeton Review* 22, no. 4 (October 1850): 586.

62. James W. Alexander, *The Breaking Crucible and Other Translations of German Hymns* (New York: Randolph, 1861). For Alexander's translation of Gerhardt's majestic passion hymn, "O Sacred Head Now Wounded," see Appendix 2.

giving rise to the missionary impetus gaining momentum at this time in American church history.[63]

The urban environment in which he labored provided frequent stimulus to Alexander's thoughts on missions. While he was committed to the support of foreign missions, he also recognized the importance of an aggressive missionary outreach to the community in which he resided.

One of his earliest observations on the missionary enterprise can be found in a letter of February 8, 1831. At the time of its writing, the renewed emphasis on a denominational missions program that followed in the wake of the split between the Old and New Schools in 1837 had not yet taken place. His letter reflects the earlier support that was shown to nondenominational organizations such as the American Board of Commissioners for Foreign Missions. Interestingly, Alexander's passion for missions had been stimulated by preaching from Psalm 72 and his reading (in German) of Hengstenberg's massive study on the christological passages in the Old Testament.[64]

> Our Presbytery will probably determine to support one missionary in the foreign field, under the A.B.C.F.M. How pleasant it would be if every Presbytery would begin to do its duty by adopting this measure. Edward Kirk's church, in Albany, which is composed chiefly of poor persons, sends regularly, once a month, $50 to the Board at

---

63. For an introduction to Puritan and early American colonial views on the "millennial hope," see Iain H. Murray, *The Puritan Hope* (London: Banner of Truth, 1971). For a background study on American millennial thought at the end of the eighteenth century, see James H. Smylie, "American Millennium Visions, 1776–1800," *Journal of Presbyterian History* 77, no. 2 (Summer 1999): 119–28. For a short study examining the relationship between millennial views and American nationalism, see Christopher M. Beam, "Millennialism and American Nationalism, 1740–1800," *Journal of Presbyterian History* 54, no. 1 (Spring 1986): 182–99. For a valuable sermon that captures the millennial optimism pervasive to American Christianity at this time, see Samuel Miller, "The Earth Filled with the Glory of the Lord," *The American National Preacher* 10, no. 7 (December 1835): 289–304.

64. Hengstenberg was an influential nineteenth-century German biblical theologian whose landmark treatment on messianic prophecy was first published in English during the 1870s. See Ernst W. Hengstenberg, *Christology of the Old Testament and a Commentary on the Messianic Predictions*, trans. Theodore Meyer and James Martin, 4 vols. (Grand Rapids: Kregel, 1956). Alexander provided an early translation of Hengstenberg's interpretation of the first promise of the Messiah for the *Biblical Repertory* in 1831: James W. Alexander, "The Annunciation of Messiah to Our First Parents," *The Biblical Repertory and Theological Review* 3, no. 2 (April 1831): 263–78. For a recent study examining the influence of Hengstenberg and related German biblical scholarship upon the faculty at Princeton Theological Seminary during the nineteenth century, see Annette G. Aubert, *The German Roots of Nineteenth-Century American Theology* (New York: Oxford University Press, 2013).

> Boston. If our Presbyteries would take this in hand, several objects would be attained: 1. The churches would feel more interest; 2. The money would be more easily collected; 3. The fears of the orthodox lest unsound men should be sent, might be precluded; 4. And piety at home would undoubtedly revive. The kingdom of our Lord Jesus Christ will come, and we are bound not only to pray, but to expect its arrival. My thoughts have been led into this channel, with much delight, by reading "Hengstenberg's Christologie," a German work, in which the prophecies of the Old Testament concerning the Messiah are taken up in order, criticized, defended against rationalists, and expounded. Having thus been led to examine them in connexion, I am smitten with their glory.[65]

As enthusiasm for city missions developed, the number of "agents" also increased. Alexander reports that some forty agents were active in the city of New York alone. "We are resolved to make a trial here," Alexander remarked.

Interest in missions was also strong among the students at Princeton Theological Seminary. Missionary societies had been formed, prayer groups organized, and correspondence with student mission groups at various college campuses initiated.[66]

> In the Seminary at Princeton, the number of young men who have devoted themselves to foreign missions, is greater than the whole number of those who have actually gone into the field in time past. This is a good indication; but are there not wonderful signs of the times, in every direction to which we can turn our eyes? May the Lord enable us, my dear friend, to live in the enjoyment of a spirit consonant with these things!"[67]

The passion that the young men at the seminary had to devote their lives to the work of foreign missions caused Alexander to reflect on his own discipleship.[68] He longed for the kind of undivided devotion that characterized their lives. He writes:

---

65. Hall, *Letters*, 1:158.
66. For a brief overview of the missionary spirit that pervaded the seminary campus, see Calhoun, *Faith and Learning*, 1:137–59.
67. Hall, *Letters*, 1:161.
68. Further observations can be found in a letter on August 13, 1831: "This is a day of solemnity in the Seminary. Six young men are just about to depart on foreign missions, and the professors and students are observing a day of fasting and prayer with them.

I have been sadly thinking this morning of my own stupidity and insufficiency. I am a barren tree, long spared, in infinite mercy; but when will it be otherwise? If I could live *one year* as I ought to live, even as some *do* live, how gladly would I give up all that there is in life. I speak my genuine sentiments when I say I know not what to do; I feel that I am a babe. On one hand is dependence on myself; it has cast me down a thousand times, so that I fear to make a resolution; on the other hand is listlessness and inaction; through the influence of which I wait, and wait, and wait—and do nothing. Let us pray for one another, as I still have a hope that we know how to pray. I have some comfort in that precious word, I John ii. 1–3.[69]

Alexander's thoughts on the missionary imperative can also be found in the pastoral directives that he delivered during an 1832 address to students at the seminary.[70] He wished to instill a missionary vision in every man seeking ordination to the gospel ministry. He believed that missions was at the heart of gospel outreach and that the work of the pastoral ministry is in essence a form of missionary activity whether it is exercised at home or abroad. In his opening remarks, Alexander stated:

> Every candidate for this momentous work should consider himself as dedicated to Christ without reserve or exception; not merely devoted to this or that function, or set apart for the more easy employments of the city, or of refined society, but yielded up to the cause of the Lord Jesus, in the spirit of sacrifice, with no limitation or evasion of his bonds. There is something indescribably attractive in the character of such a youth. He is ready, if the Lord will, to go to the pestilent swamps of Burmah, or to work at the printing presses of Malta, or to endure the still greater self-denials of teaching the American Indians, no less than to display his moving oratory before a listening crowd in the metropolis, or through the press to rouse or melt the community of readers.[71]

They are beloved youth—all of them manifesting a primitive zeal and love. The Lord go with them." Hall, *Letters*, 1:176.

69. Hall, *Letters*, 1:161.

70. James W. Alexander, "Considerations on Foreign Missions Addressed to Candidates for the Holy Ministry," in *The Annual of the Board of Education of the General Assembly of the Presbyterian Church in the United States*, ed. John Breckinridge (Philadelphia: Russell and Martiens, 1832), 125–37. Alexander's address can also be found in Garretson, *Princeton and the Work of the Christian Ministry*, 2:66–74.

71. Alexander, "Considerations on Foreign Missions," 126.

The Role of Academic Learning in Pastoral Preparation

It was also during 1832 that Alexander published an important article in the *Biblical Repertory* defending the importance of a well-regulated liberal arts program as essential preparation for the rigors of theological study at seminary. Speaking from his experience as a tutor and subsequent work in pastoral ministry, Alexander cautioned his readers not to undervalue the important mental preparation a college curriculum provides:

> Young men of zeal and piety long to be actively employed in the Lord's vineyard, and view every thing as an unwelcome hindrance, which does not appear to them to have a direct and immediate bearing upon their great work. They judge thus of many subjects indeed, which are of the greatest moment, and sometimes neglect the very discipline which their minds most need.

But it was just at this point that Alexander felt that study in the humanities, and in particular subjects such as mathematics, would prove the most helpful in refining mental acumen. He notes:

> It is only necessary here to allude to the truth that it is the intellectual habits formed by these studies which give them value in a collegiate course. Tradition attributes to Dr. Witherspoon the adage that *Euclid is the best teacher of logic*; and in this pithy saying the whole argument lies in a nutshell. When we have heard a young man decrying the study of mathematics, we have generally found that it was precisely the kind of culture which he needed to systematize his vagrant thoughts, discipline his feeble reason, and give some stability to his vacillating judgment. No man ever undervalued the science who knew any thing about it. And since the ministry of the gospel demands minds trained to habits of close and rigid investigation, there is no part of our academical education which should be more sedulously cultivated. The idle and imbecile should not be encouraged in their discontents by youth who are preparing for usefulness in the cause of the Redeemer. Let the latter take counsel of learned friends, and they will soon be convinced, that deserters alone speak evil of this cause.[72]

---

72. James W. Alexander, "On Certain Errors of Pious Students in our Colleges," *The Biblical Repertory and Theological Review* 4, no. 2 (April 1832): 232–33.

Alexander's article even dealt with the objections some might have to the learning of liberal arts rather than an exclusive concentration on the study of theology:

> In a number of instances which have come under our observation, candidates for the ministry have neglected certain important branches of learning, under the pretext that they wished to dedicate the time thus gained to the study of theology, or to active labours of religious benevolence. We are constrained to say, that the conscience which approves such a course is strangely unreasonable and unenlightened. *Festina lente* [hurry slowly] should be sounded in the ears of such precipitate theologians. In a certain sense, the study of theology should employ the whole life of every Christian: that is, he should be engaged in the daily study of the Scriptures, and of instructive and practical works. But the application to the science, *ex professo* [from the one professing], has its proper place at a later period. The wisdom of the Church has decided, that, as a general rule, the two parts of preparation for the ministry should be kept distinct. The college and the theological seminary are not to encroach upon one another.[73]

As Alexander notes, students should be willing to surrender their academic preferences to the wisdom of the church in the subject matter she feels most suited for seminarians to learn at that time in their life in order to receive the training that would best prepare them for the formal responsibilities of the ministerial office.

> It should be laid down as a principle of action by every candidate for the ministry, that his time and his talents are not his own, but belong to Christ and his Church; and in accordance with this, he should avail himself of all the light which shines in the results of long experience. These results are embodied in the ordinary literary and scientific arrangements of our colleges; and while many desire to see the academical curriculum extended, and enriched by the addition of new topics, no sound scholar will consent to curtail it in any of its dimensions. Every young man should labour, during his enjoyment of these privileges, to treasure up such knowledge, and form such habits, as the past experience of the Church has shown to be available towards the defense or propagation of religion. An erratic and imperfect course of study must always end in the same result—shameful

---

73. Alexander, "On Certain Errors," 236–37.

ignorance of many things which every minster is expected to know; habits of soft indulgence and dread of mental labour; and a mind undisciplined and unsymmetrical in its acting and growth.[74]

Alexander's wise ministerial counsel to students is also reflected in his correspondence with Hall.[75] Following his conversion in 1830, Hall felt called to leave the legal profession and begin studying for the pastoral ministry. While formal studies at the seminary were not required for ordination by a presbytery, Alexander sought to counsel his friend on the liabilities of nonresidential study. Having not completed the three-year curriculum, Alexander's remarks reflect a maturity of hindsight on what he had forfeited by an early exodus from the program. His observations can be found in a letter from October 11, 1831:

> Every day I regret that I did not take the full course there, (having been tutor, as you remember.) Now, as a private student, you would have about the same advantages that I have now, and I assure you that they can in no degree supply the want of the facilities of the Seminary. I am far from considering the mere lectures of the Professors as the most important part. I hold the benefits, arising from the relation which the students have to one another, as incalculably great, and that particular kind of life as affording an admirable discipline.[76]

Ministry with His Congregation

Like many pastors, Alexander's congregation was made up of people with varying spiritual commitments. While a number were still in need of spiritual awakening, his labors had begun to bear spiritual fruit in the lives of his congregants. He described his congregation's spiritual condition in a letter on March 29, 1831:

> My own people are in a lamentable condition, yet I have in my own feeling more encouragement than ever since I have been here, and have been enabled for some time past, to give myself almost wholly to pastoral labours; so that my breast is quite sore with the unintermitted exertion of lungs in singing, and prayer, and talking. The members of the church are evidently more awake, giving more attention to the signs of the times, and joining cordially in little

---

74. Alexander, "On Certain Errors," 235–36.
75. Alexander provided Hall a list of recommended readings and related counsel for his course of theological study. Hall, *Letters*, 1:178–82.
76. Hall, *Letters*, 1:177.

family circles for conference, religious intelligence, and prayer; but the body of the people and many in the church are dead.[77]

Alexander's letter also comments on his ministry among prisoners at the state penitentiary. Ministers had ready access to prisons, and their services to the prisoners were a welcome relief to the residents. Alexander's preaching was well received, and a number of the convicts were responsive to the gospel message. A few days after preaching to the inmates, Alexander returned and visited them in their cells. It was a ministry experience unlike anything that he had encountered before.

> For the last six evenings I have attended meetings in different precincts, each of which was more encouraging than the preceding. Last Sunday afternoon I preached to the convicts in the State's prison. A more attentive audience I never had. Every eye was fixed; no averted look, no smiles, no shuffling, and at least a dozen were in tears. I spoke from the parable of the prodigal, and they seemed to sing with peculiar life—
>
> > "Take off his clothes of sin and shame,
> > The father gives command," &c
>
> I think I never felt more the unspeakable privilege of preaching the "unsearchable riches of Christ." Last week I conversed with those who are in the cells; one of whom was once an attendant (four times only) on our Sunday School; and another (24 years old) a convicted robber. The latter is as mild and comely a youth as you could well select; yet he has twice knocked down his keepers, and nearly killed a turnkey. Both of these men heard me with attention and tenderness. Let me recommend to you, if you have not attempted it, to try the delightful experiment of taking the gospel into the cells of your prisons, and to keep notes of cases and conversations.[78]

Alexander's compassion for the underprivileged was likewise directed to the African-American population in Trenton. Unfortunately, interest in Alexander's efforts fell short of his experience in Virginia. "I have made some fruitless attempts to have a Bible class among the blacks; they are strangely averse to white interference. Since I lived in Virginia, I

---

77. Hall, *Letters*, 1:162.
78. Hall, *Letters*, 1:162.

feel a peculiar yearning over [them], and sometimes feel as if I could joyfully devote myself to laboring among them."[79]

Alexander's letter dated March 29 speaks honestly of his ongoing ambivalence with regard to the duties of pastoral visitation. Like many ministers, he could at times become despondent in relation to his pastoral obligations. "The heavy rain," he told Hall, "keeps me from a row of visits which I had intended to make at this hour, and such is my guilty disinclination to this duty, that I am almost glad of the excuse." He recognized, however, that the problem was not just a matter of temperament but a lack of love for the lost. "This and other kindred feelings convince me that I lack that love of souls which is the only permanent spur to ministerial faithfulness." While he realized that the doing of "good works" is better than the not doing of them, he wanted his actions to be rooted in the proper spiritual motives. He knew that the Lord looks not only at the outward actions but the heart motivations by which they are prompted. "Yet I sometimes feel a persuasion that the Lord will accept, for Christ's sake, a duty performed against the current of natural feelings, faithfully and tremblingly, even if it is not so much a free-will offering as a self-denial. Though I have not the experience I desire, yet I think I long for it more than for any earthly happiness."[80]

A letter written two weeks later announces the birth of Alexander's first child, Archibald George Alexander.[81] "Since I last wrote, it has pleased God to make me the father of a boy; for which, and the comfortable state in which my wife is, I desire to be deeply thankful. This event, which is an epoch in our poor little lives, took place on the morning of the 8th inst. The child is called 'Archibald George,' as simple Archibald is no designation in our family." Alexander rejoiced in God's kind provision to him and

---

79. Hall, *Letters*, 1:162–63.
80. Hall, *Letters*, 1:163.
81. James and Elizabeth Alexander had a total of seven children, four of whom died in infancy or very young. Three boys survived to adulthood, one of whom, Henry Carrington Alexander, the third-born son, became the biographer of his uncle Joseph Addison Alexander. J. W. Alexander's firstborn son was in actuality George Cabell Alexander, who lived from 1831 to 1839. A second son, officially named Archibald, was born in 1832 but died in 1834. Unfortunately, references in Alexander's letters during the 1830s do not always distinguish which of the first two boys is being referred to in descriptions of their various illnesses. To further complicate matters, Alexander's published letters only provide intermittent references to the births or circumstances of his other children. Consequently, their sporadic appearance in the narrative of his family life reflects the limited information contained in the *Familiar Letters*.

his wife and how God in His wisdom assigned such an important role to women in the conception and care of their children. "When I consider how great the sufferings of the female sex are, I scarcely know how to explain the matter, or assign the final cause, unless it be that God in great mercy chooses to apply suffering, as a means of grace to those who are intended to be useful in forming the infant mind and giving early impressions."[82]

Alexander's letter also makes note of the spiritual progress that his congregation had made since writing to Hall at the end of March:

> Since last Sabbath (our communion then occurred) we perceive something like a more awakened state of feeling amongst us. Several, I believe, to be deeply anxious, and several converted, and a number more in that peculiar state of susceptibility and attention, which is neither conviction, nor yet indifference, but a mean betwixt the two.... Still it is my hope that the spirit of grace and supplications which seems to be poured out, is but the beginning of a more extensive and gracious effusion. Fifteen were admitted to our communion on last Lord's day, ten of whom were from the Pennsylvania side of the Delaware.[83]

Denominational Concerns

Issues that had been festering within the Presbyterian Church erupted with new vigor in the 1830s.[84] A number of factors were at play in the tensions disrupting the denomination. The "New Measures" popularized by Charles Finney were only part of the problem.[85] The Plan of

---

82. Hall, *Letters*, 1:163.
83. Hall, *Letters*, 1:163.
84. The story has often been retold. For a useful introduction to the period with analysis, see D. G. Hart and John R. Muether, *Seeking a Better Country: 300 Years of American Presbyterianism* (Phillipsburg, N.J.: P & R Publishing, 2007), 91–165. For a related introductory overview of Old School and New School emphases, see S. Donald Fortson III, *The Presbyterian Story: Origins & Progress of a Reformed Tradition* (Lenoir, N.C.: Presbyterian Lay Committee, 2013), 145–64. For an informative summary of the theological issues under debate, see Calhoun, *Faith and Learning*, 1:211–55. For an important Old School critique of New School doctrinal aberrations, see Samuel Miller, *Letters to Presbyterians on the Present Crisis in the Presbyterian Church in the United States* (Philadelphia: Anthony Finley, 1833). For a modern treatment of New School prerogatives and their impact upon American Presbyterianism, see George M. Marsden, *The Evangelical Mind and the New School Presbyterian Experience: A Case Study of Thought and Theology in Nineteenth Century America* (New Haven: Yale University Press, 1970).
85. The New Measures included: "praying for persons by name, allowing women to pray and testify publicly in mixed groups of men and women (in apparent contradiction of biblical teaching in 1 Timothy 2:12), encouraging persons to come forward in an altar

Union formalized in 1801 between Congregational and Presbyterian churches introduced the modified Calvinism propagated at Yale College by Nathaniel Taylor and subsequently embraced by a number of New School Presbyterian ministers.[86] "Taylorism" was also apparent in various parachurch and missionary organizations which emerged during the opening decades of the nineteenth century, and whose services were supported in their initial stages by many within the Presbyterian Church of both Old and New School convictions.

The modified Calvinism offered by Taylor found expression in numerous Presbyterian pulpits but drew particular attention in the publications of the Rev. Albert Barnes, pastor of the First Presbyterian Church in Philadelphia, Pennsylvania. Barnes's sermon "The Way of Salvation," first preached in 1829 to his former congregation in Morristown, New Jersey, was a source of continuing controversy that shadowed his reception into the Presbytery of Philadelphia when he received a call from the First Presbyterian Church in 1830.

The matter was referred to the church courts and considered somewhat of a referendum on the theological trajectories facing the denomination. In the early stages of review, the division of opinion was more constrained regarding Barnes's theological nuances and debate related to the transfer of ministerial credentials from one presbytery to another. The denomination divided into three parties. The "Orthodox" led by Ashbel Green and his supporters wanted a conviction for deviation from the theology represented in the Westminster Confession which Barnes had taken vows to uphold. A second group, in large measure associated with the faculty at the seminary, were called Moderates, primarily for hesitating on

---

call to the so-called anxious bench, mobilizing groups of workers to visit all homes in the community, and displacing regular church services with 'protracted meetings' held for several weeks." Keith J. Hardman, "Finney, Charles Grandison," in *Encyclopedia of Religious Revivals in America*, ed. Michael McClymond (Westport: Greenwood Press, 2007), 1:171. For a representative selection of primary sources with introductions supportive and critical of New Measures methodology, see McClymond, *Encyclopedia of Religious Revivals in America*, 2:140–55.

86. For an older study on Taylor's life and theology, see Sydney Earl Mead, *Nathaniel William Taylor 1786–1858: A Connecticut Liberal* (Chicago: University of Chicago Press, 1942). For a recent treatment of Taylor, see Douglas A. Sweeney, *Nathaniel Taylor, New Haven Theology, and the Legacy of Jonathan Edwards* (New York: Oxford University Press, 2003). For an informative discussion on the theological revisions represented by Taylor and Finney, see E. Brooks Holifield, *Theology in America: Christian Thought from the Age of the Puritans to the Civil War* (New Haven: Yale University Press, 2003), 341–69.

more punitive measures even though they conceded areas of weakness in Barnes's theological statements. The remaining group, predominantly "New School" ministers, believed system subscription to the Westminster Standards was adequate and chose to reject the strict subscription requirement being used to establish Barnes's supposed theological deviations.

Alexander's initial remarks on the brewing controversy can be found in a letter of December 20, 1830. By that time, Barnes's published version of his 1829 sermon, "The Way of Salvation," had found wide circulation within American Presbyterianism. On such doctrines as original sin and the guilt Adam's descendants incurred or the extent of the atonement which Christ's death provides, Barnes's theology seemed far more complicit with the modified New England theology of Nathaniel Taylor than that of the Westminster Standards which he had taken vows to uphold. While Barnes's call to the presbytery of Philadelphia in 1830 was upheld, his sermon (referred to by Alexander as a "book") was condemned in the same year by the presbytery for its unguarded statements. The actions of the presbytery in affirming his call while condemning his published theology resulted in an appeal by Barnes to the General Assembly of 1831. Alexander's observations draw attention to the procedural matters at issue as well as some of the theological formulations at stake in the early stages of the conflict:

> As to the Barnes controversy I may say that I should feel very badly if it should ever become necessary for me to give a vote upon it. Viewing it in gross, I am clear that the measures of the Orthodox party were uncalled for, and inconsistent with their toleration of such men as * * * * * *. Their spirit has been bitter and unfraternal, yet that of the Moderate men has not been altogether dove-like. With respect to what I consider the fundamental principle of Mr. B.'s friends, viz.: that it is unconstitutional to condemn a book, without arraigning its author, and that Presbytery is incompetent to examine into the orthodoxy or heterodoxy of a member, without a regular accusation, I am fully with the present majority. The cases of Davis, Craighead, &c., are precedents which establish the principle; and I should feel free at any time, as a member of any judicature, to call up and censure any book, of any sect, by which the purity of the church might be endangered. As to the probable result in the General Assembly, I do not see how any thing can come up before that body, except the mere question of order, as to the right of examining the book. At the time when the complainants appealed to the higher court, there had

been no definitive sentence passed upon Mr. Barnes or his sermon. I see no way, therefore, in which their final decision can be adduced in the General Assembly, in any orderly manner. That body will, therefore, I hope, throw the matter out of doors, after deciding the point of order; as to which, we may presume, there cannot be much debate, unless it is taken up as a mere party question. My impressions upon reading Mr. Barnes' defence are twofold. I am gratified to perceive that he is so much nearer the truth than I had supposed. I am pained at the want of candour in many parts of that production. In illustration let me refer you to the paragraph in which he justifies his assertion, that it is easier for an unregenerate man to love God, than to hate him. His reply does not touch the objection, and involves a violent perversion of common language. Not one reader in ten thousand would have alighted upon the construction which he gives the phrases. In common candour, he ought to have taken back, or qualified those unhappy expressions. The defence of his statements on Imputation, is plainly an after thought, and the ground taken very diverse from that of the sermon. His allegations concerning the old Calvinists, are, I think, triumphantly answered in the article on Imputation in the Repertory.[87]

In correspondence written the following June, Alexander continues his observations on the controversy. While he disagreed with aspects of Barnes's theological formulations, he was even more troubled by the increasingly rancorous and judgmental spirit in which the matter was being handled.[88] Observations found in his letter on June 14, 1831, warn of the dangers being addressed, but also of even greater evils that emerge when matters of this kind are mishandled in the courts of the church or in the character assassination that can surface in public opinion.

> The great danger as to the upshot of the Barnes' controversy seems to be this: The case which is held up to public view, and which excites to a kind of phrenzy men and even babes and women is: *Must Mr. B. be sustained?* Now, though this involves the doctrinal question, yet independently of the latter, it is decided, pro or con, upon general

---

87. Hall, *Letters*, 1:155–56.
88. At about the same time that the Barnes controversy was heating up, Alexander had completed his reading of the life of Matthew Henry. He found the blend of orthodoxy and piety displayed in Henry's life a model for the turbulent period of the 1830s: "Have you read Matthew Henry's life? (by Williams, Bost. 1830). I have never read a more truly instructive, or cheering biography. Read it, for the sake of bleeding orthodoxy." Hall, *Letters*, 1:168.

and worldly principles, often those of mere feeling; and this decision once made in either direction, there is a prepossession formed which militates for a lifetime with candid search after the truth. I suspect that scores of spinsters in your city have become far more "liberal" theologians than ever Mr. B. will be. Our Princeton men are considered by certain soi-disant standard as "sneaking," "on the fence," &c. There certainly is such a thing as righteous moderation, and those who have practiced it have, as far as I know, in every age stood between two fires, incurring the wrath of both sides. It requires perhaps more solidity than some of these juvenile seignors have imagined, to keep this position where two seas meet. A crowd is a very convenient support to men of weak spines.[89]

A moderate by nature and by principle, Alexander aligned with the faculty at the seminary in their manner of adjudicating on the Barnes's case.[90] In October 1831, he reported on the unfortunate character assassination taking place in the public realm by members of the "Ultra" or "Orthodox" party. He writes to Hall:

> You are aware that the Princeton men are in very ill odour with the *extreme droite* of the Philadelphia Presbytery. The Repertory is considered as a craven publication, because it did not take sides at once on the Barnes controversy. Now all this is exceedingly impolite in the Philadelphia gentlemen. By excluding as "fence-men" all who have not fully participated in their panic, they run the risk of reducing their party to a mere handful. The truth is, the Princetonians are as thoroughly old-school in their theology as Dr. Green himself, but they are unable to see that it is the path of duty to denounce every dissentient individual, more particularly as it requires no sagacity to observe that the policy of Wm. L. McCalla, &c., can never result in the adoption of their measures by the church at large.[91]

---

89. Hall, *Letters*, 1:170.
90. The Princeton faculty and the *Biblical Repertory* alike were derided within the Presbyterian Church for the stand that they had taken during these years. The events were a matter of tremendous grief to Alexander: "The ground taken by the *Repertory* is sufficiently well known; but the spirit in which he contemplated the strife is evinced in such exclamations as, 'Oh for a corner where theological warfare is unknown!'—'The greatest heresy is want of love'—What would I have? certainly peace; if possible, unity of doctrine; then unity of organization; if we cannot be 'like-minded,' we may as least be 'having the same love,' and the way to attain this seems to be 'let each esteem others better than themselves.'" "James Waddell Alexander," 72.
91. Hall, *Letters*, 1:177.

While the Barnes case would wind its way back and forth in the church courts throughout the 1830s, the issues that it represented would ultimately culminate in the division of the Presbyterian Church in 1837 when a number of presbyteries and ministers were excised of their standing within the denomination. For Alexander, the division was precipitated, in part, by the failure of the various parties to interact on their differences in the spirit of Christian charity to which all believers are called to adhere.[92] The injury that it caused to the various parties was in certain respects irreparable. Its fruit would have long-lasting consequences in the life of the church for years to come.

Revivals

Alexander's pastoral labors in Trenton coincided with the outbreak of revivals along the eastern seaboard and inland areas as far west as Ohio and Kentucky—part of the Western frontier in early nineteenth-century America.

While Alexander prayed for and supported every Spirit-wrought work of revival, he was hesitant to support certain evangelistic practices that had become popular in the ministry of Charles Finney and his followers.[93] But Alexander was equally troubled by the way in which "anti-revival" Presbyterians could be dismissive of a true work of the Spirit because it did not fit their expectations of how it may manifest itself in a way different from what took place during the time in which their forefathers lived.

---

92. Commenting on his receipt of *The Presbyterian*, a new paper edited at the time by Ashbel Green, Alexander hoped that the magazine would be productive of spiritual good in reporting on denominational issues: "It is devoutly to be wished, that in 'contending for the faith' which is enjoined, they may not 'strive,' which is forbidden." Hall, *Letters*, 1:160.

93. For a careful study of the period and the theological issues that had emerged regarding Finney's theology and popular interest in New Measures evangelistic practice, see Iain H. Murray, *Revival and Revivalism: The Making and Marring of American Evangelicalism 1750–1858* (Edinburgh: Banner of Truth, 1994). For a broader study of Finney's ministry and related religious movements that emerged during this period of American history in western New York, see Whitney R. Cross, *The Burned-Over District: The Social and Intellectual History of Enthusiastic Religion in Western New York, 1800–1850* (New York: Harper & Row, 1965). For a study on the camp meeting revivalism whose features predated the rise of methodological practices Alexander encountered during his years of public ministry, see Ellen Eslinger, *Citizens of Zion: The Social Origins of Camp Meeting Revivalism* (Knoxville: University of Tennessee Press, 1999).

There are dangers attendant upon revivals of religion, which escape the notice of those who are most active in promoting them, while they are obvious to sharp-sighted men, who suspect the whole affair of revivals. *"Fas est a hoste doceri* [It is right to be taught even by the enemy]." It is unwise for some of our brethren to repel, as they do, all inquiry as to the prudence of their measures. A great and lamentable evil, into which weak but sometimes pious men fall, is the indiscriminate application of special means to all circumstances and cases, without regarding the principle upon which such and such measures have been instituted, with success. Thus the imitators of Mr. Nettleton make sad work by doing what they have seen him do, without possessing that almost superhuman sagacity which enables him to avoid failure, by addressing his efforts to certain principles of human nature. This is, no doubt, religious empiricism; and I constantly feel myself hampered by its existence among the more zealous part of my flock. It is like a good quack-ess of my neighbourhood, who is always saying: "take this," and "take that." It is the same error under a different form with that of the old formal, respectable, anti-revival Presbyterians. These say: "Our fathers did so and so, and we will do so too." I freely confess that I have as much doubt respecting "anxious meetings," as they are commonly called, especially as I have sometimes seen them conducted. There is a certain stage of an awakening when they are indispensable; *i.e.* where the number of seeking souls is great; but many of my brethren use them as a *means of awakening.* How far is this correct? An individual is tender and somewhat alarmed; comes with a vague impression to the inquiry-meeting; is conversed with; is visibly set apart as an inquirer; is thus self-committed; must do something, or seem to do something; is there not room for fear of evil? of hypocrisy? And from the perfunctory manner in which discourse is conducted, is there not sometimes much daubing with untempered mortar? I want the aid of your eyes and judgment in this matter, and I believe I propose my doubts in the spirit of candour. I *may* have a meeting of the kind before a week is over my head.[94]

Alexander was especially concerned to avoid the use of manipulative measures to induce men to seek salvation in Christ. He recognized how easy it would be to evoke an emotional response that may be mistaken for a true work of the Spirit in regeneration. A letter on April 23, 1831, identifies his concerns and also recommends Jonathan Edwards's writings

---

94. Hall, *Letters,* 1:164.

as applicable to the dispute agitating the Presbyterian Church regarding the "New Measures." Alexander prefaces his remarks by contrasting the ministry emphases of contemporary Edward Payson and that of David Brainerd from an earlier generation:

> Payson deeply affects me, but not as Brainerd does; in one case you have the *man* always before your mind in alto-relievo; in the other, you are directed away from him to the work of the Spirit in him. Edwards' concluding remarks to the Life of Brainerd, are wonderfully searching and appropriate at the present religious crisis.... What you say of extraordinary and doubtful measures for exciting religious feeling, tallies exactly with what I hear from ——'s anxious-meetings, and from other quarters. I dare not attempt such things, though if I should, I am persuaded I could next week say in the Evangelist that we have forty inquirers. I feel that this is a question of awful responsibility; and oh how strongly do I wish to be led aright, and to avoid cowardice and formality; but then, human souls and the cause of Christ are not surely fit subjects for these perilous psychological experiments.[95]

While he disagreed with the theological orientation of the New Measures, Alexander supported the growing interest in small group gatherings associated with revivalist emphases. Appreciative of the ministry model that John Wesley developed in eighteenth-century England to assimilate converts into local Methodist gatherings, Alexander favored the establishment of small home fellowships, or regional meetings, for the nurture of new believers.[96] "We need something like 'Class meetings' to prevent the frequent collapses after revival," he observed.[97]

---

95. Hall, *Letters*, 1:166.

96. In a review examining the organizational framework of the church's ministry, Alexander commented on the importance of "small" groups for cultivation of personal piety and mutual edification: "In addition to the communication of doctrinal knowledge, there should be a discipline to which every young professor should be subjected, the object of which should be the cultivation of the heart. If it were practicable to have every individual taken under some stated supervision and spiritual care from the first moment of his dedicating himself to the Lord, much of the defection which we now lament might be prevented. We have strong objections to the system of class-meeting, as they are conducted and abused, but to the principle of such a thorough organization we yield a most cordial assent." James W. Alexander, "Hints towards a more Complete Organization of Particular Churches, with Reference to Christian activity," *The Biblical Repertory and Theological Review* 6, no. 3 (July 1834): 404.

97. Hall, *Letters*, 1:167.

The cultivation of piety lay at the heart of the "Class meetings." It was equally central to Alexander's own thinking. As he reflected on the topic of piety, it led naturally to a concern for Hall's growth as a Christian. "My dear friend," he asked, "is your heart attaining more and more to a felt communion with the Lord Jesus Christ as your head, and source of all vital influence?" "Here, alas! I err most," Alexander said.

"Looking unto Jesus," is a motto suited to every hour. Duties performed, as I perform so many, with a legal spirit, are heavy to the soul and scarcely acceptable to God. In word or in deed to do all in the name of the Lord Jesus, *giving thanks*, rejoicing, relying on Him; this I find in the New Testament, in Whitefield, in the Tennents, in Newton, in some living men; but not in all who are zealous and bustling around me. "To know Him, and the power of his resurrection, and the fellowship of His sufferings," &c., Paul, the active Paul, seemed to think the great mark at which he might ever aim. Here I am conscious of a daily and habitual short-coming. The Christian paradox is, When most active, most dependent. The two ideas are beautifully comprised in the word: "I can do all things through Christ which strengtheneth me." When we are most abundant in labours, we feel most our dependence on God; and if we would stimulate ourselves to Christian activity, we can take no better way than to dwell in meditation and prayer on the truth that it is "God who worketh in us," &c., and that "He giveth more grace."[98]

As Alexander explained, his desire was for a deeper experience of the Spirit's work in his life. He continues:

Natural conscience and intellectual light may go very far; but to be *born again*, to have "all things become new," to have "crucified the flesh with the affections and lusts," to have the leading of the Spirit, the mind of the Spirit, the walk of the Spirit, the seal of the Spirit, the inhabitation of the Spirit; this is that which I long after, but do not often ascertain to my satisfaction.[99]

What Alexander hoped to experience in his personal life was being discovered throughout the Presbyterian Church as the number of local revivals increased. By early October, he was able to report that "revivals have visited about half our churches, and what is strange, principally

---

98. Hall, *Letters*, 1:165.
99. Hall, *Letters*, 1:165.

those of the ultra [Old School] of Newton Presbytery. In one church (Mansfield) a great revival is in progress without any new measures, not even an inquiry meeting." "I lay no stress upon this," he said, "but mention it as repelling the invidious charge of our opposing brethren that revivals are the seals of new doctrine and new measures only." He was convinced that fervent piety was essential for the success of the revivals. Spiritual factors, rather than human engineering, were at the heart of true revival. "For my own part, I believe that revivals depend not so much, as is thought, upon phases of doctrine, or petty arrangements, as upon the ardent piety and zealous labours of humble Christianity, apart from all these things."[100]

As the revivals multiplied, interest in them among Alexander's congregation grew. However, he was worried that his people did not understand what lay at the heart of true revival. Members of the congregation sought to substitute special meetings for the disciplined commitment to piety and prayer that typically precedes and undergirds an outpouring of divine grace. Alexander writes, "Some among us profess to desire a revival, but I plainly discern the prevalence of a common error among our professors; they wish to shift from themselves the responsibility of a great and united effort towards a revival, and to put all their hopes in a four day's meeting. I preached last Sunday in defence of revivals and against this error."[101]

In a related letter, written the following year on March 27, 1832, Alexander further elaborated his thoughts on the "New Measures" associated with revival meetings. At this stage in his life, he was reticent to condemn their employment in an evangelistic context. He saw them as an area of ministerial liberty that should not be used to bind the conscience of others who viewed their incorporation differently.[102] While not explicitly stated, the biblical principle guiding his practice appears to be "whatever is not of faith is sin." Although Alexander may have disagreed with some of the methodologies being used, he believed they were expressions of genuine biblical faith, however misguided in their application. Later years would

---

100. Hall, *Letters*, 1:177.
101. Hall, *Letters*, 1:177–78.
102. A letter from March 1842 provides further reflection on the approach Alexander had taken to the New Measures during the 1830s: "In regard to *new measures*, I wish I had always observed this rule, viz: 'Never vent any *general principle* about them; speak to the individual case; nor then but when forced.'" Hall, *Letters*, 1:354.

see a change in Alexander's perspective, but a spirit of charity in relation to men's motives proved determinative in Alexander's assessment at this time regarding efforts to reach his generation with the gospel message. Alexander explains his rationale:

> I wish all parties would read what Edwards says hereupon, in his work on Revivals. I dare not condemn a multitude of things, which I would as little dare to do. There is, it seems to me, an inordinate stress laid by both parties upon mere *measures*, as unreasonable as argument about mere ceremonies. On one hand a truly superstitious reliance is placed on certain methods of conducting meetings, &c.; on the other, certain measures are denounced as if they were absolutely anti-Christian. One man has anxious meetings, another anxious seats, a third calls them out in the aisle, a fourth invites them to his study, a fifth visits them at home. Here are diversities of methods, but no ground, I think for violent controversy. Various methods have been blessed, to my knowledge, in various revivals, and new ones are yet to be invented. On this subject, I think our old men are too tenacious. Nothing is worse in my estimation, *because* it is new, unless indeed it be doctrine. It is hard to determine in all cases what measures are the best, but almost any are better than total listlessness.[103]

Although Alexander would not endorse the use of New Measures as a means for church growth, he remained confident that the right use of the ordinary means of grace was sufficient for the purposes of pastoral ministry.[104] Preaching, administration of the sacraments, and prayer were at the heart of effective pastoral ministry. These, Alexander believed, were the primary means by which God gathers and nourishes His church in developing the Christian life.[105]

---

103. Hall, *Letters*, 1:186.
104. Alexander's views on the New Measures matured over time. Murray notes: "He was slow in coming to the conclusion that the new measures were not simply a mistake about methods, rather they were the direct result of the Pelagian belief about human nature which supposed that regeneration could take place by human decision. Described by a friend as 'one of the kindest and noblest' of men, it went against the instincts of Alexander's nature to believe that a crusade against orthodoxy was underway, led in several instances by men who, by denominational affiliation were expected to be upholders of the Westminster Confession." Murray, *Revival and Revivalism: The Making and Marring of American Evangelicalism*, 336–37.
105. For an important study on revival and its effects with contributions by leading Reformed churchmen and theologians of the period critical of New Measures excesses, see W. B. Sprague, *Lectures on Revivals of Religion* (Albany: J. P. Haven and J. Leavitt, 1832; repr., Edinburgh: Banner of Truth, 2007).

The March of Faith

Like her husband, Elizabeth Alexander was also susceptible to various illnesses that required a change in environment for the recovery of her health. In May 1831, Alexander's family traveled to Virginia to seek respite for the various maladies with which they were afflicted. Both his wife and little boy would remain in Virginia for a time in order to regain their strength. A letter on May 30, 1831, records Alexander's sadness over his separation from his family:

> I left my wife on Friday, and have heard nothing since from her; you will be pleased to learn that she was then convalescent, though still very, very, weak, and much emaciated. You know, my dear friend, far better than I, how severe are those pangs which reach us through a beloved one: pardon this seeming tearing open of a wound. How hard to the flesh is the lesson I Cor. vii. 29–31. I lately preached on it; but only the Spirit can write it on our hearts.[106]

By mid-June, Alexander had become ill as well. The problem was again that of liver secretions. "Mine is the yellow, bilious, liverish, dyspeptical, summer complaint—the beginning of those diseases which have already so often brought me down," he informed Hall.[107]

His son Archibald George's health was likewise a source of ongoing concern. "My child has never been well, having had strong symptoms of hydrocephalus since his birth. He is small and always sick, and cannot use milk in any form or measure," Alexander shared. "The Lord do with him what shall be for His glory! thus we try to feel, yet my heart cries aloud: 'O that Ishmael might live before thee.' Never have I much cheerful hope except when I study to resign myself and mine, totally and unreservedly, to a merciful Saviour and King." Ultimately, Alexander rested upon God's grace to sustain his family in their walk of faith. "I am myself a bruised reed, always crushed when set to sustain the right kind of work, yet through infinite grace not yet broken."[108]

A month later, Alexander was happy to report on the growth of his congregation. It was an encouraging sign, in spite of his earlier reservations about their spiritual interests.

---

106. Hall, *Letters*, 1:168.
107. Hall, *Letters*, 1:170.
108. Hall, *Letters*, 1:171.

> Last Lord's day we were favoured with the addition of eleven persons to our church, four of whom are active men. This is a good addition in a place where we have to draw upon the same congregation at all times, for we have no floating population or rival churches to select from. There are, I suppose, fifteen or twenty inquiring souls among us, and for four months the standard of piety has been quietly and steadily rising. Could this continue, it is just what I desire. I say so after having been in the furnace of new measures in the Troy Presbytery. I hope, however, that I am learning to be forbearing.[109]

Unfortunately, the spiritual improvement in Alexander's congregation was not matched with a corresponding improvement in his health. Since writing to Hall in June, his physical condition continued to deteriorate. Although some of the earlier symptoms subsided, his health had worsened. "I am perhaps as thin and feeble as you ever saw me, though relieved within a few weeks from my violent head-aches and bilious symptoms." Absent from his family, Alexander's illness turned his thoughts toward eternity. "Every hour I am made to think of death, and feel how slight is my tenure upon all that unduly engages my attention. May we so enter into the great realities of another world, as to be prepared to depart joyfully whenever the summons may come."[110]

As Alexander continued to deal with the debilitating effects of illness upon his body, he used the occasion to reflect on how a believer's faith in Christ and trust in the promises of God's Word must be allowed to guide his thoughts and feelings while undergoing a period of physical sickness.[111] Portions of an extended letter on August 6, 1831, follow:

> I have been very weak and thin for months past; and though the symptoms of disease have nearly vanished, I am so much unnerved as to be next to useless. I know of nothing so well adapted to satisfy the mind under trials of this kind, as the simple truth, that we and all our concerns are ruled and disposed of by a Sovereign Mediator,

---

109. Hall, *Letters*, 1:172.
110. Hall, *Letters*, 1:172.
111. Observations on sickness written a few years later remain of continuing value: "I have been considering the smallness of the benefit which we are content to derive from our ordinary afflictions. For instance: you and I have been sick lately; what good has it done our souls? Are we more heavenly-minded, and better fitted for communion with God? 'Yes, Yes,' we are ready to reply, 'but these are small afflictions, to which I scarcely look for any advantage.' Thus we seem to render great trials necessary; whereas, I suppose, every disquietude we meet ought to be received as a message from God." Hall, *Letters*, 1:257.

whose, I humbly trust, we are, and whom we serve, for "they also serve who only stand and wait," as Milton beautifully and consolingly expresses it. I wish I were able to speak of deeper and richer experience of the truth that it is good to be afflicted. So often have I been chastised with personal suffering, that I am at times alarmed to think that this trying visitation has so little purified and elevated my soul. Yet there have been seasons of affliction, especially of sickness, in which I have known more of the power and of the joy of religion, than ever in my life, and in which I have understood how glorious is that grace of the gospel which can "give songs in the night" of pain and weariness. An ordinary concomitant of bodily weakness is depression of spirits, and morbid susceptibility of impressions which alarm or grieve the mind. Under these, the most resolute and the best men have sometimes bowed, and it becomes important to learn how we may be relieved from an influence so deleterious to the spiritual exercises of the heart. And here I really believe, we too often undervalue the treasures of the Word of God, and especially the unspeakable gift—the crowning mercy—our Lord Jesus Christ. In times of peril and sickness, I have remarkably felt that I had made too little of access to the Saviour himself. Joy is more certainly diffused through our souls, by a simple, filial approach to the cross, than by any means which I have any idea of. This is remarkably characteristic of the apostolic and primitive experience. The triumphant hope and glorying of the apostle Paul, exhibited in the first part of the 2d Epistle to the Corinthians, seems to have flowed from such child-like faith: "We had the sentence of death in ourselves, that we should not trust in ourselves, but in God which raiseth the dead: who delivered us from so great a death, and doth deliver: in whom we trust that he will yet deliver us: ye also helping together by prayer," &c.: "As the sufferings of Christ abound in us, so our consolation aboundeth *by Christ*." The 4th and 5th chapters have revived my soul in some degree, within a few weeks past, when I have had very melancholy prospects as to my future health and usefulness.[112]

Like many who undergo a time of prolonged physical suffering, Alexander pondered the role of prayer in relation to the restoration of one's bodily health. His reading of Scripture reminded him that God is interested in our spiritual as well as our temporal needs, and that it is appropriate to pray for both.

---

112. Hall, *Letters*, 1:172–73.

> Do we not restrict our faith in prayer too much to *spiritual* blessings? I know these are infinitely the more important, and that our petitions for earthly good are to be under submission to the Divine will; but then how plain it is, that when Christ was on earth, he listened to the requests of the sick and mourning, that he never chided any one who asked healing and deliverance, as asking amiss, and that he invariably heard the prayer of all such. How plain, but how much forgotten, that he is the same Saviour now, with just the same views of poor, suffering, and sinning men. How explicit the promise, James v. 14. But however tried, it is still undeniable, that if we believe, all things shall work together for our good, and with this assurance we may pray with absolute certainty that our prayers shall be answered in kind, or in a higher and nobler measure and way than we intend.[113]

Individuals who have endured a season of sickness know the trials that it produces. It often serves to make their hearts sympathetic to their fellow sufferers. Alexander assured Hall that he would be in prayer on his behalf while reminding him of the "inheritance incorruptible" which lay before them at the end of their earthly pilgrimage—an inheritance that would outlast the loss of temporal things.

> Let me assure you that I shall endeavour to offer my feeble petitions for your temporal and spiritual welfare. My belief of the prevalence of the prayers which we make in behalf of individuals is strong. Dr. Rice remarked, in a letter of his which I lately read, that he had often, he thought, been prayed back to life from the jaws of death. He is now slowly rising from a long illness, which baffled all the means used, and all the hopes of his friends. After all, however, our prospect would be dark indeed, if we had only this world to which we might cling. Blessed be God, our anchor is *within* the vail, and our hope is of an inheritance incorruptible. To see Jesus, and with him to see all saints who have gone before, is a glory which we may expect; and the belief of this, independent of all other things, is support under the greatest of trials. All these things occur to you daily; yet they may not be without some force when coming from the pen of a sincere friend.[114]

---

113. Hall, *Letters*, 1:173–74.
114. Hall, *Letters*, 1:174.

Alexander's letter dated August 6 provided stimulus for another extended letter to Hall written a few weeks later, this time dealing with the marks of genuine piety. Hall was troubled about the low level of piety that he observed among Christians as well as himself. Alexander responded to Hall's inquiry with a brief summary of what piety in practice will look like. A pastorally sensitive issue, the ability to recognize the reality of piety in all its stages is a matter of both personal interest and pastoral obligation.[115] Alexander's observations on identifying and cultivating the life of piety bear witness to the balanced approach which he took to piety's maturation, expression in different personality types, and the circumstances in which it is exercised. He writes:

> Very deeply do I sympathize with some of your feelings, respecting the lowness of piety in many professors—above all in my self—the want of [πληροφορια], and the idolatry of this world. Still I find it more to my comfort, certainly more to my profit, to acknowledge the grace of God those manifestations of piety which *do* exist—manifestations which none but God can produce, and which are intended to show forth his glory, and therefore to be recognized by us. All the religion of Bible examples, so far as they are given in detail, is mixed and alloyed, saving only that of our blessed Saviour; and "weak faith" is a necessary term of relation and comparison, unless all faith is the same *in degree*, which would preclude the growth of our graces, and render the comparison of the "grain of mustard" nugatory. No doubt hypocrites will pervert this to their own destruction, and our reason might tempt us to elevate a standard which should make no allowance for defect, such is not the scriptural account. The fear of death is a natural sentiment, which often exists by association in hearts which have more unquestionable marks of piety than the most ardent desire of death could be. Whatever explanation we may give of it, it cannot be denied that men, of whose piety we are assured by inspiration, have prayed to be delivered from death—Psalm vi.; especially Hezekiah—Isaiah chap. xxxvii.—and God was pleased to grant this as a blessing, and holy men have rendered thanksgiving for the deliverance as a mercy—Psalm cxvi. Epaphroditus "was sick, nigh unto death, but God *had mercy on* him." The soul ought

---

115. One of the most valuable volumes Alexander's father would pen was on the topic of Christian piety. Archibald Alexander's insights on the nature, growth, and decline of biblical piety remains one of the great classics on Christian spirituality written during the nineteenth century: Archibald Alexander, *Thoughts on Religious Experience* (Philadelphia: Presbyterian Board of Publication, 1841; repr., Edinburgh: Banner of Truth, 1968).

unconditionally to submit to God, willing to live or die; but I am ready to think that more has been made of willingness to die, as an evidence of piety, than the Scriptures make of it. Long life is even promised as a blessing; I suppose for two principal reasons—1st, that we may do more for saving souls, (a work confined, for all that we know, to this life;) and 2dly, that we may attain greater piety, and thus have a greater capacity for heaven, and greater reward there. This is perfectly consistent with Paul's estimate of heaven as "far better," for the *rest* is at any moment better than the *labour*; still, the latter may be lawfully desired, in order to an increased enjoyment of the former. It is right to wish to see in all the faith of Abraham; but we see only one Abraham in the Bible, and many imperfect Davids, Jobs, and Peters. Moreover, I doubt not the same kind of faith is in exercise as often now. Understand me now, not as suggesting that we should be *content* with lower measures; by no means; but as dissenting from the doubt which you say you have of the *reality* of your own faith and that of the Christian community generally. This doubt is not, I think, encouraged by the tenor of Scripture, and tends, not to piety, but to the rejection of it. For surely the heart-rending conclusion that *all* are wrong, saps the foundation of Christianity itself. So, also, there is a sinful complaint under affliction, so sinful as to vitiate all a man's title; and a complaint (such as the hundreds of David) which is compatible with the actual vigour of entire submission. "If it be possible let this cup pass." We may say this in *faith*, and to say this is not to rebel. Chastisement would be nothing, were it not felt to be afflictive; and no affliction is joyous; *afterward* it yieldeth the peaceable fruits of righteousness.[116]

By the following year, Alexander's health was better, although he was still weak. As his health recovered, his outlook on life also improved. Early morning walks contributed to his recovery, as did the time he spent outside in nature. He wrote of his restoration to health in a communication on May 23, 1832:

By adopting the practice of going out very early in the morning, often before sunrise, I think I have become a little more vigorous. External nature, especially at this season, produces a remarkable and happy modification of my religious feelings; and after a glorious sunrise, I feel better all day. David no doubt felt the force of such influences: witness in particular the 104th Psalm, which I have

---

116. Hall, *Letters*, 1:174–76.

often read while looking upon the very pictures delineated in the latter part of it. From my little study window, I catch a glimpse of green fields (about three panes full) and eastern clouds, and this helps me in the morning. I always esteemed it a great blessing, at my father's house, to be able to look out eastward upon a thousand acres of meadow land, and a hundred and sixty degrees of hill and mountain on the horizon. I hold this to be not romance but reason.[117]

Coupled with his delight in nature was the satisfaction Alexander found while studying the book of Romans. "Just at this time I am floundering in that perilous channel, the vii. c. Romans. I am at the Greek and the versions, without commentaries, and am hoping to steer clear of radical error." "The noblest help in New Testament study," he said, "is the Greek Concordance, which is better than any dictionary. Some of our lexicons are nothing short of Commentaries; though you have no doubt observed this, just read Schleusner or Wahl upon such a word as πνευματικος. The concordance, on the contrary, makes the Spirit of God the commentator."[118]

In addition to his study of the text, Alexander had been challenged by the example of his brother for memorization of the Scriptures. "A– has just committed to memory the Epistle to the Hebrews in Greek and English, and about twenty of the Psalms in Hebrew. At his instance I have attempted a little in this way, and find it a great advantage; for I can speculate upon the meaning of a passage while I lie awake in bed, as I very often do of late."[119]

Alexander's letters from this period speak appreciatively of the work of the pastoral ministry, although he admits frustration with having his schedule interrupted. While the work could be exhausting, he spoke of the satisfaction he found in his labors on behalf of others.[120] A letter on June 19, 1832, highlights the busyness of Alexander's schedule:

---

117. Hall, *Letters*, 1:188.
118. Hall, *Letters*, 1:187–88.
119. Hall, *Letters*, 1:188.
120. Alexander's letters of this period also caution against ministerial formality: "Need I warn you not to think of the Ministry as free from temptations? The very habit of constantly dealing with Divine truth *for the use of others* is a great cause of dreadful formality; it obtunds the moral sensibility, impairs the tenderness of conscience, and dissociates the actions of the head and heart, to an alarming degree. In preparation and preaching I have often found that subjects which warmed and melted me in the closet, have flowed from my lips in the desk with some animation of manner, but with almost no

This instant I am called down by a man, who probably will sit an hour and leave me to guess why he called.—Better than I thought, for he gave me five dollars, missionary money, but kept me an hour, which I could not refuse, for I believe he received benefit, and was quickened by my suggestions. Yet I scarcely have two hours solid, except before breakfast, for spiritual nourishment. In a sickly season, I have not two waking hours in which I can sit down to read, much less to write. Once a fortnight I am knocked up by headache. Yet I love my work. O that I were more faithful![121]

Mrs. Alexander had also regained her health in the intervening months, but little Archibald George continued to have problems.[122] The ongoing health issues of his children were constantly before Alexander's mind and used by God for the maturing of his character.[123] "In estimating this letter," Alexander wrote in a communication from August 1832, "please remember that I write within full hearing of my little boy's cries. Oh! I have new understanding, since I became a father, of that expression 'As a father *pitieth* his children,' &c."[124]

A letter the following week expresses the concern that the Alexanders felt on behalf of their son:

Our little boy varies so little, except from one painful symptom to another, that I do not say much of him. We find the trial severe; more so by far than the ordinary death of a child. But we are wonderfully helped. Even now we find that "He who tempers the wind to the shorn lamb," makes our way smoother than one could suppose. We need the prayers of our friends.[125]

The combination of his son's health concerns and his own deepening empathy as a father led Alexander to develop an interest in the writing

---

emotion. Then the *trials* of the ministry to a man who has a conscience, are unspeakable. Who can ever say 'I have done all I ought for these souls?'" Hall, *Letters*, 1:197.

121. Hall, *Letters*, 1:190.

122. A second son, Archibald, was born into the Alexander home in August 1832. While it is possible that the references of concern refer to this son, they are likely in reference to Archibald George (Cabell), but this cannot be determined for certain as both boys had health issues, with those of the firstborn being the most severe.

123. "I am unable to say much about my little boy. We feel it to be a great trial: yet sometimes I taste some sweetness in the cup. O there is nothing but Christianity that enables one to *face* an affliction." Hall, *Letters*, 1:195.

124. Hall, *Letters*, 1:194.

125. Hall, *Letters*, 1:196.

of children's literature. "If my life is spared, and my pieces succeed," he said, "I will (D.V.) devote much of my time to babe's books. My health scarcely admits more."[126]

The burden that he had developed for the nation's youth weighed heavily upon his heart.[127] His earlier interest in literary refineries had given way to a passion for the spiritual welfare of coming generations through the publication of books and material written with the youngest readers in mind.[128] His thoughts on these matters can be found in a letter penned in mid-September 1832:

> My aim is to do something before I die to reach the millions of youth in our land. I have made up my mind to go for the nursery practice. Let others take the fathers and grandfathers, if I can only make an impression on the children. This I wish to do by writing; and I am not sure (though you may think it paradoxical) that I will not do more in this way, as a pastor, than if I were to set about it *ex professo*.[129]

Because of the ongoing fluctuations in his personal health, Alexander eventually felt compelled to resign his pastoral charge in Trenton. While he enjoyed ministerial labors with his congregation, he believed himself too incapacitated to fulfill the responsibilities of his office.[130] As would often prove the case in coming years, he felt a change in employment necessary for the recovery of his health. Accordingly, he resigned his pastorate in late 1832, exchanging the weekly labors of the gospel ministry for the editorship of the denominationally focused paper, *The Presbyterian*.

---

126. Hall, *Letters*, 1:195.

127. While ambitious in his ministerial goals, Alexander was careful to not overrate his self-importance: "However, the great query with all of us should be, where and how can we fit ourselves best for the Lord's work. The mere romance, even of religious effort, which tinges our views, is doubtless to be rejected." Hall, *Letters*, 1:169.

128. Alexander's interest in producing children's literature even included learning how to draw so as to illustrate his books. A review on this topic appeared a few years later in the *Biblical Repertory*: James W. Alexander, "Graphics; a Manual of Drawing and Writing, for the use of Schools and Families," *The Biblical Repertory and Princeton Review* 10, no. 2 (April 1838): 271–78.

129. Hall, *Letters*, 1:196.

130. "Although Mr. Alexander's pastoral work in Trenton was frequently diminished or interrupted by feeble health, his people would cheerfully have granted any amount of indulgence rather than part with him. But he was too sensitive and conscientious to retain his place under the circumstances." "James Waddell Alexander," 72.

The secret cause of this indisposition to certain parts of academical labour, is too often simple sloth. This it is the undoubted duty of the pious student to mortify. He should learn "to endure hardness" in mental, as well as bodily toils. "I find nothing," said David Brainerd, "more conducive to a life of Christianity, than a diligent, industrious, and faithful improvement of precious time. Let us then faithfully perform that business which is allotted to us by Divine Providence, to the utmost of our bodily strength, and bodily vigour." And it was remarked by Buchanan, in a letter to the venerable Newton, that although the mathematical studies of the university were little to his taste, and scarcely connected, by any link which he could perceive, with his future labours, yet he diligently pursued them, put a constraint on his natural predilections, and yielded himself to their absorbing abstractions as a part of his Christian self-denial. This is an example worthy of every Christian student. The "greatly beloved" Martyn was influenced by the same motives in those toils which caused him to be designated, while at Cambridge, as "the man who never lost an hour."

—J. W. ALEXANDER
1832

Chapter 7

EDITOR: 1833

In January of 1833, Alexander began a brief stint in Philadelphia as the editor of *The Presbyterian*. By the time he assumed the editorship, the paper had become an important Old School publication that addressed issues affecting the denomination. Sermons, articles, essays, and commentary on contemporary trends in theology and church polity provided readers with up-to-date analysis on the present condition and future prospects of American Presbyterianism. His editorial responsibilities with *The Presbyterian* and *Biblical Repertory* kept him busy. Thus, only a few letters were exchanged with Hall during 1833.

While Alexander enjoyed his work as an editor, he found ample opportunity to preach and work on his personal writing projects, many of which would be published by the American Sunday-School Union. He assured Hall in a letter on January 8, 1833, that "next to preaching, there is no employment I should relish more, than writing books for the Union."[1] Although he had not felt led to resign his pastorate in order to work for the American Sunday-School Union, he delighted in the opportunity to provide tracts and literature for the organization.

Observations on marriage filled Alexander's thoughts at this time. Once a loner, he had come to appreciate the joys of marital union. His marriage was a happy one. It had enlarged his outlook and deepened his appreciation for the spiritual enrichment that had been brought into his life. Hall had remarried after the death of his first wife, and Alexander encouraged him to speak openly with his new spouse on the subject of personal piety in order that the two of them might support one another in their pilgrimage through life:

---

1. Hall, *Letters*, 1:203.

> To you I need not say any thing of the unspeakable and increasing joys of Christian wedlock; joys which become purer and more exquisite as they lose the adventitious glare of early romance; joys which are increased by affliction, and raised by religion to the very summit of terrestrial blessings. You will not refuse the counsel, though it may be very familiar, when I urge on you to begin, as soon as possible, with freest, confidential, mutual, unbosoming on the subject of personal experience. I hear many husbands and wives complaining of a shyness here.[2]

Alexander's letter also reports on a revival that had broken out in a local Methodist church back in Trenton. Interest in the revival had resulted in declining attendance at his former congregation, but he celebrated the work nonetheless, having learned the biblical principle of "rejoicing with them that rejoice." Alexander was struck by the Methodist church's zeal for the salvation of Trenton's population.

> For the last three or four months, there has been a wonderful work of grace (so I must call it, notwithstanding blemishes) in the Methodist Church here. I think 150 have been supposedly converted. It goes on uniformly, and some of the changes are surprising. While our other churches suffer, I am persuaded the cause of Christ gains. Such zeal I never saw. They seem disposed to attempt the conversion of every soul in Trenton. God grant them success. I cannot but say that God is with them of a truth, though we have lost a number of hearers. It is not the minister, but the private members who have been instrumental in this.[3]

A letter from mid-January provides a sample outline of one of Alexander's recent sermons from Psalm 77:7. His use of the interrogative centers the exposition's focus—a series of "answers" provide the framework for the exposition, and a closing section lists points of application.

> I preached last night, with much comfort, from Psalm lxxvii. 7, "Will the Lord cast off forever?"—Answer 1. No. His *attributes* forbid the thought. 2. No. His *gift of Christ* forbids: "He that spared not his own Son," &c. 3. No. His dealing towards the *church* forbid. 4. No. His dealing in time past to *us* forbid. 5. No. His special promises forbid. Application: 1. To *have* this safety we must have interest in Christ.

---

2. Hall, *Letters*, 1:203.
3. Hall, *Letters*, 1:203–4.

2. To enjoy the comfort of this, we must have a good persuasion of our interest. 3. To be raised in triumph above all despondency, we must have the full assurance of hope. May such blessings be ours![4]

Like much of his earlier correspondence, Alexander's letters during this year mention various literary projects he was considering. He started, but did not finish, a work on the life of Elijah. He also expressed interest in writing on the life of Jacob, a work which was later published anonymously in 1836 by the American Sunday-School Union.[5] Among his research interests was the Missionary Concert of Monthly Prayer. Alexander found particular satisfaction in the writing of popular works for the general reading public. "I find no employment so delightful to me, as writing little books," he said. "I am determined not to put my name on them, and I even doubt whether I shall ever agree to say 'by author of so and so.'"[6]

By August of 1833, Alexander was saddened to learn about the condition of his former congregation in Trenton. While the community in which the church was located had grown, the congregation had struggled to maintain its vitality following Alexander's departure. He writes:

> I am really pained at heart about my late poor charge. They are dividing, dwindling, and scattering; cannot agree in any one; and though the place is rapidly growing, and soon to grow yet more, the congregation decays. Their appeals to *me* produce an effect which you can never know, until you have broken the peculiar cords which unite a pastor and flock.[7]

As tensions within his denomination between the New School and Old School continued to fester, Alexander told Hall that a division within the Presbyterian Church was inevitable. Writing to Hall on November 4, 1833, he remarked, "Two who are so little agreed as the old and new side, cannot long walk together. I look for a rupture with much certainty, and *rebus sic stantibus*, could not mourn over it, if it were possible to divide upon the principle of our book."[8]

---

4. Hall, *Letters*, 1:204.
5. See James W. Alexander, *Life of Jacob and His Son Joseph* (Philadelphia: American Sunday-School Union, 1836).
6. Hall, *Letters*, 1:204.
7. Hall, *Letters*, 1:206.
8. Hall, *Letters*, 1:207.

While the immediate horizon for his denomination's unity appeared bleak, Alexander saw hopeful signs among the incoming students at the seminary and college that would bode well for the Presbyterian Church's future. "New students are coming into the Seminary and College; two young men have *walked* from Tennessee, carrying all their clothes in their packs," Alexander reported. "Such men are worth helping; such men do the work of the Church."[9]

By the end of 1833, he decided to resign his position as the editor at *The Presbyterian*.[10] The polarization that marked his denomination was also reflected in the increasingly polemical spirit of the paper—neither of which was to Alexander's liking.[11] Providentially, the College of New Jersey had again requested his services—this time to serve as Professor of Rhetoric and Belles Lettres. The position was tailor made for Alexander. His experience in public oratory and encyclopedic knowledge of classical literature were a perfect match for what the position required.[12] He heeded the call and returned to his alma mater before the end of the year.

---

9. Hall, *Letters*, 1:207.

10. Hall notes, "Mr. Alexander's connexion with 'The Presbyterian' continued from November, 1832, until the close of the volume for 1833." Hall, *Letters*, 1:207.

11. "This post gave him a few months of more direct experience in the general interests of the church, and of the wide-spread and multi-farious observation which a religious journalist must exercise. But he thought that a less vexatious, and more retired department would be better suited to his taste and circumstances." Hall, *Sermons*, 50.

12. Alexander's election to the chair took place in September. An entry in his "Private Journal" for October 1, 1833, records his reaction: "I have never had an appointment which fell in more with my feelings. During some days since I had the first inkling of it. I have prayed that the Lord would not suffer me to be called unless it were right that I should go. To-day I have been in some pain, but blessed be God I had choice mercies." Alexander, *Life of Joseph Addison Alexander*, 1:315.

The eleven years (1833–1844) which were then passed in Princeton, though they were withdrawn from the more direct work of the ministry, and this solely on account of the infirmities of his health, were not absorbed in his literary office, or lost to the higher interests of the church, or to his prospective position in it. His correspondence, throughout that period, has less of the tone of the mere scholar or professor, than of a minister who, in season and out of season, was seeking to spread divine knowledge and to save souls. Submitting patiently to the Providential suspension of his employment as a pastor, and doing all that industry could do for the faithful discharge of his duties as an instructor, yet one who did not know his professional position, would conclude from his letters, that he was in the centre of weighty and immediate responsibilities for multitudes. His mind labored with schemes for the diffusion of healthful and conservative influences throughout all classes of society. The threatenings of infidelity and social disorganization, aroused his anxious efforts to interpose the Bible and Christianity as the only effectual antidote. His main hopes rested in the making of Holy Scripture the great organ of mental and spiritual development in education. And this, as usual with him, was a practical opinion. He was all the time working in that field: writing for children, for young men, for Sunday Schools; and his publications of every sort will be found marked with that strong impress of his theory, itself derived from revelation (for he never was a schemer), that draughts, pure, direct, and constant, from the fountain of inspired truth, are the most salutary and only sufficient remedy for the evils of the times.

—JOHN HALL
October 9, 1859

Chapter 8

PROFESSOR OF RHETORIC AND BELLES LETTRES: 1833–1844

It seemed as though a lifetime had elapsed from when Alexander had first accepted a call to serve as a tutor at the college and his recent appointment as Professor of Rhetoric and Belles Lettres. In the intervening years, Alexander had matured considerably. His pastoral experience, travel, publications, marriage, and work as an editor provided a rich backdrop to his new calling.

While Alexander enjoyed the work of the pastoral ministry, he thrived on the intellectual atmosphere of the college. He enamored himself to his students, quickly earning the respect of the distinguished faculty who served at the college during the 1830s.[1] A letter dated December 12, 1833, provides a glimpse of the weekly activities in which he was engaged:

> I attend the Seniors four times a week, on one of which occasions I spend about an hour in lecturing; the subject is Rhetoric and Composition. The Latin of the two higher classes is also consigned to me. At present, I have the Juniors five times a week on Tully's Orator. I

---

1. Student testimony provides record of Alexander's success as a tutor and professor: "A fellow-student of his brother Addison, and pupil of the young-looking, but extremely dignified mathematical tutor, tells me that he vividly remembers Mr. James Alexander's spare person and deep black eye, and how he would draw himself up and place a visible constraint upon his mobile features when any thing of a laughable nature occurred. His hair and his complexion were both uncommonly dark. His head was high, and somewhat narrow, and his face long and oval. His temples were finely moulded, and were unusually bare. The expression of his countenance was frank, noble, intellectual, and in a singular degree captivating and engaging. It was forever changing with his changing feelings. He always stood upon his native dignity, and seldom or never had cause to administer a reproof of misconduct. The classical felicity of his taste and of his diction were subjects of marvel. His piety was as evident as it was unobtrusive. He was eminently popular, without once letting down the bars of discipline. By many, he was beloved with an extraordinary affection; by some with an almost passionate devotion." Alexander, *Life of Joseph Addison Alexander*, 1:58–59.

occasionally lecture to them. Attend prayers every evening, preach in my turn in the chapel, and every Lord's day afternoon at Queenston. Every fortnight a literary club meets, viz.: Drs. Alexander, Miller, Carnahan, Howell, Maclean, and [B.H.] rice; Professors Dod, Maclean, Henry, Jaeger, Alexander; Tutors S. Alexander, Hart, and Wilson. It is truly a delightful soiree. On alternate weeks a strictly *Clerical* association meets. On Monday, we have a stated faculty meeting and in the evening a faculty prayer-meeting. On Tuesday evening a College prayer-meeting. On Thursday evening Dr. Rice preaches.[2]

A number of the meetings of which Alexander speaks would have taken place at the home of Charles Hodge. During most of the 1830s, Hodge was afflicted with an illness that left him homebound and largely confined to his first-floor study where the bulk of his literary labors for this period took place. Hodge's study became the center of intellectual recourse for the seminary and college faculty throughout these years. As A. A. Hodge explains:

> The fact of his long confinement, and the further fact that he was in age and general qualities the central man, the common bond of intercourse and action among the Princeton Professors of that day, caused his study to be for many years the meeting place and intellectual exchange of both Institutions. Here during all these years the faculty of the Seminary held all its meetings. Here the Association of gentlemen which conducted the Repertory met for the reading and criticism of articles, and for the discussion and decision of the policy of the Review. Here all debates and consultations of general interest were held, and here literary strangers, visitors to either Institution, were brought to meet the gentlemen of the town.[3]

In his work as Professor of Rhetoric and Belles Lettres, Alexander made use of authors such as Cicero,[4] Quintilian,[5] Kames,[6] Blair,[7]

---

2. Hall, *Letters*, 1:209.
3. See Hodge, *Life of Charles Hodge*, 239.
4. *Cicero On Oratory and Orators*, ed. J. Watson (Carbondale: Southern Illinois University Press, 1970).
5. Quintilian, *The Institutio Oratoria*, trans. H. E. Porter (New York: Putnam, 1921–1922). For a shorter treatment, see *Quintilian On the Teaching of Speaking and Writing: Translations from Books One, Two, and Ten of the Institution Oratoria*, ed. James J. Murphy (Carbondale: Southern Illinois University Press, 1987).
6. Henry Home (Lord Kames), *Elements of Criticism* (Edinburgh: Bell & Bradford, A. Constable & Co., 1817).
7. For a facsimile reprint of the 1783 edition, see Hugh Blair, *Lectures on Rhetoric and Belles Lettres*, ed. Harold F. Harding (Carbondale: Southern Illinois University Press,

Whately,[8] and Campbell[9] for learning the principles and practice of public and persuasive speech.[10] Blair in particular was one of the most popular of contemporary writers on rhetoric in use during the early nineteenth century. Blair's two-volume work *Lectures on Rhetoric and Belles Lettres*, first published in 1783, found widespread appeal on both sides of the Atlantic for its polished and comprehensive presentation.[11] While strong on the importance of literary elegance, Blair's work received scathing criticism from Alexander and faculty at Princeton Theological Seminary such as Samuel Miller and Archibald Alexander for the lifeless model of preaching which his approach embodied.[12]

As Alexander recognized, artifice and style are often conjoined when an undue emphasis is placed on literary elegance. Public eloquence and pulpit power are both compromised if literary ingenuity replaces impassioned, extemporaneous speech true to a man's nature and individual personality. True eloquence must be natural and not artificial. It is marked by simplicity of style, sincere conviction, and purposeful pronouncement. Grounded in the integrity of character represented in its speaker or author, whole cultures have been changed by its power to influence and motivate the hearts and minds of its hearers. Although

---

1965). For a modern typeset edition, see Hugh Blair, *Lectures on Rhetoric and Belles Lettres*, ed. Linda Ferreira-Buckley and S. Michael Halloran (Carbondale: Southern Illinois University Press, 2005).

8. Richard Whately, *Elements of Rhetoric: Comprising an Analysis of the Laws of Moral Evidence and of Persuasion, with Rules for Argumentative Composition and Elocution*, ed. Douglas Ehninger (Carbondale: Southern Illinois University Press, 2010).

9. For a facsimile reprint, see George Campbell, *The Philosophy of Rhetoric*, ed. Lloyd F. Bitzer (Carbondale: Southern Illinois University Press, 1963).

10. Alexander's classroom deportment and weekly preaching interests were recalled by one of his former students: "He was a master of old Latinity, and the modern humanities. We, his pupils, recall him now as, scrupulously dressed, he used to mount the steps to his lecture room in the old 'Whig Hall.' We recall the precise tones in which he used to quote Quintilian and Cicero, and would say to us students, 'Sir! Please to say something about Pericles.' While he was teaching us through the week, he loved to preach the gospel of Jesus gratuitously—down in Witherspoon Street Negro Chapel—to the children of God carved in ebony." Theodore L. Cuyler, "James Waddelll Alexander D. D. Address," in *The Alexander Memorial* (New York: Anson D. F. Randolph & Company, 1879), 20–21. Cuyler's address can also be found in Garretson, *Pastor-Teachers of Old Princeton*, 172–75.

11. Blair's work was among the recommended titles students studying at Princeton Theological Seminary in the early nineteenth century were encouraged to read. For Samuel Miller's instruction on "style," see Garretson, *Able and Faithful Ministry*, 214–27.

12. For representative criticisms, see James W. Alexander, *Thoughts on Preaching: Being Contributions to Homiletics*, ed. S. D. Alexander (Edinburgh: Banner of Truth, 1975), 273–74.

Alexander would at a later time come to realize the undue importance contemporary rhetoricians had placed on formal composition, he appreciated their observations on the parts of public speech and the practical benefits to be gained from their analysis for sermon composition.[13]

During his first year at the college, Alexander began a series of letters that were later published in 1838 as *Letters to a Younger Brother*.[14] "He began his series of letters in the Sunday School Journal, January 1834, and continued them to twenty numbers, when they were collected in a volume."[15] Similar in style to other works he produced during the 1830s, his little volume taught biblical principles through the conversational plotline of the book's leading characters.[16] A series of children's articles also appeared.[17] As with a number of his publications for children, they were authored anonymously.[18] In addition to his publications for young children, he expressed interest in writing a work on the life of Christ.

A letter written the following summer speaks of the satisfaction Alexander found in returning to his old surroundings. His health was good, and his work at the college had been productive. Writing from Princeton on July 14, 1834, he states: "I have passed the happiest summer thus far that I have known for years; let me record it as the gift of Providence. The greenness, the airiness, the fragrance, the healthfulness, the over—over—overflowing of fruits, and the otherwise varied delightfulness of Princeton, have made up for the loss or want of many urbane luxurie."

He was eager to familiarize himself with his new field of studies.[19] "I am endeavouring to get all the books I can," he said, "relating to the English Language and Literature—Anglo-Saxon, History of our Tongue,

---

13. For an examination of Alexander's approach to the study of rhetoric, see Gregory Martin Anderson, "The Religious Rhetoric of James W. Alexander: Texts and Contexts of an antebellum rhetorical tradition" (PhD diss., University of Minnesota, 1994).
14. See James W. Alexander, *Letters to a Younger Brother* (Philadelphia: American Sunday-School Union, 1838; repr., Birmingham, Ala.: Solid Ground Christian Books, 2004).
15. Hall, *Letters*, 1:209.
16. For a related title, see James W. Alexander, *Charles Clifford; or, The Children at the River Bank* (Philadelphia: American Sunday-School Union, 1834).
17. "The result was 'The Infant's Library,' consisting of twenty-four of the smallest size in which any thing in the shape of a book can be printed, and in the smallest language." Hall, *Letters*, 1:219.
18. Alexander explained his rationale: "I concealed my name to my lullabies; for the very reason which leads the Moravians to exclude all adults, when he preaches to children." Hall, *Letters*, 1:218.
19. "Like his brother at the Seminary, he gave himself no rest, and made it a point to read all great and good books that reached his hands, besides many volumes which he

History of Literature in England, History of Poetry, including specimens of old English books."[20] The writings of Samuel Taylor Coleridge were of special interest at this time in Alexander's life. "Lately I have made friends with Coleridge, at least for a time, and am reading his 'Aids' again with a peculiar sort of mystical pleasure."[21]

Of the various authors Alexander was reading, he found special delight in the writings of David Russell. Alexander found them rich in practical spirituality, and his enthusiasm for Russell is evident in his recommendation to Hall:

> I will go so far, as with more than ordinary earnestness, to recommend to you to get, *own*, put on your table, and study, a book with this title, "Letters Practical and Consolatory, designed to illustrate the nature and tendency of the Gospel, by David Russell, Minister of the Gospel, Dundee, 4th Ed., Edinburgh, 1830, 2 vols., 12mo." Who this Russell is I know not, probably a Scotch Dissenter; but I have read no human production which comes nearer my views of Calvinism: it is theology without one shred of scholasticism; orthodoxy without one film of mystification; purity without one note of ecclesiastical harshness.[22]

Alexander's interest in his new field of studies was accompanied by an increasing burden for the reform of public education. Eager to see a strong Protestant presence among the "common schools" developing in the nation's eastern states, Alexander encouraged incorporation of the Bible into the curriculums being developed.[23] Correspondence with Hall at the end of October 1834 expresses his confidence in the transforming power of the Bible for shaping American approaches to educational pedagogy:

> Let me beg you to take it as a prominent, perpetual object of selections, &c., for your Journal, to hold up the great truth, that *the Bible is the book to educate the age*. Why not have it the *chief* thing in the family,

---

could not fully commend. He was a most rapid reader." Alexander, *Life of Joseph Addison Alexander*, 1:347.

20. Hall, *Letters*, 1:213.
21. Hall, *Letters*, 1:214.
22. Hall, *Letters*, 1:214–15.
23. "For most Protestants…religious weekday schools were hardly a feasible solution to the apparent defects of the common schools. Instead, most orthodox critics continued to press for changes in the schools' curricula and texts. Many advocated the use of the Bible as the basis for courses in literature, science, and history, as well as ethics and morality." Boylan, *Sunday School*, 58.

in the school, in the academy, in the university? The day is coming; and if you and I can introduce the minutest corner of this wedge, we shall be benefactors of the race. I can *amuse* a child about the Bible; I can teach logic, rhetoric, ethics, and salvation from the Bible. May we not have a *Bible School*? Sow the seed, my dear friend, meekly, prayerfully; it must grow![24]

Alexander's initial optimism with regard to the reform of America's schools would be tempered by the broader educational direction that was taken. This refocused his interests on the strategic role that the Sunday-school movement could have on American youth in offsetting what would eventually become a more secularized approach to "common school" education.[25]

Letters from this period also respond to Hall's inquiries on preaching. In one of their exchanges, Hall asked Alexander who he thought were the best preachers from which to learn the art of sermon composition and delivery.[26] "You must not ask me who is the best sermon writer," Alexander responded. "If suddenly cornered, I should say Baxter. On second thought, Robert Hall. Then a mixture of Baxter, Barrow, and Taylor. I have read Sherlock, but never become interested." Somewhat unexpectedly, Alexander stated, "Indeed, I scarcely read sermons."[27]

Alexander's observations continue in a letter of the following week. Commenting on the differences between English, American, and French

---

24. Hall, *Letters*, 1:217.
25. "In the end, the critics settled for something less than infiltrating the schools with orthodox teachers or using the Bible as a text. Indeed, the kind of Bible-based curriculum that many of them sought became increasingly elusive, simply because common schools served so diverse a clientele. Instead, Bible reading and Protestant prayers became fixed parts of the school day, a compromise that fully satisfied neither the orthodox, who wanted more, nor the non-Protestants, who wanted less. Within this context, the Sunday school assumed increasing importance as the only institution that could correct the 'unavoidable deficiencies' of common-school education. Although often very critical of common schools for abandoning true 'moral education' in favor of mere 'mental culture,' advocates of the Sunday school generally came to agree that their institution could be 'the evangelist of the common school,' providing a specifically religious education to the youth of the nation." Boylan, *Sunday School*, 58.
26. Alexander responded to a similar inquiry from Hall in October 1829: "You ask me my opinion about preachers. I think that of the 17th century, John Howe and Barrow are the first; and of the 19th Robert Hall, whom I prefer to any sermonizer I have ever read. His sermon entitled 'Modern Infidelity Considered,' is unequalled. For deep pathos, Samuel Davies is surpassed by none, but he often sins against good taste." Hall, *Letters*, 1:137.
27. Hall, *Letters*, 1:214.

preachers, Alexander wisely emphasizes the balance that must be struck between the didactic (informational and instructive) and pathetic (emotionally persuasive and applicatory) styles of preaching if sermons are to be both informative and inspirational:

> With reference to English preachers, the best article I ever saw is in the first volume of the Edinburgh Presbyterian Review. The great defect in the Churchmen, even of their golden era, the 17th century, is Energy, including in that term both pungency and pathos. I can just now think of none but Barrow, who is powerful. Taylor is rich, and often pathetic, always brilliant and poetical, but never commanding. Those whom we (upon English tradition) celebrate, while they are argumentative, instructive, sensible, and terse, are, to my feelings, tame. A mixture of Edwards and Davies, who are all our own, would be a phoenix. Strange as it would seem to one who had not made the comparison, the French preachers have more addresses to the conscience, heart, and will, than any I ever saw in print. Bourdaloue is full of holy unction, Bossuet is Demosthenes in canonicals, and Massillon is the effusing of all great qualities into so perfect a mass that his powers are scarcely appreciated. The same things lead, I think, to the undervaluing of R. Hall. This extreme elegance makes one suspect there is no strength, because there is no ruggedness. I have Sherlock, and know some fine places in him, but as a whole he does not take possession of me.[28]

As Alexander points out, the "solid structure of Scripture truth" is the essence of good sermon proclamation.[29] "And is not this what preaching should convey?" he asked. The absence of "Scripture truth" provided explanation for the decline in powerful preaching that once marked New England pulpits.[30] "And after all, this modern New England preaching is less moving, less reaching, less awakening, than that of the preceding age."[31]

---

28. Hall, *Letters*, 1:215–16.
29. Writing at a later point on the topic of extemporaneous preaching, Alexander remarked: "I am more and more convinced, that the greatest preparation for preaching extempore, is to know the English Bible by heart." Hall, *Letters*, 1:379.
30. Among the New England preachers that Alexander enjoyed was Edward Dorr Griffin: "I think more of Griffin's sermons than I expected. They have that sort of power which arises from the extirpation of superfluous words, in a very remarkable degree. In most cases I like the doctrine; always bearing in mind that they are avowedly *awakening* sermons." Hall, *Letters*, 1:298.
31. Hall, *Letters*, 1:216.

As the months passed, Alexander's letters reveal his deepening spirituality. He sought to bring every area of his life into submission to God's purposes for the walk of faith. A letter from December 9, 1834, incorporates his reflections and speaks of his love for the Word of God. As is obvious from Alexander's remarks, no subject was off limits when it came to considering how he might learn to live a life of undivided discipleship:

> I ought to be a very thankful man, for, with "manifold temptations," I am as happy in my present site, as a miserable sinner ought to expect. I am very sure that some of us do not discipline the flesh enough in our prosperity, by voluntary abstinence from many things which are lawful but inexpedient. Paul talks (in Greek terms of force) of bringing under and subjecting the body. Might we not sometimes fast? Might we not curtail expenses and retrench style? Might we not risk a little worldly sneer for being nearer the primitive model? May we not hope for more uncommon manifestations, when we make more uncommon sacrifices to walk in Christ's steps? Austin says sweetly, *Nudus nudum sequor Christum* [Follow naked the naked Christ]. I more and more sicken at human dilutions of the Word, and love the taste of the fresh fountain.[32]

Alexander wrote to Hall a few days later to inform him about the death of his second-born son, Archibald. His letter dated December 15, 1834, is filled with the pathos of a father's love and speaks powerfully of how God's promises undergird the life of faith. In the midst of this present world that we pass through as a "vale of tears," Alexander's remarks model the robust biblical faith necessary for handling the heart-wrenching trials that can befall a Christian family.

> More to disburden a throbbing and full heart, than to communicate much good, I write to you. I know you will feel a pang, when I tell you that this afternoon, at 3 o'clock, God was pleased to take away my little Archibald—our Benjamin, the son of our hopes. Blessed be God for all his mercies! Last evening he was as well as a child could be, to appearance. About 7 he began to show symptoms of croup, which gradually advanced, in spite of the most vigorous practice of our physician, who was with us almost from first to last, until he died in our arms. His last moments were sweet; he simply fell asleep, no pang, no distortion; he lies like a lovely smiling marble. He was two

---

32. Hall, *Letters*, 1:220.

years four months old. Twenty hours' illness! A little before his death he clasped his hands and said, "I want to say my prayers." Judge what we feel. My dear friend, the tears I poured in torrents over his dying form were tears of joy—blessed be God for it! Never had I such faith of immortality. My wife and I yield with a composure, for which we can never be thankful enough, to the resumption of the precious gift. We have been in the practice of deliberately giving up our children to God, every day. O how I rejoiced in this, as I felt his last pulses, and found his precious hand turning to clay in mine.

We have too much caressed and prized this dear boy. Disappointed in our first, whom we held by a spider's thread, we counted much upon Archibald. He was lovely, and precocious. In a moment we are blasted! But why do I repeat these things? Join us in giving thanks to God for the wonderful (I will not say resignation, but) comfort we have. Join us in praising Him who can make us glory in tribulations also. Join us in prayer that we may be *kept* in faith. "Hold thou me up and I shall be safe."

I wish to learn the lesson of this dispensation. I wish to be more entirely consecrated to the work of God. If God write us *childless* (An awful word now—once it seemed a trifle) I will try to find children in the Sunday School. O my friend! I have a dear child in heaven! Only a few hours in heaven! Is not this an honour—a joy—a triumph? let me then determine to lead a heavenly life here. When shall we "use this world as not abusing it"? When shall we who have wives, live as though we had none? A little while and all these shadows will fly away, and we shall find ourselves amidst the realities of eternity. For some time previous to this dispensation, I have found myself under a leading to thoughts more serious than common; greater desires to cut off superfluous pursuits, to take up unaccustomed crosses, and to cultivate humble love. Alas! how little have I succeeded in doing so.[33]

1835

Although Alexander's formal responsibilities were those of Professor of Rhetoric and Belles Lettres, he continued to produce important articles on the work of the pastoral ministry. In early January 1835, his insightful article "The Lord Jesus Christ the Example of the Minister" was first published in the *Biblical Repertory*.[34] In a simple but profound way, he reminds

---

33. Hall, *Letters*, 1:223–24.
34. James W. Alexander, "The Lord Jesus Christ the Example of the Minister," *The Biblical Repertory and Theological Review* 7, no. 1 (January 1835): 97–109. Alexander's article can also be found in Garretson, *Princeton and the Work of the Christian Ministry*, 2:53–65.

his readers how Christ's character is determinative for clerical behavior. Viewed against the backdrop of developing clerical conflict within his denomination, Alexander's study is a timely word of exhortation to his fellow clergy to live up to the calling for which they had been set apart.

Alexander's letters from early spring express a growing frustration over the tensions within his denomination. By temperament and conviction, he was reluctant to become embroiled in the developing polarization between New and Old School positions. "Every day I live I become more sick of controversy; I cannot persuade myself that the Church was meant to be kept always in hot water. As to our own church a split seems inevitable," he said.[35]

In his judgment, the controversy had shifted the denomination's missionary priorities at the expense of interest in the salvation of the lost.[36] "I honour the men who seem to be laboring *directly* for the conversion of souls," he told Hall.[37] The testimony of Christian example and zeal for doing that which was right in God's eyes, he thought, would be more beneficial to the church's collective witness than the acrimony that characterized the current conflict.[38]

Correspondence from mid-April 1835 elaborates Alexander's convictions on the importance of pious behavior during times of church conflict. Without minimizing the dangers of doctrinal declension, he was equally troubled by the damage that ungodly behavior causes to the church's witness. Like the apostle Paul, he was committed to "speaking the truth in love." He writes:

> At judgment I heartily believe that some heresies of heart and temper will be charged as worse than heavy doctrinal errors. To you I may say this, because you understand me as holding, not merely that the tenets of our church are true, but that they are very important. But I

---

35. Hall, *Letters*, 1:226.

36. "The strength of Presbyterianism, its tendency to increase, has, I think, always been in proportion to its keeping clear of polemic preaching, sectarian propagandism, and supplanting and proselytizing ways; and in times when its direct aim was at converting souls." Hall, *Letters*, 1:363.

37. Hall, *Letters*, 1:226.

38. Alexander expressed similar thoughts in relation to the Presbyterian Church's testimony regarding Roman Catholicism: "If, instead of reviling the Catholics, we would surpass them in schools, in personal charities, in persevering missions, and in the preparation of our ministers, I believe we should make more head against them." Hall, *Letters*, 1:226.

see how easy it is to "hold the truth" in rancor, and hate, which is the grand error of depraved human nature, yea, and of diabolism itself.[39]

Alexander's letter continues by pointing out the opportunities for outreach that were being squandered amidst the conflict. To a certain extent, he viewed the "New Measures" as a matter of indifference, as long as they were not mistaken for or substituted in place of a genuine work of the Spirit in regeneration.[40] "Sometimes there seems to me to be an opening just now for a united attempt to awaken religious feeling in the churches, without the shibboleths of measures. Surely too much has been made of these measures, both pro and contra."[41]

Although committed to addressing the issues that his church was facing, local matters were of more immediate concern to Alexander than the denominational squabble that surrounded him. Of particular interest was the opportunity to preach to the African Americans who attended worship at the First Presbyterian Church. As construction on a new building for the predominantly white congregation began, the eighty African American worshippers met at a separate location. Having preached with great satisfaction to the slave population in Virginia, Alexander relished the opportunity to be regular pulpit supply for the African American congregation. While he thought his preaching "too long" and his practice "defective," he was encouraged by his new ministry setting. "I believe my happiest hours are spent on Sunday afternoons in laboring among my little charge [his African American congregation]. I am humbled when I think how little effect results from my discourses."[42]

His letter also comments on the colonization movement and his deepening opposition to the institution of slavery.[43] Earlier reticence regarding the plan of colonization has given way to a modified endorsement of the effort.

> I was not pleased with the spirit of the Colonization meetings in New York. I am tending towards a middle ground which neither

---

39. Hall, *Letters*, 1:227.
40. A few years later Alexander would write: "I am disposed to make a stand on this position, viz., that wherever our church has made great advances, it has been by the pressing of *converting truth*." Hall, *Letters*, 1:379.
41. Hall, *Letters*, 1:227.
42. Hall, *Letters*, 1:227.
43. For a brief overview of the approach that faculty at Princeton Theological Seminary took to the vexatious issue of slavery, see Calhoun, *Faith and Learning*, 1:323–32.

party will allow: *i.e.* I abhor slavery, and think the public mind should be enlightened, and every lawful means immediately taken for an eventual and speedy abolition; but I also approve of the plan of Colonization, on ground altogether distinct from the question of slavery. Thus I open my mind to the full, legitimate impressions of all the anti-slavery arguments.[44]

Acknowledging that a solution for the abolition of slavery was complex, Alexander believed the South had brought the problem upon itself in ways that could have been prevented if earlier action had been taken. Correspondence from November 3, 1835, expresses his concern. "And though I conceive the anti-slavers to be rash and pragmatical, yet I think the arrogance of the South is palpably their worst policy. This wedge is in, and drives deeper year by year."[45]

Alexander was happy to report on the success of his children's books. Despite his literary gifts, Alexander found the genre a difficult one to master. "Do you know that my grand difficulty in making baby books has been that of getting few enough words in a page?" he asked.[46] Nonetheless, while the work was challenging, the outcome was rewarding. He believed the writing of Christian children's literature to be one of the most valuable legacies one could leave for future generations.[47] "The spread of my little books is pleasing to my mind, as it flatters my hope of not dying without leaving some few souls the better for my having been born." "Rejoice, my friend," he wrote to Hall, "in the station you hold; never let the truth grow stale in your estimation, that what we do for infants, we do for the best interests of man, in the most hopeful way."[48]

By December of that year, Alexander found that the editorial responsibilities of the *Biblical Repertory* had consumed the majority of the time he had set aside for personal writing.[49] "I am particularly full of writing,"

---

44. Hall, *Letters*, 1:228.
45. Hall, *Letters*, 1:234.
46. Hall, *Letters*, 1:232.
47. Alongside his work as an author, Alexander engaged in pastoral ministry to children and their parents in the areas surrounding Princeton during his time as a professor at the college. A passing reference in a letter from September 4, 1835, records his activity: "On Sunday, I hope to preach to the children of a rural district, and to parents; also catechize." Hall, *Letters*, 1:231.
48. Hall, *Letters*, 1:231.
49. A contemporary notes Alexander's prodigious literary output: "Besides his articles in the *Repertory*, he always had something in hand for the Sunday-school Union, or

he said, "I have been a full month kept from any other writing by preparing for the Repertory."[50]

Alexander's teaching responsibilities, research, and sermon preparation also filled much of his weekly schedule.[51] The student body now numbered over 200, and Alexander had been forced to divide some of his classes to accommodate the growing number of undergraduates.

> I have lectures to write, and preach at least every Sunday, besides preparing four chapters for Bible classes each week, and conducting two private classes in belles-lettres in addition to my official task, and my constant private instruction of two boys in my study. I have just done a most lengthy investigation of the Servetus affair, in which I have wearied through some thousand pages. The collateral information I have thus got of Calvin's character, is very delightful.[52]

1836

The first installment of the *Biblical Repertory* for 1836 saw publication of Alexander's historical review of the life of Michael Servetus.[53] One of many articles Alexander would produce during the 1830s, the review evidences a careful mastery of the primary sources in his interaction with the author's presentation.

By late May 1836, Alexander's study of church history had convinced him that the spiritual vitality of the church's witness is often in disproportion to its emphasis on church polity. As he reflected on the impending division within his denomination, he came to recognize that as important as the church's polity is, it may not be an indication of genuine spiritual life among its constituents. Outward forms must always be accompanied by a vital, inner piety if the proper balance is to be maintained between

---

for the booksellers, or newspapers, aiming at the moral and social improvement of the young and of the laboring class." "James Waddell Alexander," 73.

50. Hall, *Letters*, 1:235.

51. "His literary reading kept up to the wide range which it had so long taken, and which his duties in the class-room required of one who was not satisfied to take his preparations at second-hand; for he contrived to subordinate every occupation to practical use: thus, he took lessons in drawing, that he might the better assist in the illustrations of his books for children, and pored over Greek tragedy in the hope of gaining a more accurate knowledge of New Testament grammar." "James Waddell Alexander," 73.

52. Hall, *Letters*, 1:235.

53. James W. Alexander, "The Life of Michael Servetus," *The Biblical Repertory and Theological Review* 8, no. 1 (January 1836): 74–96.

the church as an organization and as a living spiritual organism.[54] A letter written from Princeton on May 30, 1836, includes his observations on this subject:

> It seems to me, in looking over the history of the church, that the real progress of religion has been in a very small degree dependent on the spread or permanency of any external form of polity. The external form has shot out great branches, and taken root, while at the same time the spirit of religion has become almost extinct; witness the Romish church, the Anglican church under Queen Anne, and in Virginia. The external form has, on the other hand been violated and trampled on, while the spirit of religion, taking a large view, has made immense progress; witness the *early* Reformation; the Moravian offset from Lutheranism, and the Wesleyan Reformation in England. This thought runs beautifully through the whole of Neander's Church History. He looks for the unity of the church in something internal.[55]

Besides his thoughts on church polity, his letters to Hall during 1836 also address the topics of prayer, divine guidance, and the practical benefits of bereavement. Alexander's observations on divine guidance can be found in correspondence on July 19, 1836. Written from the vantage point of personal experience, his counsel to Hall succinctly summarizes the manner in which personal obedience intersects with the activity of prayer in a believer's life:

> We are all too apt, however to give an undue weight to selfish considerations in making our election of our lot, and our satisfaction of mind is therefore all the greater when we can feel that we choose the humbler and thornier path for Christ's sake. Having been repeatedly called to this anxious sort of inquiry, I have come to this result: that when we pray for guidance, we *receive* it, but do not always know, even when we take the decisive step, that it is just the right thing; we leap, so to speak, in the dark, or in the best light we have, and then find ourselves on solid ground, and are ultimately convinced that what we did was "of the Lord."[56]

---

54. A letter written the following year in April 1837 elaborates Alexander's thinking: "I see but one plan, and that I have often stated to you: *Reduce the Church to its constituent Presbyteries*. These are all that are essential to the notion of a Presbyterian Church. These may coalesce as they see fit." Hall, *Letters*, 1:251.

55. Hall, *Letters*, 1:239.

56. Hall, *Letters*, 1:241.

A letter from the following November draws helpful lessons from the experience of bereavement useful for ministers in their pastoral care to the downtrodden and grieving.

> I am sensibly affected by the peril and the escape of — —, and unite with you in giving thanks. No doubt, you already feel the lesson to be better than many volumes, and many sermons. You will probably never lose the benefit of these softening and humanizing scenes. "By these things we live, and in all these things is the life of the spirit." And do not charge me with meaning to take an ungenerous advantage of you in an argument, when I say with earnest conviction, that such experiences better fit a man for feeding Christ's sheep, than even the ascetic *devotions* of a bachelor. If I have ever made any "proof" of my "ministry," it has been in the house of mourning, and by means of knowledge learned in the same. The thought has occurred to me, that the angels, although perfect in holiness, cannot have *that* perfection of holiness which saints have, inasmuch as they have never known the discipline of tears. They cannot know what it is to bleed with a wife or a child. And analogously, how much is contained in that character of our high-priest, that he was "tempted in all points like as we are." My thoughts run more naturally in this strain, because we have two sick children.[57]

A month later, Alexander sought to give encouragement to Hall upon the death of one of his children. Alexander's counsel is exemplary for its model of pastoral compassion to the grieving. Brief but substantive, Alexander's letter on December 27, 1836, speaks tenderly to Hall's circumstances, urging him to focus upon the consolation that can be found for Christian families at such a time as this in the "covenant of grace." He writes:

> Last night, after returning from Brunswick, where I had been for three days, I received the paper you sent me, containing the news of your bereavement. May the Lord make it an abundantly useful dispensation! I might dwell on the fact that the increasing afflictions of your child made it desirable that she might be transplanted to a more genial climate, if I did not know how little this consideration has to do with our affections, or if I had not learned by experience that the feeblest is always the darling of the parent's heart. A better rest for your mind will be found in considerations purely evangelical, and

---

57. Hall, *Letters*, 1:245.

connected with the covenant of grace. This stroke is a part of the gospel compact. It has been, I doubt not, sent, and sent at this time, with a specialty of purpose, as to your sanctification and salvation. In the belief of this, I am less disposed to suggest topics for your consideration, than to direct you to listen to that voice of the Spirit which accompanies the stroke. If you carefully observe what great truths of Christianity are at this time most weighty on your soul, or most precious, you will find it good to note these, and treasure them up for future contemplation and practice. In these seasons of night we are permitted to discern those stars which are hidden by the glare of day. Such sins also as now weigh upon your conscience may be those which the dispensation is intended to cut away. After all, it is safest to put the word of God into your Hands, and to leave you to imbibe those truths for which your heart shall manifest the greatest affinity. "I will hear what God the Lord will speak."[58]

1837

With the advent of a new year, Alexander's thoughts turned to practical questions relating to a minister's salary. He feared that worldly values were taking root in his life to the detriment of his personal piety. Of particular concern was the ever-present temptation for more money. "Truly and unaffectedly I am alarmed at these things, and most of all alarmed at what I discern in myself, of desires for more ease, style, and luxury than is compatible with the sincere preaching of self-denial." The dangers affecting the Presbyterian clergy were real, and he felt it did little good to spend time criticizing the Catholic clergy for similar issues at a time when one's own house needed to be put in order. "It is in vain for us to cry out against the luxury of Popish priests, in the face of such things. I believe, that the majority of Popish priests are poor and live low." In comparison to other professions, Alexander felt there was little cause for complaint in relation to the standard of living many Presbyterian clergy enjoyed. "It is also vain for us to prate about the self-denials of the ministry," he said.[59]

---

58. Hall, *Letters*, 1:246.
59. Hall, *Letters*, 1:247.

Popular Literature and the Reading of Scripture

A letter written from Princeton on March 10, 1837, describes Alexander's growing alarm at the proliferation of trite novels and magazines beginning to flood the public in the 1830s. He believed their content detrimental to the life of piety and interest in study of the Scriptures.[60] As a matter of first importance, he believed that the reading of the Bible should take priority over every other kind of literature, no matter how beneficial.

> No conviction of my soul gains more strength than that our great study should be *The Bible*. I reproach my butterfly mind every night, for her idle excursions. Yet one consolation I certainly find: though I am much away from my Bible, as I am much away from my wife and boys, yet when I *do* get back I feel that I love them mightily. O how! how! how shall we check the waste of mind upon the ever-increasing frivolities of literature! Literature needs a Deluge. We are antediluvians in this regard. Is God about to banish our impertinent rivalry of *his* book by sweeping our books away? by war, discord, or other calamity? I hope not. Let me begin reform at home. I am ashamed of piddling all my days among periodical scraps, and short-lived nothings, while whole tracts of Scripture remain unexplored.[61]

In a related letter, Alexander spoke of the delight he had in the reading of Scripture. In relation to uninspired writings, he found no comparison. "There are occasions on which I feel a distrust for all books but the Bible, as feeling that the best communications of men come to me modified by the discipline of a sect or the idiosyncrasy of an individual." "The liquor," he said, "has the tang of the cask. This I feel most as it regards books of experimental religion; sometimes turning over successively the stirring or tender productions of Catholics, Methodists, Moravians, and Presbyterians, and then resorting at last to the infallible source of all."[62]

Concentrated study of the Bible, Alexander counseled Hall, was essential for Christian growth and absolutely vital for those called to

---

60. The previous year Alexander had produced a helpful review of volumes published by the American Sunday-School Union that he felt beneficial to the reading public: James W. Alexander, "Descriptive Catalogue of Books, and other Publications of the American Sunday School Union: designed for Sunday Schools, Juvenile, Family, and Parish Libraries, and for General Reading," *The Biblical Repertory and Theological Review* 8, no. 1 (January 1836): 96–114.

61. Hall, *Letters*, 1:249–50.

62. Hall, *Letters*, 1:256.

be instructors of the Word of God.[63] "The one great rule for bible-study appears to me to be this; Read the text—the text—the text. Read it over and over, over and over. Read continually and largely. Thus while particulars become impressed by repetition, we do not lose the general connexion." The Puritans, Alexander observed, devoted their lives to the study of the Scriptures, and their ministries reflected the fruit of their labors. He writes:

> No men ever lived, me judice, who knew the tenth part as much of the contents of the Bible as the Puritans, and thus it was they read it. They were never without their little Bibles. Among them I regard Charnock as far the most wonderful in this regard, and Flavel next. To my taste Flavel is the most uniformly interesting, engaging, and refreshing writer on religion, ancient or modern. I always feel that I am talking with a Christian, fresh and ruddy, in perfect health and spirits, with no cloud or megrim, and with every power available at the moment.[64]

Revivals

Commentary on the ongoing influence of local revivals also finds expression in his correspondence from 1837. While describing the effects that the revivals were producing, Alexander notes the Calvinistic conviction that undergirded the content of the preaching and the manner in which new believers were assimilated into the life of the church. A communication from June 1837 highlights his participation in the meetings taking place and the effect that his preaching had on his hearers:

> I could not get down to the city, because when I was not teaching, I felt constrained to be in New Brunswick, to aid Bro. [Jos. H.] Jones, one of my most intimate brethren, for whom I have within ten

---

63. Even passages that may not be "clear" produce their effect in ways a reader may not expect: "Quere: may we not receive a hallowing impression, though vague and unrepresentable in words, from portions of Scripture which we do not understand, such as Ezekiel, Canticles, or Revelation? And may not this be part of their intention? This struck me mightily last night, while reading some picturesque passages in the original Apocalypse." Hall, *Letters*, 1:233.

64. Hall, *Letters*, 1:256. Charnock and Flavel's collected works remain in print. See Stephen Charnock, *The Works of Stephen Charnock*, 5 vols. (Edinburgh: Banner of Truth, 2010); John Flavel, *The Works of John Flavel*, 6 vols. (Edinburgh: Banner of Truth, 1968). For a recent biography on Flavel's life and theology, see Brian H. Cosby, *John Flavel: Puritan Life and Thought in Stuart England* (Lanham: Lexington Books, 2014). Flavel's writings were instrumental in Archibald Alexander's conversion and remained a family favorite among his own children.

days preached six sermons, and attended as many meetings more. That ultra old school town is shaken by a great awakening, still in blessed progress. In the Baptist Church 109 have been baptized; others inquiring. In the Dutch Church (Dr. S.B. How's) 35 have been admitted; perhaps as many more awakened. In Jone's Church, some 70 entertain the Christian hope, and about 30 are awakened. In Rutger's College, out of 80 youths, 68 are thought to have believed in Christ.... After so many years of preaching with comparatively little visible effect, it was a gratifying and unspeakably gracious favour conferred on me, to allow me to witness some remarkable instances of apparent fruits. And still more, the whole tenor of this revival has been very pleasing to me, as confirming that high Calvinistic view of the gratuity of salvation, and the efficacy of the "gospel," as contradistinguished from "obligation," in which I grow day by day more exclusively rooted.[65]

The record of the revivals that were occurring is documented in correspondence from the following month. Writing to Hall from New Brunswick on July 13, 1837, Alexander details the widespread effect of divine grace taking place in the surrounding communities.

Yesterday I came hither; my third visit to this revived church. The work of the Lord is still advancing here, though the phase of divine influence is somewhat varied. As might be expected, the number of awakenings is smaller; but some of the most remarkable conversions have occurred within a day or two; including several professional men, and other persons of great influence. The Baptists have immersed a hundred and fifty. The Dutch number some 50–70 converts; the Presbyterians 130–150. The Methodists have a great excitement. All the students of Rutgers College but five or six are now hopefully pious. I perceive no one thing in the Presbyterian church which is undesirable, nor any flagging in the prayers or efforts of pastor or people. In the Sunday School the state of feeling is more full of promise than it has been at any time. All day, and much of the night, Mr. Jones is engaged with inquirers. Over the river, in Piscataway, and Metutchen, also in Plainfield, and (somewhat) in Rahway, there is revival. These influences, except in the case of Bound Brook, have been most extensive among the Baptists. There has been here no veiling or modifying of high Calvinistic tenets, in order to keep the sinner under the yoke of obligation, or to precipitate the resolved

---

65. Hall, *Letters*, 1:252–53.

efforts of his own soul, as abstracted from Divine power. The doctrines which have been blessed are the "primer doctrines," taught in the old way, and in old phraseology. Indeed I may say of the preaching, what Brainerd says of that which was used to awaken his Indians: "It has been from first to last a strain of gospel invitation."[66]

Denominational Division

Amidst the growing influence of local revivals, Alexander also had to contend with the recent division of his denomination which occurred during the General Assembly of 1837. At the annual meeting of the Presbyterian Church, an Old School majority effectively voided the 1801 Plan of Union between Congregational and Presbyterian churches while excising presbyteries and synods, especially in upper New York State, of New School persuasion. Alexander was optimistic that the division would be productive of spiritual good. While the separation was painful, he recognized that the advance of the church was often accompanied by spiritual conflict.[67] Writing in early August 1837, he remarked:

> I hope I shall never so far undervalue charity as not to lament the false fire kindled in church controversies; but I comfort myself with the thoughts, that what we love we always contend for; that the most flourishing seasons for piety have been those of the most active debates: witness the days of Augustin, of Luther, of the English Nonconformists; that the conservative principle of Protestantism is discussion of all points; and that the friction of debate is temporary, while the gain on the side of truth is permanent.[68]

While the divisions within his denomination were a source of grief, Alexander continued to find pleasure in his ministry to the African Americans. During the time that the new sanctuary was being constructed, the majority of Caucasian communicants felt that it would be best if a facility were located where the African Americans could continue to meet separately rather than returning to the main congregation when the construction was complete. With abolitionist sentiments on the rise, Alexander felt it a prudent move that would ensure peace within the congregation's constituency. A letter from mid-November 1837 updates

---

66. Hall, *Letters*, 1:254.
67. Alexander would later write: "Fierce orthodoxy burns as well as warms, but Christlike gentleness sheds life all around it." Hall, *Letters*, 1:313.
68. Hall, *Letters*, 1:254–55.

Hall on the challenges that confronted integrated worship at the First Presbyterian Church in Princeton.

> We have a new and handsome church edifice. While it was building the negroes worshipped apart, in a little place of their own. The majority of the pew-holders wish them to remain as a separate congregation. By-the-bye, we are said to have a larger proportion of blacks in our population, than any town in the free States. If they come back, they will take up about half the gallery. There are about 80 black communicants. I am clear that in a church of Jesus Christ, there is neither black nor white; and that we have no right to consider the accident of colour in any degree. Yet I think the blacks very unwise in insisting on such a privilege now. Some years ago there would not have been the slightest difficulty in admitting them, but in consequence of the abolition movements the prejudice of the lower classes of whites against the blacks has become exorbitant and inhuman.[69]

Alexander's ministry with the African Americans continued to prosper in the coming years. By 1840, "a special building was constructed for the use of the black members, and finally in 1846, the session reported that ninety people were dismissed 'to form a church under the name of the First Presbyterian Church of Colour of Princeton.' In 1848 the name was changed to the Witherspoon Street Presbyterian Church."[70]

1838

Alexander's first letter of the new calendar year was written on January 9, 1838. Among the matters discussed was the topic of extemporaneous prayer. He was troubled by the lack of focus and unnecessary repetition with which it was often accompanied. He appreciated the benefits that set forms for prayer provided but wished to limit the frequency of their use in public worship lest the vitality of the service be replaced by a liturgical formality void of spiritual life.

> No one groans more than I under the abuses of extempore prayer. How much time is lost, how much weariness produced, by periphrastic introductions, diffuse dilutions, and vain repetitions. Many pulpit prayers are largely made up of passages evidently meant to impress truth on the auditor. Whole strains of this sort: "O Lord,

---

69. Hall, *Letters*, 1:260.
70. See Calhoun, *Faith and Learning*, 1:330.

may sinners feel that time is short; that this is the only season for repentance; and that unless they believe, &c., &c." A man might thus tell his Maker what to make sinners feel through the whole extent of the catechism: "May we feel that our chief end is to glorify God and to enjoy him forever." I nauseate all such perversions. Still I never could submit to one stereotype form for every day of my life. I should be pleased to have a few forms, varying, we may say through a month, expressing those things which we are to pray for always, with license to use a short extemporaneous prayer besides: this is exactly the Lutheran method.[71]

Although his work as a professor at the college consumed the bulk of his time, Alexander was as devoted to the little congregation of African Americans who met together on Sunday afternoons as any pastor who serves a full-time charge. He found tremendous freedom in his pulpit ministrations among them in ways he had not experienced with the other congregations he had served. Unfortunately, not everyone in Princeton was supportive of his ministry to the African Americans:

I find much comfort thus far in preaching to my Africans. The house is crowded by decorous and attentive people, and it seems a little like being a missionary. Then one can enjoy a total "abandon," and use every mode of address or illustration, without the dread of blundering. Strange as it may seem, I have already met with some insult, as the preacher to the blacks, in returning from their place of worship: it was from some of the lowest of the white canaille. One case of very powerful awakening has occurred under my unworthy labours.[72]

By the summer of that year, Alexander had secured better lodgings for his family. The house he acquired had belonged to a professor named Rev. Dr. John Breckinridge who taught at the seminary, and the house had been sold following the latter's wife's death. Alexander was pleased with the new home, although he found the walk to work somewhat fatiguing during the warm summer months.[73] A letter from July highlights the Alexander family's delight in their new lodgings:

---

71. Hall, *Letters*, 1:261–62.
72. Hall, *Letters*, 1:262–63.
73. Alexander's letter also mentions the "extended" members of their new household: "We have been two days in our present residence, and are thus far well-pleased, except with the amazing increase of housewifeship. It is something of a job to keep out of

There is some difference between being moved, and being fixed, or I should say we were established in our new place. I believe you know it whereabout. Every object is painfully commemorative of its late beautiful owner: we even have her flowers; and the magnolia which stands near our back-door, it was almost the last of her worldly deeds to have planted. The house is far too large for my family or furniture; but the terms were such as I felt no right to decline, especially as by acceding to them, I should be doing all I could for ——, and at the same time introduce my own children to better air, ampler space, and goodlier prospects. The walk to College, in the hot season, is dreadful even to my imagination; how I shall endure it, I know not: but I am somewhat satisfied that I have come hither without self-seeking—and the Lord will provide.[74]

Another of his letters from July 1838 provides interesting reflections on the difference in preaching style between himself and his father Archibald Alexander. J. W. Alexander believed that didactic instruction in preaching had given way to hortatory models of exposition that failed to provide sufficient biblical substance in pulpit proclamation.[75] "Hortation," he said, "seems to me to be the pulpit-error of the age, which has emasculated the church." Hall notes further:

In a postscript to this sentence, dated August 4, he adds: "Yesterday I heard my father preach to our students on Eccl. xii. 1, a text which I had handled a few weeks previous before the same hearers. I was never more humbled, nor more struck with my own past fault in this line. *My* discourse was all appeal: his was all argument, even bare and quite dialectic in places. My sermon was like a flash in the pan, and his like a ball *lodged*, lodged where to work afterwards."[76]

As he reflected on this topic, Alexander concluded that his own preaching had fallen short of the ideal in this regard.[77] More doctrinal

---

mischief three cats, one dog, forty fowls, and mice *ad libitum*; the latter having declared independence during the late troubles and vacancy." Hall, *Letters*, 1:267.

74. Hall, *Letters*, 1:266–67.

75. An article published in the *Biblical Repertory* earlier that year examines the history, practice, and benefits of expository preaching: James W. Alexander, "Remarks on the Disuse of Expository Preaching," *The Biblical Repertory and Princeton Review* 10, no. 1 (January 1838): 33–55.

76. Hall, *Letters*, 1:268.

77. In a separate context Alexander wrote: "It does little good to awaken mere conscience, without reaching the heart. We know better what we ought to do, than we feel

content, he believed, should have been included in his pulpit ministry. "In this matter of preaching, with which I began, I feel quite earnest, as believing that most of my earlier sermons were constructed on a wrong principle. I would be plain, but O, I wish I had *fed* my hearers with more truth, and given them less harangue."[78]

Charlotte Court-House
By early October, Alexander had returned to visit his friends and former congregation in Virginia. His love for the slaves continued unabated, and he took every opportunity to preach the gospel to them during his visit.[79]

A letter from October 19, 1838, written while at Charlotte Court-House, describes his ministry among the slaves:

> I have, as a general plan, conversed particularly and pointedly about religion, with every negro whom I could get alone, in walks, rides, &c. I have been tenderly affected in so doing. Many seem to me to be genuine saints. Many show that they have been seekers for years on years, but have never been directed, privately, by any competent person. In every case they are as perfectly accessible as my Henry. Even where they are wicked, they listen, and their conscience is prompt.[80]

Alexander was eager to see the slaves evangelized and sought to promote their spiritual interests among his friends in the South. He saw the vitality of genuine faith demonstrated in their public assemblies and was confident of the work of the Spirit in their lives. His compassion for the slaves is especially evident in his October 19 letter. An extended extract provides an illuminating glimpse into the spiritual vitality of the African American population in Virginia during the 1830s:

---

motives to do otherwise. I think this the great difference between New England, and the best Old England preachers of the best time. It is wonderful how different is the strain of address to Christians in the New Testament epistles." Hall, *Letters*, 1:343–44.

78. Hall, *Letters*, 1:268.

79. Alexander's ministry to the slaves coincided with a lengthy review of the life of William Wilberforce which appeared in the October edition of the *Biblical Repertory*. It is likely that Alexander's ministry to the slaves had been galvanized by his reading of Wilberforce's efforts to eliminate the institution in British society: James W. Alexander, "The Life of William Wilberforce," *The Biblical Repertory and Princeton Review* 10, no. 4 (October 1838): 560–602.

80. Hall, *Letters*, 1:271.

The scene we saw in Locust street [a religious excitement] is acted at every meeting. Yet even among these, I am sure, Christ hath his sheep. A hundred lay missionaries might now go into this field and convert thousands. They ought to be Southern men, and the South ought to furnish them forthwith. I am so filled with this, that I try to introduce the theme in every circle. Mrs. Le Grand lodges and boards a good Episcopalian (a Connecticut man, but twenty years in Va.) awaiting orders, for this business among her slaves. He has this moment returned, on foot and through a smart rain, from the overseer's house two miles off, where he instructed a group of fifteen last night. Now it is my deliberate belief, that more of these slaves are likely to go to heaven, than of an equal number of servants of pious people in our Middle States: and such being the hopefulness of the work, how earnestly ought Christians to engage in it! Thousands might be got to attend public preaching, as hundreds now do. The law (thanks to the meddling of anti-slavery societies) forbids schools, and public teaching to read; it was not so when I lived here: but I hold it to be our business to *save their souls*; and however criminal slavery may be, I see with my eyes that God has so overruled it, as that the slaves are more open to Gospel truth than any human beings on the globe. They are, I know, under temptations to hypocrisy: but grant they are pretending more than they feel, one has nevertheless the chance to lodge truth in their minds. The instances of this are affecting. In one short walk yesterday, I had talks with two men. One was loading his wagon with billets of wood, in a clearing of the forest. As he hung over the side of the wagon, his face beamed with the expression of sincere and intense emotion. He declared he had "long, long, yes for many years, desired to have true religion. Yes," said he, "master, true religion—that sort of religion which will do when I lie on my death-bed." I read over and over to him Matt. v. 6, commenting, &c. This occurs daily, and this is easy work, and work which anybody may perform. This is, moreover, the best preparative for freedom.[81]

Princeton

Once back in Princeton, Alexander continued his research and preparation of lectures. Sensitive to the growing influence of German philosophical thinking on American theological discussion, he completed an important article titled "Transcendentalism," which was subsequently copublished

---

81. Hall, *Letters*, 1:271–72.

with Professor A. B. Dod in the January 1839 issue of the *Biblical Repertory*.[82] Alexander recognized the threat transcendental thought posed to biblical orthodoxy if its tenets were embraced.[83] Identification of the threat was not a cure, however; ultimately, the best remedy against the dangers of skeptical unbelief was regular study and appropriation of biblical teaching into one's heart in order to safeguard against transcendentalism's insidious influence on the life of faith and simple trust in the doctrines of Scripture. He writes:

> I am deep in grubbing among German metaphysics, to write an article for the Repertory, against the attempts to introduce their poison among us.... The more I read of human philosophy, the more I prize the childlike spirit; the more I love the book of books. Like Goliath's sword, "there is none like it." Why are we not more devoted to the study of it? Can we do a better work than to get people to read it?[84]

In a related context, Alexander would later write:
> I think it is too much our way to rank modern philosophers who reject the Gospel, with ancient sages who did not know it. But if Plato is in hell—how far nearer absence of pain must he be than Gibbon! The former having almost guessed at truth without revelation, the latter, after a perfect education in it, having rejected it! The grand error of free-thinkers, and that which, I think, should be pressed home upon them, is their obstinate persistency in going blindfold when a light from heaven is offered to them. Suppose a man should profess to doubt all the acknowledged principles of chemistry and

---

82. Hall notes: "This became the paper (65 pages) on *Transcendentalism* in the number for January 1839. One part of the argument (reviewing Cousin) was prepared by the late Professor A.B. Dod." Hall, *Letters*, 1:274. See also James Waddell Alexander and William H. Dillingham, "Elements of Psychology, included in a Critical Examination of Locke's essay on the Human Understanding, with Additional Pieces 2. Introduction to the History of Philosophy 3. An Address delivered before the Senior Class in Divinity College, Cambridge, Sunday, 15th July, 1838," *The Biblical Repertory and Princeton Review* 11, no. 1 (January 1839): 37–101. For a recent study on the rise and influence of Transcendentalism that includes observations on Alexander and Dod's article, see Philip F. Gura, *American Transcendentalism: A History* (New York: Hill and Wang, 2007).

83. The period saw rapid change in traditional Protestant theology and the emergence of new denominations and religious cults. Alexander sought to address these changes while seeking to preserve the confessional foundations upon which his denomination had been established. For useful overviews of these developments, see Paul K. Conkin, *The Uneasy Center: Reformed Christianity in Antebellum America* (Chapel Hill: University of North Carolina Press, 1995).

84. Hall, *Letters*, 1:274–75.

blow himself up, by going into a foul mine, when a thousand safety-lamps has been offered to him. Our minds are too often disposed to regard that as venial, which God regards as heinous. Perhaps the very rejection of such a book as the Bible, even without a word of external evidence, is proof positive of enmity to God. Pride of understanding ruins learned men by hundreds and thousands; it is destroying, I fear, all the philosophers of Germany. To become as little children is a great attainment. May it be ours!"[85]

Happily, Alexander's disillusionment with German metaphysical speculation was offset by the spirituality that he encountered in the writings of Calvin. Of the books that Alexander read for sermon preparation, he especially prized Calvin's commentaries for their exegetical insight and spiritual disposition.[86] "Among many commentators, whom I have to consult, I find none like Calvin—he oftenest beards the real difficulty, and oftenest knocks it down, and drags it out."[87]

1839

With the academic year back in session following the Christmas season, Alexander found himself quite busy. "I write at a hand-gallop," he told Hall. "I have preached five times in eight days, lectured four times, examined a class, made a Tract speech, and heard seven recitations."[88] While fully consumed with his responsibilities as a professor, he continued to maintain a rigorous preaching schedule. He loved preaching and eagerly sought out opportunities to proclaim God's Word.[89]

The influence of New Measures revivalism continued to be a source of ongoing theological concern. In the intervening years, Alexander had come to recognize the corruption of church life that had taken place where its methodology had been incorporated into the ministry philosophy of local congregations. In a review of Gardiner Spring's contemporary work *Fragments from the Study of a Pastor*, Alexander provided

---

85. Hall, *Letters*, 1:307.
86. In another context Alexander wrote: "Of all the commentaries I have examined, there is the most constant glow of piety in Calvin, this without setting his pious remarks by themselves." Hall, *Letters*, 1:367.
87. Hall, *Letters*, 1:276.
88. Hall, *Letters*, 1:276.
89. In a footnote, Hall notes that "during the term of his Professorship, Mr. Alexander preached, on average, sixty times each year." Hall, *Letters*, 1:276.

a descriptive analysis of the methodology of New Measures revivalism and its deleterious effect upon the churches. He agreed with Spring's theology of experiential preaching. He was optimistic that the tide had now turned toward an interest in preparing messages marked by substantive expository content in place of the hortatory harangues common to pulpit ministries which had embraced New Measures evangelistic methodology. He writes:

> It is but a few years since we were in all the din and consternation of the new-measures; during this the pulpit was neglected, except when in the so-called "protracted-meeting" it was employed, not to instruct but to electrify, and when the serious exposition of scripture was sacrificed to a strain of scriptural objurgation and ill-bred menace, which was called pungent, close, and to the conscience. During this agitation, the regular stated instructions of God's house, such we mean as admit of being kept up with a healthful glow for years, and the deliberate education of the church in the full course of biblical knowledge which is the true end of the pastoral office, and which can be secured only by men mighty in the scriptures, and meditating in them day and night, were undervalued and set aside, in favour of a kind of harangue which needed no preparation, and which aimed at "breaking down" the sinner as it was significantly termed. This whole bubble has burst. The leaders in this mighty revolution have slunk into corners, and those good and unstable or ambitious and mistaking men, whether preachers or professors or presidents, who were high in the praise of the Reverend Professor Finney or the Reverend President Mahan, are too happy to have the whole thing forgotten, and to have no inquiry made respecting the time and place at which they sorrowfully turned back from that hurried multitude which has since gone on to Perfection. This inundation has passed and receded, we hope for ever, but it has left its slime; and not only some of its canting phrases, but some of its opinions abide, and must be purged away. Do we not still hear many speak of *pastoral labour* as if the only proper labour of the pastor were his dealing with individuals or with families? Is there not still a craving for those paroxysms which to both preacher and people were an excuse for retiring from calm and spiritual labouring in God's holy truth? Is there not a readiness in many to believe that the old way of Christianity is an obsolete way, and that the spirit of the age requires high stimulation instead of never-ending instruction? Where these things may be affirmed with truth, there is much to be unlearned. We must honour God's institution, and especially abide

by his word, or we shall be liable, at the very next rise of the tide, to be swept away.[90]

As Alexander was careful to note, the strength of the Reformed pulpit heritage was to be found in its commitment to careful study of the Scriptures in preparation for a God-honoring, Christ-exalting pulpit ministry. He quotes with approval the words of Puritan minister Stephen Charnock: "It cost Christ his life to save, and what if it cost me *my* life to study for him?" The same mind-set was true of the early New England clergy. Thomas Shepard, Alexander observed, spoke in even stronger terms: "God will curse that man's labours, that lumbers up and down the world all the week, and then upon Saturday in the afternoon, goes to his closet; when, as God knows, that time were little enough to pray in, and weep in, and get his heart into a fit frame for the duties of the approaching Sabbath." "From the instructions of such men the Reformed churches gained a strength which even the palsy of our modern day has not been able wholly to destroy."[91]

By late March, Alexander's correspondence takes on more serious tones in relation to the illness of one of Hall's children. "I have felt anxious for a week or more about your family, and not the less so, since your note by my father," he said. Wishing to encourage his friend, he wrote:

> I sincerely hope you may be carried through this trial without a bereavement; but if not—I have nothing I can say but to recommend to you absolute and filial submission: I hope you know its necessity and its virtue; and I doubt not a moment the trial is meant to go a certain length towards slaying the body of sin in you and ——. In the ordinary course of gracious discipline nothing seems to kill sin in us so surely as these stripes. May they be few and light![92]

Tragically, Hall's daughter did not survive the illness. Following her death, Alexander wrote on behalf of his family to encourage Hall and his wife during their time of grief. Alexander's letter on April 9, 1839, embodies the pathos that only those who have lost their own children can express.

---

90. James W. Alexander, "Fragments from the Study of a Pastor. By Gardiner Spring, Pastor of the Brick Presbyterian Church in the City of New York," *The Biblical Repertory and Princeton Review* 11, no. 1 (January 1839): 112–13.
91. Alexander, "Fragments from the Study of a Pastor," 107–8.
92. Hall, *Letters*, 1:277.

I have not for some days written to you, being doubtful in what strain I should address you, as I could hear nothing about your child, and it is only this hour that I have learned that it has pleased God to take her away from you. Let me assure you, that my wife and I sorrow with you, as knowing in some measure the heart of bereaved parents. In such times one can only say "It is the Lord." Here is our stay in every affliction. "The Lord reigneth." "It is well." It has fallen to your lot to have a number of family afflictions, and no doubt they have been, whether you know it or not, among your greatest blessings. No one can rejoice in such strokes, in themselves considered; but when viewing them in connexion with great grace vouchsafed along with them, we may "glory in tribulation also." The stroke must be heaviest, as it is most unwonted, to the afflicted mother. Here, if any where, "the heart knoweth its own bitterness;" and I would not intermeddle; but even here grace does often so soothe the agonized heart, as to bring joy out of the midst of grief. Our dear children are not lost, but sent before. They await our coming, and perhaps rejoice, not merely as redeemed creatures, but as *ours*; as bone of our bone, and flesh of our flesh. Probably they know more of us, than we of them. Certainly they know more of Christ. You are familiar with the expressions of Jeremy Taylor and Leighton, concerning the loss of children: they are both touching, but Taylor's the most so; for he had many children, and all his sons died before him, while Leighton was a bachelor. "No man can tell" (says Taylor) "but he that loves his children, how many delicious accents make a man's heart dance in the pretty conversation of those dear pledges—their childishness, their stammering, their little angers, their innocence, their imperfections, their necessities, are so many little emanations of joy and comfort, to him that delights in their person and society." I trust that Mrs. Hall and yourself will be enabled to receive just that measure and kind of benefit which it seems to be the Master's will to communicate.[93]

Not long afterward, the Alexanders would also be faced again with parental grief upon the death of their firstborn son, "Archibald" George Cabell Alexander.[94] Always a sickly child, the boy had been spared an early death but still died prematurely having suffered from congenital hydrocephalus. The brevity of Alexander's remarks to Hall evidence the

---

93. Hall, *Letters*, 1:277.
94. The experience led Alexander to publish "Scriptural Account of Suffering Parents" in the Sunday School Journal. The two articles were written to encourage families who lost children to a premature death. See Hall, *Letters*, 1:280.

affection he and his wife had for their little one. "I may say, with hope of being credited, it is a loss to part with even so distressed a child. His little bird-like voice was the first morning sound we used to hear. The Lord has done well and mercifully to us, and especially to him."[95]

As the months hurried by, Alexander was encouraged to report on the numbers of students enrolled at the college and seminary. Some two hundred fifty young men were in attendance at the college, while accession to the seminary was near fifty, the "third largest" Alexander observed.

Accompanying his interest in ministry outreach to the camps and schools in which soldiers resided, Alexander continued to work on popular treatments of the Christian life written for the working class.[96] While capable of writing highly specialized articles addressed to the academic community, the bulk of Alexander's literary efforts were directed to the ordinary citizen.[97] Correspondence from August 15, 1839, updates Hall on the progress he had been making on a companion volume to his work of the previous year titled *The American Mechanic*. Alexander viewed the work as a kind of popular apologetic intended to help simple believers remain grounded in biblical teaching lest they succumb to the popular forms of unbelief that vied for their allegiance:

> I should like to advise with you a little about the sequel to the American Mechanic, which I have been preparing, ["the Working Man."] The plan is just the same, but I have pitched the tone of it two or three degrees higher, as to style, allusion, &c. Still I wish it to be a book for the working classes. I feel encouraged to bestow such little labours as I may be able to put forth, more and more on the working classes, the rather because they are the great object of the infidels, socialists, agrarians, Owenites, Wrightites, and diabolians generally.[98]

---

95. Hall, *Letters*, 1:280.

96. Alexander was able to produce a large number of books for the American Sunday-School Union *currente calamo* (i.e., requiring little consultation or research). He writes, "For unless I can make my Sunday School labours a sort of recreation, it is impossible for me to persevere in them." Hall, *Letters*, 1:255.

97. In a related context, Alexander asked Hall: "What do you think of a Sunday School Book called the Farmer's Boy, or some such title, of some length, intended to be a manual for young fellows in the country, connecting all agricultural operations with the corresponding Biblical facts, and giving a spiritual, but natural turn, to the works and changes of the husbandmen? I meditate [on] something of this sort." Hall, *Letters*, 1:257.

98. Hall, *Letters*, 1:283.

Besides works of popular apologetics, Alexander also wanted to produce literature that would be of benefit to the elderly. He shared with Hall the kind of book he thought should be written to help guide them in the life of piety. "A book ought to be written with this title: 'The Aged Christian's Book: printed in large type for the convenience of old persons.' It should be in the largest character available. Such topics as these: The Trials of Old Age; The Temptations of Old Age; The Duties of Old Age; The Consolations of Old Age, &c., &c. It should be a large book with little matter in it."[99]

In addition to his ministry with the Witherspoon Street congregation, Alexander also conducted pastoral visits in the outlying area around Princeton. Some of his stops were among the most destitute situations. His record of a pastoral visit in early December describes the devastation that alcohol had brought upon the family. It also identifies his increasing concern for the destructive effects which alcohol can have on society at large. Writing from Princeton on December 9, 1839, Alexander describes the scene he came upon and the impact it had on his conscience:

> I was called the other day to see a dying man several miles out in the country. It was a wretched hovel of a place, reminding me of some of Crabbe's inimitable descriptions. Neither the sick man nor any of his household could read, and they were as ignorant as heathen. The front door of the house was unhinged, and merely lying up against the posts. We need such a districting of all our neighbourhoods as should infallibly bring every such place under inspection. This work has been tolerably well done around here, but this man has been almost always drunk until he was seized with consumption. I wish in my soul that all the alcohol could be annihilated. Every day exposes to view more and more its horrific, soul-destroying power.[100]

On a more encouraging note, Alexander reported on the positive benefits of psalms and hymns for nurturing the life of piety. In the absence of being able to read, African American spirituality, Alexander noted, had depended largely on the theology of their songs to preserve biblical orthodoxy and pass the faith along to coming generations. A letter dated December 21, 1839, records Alexander's developing appreciation for hymnody in cultivating a strong spirituality:

---

99. Hall, *Letters*, 1:255.
100. Hall, *Letters*, 1:286.

I have near me a (black) parishioner, not long for this world, a young woman, whose case will, I think, some day, make an interesting article for the S. S. Journal, or for a book, as showing the value of Sunday School texts and especially hymns, on a dying bed. We, who pretend to be refined folks, greatly undervalue hymns and psalms. Now I have often observed, that, from the natural fondness of the common mind, and the infant mind, for metre and rhyme, the great body of theology and experience in the lower classes is preserved in the shape of hymns. They read the psalm-book, they repeat and sing the verses, &c. Hence we should not neglect sacred song, I mean the plain sort, with our children and scholars.[101]

No doubt with an eye to the aforementioned observations, Alexander told Hall that he wanted to direct the remainder of his literary efforts to the basics of biblical belief. The same, he hoped, would be true of the style in which he would preach. He commended both to Hall, confident that it was the path of duty and the approach that would prove of greatest spiritual benefit to the people who would sit under their ministries.[102] He writes:

> My present feeling is that I will write no more irreligious books. Life is short. The great work is to save souls. All our economical, political, and literary reformations are mere adjusting of the outer twig; religion changes the sap of root and trunk. This I never felt more than now. I see that when a people become godly, all the rest follows. In the same connexion I see the value of preaching. Let me earnestly exhort you, on the strength of my own sad experience, not to allow yourself to trust to a flow of extempore thought and expression in the pulpit, but to labour *every* sermon, however obscure or ignorant the auditory may be. Drs. Skinner and Spring have proved what can be done by devoting all one's soul to the simple work of sermon making. I wish I had done something of the kind.[103]

1840

Alexander's eagerness to become a more effective preacher continued with a series of observations on the work of the ministry which may be

---

101. Hall, *Letters*, 1:289.
102. Alexander frequently emphasized the importance of careful preparation for a God-honoring pulpit ministry.
103. Hall, *Letters*, 1:289.

found interspersed throughout his letters of 1840. He deplored his ineffectiveness in preaching. He attributed his weakness to a kind of clerical formality that placed greater emphasis upon the *composition* of a message than the actual *purpose* of preaching. He records his thoughts in a letter from January 18, 1840:

> I don't like "fine" preaching, or preachers; and (lest you should think I like any thing) let me add, I don't like myself, or my past or present ways, especially my having made so much of *preparing* as scarcely to have begun to work; my having labored so much *indirectly* when I might have done the same *directly*; my having set the soul's salvation too far off. O if we could live one real year of effective gospel service, we might be willing to depart. Preaching Christ is the best, hardest, sweetest work, on this side of beholding him. I trust we shall do both.[104]

Alexander drew inspiration for his preaching style from the writings of the Puritan minister Richard Baxter.[105] "I think I would rather write Baxter's English," he said, "than any I know, though I would not wish to write always what he has done. He well describes his own style: 'May I speak pertinently, plainly, piercingly, and somewhat properly, I have enough.'"[106]

In addition to the need to write clearly in order to speak effectively, Alexander also recognized the difference between the formal preparation of a sermon for publication and the actual delivery of a message. The true power, that is, the *life* of a sermon, can never be captured in a printed transcript:

> It is as easy to paint fire (says old Gurnall) with the heat, as with pen and ink to commit that to paper which occurs in preaching. There is as much difference between a sermon in the pulpit, and printed in a book, as between milk in the warm breast, and in a sucking-bottle. It may not be so with such preachers as —— or —— whose discourses have sometimes been preached in the pulpit then delivered at a commencement, then published in the ——, and then issued as the Preface to a work. In my notion a sermon is a sermon, and nothing

---

104. Hall, *Letters*, 1:291.
105. For the best analysis of Baxter's theology and influence, see J. I. Packer, *The Redemption & Restoration of Man in the Thought of Richard Baxter: A Study in Puritan Theology* (Vancouver: Regent College Publishing, 2003).
106. Hall, *Letters*, 1:303.

else; if you make it with any thing ulterior in view, you destroy it as a sermon. It is death to a good sermon, as to a good love-letter, to publish it. It is dead beer, sour champagne, cold coffee, an effete cigar, a daguerreotype portrait.[107]

Despite his evident gift for preaching, Alexander sometimes declined invitations to speak at special events for fear that he would not be able to effectively deliver his message.[108] Having turned down an invitation to preach the annual sermon for the American Sunday-School Union in May 1840, he explained his decision to Hall: "It is with much pain that I bring myself to say the aforesaid. But I am sincere in it. I am conscious of no special ability on set occasions; I suffer distresses, which to many would be inconceivable, while such an engagement is pending."[109]

As with many of his fellow pastors, Alexander was also subjected to anonymous notes of criticism that arrive at the pastor's home. "Have you arrived at that stage of ministerial experience," he asked Hall, "at which one receives anonymous letters, telling him to preach this, or preach that?"[110]

His reflections on preaching and pastoral ministry lent themselves to observations on the growth of piety in the human soul. A letter from March 1840 records his observations and the recommendations he made to Hall regarding the benefits of keeping accurate records to assist one's ministerial labors. He writes:

> In religious things, no genuine record of a soul's history, or of any segment of it is unimportant. God's way of working is always marked and self-consistent. In a real history, I care not of what, the parts hang together in a definite relation like the limbs in a human body, or the features in a face; the connexion in a fiction is often forced and sometimes impossible. *Corollary.* 1. We ought to keep an eye open perpetually for religious facts. 2. We ought to record them. 3. We ought to record them with great care, in cases where the enormity of the transaction, or some delicacy of circumstances, absolutely forbids their publication *at present*. These are the very facts which are often most striking and valuable. Lay them by, and a year or two

---

107. Hall, *Letters*, 1:305.
108. Alexander also recognized that reticence can become an excuse for fulfilling one's calling as a minister: "We are all of us in danger of undervaluing the importance of our posts, and our means of usefulness." Hall, *Letters*, 1:293.
109. Hall, *Letters*, 1:296.
110. Hall, *Letters*, 1:297.

hence, they may be brought out with much force. 4. Ministers ought to keep a record of "cases" in their pastoral practice. That they do not, either mentally or verbally, argues a certain skepticism as to the reality or moment of the exercises. These thoughts have come on me with increased impression within a short time; and as I have lost some fifteen years' use of them, I give them over to you.[111]

Alexander's letter also includes some helpful thoughts on parenting. As he grew older, he developed more decided convictions on how to best prepare children for the challenges of living in an ungodly world. He was appalled by the evident lack of piety in the lives of children who had been raised in godly homes. Vigilance against the inroads of worldly thinking and values was of course necessary, but even more importantly, Alexander felt that a parent's life needs to embody the self-denial and cross-bearing spirit from which their children can learn the true meaning of piety. Children learn best by example and will replicate the patterns of behavior that they have learned from their parents:

> As I grow older as a parent, my views are changing fast as to the degree of conformity to the world which we should allow in our children. I am horror-struck to count up the profligate children of pious persons, and even ministers. The door at which those influences enter, which countervail parental instruction and example, I am persuaded, is *yielding to the ways of good society*. By dress, books, and amusements, an atmosphere is formed which is not that of Christianity. More than ever do I feel that our families must stand in a kind but determined opposition to the fashions of the world, breasting the waves, like the Eddystone Light House. And I have found nothing yet which requires more courage and independence than to rise even a tittle, but decidedly, above the *par* of the religious world around us. Surely the way in which we commonly go on is not that way of self-denial and sacrifice and cross-bearing which the New Testament talks of: "then is the offence of the Cross ceased." Our slender influence on the circle of our friends is often to be traced to our leaving so little difference between us. I plead guilty to every count.[112]

As Alexander ruminated on the example that his life provided, he wrestled with the question of whether he should support a pledge to refrain from the use of alcohol—both as a Christian and as a minister

---

111. Hall, *Letters*, 1:297–98.
112. Hall, *Letters*, 1:298–99.

of the gospel.[113] At the time Alexander wrote, the antitemperance movement was making great strides and enjoyed the support of numerous clergy and laypeople. "I am at a great loss what to do about the Temperance Question," he wrote to Hall.

> My sole difficulty is *Pledge or no Pledge*. As to the Wine Question, it has long seemed to me frivolous to stand over the corpses of a thousand drunkards asking whether their brandy had water or wine in it. I am made up in mind and conscience to avoid the means of drunkenness in my family. On this I have acted some months. We have dozens of young men in and about Princeton who are drunk every little while, and always on wine. Our students commonly begin on malt-liquors. But I am not so clear as to the Pledge. I do not see my way plain as to taking the high ground respecting morals, which some do. And I abhor as hell the doctrine that our blessed and omniscient Saviour can be conceived to have made wine *ignorantly*. That the wine he made was intoxicating, I believe as fully as I do that he made it. Our students need an example. I am really at a loss. We need divine direction at every step, and for want of seeking it, and waiting for His counsel, (Ps. cvi. 13,) we so often rush into errors.[114]

Alongside his desire to bear witness to his friends and family on behalf of Christ, Alexander continued to look beyond the horizons of his community for the ways in which the gospel message could go forth to the various continents. In the aftermath of British colonization and conquest, the English language had taken root in numerous countries around the world. Alexander thought Christian missions should follow in the path of colonization that had already been blazed.

> My mind expands when I look at the mighty conquests of our language. If we could only pour in the gospel with this tide of conquest and colonization! Since, in our day, God so signally blesses colonies for the spread of civilization, ought we not to follow the lead of Providence, and strike in as much as possible with the divine plan? The hope of great effects is more reasonable from such efforts than from insulated assaults on the mass of heathenism.[115]

---

113. By July 1842, Alexander had resolved the matter: "I am no longer a member of any Temperance Society of any sort, except that which is 1,800 years old." Hall, *Letters*, 1:358.
114. Hall, *Letters*, 1:299.
115. Hall, *Letters*, 1:301.

A brief note written during the spring records Alexander's satisfaction regarding the establishment of a permanent house of worship for the African American congregation in Princeton. The building was dedicated on Palm Sunday 1840. "We dedicated our [Presbyterian] new African meeting-house yesterday." "A pleasant 'season,'" he reported, "and really delightful singing."[116] A few months later he would write of God's unusual providence in the worship services of the congregation: "I am not without reasons for thinking that the last sermon I preached to the blacks was the means of awakening the only white person present. Strange are the ways of Providence!"[117]

One of Alexander's letters from this period reports on the invitation he received to accept a call to Prince Edward, Virginia. The college and seminary atmosphere were of interest, but ultimately Alexander declined. "I am in pain to know what is my duty," he shared.

> I have always sat in my present chair with a feeling that it was right only as a refuge during ill-health. At present, through great mercy, I am perhaps only for a short interval, in the enjoyment of the best health I have had since I left College. I think I can say, *ex animo* [from the heart], I wish to go where I may most fully exhaust my talents, *quantulacunque sint* [however small they be], in the service of Christ. It may seem strange to you, that no invitation has shaken me more.[118]

Following a busy academic year, Alexander and his family journeyed to Virginia during the fall of 1840 for a time of vacation.[119] A letter from Charlotte Court-House written in late October 1840 speaks of the "great religious excitement" that had taken place in the area. Alexander notes that one hundred five converts "of different sects" had been added to local churches. Twenty of these had joined the Presbyterian congregation. "The feeling extends on every side to neighbouring congregations," he said. "The new measures are rift, but connected with old doctrine, except in the case of the Methodists."[120]

---

116. Hall, *Letters*, 1:301.
117. Hall, *Letters*, 1:307.
118. Hall, *Letters*, 1:303.
119. A letter on August 4, 1840, details the busyness of his schedule: "This morning I attended a funeral, sat at Dod's *examen*, heard a long recitation, and, after a bit, examined 76 fellows in Latin, came home *exanimatus*, drank three cups of strong tea, played half an hour on a flute, and feel better this moment than I did when I got up." Hall, *Letters*, 1:311.
120. Hall, *Letters*, 1:314.

A final letter for the year comments on the ministry taking place among the slaves in Virginia. In a letter from December 1840, Alexander remarks:

> I know of five or six men who are silently wearing out life in most devoted labour among the slaves. Slavery must and will end; I hope peaceably; but, anyhow, we ought to save the souls of this generation. There are 1,700 black Baptist communicants in Richmond. Of these as many are elect souls, I believe, as of any 1,700 of white Baptists, taken at random.[121]

1841

Among the anecdotal stories found in Alexander's correspondence of 1841 is a surprising account of a Methodist preacher who called on Alexander's father, Archibald Alexander, during Christmas day to inform him that he was unconverted and in need of salvation!

A number of entries during the year address matters related to reading and literature. Alexander wisely observed that the books most likely to affect a man's thoughts are the ones with strong emotive power. "I grow in my conviction, that in our day, when men have a thousand things to read, and won't read long at any thing, the books which reach the mass and colour its opinions, are not books of research, but books of feeling, or point, even of eccentricity; books written with a gush, *currente calamo.*"[122] Among ancient writers, Alexander found Cicero, Ovid, and Seneca helpful in this regard.[123]

In a related context, a letter from September 1841 voices Alexander's ongoing alarm over the danger that "ephemeral" literature poses to the life of piety and the cultivation of critical thinking skills. Of particular concern was the influence of newspapers for diluting interest in serious mental reflection. In his opinion, the damaging effects of newspaper reading exceeded that of novel reading. Newspapers were ubiquitous in ways that novels were not. Alexander notes the irony of his criticism: both he and Hall had served as editors of newspapers!

---

121. Hall, *Letters*, 1:319.
122. Hall, *Letters*, 1:323.
123. Speaking of Cicero, Alexander remarked: "In all classical antiquity, so far as I have any glimpses, there is no better reading for youth, as I am sure in all pagan history there is no better character. This I say the more readily after a careful perusal of his familiar epistles." Hall, *Letters*, 1:239.

I am seriously convinced that more harm is done by newspaper-reading, than by novel-reading. I know men who spend 2—6 hours daily over newspapers. There is no other production so heterogeneous and incoherent; there is none in which we read so much that is not even interesting. Probably each of us spends a hundred hours of morning-time per annum, on 1, Repeated matter; 2, Accidents; 3, Crimes; 4, Idle narrative; 5, Unintelligible or useless statements; 6, Error and False-hood; 7, Advertisements and proper names. What better recipe for making a weak mind addle? We take the tone of our company. Suppose a man's bosom-friend to talk an hour a day, exactly like his newspaper. I am told Dr. Wilson used to read only a small weekly sheet; and I have heard that Mr. Wirt, during his most active forensic labours, spent three years without reading a newspaper. But this is talk from one Ex-editor to another.[124]

Rooted in the Reformation
During his time as a professor at the college, Alexander's reading interests included the correspondence of the Protestant reformers. In the lives of Protestant ministers such as Ulrich Zwingli and John Calvin, he found an example of faith both inspiring and convicting.[125] Few historical accounts moved him as powerfully as did the stories of the Protestant reformers in their service to Christ and His church.

I find by reading Zuingle's letters, that he was a polished scholar, as much so as Erasmus or Melancthon, intimately acquainted with all the ancient classics, holding correspondence in Greek and employing a Latinity which is as nervous and elegant as that of Calvin. He had a heroic courage, and remarkable prudence. The edition I am reading gives the letters *to* as well as *from* him, so that I am quite

---

124. Hall, *Letters*, 1:338–39.
125. Alexander's interest in Calvin resulted in multiple reviews of recent biographies on the French pastor: James W. Alexander, "The Life of John Calvin, the great Reformer. By Paul Henry, Pastor of the French Church at Berlin. Volume I. 1835; *Joannis Calvin, Thod. Bezae, Henricis IV. Regis, aliorumque illius aevi hominum Literae quaedem-nondum editae. In memoriam sacrorum Genevensium ante tria saecula emendatorum ex autographis in Bibliotheca Ducali Gothana, editit* Car. Gottl. Bretschneider, Th. et Ph. D. etc. Lipsiae, 1835. 8vo. pp. 228," *The Biblical Repertory and Princeton Review* 9, no. 1 (January 1837): 29–88; James W. Alexander, "The Life of John Calvin, The Great Reformer. By Paul Henry, D.D. Berlin. Volume II. 1838," *The Biblical Repertory and Princeton Review* 11, no. 3 (July 1839): 339–69. For a related review of Zwingli's works, see James W. Alexander, "Huldreich Zwingli's Werke. Erste vollstandige Ausgabe durch Melchoir Schuler und Joh. Schultness. Zurich.—Huldrici Zuinglii Opera. Completa Editio prima, curantibus Melchiore Schulero et Jo. Schultessio," *The Biblical Repertory and Princeton Review* 13, no. 2 (April 1841): 197–231.

transported to Reformation times. This is what I like. No novel can awaken an interest like these realities.[126]

The appreciation Alexander had for the leaders and theology of the Protestant Reformation was matched by his love for the history of Protestant hymnody.[127] The reformers not only wrote great theology but were also instrumental in the renewal of public worship through the incorporation of psalms and contemporary hymns in congregational praise. The reform of public worship became the inspiration for a Christ-centered hymnody that influenced generations of hymn writers in the years during and following the Protestant Reformation. Of the various hymn writers, Alexander favored the works of Paul Gerhardt. "For facility, vivacious sparkle, a cheerfulness almost mirthful, a pathos that melts in sighs, the purest evangelical matter, and the flame of sanctified passion, all in the most nervous, heart-reaching idiom of the market place and the hearth, we have never seen anything equal to Paul Gerhardt."[128] "There are no hymns, for unction, like the German," Alexander said. "I read them liturgically. They are pure outgoings of gospel feeling. The best I know are old Paul Gerhardt's."[129]

Alexander believed "the merit of Paul Gerhardt...akin to that of Luther, after whom and Hans Sachs he may be said to have formed himself, but with a facility, melody and fancy, altogether unreached by those great men."[130]

> Reference to any hymn-book of German Protestants will show how largely they have been indebted to Gerhardt. In this respect he has been to all Germany what Charles Wesley was to the Methodists. The greatest hymns in the language are confessedly those of Gerhardt; his place is as indisputable as Shakespeare's among dramatists, and for reasons which make him quite inaccessible by means of any version. Of his spiritual compositions, a large number continue to be sung, in no respect obsolete after two centuries. Nowhere do we find deeper lamentations over sin, more tender and believing and

---

126. Hall, *Letters*, 1:324.
127. Alexander's appreciation for German hymnody found expression in an informative introduction to its history first published in 1850: James W. Alexander, "German Hymnology," *The Biblical Repertory and Princeton Review* 22, no. 4 (October 1850): 574–602.
128. Alexander, "German Hymnology," 586.
129. Hall, *Letters*, 1:323–24.
130. Alexander, "German Hymnology," 586.

elevated addresses to Christ as dying and reigning, or a richer variety of consolations for sufferers of every class.[131]

Alexander sought to incorporate the best of the German Protestant hymnology into the public worship of the congregations he served and the personal worship practice of his family. His theology of worship is well-represented in his summary analysis of the hymnody that emerged during the Protestant Reformation in sixteenth-century Germany.

> German hymns, at the time of the Reformation, were, as we have said, to a great extent doctrinal; they were religious tracts in verse, and vehicles of the revived truth in every land. At a later period, especially under Gerhardt, while there were still many didactic pieces, often of inordinate length, the church hymn took a new form, which became normal. Hence the spiritual songs of Germany are characteristically emotional; and abound in direct addresses to God, and especially to the Lord Jesus Christ, expressive of the warmest evangelical feeling, and contemplating the Redeemer in all his offices, but chiefly as dying for our sins. Some of these are touching beyond expression. Sometimes they involve the peculiar tenets of the old Lutherans, but seldom offensively. All our indignation at Gerhardt's zeal against Calvin vanishes, when we sing one of his Passion-hymns. Such strains could have issued only from a spiritual church, and hearts filled with genuine emotions of grace. Even those too familiar expressions, which severe taste would reject, are products of unfeigned attachment; and are not without parallel in the stanzas of Watts and Hart. Generally speaking, the best German hymns concerning the person and sufferings of our Lord are marked by pure and reverent and spiritual affection. If German Christianity of the old stamp lays more stress than is common in America, on personal love for the Lord Jesus Christ, and on the sorrowing contemplation of his cross, it is only because we have too deeply felt the influence of northern theology, and the balance of advantage is clearly against us.[132]

The recovery of biblical faith that characterized Protestant spirituality was rooted in a simple trust in the promises of Scripture. Confidence in the Word of God lay at the heart of the sweeping moral and cultural transformation that took place in the countries influenced by Protestant

---

131. Alexander, "German Hymnology," 587.
132. Alexander, "German Hymnology," 600.

theological teaching. What was true for the Reformation period, Alexander observed, remains true for every generation of Christians who seek to learn the message of Scripture. Like the reformers, childlike simplicity is essential for appropriating the true meaning of the text to life.[133] A recurring theme in his correspondence with Hall, Alexander's reflections can be found in a letter on March 5, 1841:

> How much we lose in reading the Bible, by not having that fresh feeling of novelty and interest which they had in the apostolic age, and even at the reformation; we come to the book already acquainted with its contents, in its most important parts. Perhaps the best way to gain something of this vividness is to read large portions without any human comment, and in as complete forgetfulness as we can attain of our own age. Latterly I have more frequently thought than I used to do, that we make too little of the Holy Spirit's agency with the Scriptures as indispensable, perpetual, immediate. Do we not in fact read the Bible as if our unaided powers would secure us from error? Few texts have been oftener in my mind than I John ii. 26, 27; especially in reference to the diversity of opinions which men profess to derive from the Bible. The "Word *and* the Spirit" conveys the true doctrine.[134]

Forging a Pastoral Identity

While Alexander enjoyed his work as a professor, he wrestled with whether his true calling was that of a preacher.[135] He often found himself

---

133. "Sometimes we are ready to wish it were possible to travel backward on our line of experience, to that point in childhood when gospel grace first came to our cognizance; or else to stand in the position of some serious inquiring heathen who opens his ear and heart to the news of a redeeming God; that by either of these ways we might get rid of the dullness and indifference which our worn and jaded souls derive from long hardening of custom." Alexander's remarks can be found in his sermon "God's Great Love to Us": James W. Alexander, *Sacramental Discourses* (New York: Anson D. F. Randolph, 1859; repr., Edinburgh: Banner of Truth, 1985), 32. For a recent treatment analyzing Old School Presbyterian sacramental theology in the preaching of James W. Alexander, see Hughes Oliphant Old, *Holy Communion in the Piety of the Reformed Church* (Powder Springs: Tolle Lege Press, 2013), 716–39. For an earlier but related treatment on James W. Alexander's communion discourses, see Hughes Oliphant Old, *The Reading and Preaching of the Scriptures in the Worship of the Church, Volume 6, The Modern Age* (Grand Rapids: Eerdmans, 2007), 271–81.

134. Hall, *Letters*, 1:325–26.

135. Alexander viewed his work at the college a period of respite from the fatigue of pastoral labor, but he always knew that he could not use the position as an excuse for not returning to full-time pulpit ministry once his health was strong enough for the rigors of the pastorate.

ambivalent about a return to pastoral ministry. He attributed his reticence to pride. He writes:

> I am convinced, that in the sight of God, my declining to preach as a candidate has often been a sinful tribute to my own pride. We ought to be as willing to seek a place of labour for Christ, as the people to seek our services. This is my serious opinion, after having long acted on the other and the worldly plan. True, a man's reputation is a talent, and should not be jeoparded by his making himself cheap.[136]

His reflections were precipitated by an invitation from his former church in Trenton to return as their pastor. The congregation desperately wanted Alexander back. The intervening years since his departure had been ones in which the congregation struggled to find its footing. While Charles Hodge was opposed to Alexander leaving his position at the college, Archibald Alexander felt that his son's return to the pulpit would be appropriate, provided certain conditions were met. "My father says, 'The pulpit is your proper place. You have health enough at present, and have no right to count on future contingencies; but the people cannot support you, and you ought not to stir a step, without explicit arrangement on this head.'"[137]

In the end Alexander determined to decline the offer. As matters turned out, the congregation then directed its interest to John Hall and extended him a call to serve as their next pastor.[138] The relationship between Hall and the congregation in Trenton was a happy one and provided many fruitful years of pastoral labor for congregation and pastor alike.

Unbeknown to the congregation at Trenton, Alexander worked with Hall to improve his preaching style. A concerned parishioner had contacted Alexander after Hall's arrival in the hopes that he might be of assistance in helping the new pastor to become a more effective communicator. Alexander counseled Hall to be less constrained in his delivery. A stilted style lacking emotion would never ingratiate a preacher to his hearers, he explained. A letter dated June 6, 1841, provides the context for his counsel:

---

136. Hall, *Letters*, 1:329.
137. Hall, *Letters*, 1:331.
138. Hall's ordination and installation service took place at the First Presbyterian Church of Trenton on August 11, 1841. Alexander's stirring ordination charge to Hall can be found in Appendix 1 to this volume.

In a letter of ——, there is a suggestion which I cannot convey to you better than in his own words: "Pray tell Mr. Hall, if you can, to let on steam in his preaching. He certainly can do it, to such extent at least as to remove all appearance of deficiency." I accord in this, and it is the only point respecting which I have heard any misgiving expressed; and I would not mention it if I were not assured that it is perfectly within your power to remove the difficulty at once. You utter voice enough, I am persuaded, but there is a want of sharpness and percussion in your utterance, which causes the stream of words to flow indolently and somewhat indistinctly, and this is seriously the case in the cadence of every period. Perhaps every thing will be accomplished, if you give yourself up with a greater *abandon* in delivery; as there is no possibility of your laying yourself open to the charge of being theatrical, affected, or extravagant.[139]

Alexander was also careful to remind Hall about the importance of pastoral visitation—especially at the beginning of a new pastorate. Disciplined pastoral visitation acquaints the minister with the needs of his people while at the same time helps him acquire moral capital in the eyes of the congregation. Even average preachers will be more readily accepted if the congregation knows that the minister loves them and has their best interests at heart.

The only other point is one in which you cannot be too much interested. The Trenton people lack frequent pastoral visits. They need this, and they look for it. I have told them that in my opinion you would not be backward in this class of duties; and my private judgment is, that you have advantages in this particular. Such is the character of the people, that they would be satisfied with inferior pulpit performances, if these were accompanied with a free and easy social intercourse.[140]

At the time Hall was beginning his new labors at Trenton, local revivals were continuing to break out in areas around Princeton. Alexander preached in a number of the congregations that were experiencing revival. His observations on what he witnessed and heard by way of report can be found in his correspondence on August 30, 1841:

---

139. Hall, *Letters*, 1:333.
140. Hall, *Letters*, 1:333.

I have had a good deal of preaching labour lately, as all around us, in the country, there is a state of great awakening. In Mr. Comfort's congregation, I dare say, there are seventy or eighty inquirers, and perhaps thirty who have believed. It is thus far remarkably free from any the least new doctrine, new measures, noise, enthusiasm, and opposition. In Mapleton, a neighbourhood between us and Kingston, on the Canal, it is believed that every person above ten years of age, is seriously concerned. Here the awakening commenced; and in some degree through the labours of a half-witted bound boy, who would not rest till he got meetings established in a certain schoolhouse. In the Rocky Hill district north of this, and at Centreville north-west of us, each about four miles off, there is a like appearance of good. In the former place, I knew of four blind persons in one house converted. The seriousness is extending itself into the Blawenburg Dutch Church, (Mr. Talmage's). Some of the very worst and most hopeless men in our countryside have been brought to Christ. I spent Thursday night at ——, where five children (all he has) are seemingly renewed. In Princeton-proper, I know of but three or four persons inquiring; but I think more of the communicants are stirred up, than I have observed for ten years.[141]

Besides his itinerant preaching, Alexander continued as regular supply at the African American congregation in Princeton. "There is some encouragement among my blacks," he wrote to Hall in a letter from September 1841.[142] While he was encouraged by the spiritual vitality of the congregation, Alexander sought to avoid the manipulative techniques common to "inquiry meetings." "I am very dubious about inquiry-meetings, and my doubts are always greatest while they are going on." He felt it better for the pastor to engage in personal visitation rather than attempting to minister to the needs of the human soul in a public gathering with all its distractions. He writes:

> If admitted, I am clear that no one but the pastor should ever talk with the inquirer; especially, that ignorant or foolish helpers should not bring their trowel and daub. The natural, the scriptural, and the safe way, is for the pastor to see them at his house or theirs. But then

---

141. Hall, *Letters*, 1:336–37.
142. In a letter written a few weeks later, Alexander notes: "As many as eleven of my Africans are under serious impressions. In College we have had no excitement, and not even an inquiry-meeting, but a wide-spread seriousness, daily short prayer-meetings, and much private conversation." Hall, *Letters*, 1:340.

this great means of excitement must be foregone, and this is really the reason why ministers cling to it.[143]

Family Matters

As in previous years, Alexander's family traveled to Virginia in late autumn for respite amidst family illness and deliverance from the cold November weather common to New Jersey at that time of year. A letter written in mid-November 1841 reports on the family circumstances:

> Our journey to Virginia, and my return, were accomplished with much less trouble, danger, and fatigue, than I had feared. The kindness of Providence was signal towards us, in regard to weather, conveyances, and the like. I trust my little flock is safely folded in Charlotte. I do not desire soon to have a trip of the same solicitude, yet I feel it be a sacred duty to record the loving-kindness of the Lord in every part of it. My situation here is lonely enough, and I feel it more than if I were alone in another house.[144]

The forced separation was painful to Alexander. He loved his family and missed their company. Just as he sought to make "spiritual improvement" from his illnesses, he hoped that he might benefit in the same way from their absence. "I take breakfast and tea entirely alone. You can't tell how I miss the children," he said. "What a doleful place is a childless house. Let me assure you that to have a sick wife 400 miles off, is no small trial; I hope it may do me good."[145]

In his final letter of the year, written on December 8, 1841, Alexander spoke of the benefit he had gained from the reading of a classic biography on the Puritan minister Joseph Alleine.[146] "I have not for a long time seen a book, so well adapted to awaken the heart and conscience of a minister," he told Hall, "or so well deserving to lie on his table, as the Life and Death of Joseph Alleine, written by Baxter and others, and lately printed by Carter."[147]

---

143. Hall, *Letters*, 1:338.
144. Hall, *Letters*, 1:340.
145. Hall, *Letters*, 1:341.
146. Richard Baxter, *The Life and Letters of Joseph Alleine* (New York: Robert Carter, 1840; repr., Grand Rapids: Reformation Heritage Books, 2002).
147. Hall, *Letters*, 1:341.

1842

Insights into Alexander's method of personal Bible study can be found in an opening letter of January 5, 1842. His method was to immerse himself in a passage of Scripture, allowing the truths of which it speaks to take life in his soul. He writes:

> I have just been reading over, at one sitting, the epistle to the Colossians. I have done so many times within a month, both in Greek and in all the translations I have, which are more than ten. This way of frequent reperusal, continuously, I learned of my father, many years ago. It is well to intermix it with critical study of the same portion. I like to confine myself to one book for a time, and as it were, *live in it*, till I feel very familiar. I usually find great satisfaction during such a period, in preaching from such a book, thus studied.[148]

Ministry to the Slaves

With the harsh winter months behind him, Alexander journeyed to Virginia to be with his family. Having arrived at Charlotte County in early March, he once again took up his ministry to the slaves. He enjoyed preaching to them and was encouraged to learn of the Methodist preachers also devoted to ministering to their spiritual needs.[149] "I have been preaching a good deal to the negroes, a delightful work, promising, I think, as much good as any labour a man can engage in," he said. "Within a year or two much more attention is paid to this, especially by some of the Methodists. A preacher, named Skidmore, himself a slaveholder, has some thirty plantations under his charge, at one of which he preaches *every evening*. He enrolls the names, and conducts every meeting of the slaves on the plan of a Class-meeting."

The worship services of the slaves were especially inspiring to Alexander. "I am much affected by the negro singing," he said. "There is a softness in their voices, which penetrates me, and in these meetings they all sing, down to the infants."[150]

---

148. Hall, *Letters*, 1:347.
149. Alexander's continuing interest in the religious instruction of the slaves can be found in a review article contributed to the *Biblical Repertory* a few years later: James W. Alexander, "Proceedings of the meeting in Charleston, S.C., May 13–15, 1845, on the Religious Instruction of the Negroes, together with the Report of the Committee and the Address to the public," *The Biblical Repertory and Princeton Review* 17, no. 4 (January 1845): 590–606.
150. Hall, *Letters*, 1:351.

A letter written on March 21, 1842, recounts the services Alexander participated in. "I attended two full services, right on the back of one another: the last one was a funeral sermon of a black. I had a large collection, and preached from 'Thou fool, this night, &c.' Great attention, and hysterics in at least seven. The singing was transporting; positively I never enjoyed any thing more at the Musical Fund."[151]

Similar remarks can be found in another letter from this period. "Poor souls, their hearts go forth almost always in hymns. The other night, after preaching to an unmixed negro flock, we sang 'When I can read my title clear,' &c., and the feeling I caught was almost that of enthusiasm. Every voice joining, all loud, and all true enough in tone to have satisfied Haydn."[152]

The spiritual needs of the slaves absorbed Alexander's interest during his time back in Virginia. He was burdened by their circumstances and sought to give himself to their spiritual interests. He honored the integrity of their spirituality, holding them in a higher esteem than himself for their attainments in the life of piety and evident love for one's neighbors. We can only imagine the affectionate interchange of Christian love that took place between the Alexanders and the African American slaves during their visits to Virginia. The bondage imposed by culture could not dissuade a union in Christ that transcends race and time:

> Nothing so much engages my thoughts as the spiritual case of the negroes. I seize every chance to preach to them. Of no people, I think, is a larger portion regenerate. They are unspeakably superior to our Northern free blacks, retaining a thousand African traits of kindliness and hilarity, from being together in masses.... I do believe that there are a dozen on this estate who would risk their lives in an instant for my wife. They are, under ordinary masters, a happy people. Their chief suffering is from cold weather. In summer they are always well, plump, and joyous. The only thing I am anxious about *for them*, is their illumination. Several wait on my wife, who are as well-bred and (in heart) refined as ladies.[153]

An extended quote from a letter written on March 25, 1842, while at his old residence with Mrs. LeGrand, reveals Alexander's aspirations for

---

151. Hall, *Letters*, 1:352.
152. Hall, *Letters*, 1:355.
153. Hall, *Letters*, 1:353.

the slaves' emancipation and ongoing spiritual needs.[154] While desirous of their emancipation, Alexander weighed the liabilities sure to incur if the slaves and country were not suitably prepared for the personal, public, and cultural transition that would take place whether through gradual or immediate emancipation. Even Christians in the South who favored the end of slavery recognized the cultural chaos that would unfold if the slaves were not prepared for the responsibilities of self-subsistence. Alexander directed his efforts at preparing the moral convictions and mind-set of the slaves in shaping their values and commitments for a successful transition as a free people who might enjoy the full benefits of American society. While not undervaluing the physical freedom that he longed for the slaves to have, Alexander properly recognized the priority of the moral foundations necessary for a free society to survive and flourish. In this respect, racial boundaries were of secondary concern for Alexander in relation to the immediate needs of the salvation and sanctification of the human soul.

> My mind has been, and is, filled with the negroes. What I say on this point I say with, I do believe, as much love for the race as any man feels; and with an extent of observation perhaps as large as I can pretend to on any subject, having seen the worst as well as the best of their condition. And the result of all, increasingly, is, what you I am sure would agree to if you were on the spot, that the *average physical evils* of their case are not greater than of sailors, soldiers, shoeblacks, or low operatives; while their *moral evils* are unspeakably great. My point is this, then: The soul of the negro is precious and must be saved. Aim at this, at this first, at this directly, at this independently of their bondage, and the other desirable ends will be promoted even more surely than if the latter were made the great object. A gradual emancipation is that to which the interior economy of the North-Southern States was tending, is tending, and will reach; it is desirable; in my view it is inevitable; it is craved by thousands here; but an emancipation even gradual may arrive in such sort as to leave a host of blacks to be damned, who, by the other means, may

---

154. Alexander's ongoing compassion for the slaves can be found in a letter written some years later on April 30, 1850: "I wish this new invention about spinning flax by steam could come true; it would be a death-blow to cotton slavery. Our anomalous political state, as to this question, seems to offer no light in the future. I pity the poor free negroes from my heart; and wish we had taken a more generous course in regard to their church accommodation." Hall, *Letters*, 2:132–33.

be Christianized, while their eventual freedom is not less certain. It is the salvation of the slave, which is infinitely the most important, which moreover Southern Christians *can* be led to seek, and of which the very seeking directly tends to emancipation. I say this, on the obvious principle, that when the owner by seeking the salvation of his slave, gets (as he must) to love him, he will not rest (I speak of the mass) without trying to make him a free-man. I cannot describe the pleasure I have had in preaching and talking to the slaves: if I have ever done any good, this is the way.[155]

Princeton Again

Although Alexander appreciated his denominational heritage, he was not always interested in attending the work of its General Assembly. While he supported the importance of good order in church government, the business docket could easily exhaust his patience. A humorous entry on this topic is found in a letter written from Princeton in early June 1842, following his attendance at that year's General Assembly: "I heard Krebs [in General Assembly] open the defence of the [wife's sister marriage]. He spoke all Wednesday afternoon, and much of yesterday morning. Then arose Colin McIvor and declared that he could say his say in four hours. I fled. It is now several years since I was, even as a hearer, in the Assembly: I have no lust for going again."[156]

Of greater importance to Alexander that summer was the return of his family from their time of recuperation in Virginia. His family's extended absence caused him to reflect on God's kindness and the privileges of the salvation that he enjoyed through His mercy. It led Alexander in a letter on June 30, 1842, to comment upon the life of piety to which he and his family should devote themselves:

> Yesterday was exactly eight months since I took my wife away. That she should, at last, have got home, even as well as she is, should mark the day *albo lapillo* [white stone] of thankfulness. The events and anxieties of the last twelvemonth have given me deep thoughts about myself, and about life. I rejoice that as I grow grayer, I do not feel, as —— lately told me he felt, a growing distrust in my kind. On the contrary, I have so lived upon kindnesses, in time of need, and often from strangers, that I can only attribute the whole to that

---

155. Hall, *Letters*, 1:354.
156. Hall, *Letters*, 1:357.

system of inexplicable divine favour, which follows and overwhelms us, despite our manifold sins and provocations. And feeling, I do think, a firmer purpose to spend my remnant of life in service, and a stronger hatred to the unslain body of death within me, I cling more to the freest views of the Divine salvation; and more and more seek to behold the gift of Christ as the gift of every thing: I Cor iii. 22, 23. Surely there must have been somewhere, in the teaching of the Reformers, a wonderful spring, to act so powerfully and rapidly and widely. I think I find this, when I read in their works, especially those of Luther, certain declarations which are less frequent, earnest, and prominent, in later reformed writers, even those who adhered to the same confession; especially *free justification*; change of *state*, as distinct from change of moral character; which latter was as much insisted on by good Romanists. It was the same thing when Whitefield and Wesley preached; and in this they agreed; and there was the same effect. And I am convinced, that just so far as we seek to save God's free grace in justifying from abuse, by any condition in the sinner, except simple reception of Christ, which is only a condition-sine-qua-non, the more we produce practical Antinomianism. No communities have ever been so thoroughly moral as those who were most evangelical—I mean the least legal: *e.g.* the Scotch, in their best days: when everybody was externally Christian. The universal offer of a present, free salvation, to every son and daughter of Adam, for Christ's sake, is what I hold for *Gospel*; it is the good news which made the Reformation, which makes every true revival, and which makes us work, if we ever work what is right. It is the favourite topic of the old Calvinistic preachers of the 17th century; and of Boston. Some of these thoughts have been suggested to me, by reading McCrie's life by his son.[157]

An unusual entry found in a letter dated December 1842 concludes Alexander's correspondence for that year. While brief, his remarks shed light on the religious practices of the African Americans in relation to the presence of demonic spirits amongst their community. From Alexander's report we learn that the event he describes was often replicated in other meetings. He writes, "The black Methodists here practice orgies. The other day or night a wench was brought into their church, on a bier, laid out, and *in a trance*. During the exorcism she sat up and spake. My

---

157. Hall, *Letters*, 1:357–58.

mother's black maid speaks of it exactly as if it were a miracle. They have carried off a large portion of my congregation."[158]

1843

While Alexander read widely in the field of church history, he continued to have a special interest in works covering the development and progress of the Protestant Reformation. Among the various Reformation histories available in Alexander's lifetime was a multivolume work by the Swiss historian and educator J. H. Merle D'Aubigne.[159] D'Aubigne was one of a group of young men converted under the ministry of Scottish Independent preacher Robert Haldane who later went on to become internationally recognized scholars.[160] His work accentuated the underlying spiritual dimensions of the Protestant Reformation while providing an encyclopedic narrative of its impact on Europe.[161] In a letter from January 1843, Alexander recommended the set to Hall.

> If you have not Merle's History of the Reformation, mention to me your deficit. By all means circulate it, and by all means Carter's edition. I heard my good old father say yesterday that no book in our day he thought was doing more good. He puts the Reformation on its true ground, *i.e.* Luther made his great business the declaring of *saving doctrines*, (we lack a phrase here; I mean the truths which the soul converses with in the article of conversion,) and these went on triumphant, destroying popery, till (—when? for this is the great point) in every country the Reformers took another way, either controversy about minors, or political agitation.[162]

---

158. Hall, *Letters*, 1:361.
159. For Alexander's enthusiastic review of D'Aubigne's history of the Reformation, see James W. Alexander, "History of the Great Reformation of the sixteenth century, in Germany, Switzerland, &c.," *The Biblical Repertory and Princeton Review* 14, no. 1 (January 1842): 119–29. For a careful review of D'Aubigne's life and approach to the writing of Christian historiography, see John Roney, "Jean Henri Merle D'Aubigne," in *Historians of the Christian Tradition: Their Methodologies & Influence on Western Thought*, ed. Michael Bauman and Martin Klauber (Nashville: B & H Books, 1995), 167–89.
160. For a history of the Haldane brothers and their profound influence on nineteenth-century evangelical culture, see Alexander Haldane, *The Lives of Robert and James Haldane* (1852; repr., Edinburgh: Banner of Truth, 1990).
161. For a digest of D'Aubigne's thought on this topic, see J. H. Merle D'Aubigne, "The Voice of the Church One under the Successive Forms of Christianity," in *Classic Reformed Discourses and Essays* (Birmingham: Solid Ground Christian Books, 1995), 223–48.
162. Hall, *Letters*, 1:363.

In a separate context, Alexander explained the value of D'Aubigne's historical narrative in relation to the life of piety.[163] His thoughts on religious historiography were similar to D'Aubigne's and would later find expression in his work as a professor of church history at Princeton Theological Seminary.[164]

> We commend these most engaging volumes to every class of our readers. If sometimes, from the stirring nature of the recital, they should imagine that they are perusing the inventions of romance, they must attribute this to the skill of the historian, assured by his perpetual citation of original authorities, that every statement is drawn from authentic memorials. The book breathes the spirit of piety, and of that piety which is not indifferent to truth. There is no attempt to conceal those doctrines which offend the natural heart, and which, after being the powerful weapons of Luther and Zwingle, have been laid aside by so many of their successors. The history is evidently written in the very spirit in which its great deeds were enacted. That such a spirit is reviving in France and Switzerland, especially at a time when, as in the Canton of Vaud, the ancient landmarks are suffering violence from the hand of infidel governors, is matter of thanksgiving and of hope.[165]

In his correspondence for that month, Alexander noted his disagreement with a certain writer's opinion that "the only preaching which will meet the demands of the awakened public mind, is the metaphysical." "In every age," he said, "the interest has attached to just that preaching which most directly reached the affections and passions of souls inquiring what must we do to be saved. This I think historically incontestable."

---

163. See D'Aubigne, "The Study of the History of Christianity, and Its Usefulness in the Present Day," in *Classic Reformed Discourses*, 152–73.

164. Alexander's ongoing enthusiasm for the value of D'Aubigne's writings can be found in a letter in May 1845: "I would rather preach Christ, by such a history as Merle d'Aubigne's than by many sermons; yet men judge differently, from going by names instead of things." Hall, *Letters*, 2:33. D'Aubigne's histories of the Reformation remain in print. See J. H. Merle D'Aubigne, *The History of the Reformation in the 16th century*, 3 vols. (Harrisonburg: Sprinkle Publications, n.d.); *The History of the Reformation in the Time of Calvin*, 4 vols. (Harrisonburg: Sprinkle Publications, n.d.). For a stimulating lecture addressing the ongoing value of Calvin's life and work, see J. H. Merle D'Aubigne, *Let Christ Be Magnified: Calvin's Teaching for Today* (Edinburgh: Banner of Truth, 2007).

165. Alexander, "History of the Great Reformation," 129.

"A mix of Baxter and Flavel," Alexander stated, "would be my highest wish as a preacher."[166]

As he often did in his letters to Hall, he shared observations from passages of Scripture that he was currently studying. In January 1843, it was from the book of 2 Corinthians: "I do not know a book of Scripture so consolatory as 2 Cor. Lately I culled the passages in it describing the writer's troubles, and was amazed; but the consolation is like sunshine over all, and everywhere the same—Christ. Cheerful religion is most like Scripture, and, as Dr. Hodge says, joy is an oil to every wheel of the machine." Authors who reflect this outlook were the ones Alexander found most helpful for motivating him to pursue a life of piety. "Hence," he said, "I look with all but envy on such writers as Flavel, Bates, Philip and Matthew Henry, Romaine, and John Newton; they put me into working gear sooner than Brainerd, Payson, and the American school."[167]

For Alexander, the Puritans were not only inspirational, but also exemplary in their model of pastoral diligence. In comparison to American pastors serving rural pastorates, Alexander believed the Puritans far more diligent in Bible study and public exposition. "Don't you think our cities are rather feebly manned?" he asked. "O that our country-ministers would only aim at more learning and piety! Most of the great Puritans were in the provinces. So it was in old New England. But our country-pastors think themselves exempt from all scriptural research."[168]

Health Matters Again

While never a large man, Alexander's weight had dropped to 132 pounds by early spring. He did not seem too concerned about it, although it was likely a precursor to other problems that would occur in the coming months. He continued through his regular responsibilities at the

---

166. Hall, *Letters*, 1:364. Baxter's voluminous writings remain in print. See Richard Baxter, *The Practical Works of Richard Baxter*, 4 vols. (Ligonier: Soli Deo Gloria, 2000).

167. Hall, *Letters*, 1:364. For Bates's collected works, see *The Complete Works of William Bates* (Harrisonburg: Sprinkle Publications, 1990). For the works of Matthew Henry, see *The Complete Works of Matthew Henry*, 2 vols. (Grand Rapids: Baker Books, 1997). Philip Henry, Matthew's father, wrote a number of works, the most popular of which is *Christ All in All* (Swengel: Reiner Publications, 1976). Of Romaine's various publications, see especially William Romaine, *The Life, Walk, and Triumph of Faith* (Cambridge: James Clarke, 1970). For Newton, see *The Works of the Rev. John Newton*, 6 vols. (Edinburgh: Banner of Truth, 1988).

168. Hall, *Letters*, 1:366.

college during the spring without interruption. Correspondence from June lists some of his duties: "I write a fresh lecture every week on Latin literature, which I read to the Sophomores, over and above their regular recitations."[169]

By mid-July, his health, however, had begun to take a turn for the worse. His condition also affected his ability to preach. A letter written from Princeton on July 19, 1843, informs Hall about his deteriorating health. "I have been very much debilitated this summer, and lately, for the first time in my life, had to sit down in the midst of a sermon, from a sudden affection of the head."[170] Ashbel Green filled Alexander's pulpit during one of the Sundays in July in order to allow Alexander time to recuperate. "Last Sunday afternoon Dr. Green preached to my Africans. Though his voice was laboured, the sermon was excellent, and towards the close very impressive."[171]

In Support of Cowper

Alexander took time in a letter written during November to debunk a recently published article critical of William Cowper's melancholy. Cowper's hymns and poetry had been helpful to Alexander, and he felt the criticism of the author was unwarranted.

> In Charlotte Elizabeth's Magazine, this dashing woman declares Cowper's melancholy to have been a judgment on him for translating Homer: an odd prolepsis, surely, inasmuch as he tried to hang himself shortly after he was of age, and never thought of his translation until he was more than fifty. All she ever will write will do less for the gospel than Cowper's Task, Truth, Charity, Expostulation, and Hymns. His translation, like his other works, was the refuge from a madness, which but for this would have driven him to suicide, or at least to the cells. Though he is not our only Christian poet, he is certainly (of the great ones) our only evangelical one. The cruelty of the aspersion is affecting. The woman is deaf herself. When Charles the Second taunted Milton with losing his sight, as a judgment, Milton reminded him that his majesty's father has lost his head. And when Warburton, in a like vein, told old Quin, that all the regicide judges

---

169. Hall, *Letters*, 1:375.
170. Hall, *Letters*, 1:375–76.
171. Hall, *Letters*, 1:376.

came to a bloody end, the actor replied, "The same, your lordship may observe, is true of the twelve apostles."[172]

William Cunningham

Portions of a letter dated December 30, 1843, provide interesting observations on a recent visit to the Princeton Seminary campus by the renowned Scottish theologian and preacher William Cunningham. Cunningham's leadership had been instrumental in the Disruption of 1843 that took place among the Presbyterian churches in Scotland, and from which the newly named Free Church had emerged. A brilliant mind, committed churchman, and outstanding preacher, Cunningham was held in high esteem among American Presbyterian theologians for his reforming influence. Alexander writes:

> Dr. Cunningham has been here for several days; but this is not his main visit. He is altogether the most satisfactory foreigner I have seen. By the Scotch papers I perceive he ranks among the first four or five in the Free Church. Height about 6 ft., and large in proportion; a stout but finely formed man; very handsomely dressed, and in an eminent degree the gentleman, in every thing but excess of snuff. Age, I reckon, about 41; spectacles. A shock of thick curly hair. He has no airs of patronage. Powerful reasoning and sound judgment seem to be his characteristics; and he is a walking treasury of facts, dates, and ecclesiastical law. I heard him for an hour, on Friday, in a speech to the students. Indescribable Scotch intonation, (but little idiom,) and convulsion of body, but flowing, elegant language, and amazing power in presenting argument. Though his manner is rugged and uncouth, and he has no sign of imagination, yet when he gets on tender topics of religion, he is so scriptural, and so sound, that one is affected by what he says. I have seldom listened to a man with more instruction.[173]

Alexander greatly enjoyed the visit of Cunningham to Princeton. Cunningham represented what was best in the Scottish theological heritage and was exemplary as a preacher. In Alexander's judgment, Cunningham was one of the greatest speakers he had heard.[174]

---

172. Hall, *Letters*, 1:384.
173. Hall, *Letters*, 1:386.
174. Alexander valued Cunningham's observations on the different preaching styles that marked the conservatives and moderates in the Scottish church: "Cunningham says

At about the same time that Cunningham had visited the seminary, another great Presbyterian leader lay ill in his home a few doors away from the campus. Samuel Miller was in his early seventies, and the ravages of time were beginning to take their toll on his health. "I am concerned at having to say that good old Dr. Miller is quite ill, with pleurisy," Alexander informed Hall. "The loss of him would be a sad blow to us. I think him one of the most conscientious and pious men I ever knew. His behavior in a parlour-controversy is an example to every one, and has often put me to shame."[175] Fortunately, Miller would recover from his illness and enjoy another six years as a professor at the seminary.

1844

Cunningham's visit the previous year may have prompted Alexander to reexamine the history of preaching and the particular styles of delivery most blessed by God. What he discovered had more to do with the content of the message than the difference in delivery style among preachers. He comments on his research in a communication on January 25, 1844: "I have taken some pains to examine the series of texts preached on by Whitefield and Wesley: few of them are odd, or even uncommon; they are the familiar, evangelical, everlasting verses, which God has owned in all ages."[176]

Observations on church life highlight letters from February and March of 1844. Alexander noted a heightened interest in religion among the community but did not believe it should be characterized as a revival. A letter written in February includes observations on the health of his family and the growing religious interest:

> A bad sore-throat prevails here. My father *has been* seriously, perhaps dangerously, ill with it. There is certainly a more general attention to religion here than I have ever known, but nothing like excitement. Scores of persons, who have neglected ordinances for years, come to every thing. Some of our most substantial men and women are affected. I suppose a hundred copies of the "Way of Life," [by Dr. Hodge,] and the "Great Change," [by Dr. Redford,] have been sold

---

the prejudice against reading sermons is still very general in Scotland, and that committing to memory is the prevalent method; the Moderates have always read." Hall, *Letters*, 1:387.

175. Hall, *Letters*, 1:387.
176. Hall, *Letters*, 1:387.

here within a few weeks. The latter has been blessed to the awakening of a number. A most visible effect has taken place on our tavern-haunters. In college we have little appearance of revival.[177]

Alexander's congregation in Princeton was also experiencing an upsurge in religious affection. A number of new people were engaged to join the First Presbyterian Church. Among the stimulants to religious interest was Charles Hodge's little masterpiece on Christianity, *The Way of Life*.[178] Alexander notes in a letter in early March 1844 the increased interest in prayer that was taking place:

> Next Sunday is our Communion. About thirty will make profession of faith. The seriousness is not abated. It is a remarkable fact, that no one means of awakening has been so much blessed here, as the putting of books into people's hands; especially, "The Great Change," and "The Way of Life." We have had no inquiry-meetings, and latterly no increase of preaching. Domestic prayer-meetings have been a good deal multiplied.[179]

Pastoral Consolation

Among the letters from 1844 is correspondence from April providing Hall encouragement upon the death of his brother George. Alexander's letter is full of tender scriptural counsel appropriate to the occasion. A master wordsmith, Alexander's remarks betray the simplicity of thought so necessary at times of family bereavement.

> Though I thought a great deal about you, I did not dare to write until I received John's letter, which contained such comfortable statements, that I feel as if the opening were plain. I need scarcely say I sympathize with you and your mother, most deeply, under this affliction. It is true of your family, as of ours, that death has spared you long, only to make the blow of bereavement more severe. My recollection of George goes back to a very early period, and my renewed acquaintance with him, not many months ago, brought me to still nearer acquaintance with his kind and affectionate qualities. But I will not enlarge upon those considerations, which only serve to aggravate your loss. I know you feel it in your inmost soul. I know

---

177. Hall, *Letters*, 1:389.
178. Charles Hodge, *The Way of Life* (Philadelphia: American Sunday-School Union, 1841; repr., New York: Paulist Press, 1987).
179. Hall, *Letters*, 1:390.

in some degree, what an interest you took in your brother's prosperity, and that his death must inflict a corresponding wound. And I think it very likely, that under the first impulse of the trial, you find yourself the subject of entirely new experience, and in danger of being "swallowed up of overmuch sorrow." And a certain time must elapse, before you can respond altogether to those statements of divine truth, which are applicable to your present condition, and which you will afterwards feel in all their force. It is my wish and prayer, that you, and your bereaved mother, and all the family, may be—not simply *comforted*—but what is infinitely better, *sanctified* by means of this affliction. For surely, if George is in heaven, as we are permitted to think he is, what have we more to wish for him? what have we more to wish for ourselves? Don't think of him as suffering, and dying—all that is past—it is no more to him than the suffering of your infancy is to you—think of him as "with Christ," "present with the Lord,"—adoring the infinite grace which saves sinners. The moment he departed, all the anxious prayers you ever put up for him were in an instant answered. Now let me very earnestly recommend to you, as a duty you owe to Christ, not to brood over the dark part of a dispensation which has so very bright a side. O that we may all be led to look more at the slightness of the hold we have on friends, and be prepared to go with them!

I have said these few words, not as believing there was any information to be given you, but as a testimony that you are not forgotten in your afflictions. And I beg that you will assure your mother and sister of my tender condolence. But how shall I speak of his widow? The Lord must comfort her; I trust He does; I am sure He will. I felt disposed to write to her, but did not feel that I had any call to intrude in this way, so soon after an unspeakable trial.

Every member of my father's family feels the blow which has fallen on yours. We have ourselves had a great loss, in the death of Aunt Rice. God grant that each of us may be prepared in the day of His coming![180]

Pulpit Inquiries
In the spring of 1844, Alexander received an invitation to preach at the Duane Street Church in New York City. The congregation had expressed interest in securing Alexander as their pastor, but, for various reasons,

---

180. Hall, *Letters*, 1:393–94.

Alexander had resisted their overtures.[181] He expressed his dismay with their inquiry in a letter dated May 8, 1844:

> Very much against my wish, I have to preach in New York [Duane Street Church] next Sunday. Some time ago they wrote to my father, to know whether I would entertain a call from them. I answered, through my father, very decidedly, in the negative. On the strength of this, I accepted, with other here, an invitation to preach for them. Now I learn, with regret, that they still mean to press the matter. I earnestly begged off, but they would not allow it.[182]

The church's interest in Alexander continued into the summer months—much to his dismay. He shared his perturbation with Hall in a communication from late June 1844:

> I have a disorder which has relaxed me a good deal. I have also had a call from Duane St. which has a similar effect. I have to speak at New York the day after to-morrow, and Commencement is just over. These are reasons enough for not writing before, and for not writing eloquently now. The New York business I should settle very speedily, if it were left to my feelings; my friends, especially my father, warn me against a hasty determination.[183]

Correspondence from a few days later on July 4, 1844, elaborates Alexander's perplexity as to what he should do:

> We are all packed up for the Cape. This business of the call has given me unspeakable anxiety. The twofold solicitation, if I may so call it, makes me pause and ask, whether Providence does not mean to unsettle me from my semi-secular post. On examination, I do not find that I am drawn New York-ward, so far as I know, by an attraction of a worldly nature. Ease, quiet, friends, retirement &c., are all *here*. I do feel a strong desire to preach. I am in a strait.[184]

---

181. Alexander's family was content with their life in Princeton. The children especially enjoyed the rural life that the town provided: "One of our hens has eight ducklings. Three other hens are mothers, and two more will soon be. I never alighted on any home-attraction, which is so fertile in amusement for the children. Feeding, eggs, chicks, and ducklings, give them never-ending variety; especially as we have a regular Chicken College, roll-call, lectures on Clucking, Swimming, &c. Let me recommend a coop in your back-court." Hall, *Letters*, 1:395.
182. Hall, *Letters*, 1:395.
183. Hall, *Letters*, 1:396.
184. Hall, *Letters*, 1:397.

To complicate matters further, a Congregational church in Boston, Massachusetts, had also contacted Alexander regarding their interest in securing his pastoral services. A historic congregation, the Bowdoin Street Church would have afforded Alexander opportunity to minister in one of America's most historic colonial cities.

Alexander concentrated his prayers on whether to pursue conversation with the Duane Street congregation or the Bowdoin Street Church. While on vacation in Cape May, New Jersey, during July 1844, Alexander spoke of his growing interest in serving a pastoral charge in New York City.

> I have had great anxieties about my duty in regard to Duane St. I have very earnestly wished to be fully employed in the work of the ministry; but I never thought of so responsible a charge. My visit to New York greatly impressed me with the mighty field on which even a moderate man might operate from that centre. I have no notion of abandoning the down-town, which, to me, is the city proper, in both New York and Philadelphia.[185]

The invitation to serve the Duane Street congregation began to weigh heavily upon Alexander's mind. He realized that he could not let creature comforts determine his decision. He sensed the call was from God and that to decline it would be against God's will for his life. He was a pastor at heart and a preacher by calling, and he knew that he could not remain at the college indefinitely. A letter written from Cape May on July 15 reveals the struggle in which he was engaged.

> The call from New York weighs more heavily on me. To go thither, I plainly see, will cut up by the roots my goodly tree of literary shade and family quiet, and deprive me of a support from parents, brothers, and elder ministers, on which I have leaned most pleasantly, but too long. I shall, if I go, seem to many to go for the gaud of a large stipend; this is of no weight, however, in the great account. If I go, it will be under this feeling, which I own grows upon me, *I dare not stay*.[186]

As the new college semester began in August 1844, Alexander became convinced that the call to New York was the correct choice to make. While

---

185. Hall, *Letters*, 1:398.
186. Hall, *Letters*, 1:399.

the Bowdoin Street Church had its allurements, the Congregational polity to which the congregation was committed precluded serious interest on the part of Alexander. Although he was at times frustrated with Presbyterian polity, it was the ecclesiology to which he subscribed and felt most at home.

Alexander also found arguments for remaining at Princeton inadequate. Apparently, a number of friends and faculty felt he could be of greatest service as a professor. Whether intentional or not, their reasoning in some manner or another tended to downplay the importance of a pulpit ministry in relation to that of an academic post.[187] Alexander was not swayed by their opinions. As a preacher, he was confident of the pulpit's power to change men's lives and determine the destiny of a nation in ways that an academic post, for all the good it might do, could not achieve.[188] Alexander's thoughts can be found in correspondence on August 9, 1844:

> The college opened yesterday. Thus far, about fifty matriculates. It is a sign of getting old, that I find numbers of my old college friends bringing sons on. All the *letters* I get from Boston indicate unanimous welcome. I do not think of turning Congregationalist, and they say nothing of turning Presbyterian; that settles the point, so far as I can see it with my present facts. Dr. Hodge, Prof. Henry, Mr. Packard, and Dr. Maclean, are the only persons who strenuously oppose my leaving Princeton. But, in my heart of hearts, I think they all, in their calculations, discount too liberally from the value of

---

187. A report Alexander completed earlier that year on ministerial education affirms the importance he attached to preaching: "The great, appointed, tried and permanent means of giving men the gospel, is the ordinance of preaching. Other agencies have done their part, as invaluable aids, but this it is, which has been essential and universal, and which, as divinely ordained, will so continue to the end of time. The pious admonition, the tract, and even the written word, are not so generally the instrument of great increase. It was the institution of preaching, which, under God, wrought the astonishing changes in the first age, in the spread of religion through all the countries which became truly Christian, in the Reformation from popery, and in the diffusion of our own church in the British isles and in America." James W. Alexander, "Annual Report of the Board of Education, of the Presbyterian Church, in the United States of America. Presented May, 1843," *The Biblical Repertory and Princeton Review* 15, no. 4 (October 1843): 587.

188. "Consider the influence of the pulpit. It may be said with scarce a figure, to occupy popular attention one day in every seven; in other words, four or five whole years in a generation of men. The faithful hearer listens to a hundred discourses every year. The faithful pastor is therefore more engaged than all other men, in moulding the common mind." Alexander, "Annual Report...Presented May, 1843," 589.

the *preached* word. Several of them are men whom I scarcely dare oppose, in a prudential question; yet, in my most solemn hours, I declare to you, their arguments have little weight with me, because I so profoundly believe *preaching* (including parochial teaching) to be God's great ordinance. O how much I need prayer and counsel! I am, after all, undecided.[189]

Alexander informed Hall of his decision to resign his professorship and accept the call to Duane Street in a letter on August 21, 1844.

I have asked myself repeatedly *ubi gentium* [where in the world] you are, that you do not reply to my last esteemed favour. Not to keep you in darkness, I now break through my silence, to say that I have accepted the call to New York. I feel, as you may imagine, almost terrified at what I have done. Yet I have no doubt as to the moral rightness of what I have done: success is a different thing. "Events are God's." The last two or three months have been a season of mental struggle. I have had to breast a current of advice and powerful reasoning, from some friends of ours, who are no mean argumentators, against my intimate convictions; and I have felt with them, that leaving Princeton is leaving *home*. At the same time, even in view of possible failure, I have quite a comfortable hope that God will not forsake me, and this sustains me more than usual.[190]

A final letter from his time at the college speaks of his excitement in visiting New York and viewing the sights that surround it. His communication on September 11, 1844, is filled with the wonder of a child at the sight of some new adventure that is about to begin.

I resisted all housing, &c., went to New York, Staten Island, &c; but it is obstinate. I must stand ready to see the prediction of some verified, as to my capacity for pastoral labour. Staten Island is another Isle of Wight. I was altogether surprised and enchanted. A very gem: sea, bay, rivers, vales, mountains, incomparable verdure, villas, absence of all high-roads and noise. From one point, you see the Atlantic, New York, Brooklyn, Newark, Elizabethtown, Rahway, and immeasurable tracts of sea and land.[191]

---

189. Hall, *Letters*, 1:400.
190. Hall, *Letters*, 1:400.
191. Hall, *Letters*, 1:402.

But the trip was more than a sightseeing excursion. Housing had to be secured and plans made for his installation by the regional presbytery. A series of brief sentences summarize the flurry of activity in which Alexander was engaged:

> In New York I overworked myself, looking for lodgings, and found none answering all conditions. Therefore, by urgent advice of my elders, I took a house, 83 White Street, east of Broadway, between Broadway and Elm Street, south side of White; two stories: look at a map of New York; you will see the yards are larger than usual there. But how unlike a Philadelphia house! $600 rent. After I had taken it, I learned that its first occupant had been the first pastor of our church, Dr. Romeyn. Installation probably Oct. 3. But not unless we hear from Moderator Webster pretty shortly.[192]

---

192. Hall, *Letters*, 1:403.

I am more and more persuaded, that a man who walks "in the Spirit," must often seem to himself and others to walk alone. I mean he must follow leading towards paths of feeling and conduct, remote from the precedent and fashion even of good people. Don't we find things, in Christ's teachings, which if all our books, and human patterns, and diaries were forgotten, would lead us further and in other directions than we have gone? and is not this accompanied with an inward feeling, that what is thus indicated is true, and right, and sanctifying? In regard to the care of souls, I am constrained, after trial, to give over wearing other men's clothes, however much better than my own. I have found pain and barrenness in every attempt to do things by the approved methods for getting up "an interest," &c. Truths, found in Scripture, and affecting my own mind, freshly, strongly, and as it were newly, I mean coming to me, after frequent perusals, as living words of God, verifying themselves in my experience, are those which, when simply spoken or preached, seem to reach other people. Suppose the result is not the awakening of A[,] B, or of any body on the spot; suppose no revival ensues: my growing judgment is, that the utterance of such truth will accomplish God's end on his elect: "for they know His voice." Surely, in our craving for effect, we lose the value of such remarkable passages as John x.27; 2 Cor. iv.2, 3; 2 Thess. ii.10. Simplicity, in following Christ as a teacher, is worthy of our consideration.

—JAMES W. ALEXANDER
May 3, 1845

Chapter 9
DUANE STREET CHURCH: 1844–1849

Alexander was installed as pastor at the Duane Street Church on October 3, 1844.[1] His installation was almost nineteen years to the day from when he was first licensed to the gospel ministry. A letter written by Alexander following his installation gives thanks to "benignant Providence" for the kind welcome which he and his family received from the congregation.

The Alexanders had just arrived in the city and were staying with friends until their rental house was available, but they were eager to begin meeting with their congregation. Alexander himself also looked forward to using the back room on the second floor of their new home for his study—"the chief room," he said, "in a parson's house."

The responsibilities of the charge quickly filled Alexander's daily schedule.[2] Multiple sermons on Sunday and the monthly concert for prayer on a Monday are noted in one letter entry.[3] A separate correspondence lists Monday meetings with a "Mission-committee, one Seamen's

---

1. Archibald Alexander delivered the installation sermon. Dr. Potts presented the charge to the pastor; Dr. Krebs, the charge to the congregation. Dr. Gardiner Spring provided the closing prayer. Archibald Alexander's sermon was later published in 1853: Archibald Alexander, "Rightly Dividing the Word of Truth," in *The Princeton Pulpit*, ed. John T. Duffield (New York: Charles Scribner, 1853), 29–47. Alexander's sermon can also be found in Garretson, *Princeton and the Work of the Christian Ministry*, 1:241–52.

2. J. A. Alexander urged his brother to make judicious use of his time in addressing the vast ministry needs he now faced in a city environment: "He had great sympathy with his toiling brother in his new and heavy cares; and sometimes exhorted him to take summary measures with the troup of idlers, busybodies, and charlatans who devoured his time, and cut him off from the smallest chance of rest or leisure." Alexander, *Life of Joseph Addison Alexander*, 2:595.

3. "Dr. Alexander preached his first sermon, after the instalment, October 6th, from Psalm li. 12; and in the afternoon from Matthew xi. 16-19." Hall, *Letters*, 2:5.

committee, one Church-extension-committee, and one prayer meeting of ministers."[4] Tuesday evenings were devoted to a weekly lecture at "half-past seven, in the basement" of the church building.[5] A prayer meeting was held each Thursday, and on Saturday mornings Alexander catechized the children of his church for an hour beginning at 9:00 a.m. He took special delight in his catechism class.[6] "I find it my pleasantest hour in the week," he remarked.[7]

The members of his congregation were eager to meet with their new pastor. "Our door bell hardly ceases to vibrate," he wrote.[8] "Visitors knock and ring 'frae morn till e'en.'"[9] In order to facilitate pastoral visitation, he requested his congregation to furnish him with their names and addresses.[10] He was encouraged by their interest in spiritual matters and was optimistic for the future of his ministry: "Unless I err, there is a great desire for real pastoral attention, and for Christian profit."[11] A letter from the following June provides a vivid description of the environment in which his new pastoral ministry was exercised:

> Yet I cannot describe what I see in my walks in certain streets: dunghills, nakedness, dead dogs and cats, offal, garbage, leprous folk, lazars, magdalens. The stench, in some quarters, is mephitic. The single element of water (*nota bene*, not Croton) flows, and floods, and smells in a manner unmentionable. Cloacina herself must preside in and about the park and it purlieus. Nobody ever cares about this or

---

4. Hall, *Letters*, 2:61.

5. Alexander began a series of lectures on the book of Hebrews which "extended from October 29, 1844, to February 23, 1847." A total of sixty-two lectures were delivered at the time the series was completed. Hall, *Letters*, 1:41.

6. A letter written a few months later states his commitment to catechetical training: "I am much delighted with old John Brown's Explanation of the Catechism. My catechetical class delights me more and more. I wish I could hope as much from my sermons. When I compare professor with professor, what a difference between those who were taught early, and those who were not!" Hall, *Letters*, 2:25.

7. Hall, *Letters*, 2:12.

8. "Addison says I should practice self-denial—at the door." Hall, *Letters*, 2:30.

9. Hall, *Letters*, 2:30.

10. Alexander was eager to increase the number of active elders in his congregation: "I am anxiously concerned about new elders, having only Messr. Auchincloss and Beers. I have never had any one to pay a visit of introduction with me; still I am getting on." Hall, *Letters*, 2:12.

11. Hall, *Letters*, 2:7.

any thing similar, for it is characteristic of a New Yorker to feel like a stranger within his gates: no *esprit de corps*, no responsibility.[12]

While life in the city was marked by poverty and destitution, a variety of Christian initiatives had emerged to address the spiritual and social problems endemic to urban life. Alexander was amazed at the number of organizations ministering to the city's population.[13] "The undercurrent of religious activity in this city strikes me with unexpected force, as strong and branching into a vast number of charities. I did not conceive that so much was effected in regard to seamen, tract distribution, and care of poor."[14] He was particularly impressed with the amount of tract distribution taking place and the evangelistic outreach of the Methodists. "*Me judice*, the Methodists are doing more than all of us, in evangelizing this Sodom. The monthly visits of the City Tract Society's distributors, is the most wonderful and blessed agency; the half had not been told me."[15]

Although he was pleased by the various ministry initiatives he observed, Alexander was troubled by the sectarian partisanship that he witnessed among New School Presbyterians. "Certain New School men," he said, "are bent on awakening a New School sectarism, as against all Union Societies. They mean to have a Publication Board. These jealousies are horrid." He believed their actions divisive and injurious to the spiritual welfare of the church. In his judgment, organizational busyness had replaced the cultivation of heartfelt piety. Underlying the surface symptoms was a decline in spiritual affection for the upward calling in Christ to which all believers are to aspire. Alexander writes:

> I do not wonder that some pastors feel themselves at length constrained to do all their works within their own parish. I cannot but think that spiritual religion is at a low ebb in our churches in this city. Never have I heard, in the same amount of visiting, so little savoury discourse. I believe Puseyism triumphs, (not because

---

12. Hall, *Letters*, 2:33–34.
13. "In transferring his abode for the first time to a great city, and assuming the charge of a large congregation there, it was to be expected that a man of Dr. Alexander's piety, philanthropy, and conscientiousness would not only be surprised in the contrast with his secluded life hitherto, but that he would be more deeply affected at the new phases of misery, ungodliness, and disproportionate Christian zeal, than one who had become familiar with them all." "James Waddell Alexander," 74.
14. Hall, *Letters*, 2:9.
15. Hall, *Letters*, 2:10.

Presbyterians fight so little, brag so little, and stickle so little; so saith ——,) but because our actual state, in Presbyterian churches, *has so little to awaken and fill the affections.* Old spiritualism (Pollockism)…is no more. Revivalism is no more. The only activity visible is a mere business bustle in regard to organisms and agencies. Must we not go deeper than we have gone? I am deeply affected with a sense of this. But how to begin? *At home,* we need most of all. I have shut up books, and live in the streets and houses, all the available hours of the day.[16]

Obstacles to Effective Pastoral Ministry

Alexander was equally disturbed by the ineffective witness of Old School Presbyterianism. It too, he felt, lacked the spiritual stamina that once characterized its confessional forbearers.[17] "The savour of the old-schoolism is not good here. Many have never seen old-schoolism allied to any zeal, and have all their early associations connected with new measures."[18] In a letter dated April 28, 1845, he bemoaned the spiritual condition of the pulpit ministry of his denomination:

> What—what is the matter? something is surely wrong with us. Is it that we are all too stiff, unreal, formal, routine-ish, in our ministry? Is it that we copy others? that we do not copy primitive ways? that we do not act out our Bible-persuasions? that we are cowardly about the world? that we seek the subordinate church and congregational ends, instead of the principal ones? Whatever it be, our churches are in a heavy, slow state; wheels deep in ruts and mud. Our preaching, I feel it, is too little like earnest talking; we are too unlike, in and out of the "sacred desk."[19]

In Alexander's judgment, a number of factors had contributed to the loss of zeal he witnessed in his denomination: Moderatism, the revivalist theology of Charles Finney and his adherents, and the increasing influence of authors such as Coleridge and Emerson. Although different in

---

16. Hall, *Letters,* 2:8–9.
17. A letter on April 17, 1845, hints at his frustrations: "I do not know that I have ever been in a busier week. Besides more patients than common, and usual parish cares, we have had the presbytery these days; have talked the ordinary twaddle on points of order, and have licensed nine probationers." Hall, *Letters,* 2:27.
18. Hall, *Letters,* 2:15.
19. Hall, *Letters,* 2:29.

perspective, they were all complementary in serving to undermine the vitality of spiritual life among professing Christians.[20]

Alexander's letters frequently mention the detrimental influence that "Moderatism" had upon the spiritual pulsebeat of the churches.[21] In effect, the institutionalizing of the church's presence compromised its spiritual vigilance as interest in outward forms, ritual, comfortable facilities, and the transformation of public worship into entertainment all gutted the spiritual purposes for which the church had been established.[22] Moderatism was formal religion absent from the presence of the Spirit of God—the "form of godliness without the power thereof."

> I think I am not censorious, nor chagrined, in judging that religion in New York runs very much towards externals. Fine churches, pews, and music, fine sermons, fine "enterprises," viewed in the same light as stock-company concerns, fine collections; such are the stimulating ideas. "Moderatism" is the *terminus ad quem* [point to which]. So far as my researches go, Presbyterianism has never and nowhere made striking advances, except when the body of preachers and people has been animated with a zeal for truth and saving souls, such as at the very time has been a little too strong, methodistical, pietistical, enthusiastical, in the eyes even of many sound, good sort of brethren. When we substitute for this secular stimulants, wealth, apparatus, ritual, decorum, letters, or oratory, we find that these (at least in the apprehension of the million) exist in greater force among the Episcopalians. Nor do we mend the matter by fighting these last, on questions of difference. Our real aggression has always been by warm pushing of our evangelical tenets.[23]

"Moderatism" could just as easily compromise a clergyman's spiritual priorities. Hall had warned Alexander about its danger when he accepted the call to serve at the Duane Street Church. Fashion and affluence were aspects of Moderatism that ministers could easily succumb to in their

---

20. "But Alexander is far from laying the blame for conditions wholly upon others. The people had seen little evidence of the older evangelicalism for some years. In a city whose population was to reach around 800,000 by 1858 only Gardiner Spring's church remained a dominant influence among the Presbyterians." Murray, *Revival and Revivalism*, 338.
21. "We are dying of *Moderatism*." Hall, *Letters*, 2:12.
22. "Religious showmanism is the order of the day; a church, an organ, a poll of hair, a neat stock, a ditto hand, a gown; these are thy gods, O Israel!" Hall, *Letters*, 2:29.
23. Hall, *Letters*, 2:74.

desire to be like the wealthier members of their congregations and city. The allurements that a city provides to pursue wealth and status have ruined many city ministers.[24] Likewise, the respect shown to a minister's office and recognition for his gifts of public eloquence may lead to a misdirected sense of his self-importance. "I am convinced you are right about the place ministers seek to occupy in society," Alexander wrote to Hall. "One loses nothing, either, by being behind the fashion. Paul, or Luther, or Swartz, would perhaps have been poor Mentors about a visiting card, or a sack-coat. Their tea-service was perhaps humbler than a Methodist's."[25]

Ironically, the spiritual indifference created by material affluence was paralleled by man-centered efforts to grow the church. As the New Haven theology propagated by Nathaniel Taylor found popular appeal through Finney's preaching and publications, the meaning of revival, teaching on conversion, and understanding of growth in the Christian life took on new definitions in relation to the role that man can play in effecting his salvation and maturation as a Christian.[26] Here, too, preaching had become a form of entertainment, and salvation became a result of man-centered effort dependent less on the Spirit's sovereign initiative than the use of technique in soliciting human response. Troubled by the direction that certain ministers had taken in attempting to reach their community, Alexander resolved to keep before his heart and mind the high calling of the ministry and the proper manner in which it is to be conducted.[27] He writes, "In New York, the result of the former exciting

---

24. Alexander felt the same to be true for the churches: "I am appalled at the extent to which our city churches have become machines for raising money. Every month a stated collection, and almost weekly calls between-whiles. Now, aside from any selfish feeling, is this right? Is it the ideal of a true gospel state? Is not most of these sums given by worldlings? Is not the pecuniary association kept rankly, to the hurt of piety? These are questions more easily asked than answered. Ecclesiastico-politico-economy wants an Adam Smith. More equalization is certainly one thing we ought to aim at." Hall, *Letters*, 2:16.

25. Hall, *Letters*, 2:15.

26. Finney's theology of revival found expression in a series of lectures published in 1868. Charles Finney, *Lectures on Revivals of Religion* (New York: Fleming H. Revell Company, n.d.).

27. Alexander found encouragement in his work as a pastor from reading the life of Robert Murray M'Cheyne. The power of M'Cheyne's pulpit and pastoral ministry stood in stark contrast to much contemporary American pastoral practice: "The life of McCheyne humbles me. What zeal and faith! What a proof that Old Calvinism is not insusceptible of being used as an arousing instrument!" Hall, *Letters*, 2:11. M'Cheyne's biography remains in print: Andrew Bonar, *Memoir and Remains of Robert Murray M'Cheyne* (Edinburgh: Banner of Truth, 1978).

revivals is seen, even in good men, in the making all religion consist in evangelical *effort*. Some are very busy saving souls, with all the dialect and levity and coarseness of Maj. Downing. I feel my own defects. I desire to be a parish-minister, wholly, and with all my soul."[28]

In addition to Moderatism, revivalism, and the influence of the New Haven theology, Alexander also expressed concern in a letter on December 2, 1844, about the shift in temper taking place among the students in Princeton. The "spirit of the age" had found entrance into the hearts and minds of students at the college and seminary through the literary influence of Unitarian and transcendentalist thought in ways that the church may not have expected. "Listen to the talk of our divinity-students; it is of Coleridge, Emerson, &c.," he said. He feared for the future of the church's pulpit ministry surfacing in the reading interests and spiritual culture of the seminary students:

> Much talk in Princeton of the amazing genius of a young poet. He belongs to the set which may be said to constitute the "New America." They go for metaphysic, Coleridge, almost for Spinoza. They laugh at Locke, Reid, Stewart, &c. They undervalue Newton, and Bacon. They applaud Plato. They care less, than they once did, for prayer-meetings, missions, &c.[29]

"Keep your eye on this," he told his friend. "How much we need to stick by the plain declarations of the written word! Reading McCheyne makes me feel how defective we ministers are, in helping one another in the main point."[30]

Reflections on Preaching

While Alexander preferred an extemporaneous preaching model, he also recognized its liabilities. His brother Addison Alexander, on the other hand, felt written manuscripts more suitable to his own gifts of public utterance.[31] During August 1844, James and Addison spoke about the

---

28. Hall, *Letters*, 2:12–13.
29. Hall, *Letters*, 2:12.
30. Hall, *Letters*, 2:12.
31. "The Rev. James W. Alexander once remarked to me…that he and his brother Addison were differently constituted as to this matter; for that in his own case the imagination was never more stimulated than in extemporary preaching; whereas in the case of Addison the reverse was true: the embarrassment of appearing before an audience without notes of any kind, or some other cause, hindered the movement of his imagination,

subject. Both agreed that one of the problems of the extemporaneous style is the natural tendency for the preacher to provide unnecessary self-referential filler at the outset of his message, drawing more attention to himself than the Savior he is called to represent. In this regard, both men found their father, Archibald Alexander, exemplary for his persistent refusal to draw attention to himself through stories, jokes, or personal aggrandizement on his ministry successes in the extemporaneous style of preaching which he modeled. Notes from the conversation were preserved and included in the biography of J. A. Alexander.

> Almost all extemporaneous preachers have this fault: they talk about the *way* in which they are preaching. Thus: "After a few *preliminary remarks*, I shall proceed to," etc.; or, "What I shall lay down will take the form of general principles." "I come with hesitation," etc. "I shall be more brief on this point." "You will observe that in this discussion I do so and so." Avoid all such observations. More generally still, avoid all that brings the speaker's personality before the hearer. A better model than our honoured father, in this, there could not be.[32]

While references in his correspondence at this time suggest that at least one of the sermons delivered each week was read in order to satisfy Northern pulpit expectations, Alexander had not abandoned his earlier commitment to an extemporaneous preaching style which he had learned while serving as a pastor in Virginia. If anything, his convictions regarding the approach had only been further reinforced by his recent pulpit endeavors.

Of even greater importance than the style of a minister's preaching is the more fundamental matter of the spiritual disposition of the heart. In his observations on preaching, Alexander continued to emphasize how essential the preparation of the preacher's heart was for powerful pulpit proclamation. The best preparation for effective preaching is a growing mastery of Scripture and investment in the "culture of the heart." Correspondence from December 2, 1844, explains his thinking:

---

though the excitement of speaking greatly encouraged and excited other powers, such as the memory, the reason, and the faculty of rapid, exact, fluent, and felicitous expression. Writing was on the whole, a greater stimulant than speaking, in the case of the younger brother." Alexander, *Life of Joseph Addison Alexander*, 1:462.

32. Alexander, *Life of Joseph Addison Alexander*, 2:594.

I read one sermon a week; with a growing persuasion, that written sermons have undoubted points of superiority; but that these are all *worldly*. I more and more believe (my practice belies it) that (1) constant Bible-study, using Scripture to explain itself, and (2) culture of the heart, by prayer, &c., are the great preparation for the pulpit. O for a generation of the old sort of preachers! Matt. Henry, Newton, Cecil, &c.[33]

A letter from December 9, 1844, elaborates on the model of preaching that Alexander was describing. "I meant," he said to Hall, "such Presbyterian pastors and preachers as were known to our fathers." While acknowledging their homiletic peculiarities, Alexander gave rationale for their sermonic style:

> I would not demand that any of us should adopt those peculiarities which belonged to the age and fashion of the Puritans; their "pun-divinity," as Charles Lamb called it. Nor do I deny that they sometimes introduced inconvenient niceties of distinction. Yet even in respect to these, I believe it may be taken as universally true, that every distinction arises from some new error to be opposed. The Apostles' creed sufficed, till Arianism arose. Sabellius made other distinctions necessary, and so on to the end of the chapter. Some of the distinctions of the Reformed Theology, and even of our Confession, have become obsolete, but new ones have taken their place, and the number does not seem to be lessened. But the technical formulas of these nonconformists and Scotch Presbyterians are not the things I would imitate. One good characteristic, however, of this whole class, I do wish we had in greater measure; they not only held Scripture truth, but they associated it with Scripture *language*. Their writings teem with Bible phrase and Bible figure; a necessary result, in any age, of affectionate devotion to the book. For this I love them; and, in my best moods, in this I feel myself sliding into imitation of them. I do *not*, I own it, think even the Puritan writers, as a body, chargeable with overlaying the truth, or complicating its simplicity. True, they pursue doctrines into minute ramifications; the necessary consequence of their dwelling so profoundly on them. The *general* statement of a doctrine is, I know, true; it is, also, more intelligible, and more fit for a beginner; but the fault of modern divinity is that it too seldom gets beyond these generalities.[34]

---

33. Hall, *Letters*, 2:12.
34. Hall, *Letters*, 2:13.

Alexander also recognized the importance of preaching "the whole counsel of God" in a manner that is comprehensible and doctrinally thorough. In his assessment, the preaching of New School ministers and the revivalist emphases of Charles Finney were guilty of imbalance in failing to present the entirety of biblical revelation. While Alexander felt their evangelistic interests commendable, he believed that gospel preaching should address matters of Christian growth with equal emphasis in order that new converts might grow into mature believers.

> The *general* statement of a doctrine is, I know, true; it is, also, more intelligible, and more fit for a beginner; but the fault of modern divinity is that it too seldom gets beyond these generalities. Jay represents such a truth as this, "Christ died to save us," in a thousand ways, and each of them coloured with some Scriptural phrase, figure, or example. Some of us, if we taught the same, would scrupulously avoid every such vehicle, and would translate the bible-dictions into that of philosophic elegance. The former I think most luminous, most interesting to common minds, and most safe. It is a great merit of this way, that it is prized by our Stuarts, Pollocks, and Woodruffs, [humble parishioners]. It is the way which made them just what they are. If all our youth were bred in this way, all our old folks would relish it, as the Scotch peasantry actually do. The reverse method, though simpler, and less liable to the charge of cant, has never produced as desirable fruit. And we must not take as our model the way which pleases such as are, by the supposition, uninstructed. We must interpose some long words in the child's lesson, or he will never know any but the short ones. And I cannot help thinking it one of the chief faults of the New School or revival era, that its plan of teaching had respect too exclusively to the initiation of new converts.[35]

In Alexander's estimation, the most important truths of Scripture were the ones often preached the least.[36] He elaborated his concerns in correspondence from March 1845:

> My lectures on Hebrews give me more and more comfort; and I am pleased to observe an increased attendance of men. Looking back—for I have now passed the XL—I lament many things in my

---

35. Hall, *Letters*, 2:13–14.
36. "The Gospel is not attractive enough for people now-a-days. Ministers must bait their trap with something else. The old-fashioned topics are seldom heard. This diminishes one's wonder at the small progress made in spirituals." Hall, *Letters*, 2:48.

> preaching; and among these that I have not from the beginning aimed at the *greatest subjects*. Two things keep us from this: 1, a diffidence about treating them, because they are great; 2, a dislike to topics which seem so familiar. By the great topics, I mean, not the outworks of Christianity, but the citadel; the Fall, the Atonement, Faith, Judgment. The same remark applies to the famous parts of Scripture, the Crucifixion, the Good Samaritan, the Ten Virgins, &c. We are in danger, from neglect of this, of passing our short lives in frittering away at the appendages of the Gospel.[37]

Both the content (matter) of what is preached and the style (manner) in which it is presented were critical to Alexander's thinking for what makes preaching powerful. As the former Professor of Rhetoric and Belles Lettres at Princeton, Alexander valued the importance of careful word selection and composition, but he also knew that something more is necessary in the public proclamation of biblical truth.[38] As preaching is by nature a spiritual activity, Spirit-wrought empowerment is essential for the word to be *preached with power* as well as *experienced in power* by one's hearers. Spiritual anointing, more than anything else, is essential for the Word to go forth with power from a preacher's lips.[39]

> What we seem to want here, is not polish or literature in sermons, but something earnest, real, and affectionate; something to make the people hear as if some truth of transcendent present interest was set forth. Never was I more convinced that in order to this there is nothing so necessary as a direct and specific influence from on High.

---

37. Hall, *Letters*, 2:25.
38. Alexander's thinking on the role of literary elegance in relation to pulpit eloquence had undergone revision from earlier years: "How odd that we learn to write English from Scotchmen; viz., Kaimes, Campbell, and Blair. After teaching them ten years, I am just learning how they have betrayed me. Fear of provincialisms drives them (as us Americans) into prudery; just as parvenus dare not dress plain. Think of Blair's nonsense about the evil of ending a sentence with a particle! E contra, read Shakespeare's 'ills that flesh is heir *to*,' or the sentence cited by Lord J. Russell, 'Shall there be a God to swear *by*, and not to pray *to*?'" Hall, *Letters*, 2:23.
39. Alexander often sought his father's counsel on the subject of preaching: "The words of my good father become more and more precious to me, like the books of the Tarquinian Sibyl; I therefore copy what follows from his last letter: 'As to the effects of the truth preached, never doubt that every faithful sermon will produce its effect; it will not return void. Give it efficacy by prayer. If you have any persons in the church who are mighty in prayer, engage them to pray for the success of the gospel. Payson instituted little circles, called "Aaron-and-Hur societies," the sole object of which was to pray every Sunday morning for the success of the word preached.'" Hall, *Letters*, 2:44.

Rhetorical interest is impotent. There was great interest under the Finneyitish revivals, but it was not evangelical, and I am working among its bitter fruits every day. There is a wonderful vitality and permanency in experience which is built on the preaching of Christ.[40]

As a corrective, Alexander thought contemporary Scottish preaching exemplary of the proper approach to a God-honoring pulpit ministry. "The style of sermons in the Scottish Free Church seems to be the thing," he observed.[41] He viewed the experiential, applicatory approach of Scottish preaching in direct contrast to much of American pulpit oratory influenced by "New Measures." "When the new divinity converts grow cold, they are colder than ice, nothing but a biting censoriousness. I had no idea, even in Jersey, of the modifications wrought in the religion of this city, by the overwrought revivalism of past years. Some, even of those who were once fiery, have degenerated into pulpit-metaphysicians, subtile, and elegant."[42]

While various "forms" may be employed in the composition of a sermon, in the final analysis even literary preferences must give way to a style that flows naturally from a man's personality and gifts in order that his preaching may be most true to the way in which the Lord has shaped him for His service.

> Though given to quotation myself, I think it below the highest method. There is more in a man who spins all out *e propriis visceribus* [from his own heart]. This has often struck me in my good father,— no scraps, no pretty "phrases," no poetry, no Latin sentences. The other way is a sign of weakness: *habeas confitentem reum* [you have a confessing defendant]. Yet still more am I convinced that a man must be himself, and that he gains by following his bent.[43]

Alexander's convictions on this topic can also be found in a review first published in the *Biblical Repertory* during 1839. There, he writes:

> None but a very ignorant or a very self-sufficient man could dream of enjoining his own plans to every one. Indeed, as no really able

---

40. Hall, *Letters*, 2:62.
41. A review article on contemporary Scottish preaching appeared in the *Biblical Repertory* during 1849: Archibald Alexander, "The Free Church Pulpit," *The Biblical Repertory and Princeton Review* 21, no. 1 (January 1849): 82–97.
42. Hall, *Letters*, 2:62.
43. Hall, *Letters*, 2:46–47.

preacher sermonizes exactly like any body else, so no two methods of preparation can be exactly alike, except among pitiable imitators. The individuality and subjective character of a man must let itself out, before he can ever do any thing great; he must be himself. And therefore we shall never think of wasting argument upon the race of dictators, who maintain that every sermon must be written out in full, or on the other hand that no sermon should be written out in full; until we alight on one of them who shall preach as ably and successfully as Whitefield and Hall who never wrote, or as Edwards and Davies who wrote always; and as silently shall we listen to all prescriptions that discourses should have no declared partition, or that each shall have just as many "heads" as Cerberus. For talents differ, modes of thought, feeling and elocution differ, auditories differ, and therefore preparation will differ. But preparation of some sort, and that stated, laborious, life-long preparation, there must be.[44]

Pastoral Reflections

Alexander enjoyed the work of pastoral ministry. He loved his people and sought to minister to both their spiritual and temporal needs. He felt a special burden for the underprivileged and disadvantaged.[45] He was especially sensitive to the loss of human life through accident, illness, or age.[46] A conscientious pastor, he often reflected on the lessons he was learning about his own spiritual condition and the most profitable means of ministering to his congregation.[47]

He took special delight in the gospel message and longed for its reception by his hearers.[48] He reveled in gospel truth even as he delighted in

---

44. James W. Alexander, "Fragments from the Study of a Pastor. By Gardiner Spring, Pastor of the Brick Presbyterian Church in the City of New York," *The Biblical Repertory and Princeton Review* 11, no. 1 (January 1839): 108.

45. "The condition of our vicious poor is very dreadful. When I think of the hunger and nakedness of some, I cannot lie down in my warm bed, without a feeling akin to shame." Hall, *Letters*, 2:91–92.

46. "The loss of good Mrs. Rice, gives me many serious feelings. The more I think of it, the more I believe, that such quiet, and meekness of well-doing will be more prized in 'that day,' than many brilliant qualities. How much better than the self-tormenting pride we have known in some families." Hall, *Letters*, 2:86–87.

47. "Hardly anything so raises my pride and indignation, as when ministerial independence is assaulted in my person; but I continue to have difficulty in knowing how the line lies between the man and the minister. In regard to the latter, we are authorized to take high ground." Hall, *Letters*, 2:79.

48. "How humiliating it is to find that I am pained, when I learn that M or N does not like my teaching, yet am so calm, when all the alphabet, for years, reject my Master's message!" Hall, *Letters*, 2:61.

the death of Christ on his behalf.[49] The atonement was at the heart of the gospel message and a source of great comfort to him. He writes:

> I am now in the 8th chapter of Hebrews. I have never had an exercise more acceptable. To myself, I trust, it has been useful, as leading me to dwell much on the very marrow and riches of gospel grace. One thing, to my mind, above all others, grows in centrality (*ut ita dicam* [so to speak]) among converting doctrines; the infinite, sovereign, freeness of grace, through the death of Christ. Within a few days I have been directed to several persons, who, I think, are savingly exercised.[50]

Alexander's self-effacing honesty about his personal spiritual dereliction as a minister and desire to do that which is pastorally proper can be found in a letter from February 1846. He knew how easy it was to compromise his principles in order to be accepted by his parishioners—even if it came at the expense of having a clear conscience. This was especially the case in the relational disputes that can develop between members of a congregation. Like many pastors, Alexander found himself placed in the middle of personality conflicts within the church. As often happens, each side solicited the pastor's support in defense of their position:

> One of the unreasonable demands on a pastor is, that he should like and dislike the people whom A, B, and C dislike. I try hard to let no prejudices or bickering affect me. But oh! what a disposition, in ourselves and others, to be censorious; to see faults before excellencies in our neighbours; to applaud ourselves tacitly, by criticizing others openly, as to the points where we feel less vulnerable! I know no Scripture precept harder than that, "Let each esteem other better," &c. Sometimes I am painfully affected with the consciousness that this or that duty, which I have performed, would certainly have been neglected or deferred, if no human being were to have known it. I wish I felt more the force of the phrase, "the praise which cometh from God."[51]

---

49. A succinct summary of Alexander's thoughts on the atonement can be found in his review of a recent work by the Rev. Dr Gardiner Spring: James W. Alexander, "The Attraction of the Cross, Designed to Illustrate the leading Truths, Hopes, and Obligations of Christianity," *The Biblical Repertory and Princeton Review* 18, no. 1 (January 1846): 158–75. For an earlier discussion on the *extent* of the atonement, see Hall, *Letters*, 1:149–50.
50. Hall, *Letters*, 2:43.
51. Hall, *Letters*, 2:47.

Engraving of J. W. Alexander, age forty (1845), during his pastorate at Duane Street Presbyterian Church.

ENGRAVING BY A. H. RITCHIE.

A letter on October 12, 1846, talks of the particular trials that ministers experience which help prepare them not only for the responsibilities of their office but also for the care of their family members at home.[52]

> My measure of experience teaches me, that it is God's method never to leave me long in a season of such freedom from anxiety as shall make me forget my dependence. You know something of what it is to preach under such burdens, and to go home afraid to open the door. At such times, one thought predominates: *my sin*. Is not this one chief end of trials? I sometimes sink, but, I think, I do not rebel. God is just, and he is good. We, who teach others, need a peculiar discipline. I am thankful that my domestic trials, on the review, seem all right. Yet I confess to you, my anxieties are almost always inordinate; nor do I grow any wiser. It is, no doubt, wisely ordered, that we suffer in those we love. I did not intend a sermon; but I have thought more of your trials, amidst my own. Is there not a lesson in this also? When we pray for a more useful ministry, God answers us by stripes which we did not expect; but they fall from a gracious hand.[53]

Alexander's administration of the communion meal also provided opportunity for self-examination of his spiritual state. He used these occasions to reflect on his growth in the Christian life and the conflict involved with the presence of remaining sin in his heart.[54] Correspondence from May 8, 1847, reveals the spiritual challenges with which he struggled:

> Our communion is coming on, without one addition on examination. This causes "searchings of heart." I feel no disposition to look at other parties' share of the blame. From my soul I say, *confitentem habes reum* [you have a confessing defendant]! On an examination of my preaching, I do not see any thing in doctrine, topics, or application, (not withstanding grievous defects in zeal and faith,) which

---

52. Alexander's observations found in his letter on October 12, 1846, were written against the backdrop of a period of severe depression which he acknowledged to Hall in a letter of the following month: "I have had for months a case of mental anguish beyond all I ever saw described, unless it be Bunyan's man in the cage, or Cowper's latter days." Hall, *Letters*, 2:59.

53. Hall, *Letters*, 2:58.

54. A letter written a few months earlier expresses his intentionality on this matter: "There are, I think, no services in which we need a prescribed schedule, more than those which come often, as for example, sacramental preparations: they are apt to be the same thing over and over. For many months I have been going over our Lord's own preparatory words and acts, in the Gospels." Hall, *Letters*, 2:45.

I condemn myself in: yet I am not "hereby justified." This day of festivity has found me very sad, at times, in the survey of every sort of temper almost or quite as bad as years ago. Few things startle me more than this *permanency* of one's inward features: the same man, the same nature, in a degree. If it were not for other, and sometimes countervailing tendencies, I might well doubt whether any new nature exists. If I have any experience it fully agrees with the exegesis which ascribes Romans vii to a believer, who "delights in the law of God after the inner man."[55]

One of his letters during his time at the Duane Street Church sought to encourage Hall upon the death of Hall's sister. Illness and premature death were common in the nineteenth century in ways not appreciated today. Following some encouraging words regarding her Christian character and convictions, Alexander reminded his friend of the lessons to be learned upon the death of a loved one:

These gathering shades on our path, as we go onward, tell us that "the night cometh." I look back to the days of Sixth street [his earlier visits to Philadelphia], and my eyes fill with unaccustomed tears. What manner of persons ought we to be, &c.? How many of our cares and anxieties are very vain, when seen in the light of coming things! Under a gracious influence, our character is no doubt formed by successive dispensations of this kind. It is a new immersion, and we come out with a grave tinge. I feel unusually serious under this sudden news; and as yet know no particulars.[56]

Alexander's wise pastoral counsel on the topic of anxiety can be found in a letter written to Hall dated March 16, 1846. Half a year had passed since the death of his sister, and Hall was now troubled with some new health issues confronting his family for which he feared the worst. Alexander's transparent counsel evidences the manner in which he entrusted his own family to God's care:

It was only at a later hour this evening, on my brother Henry's return from Princeton, that I heard of your recent anxiety. And now I do sincerely hope that all cause of serious apprehension is removed, and that you will feel at ease to write me soon that you are giving thanks for great deliverance. I say this with the more feeling, as for

---

55. Hall, *Letters*, 2:68.
56. Hall, *Letters*, 2:37.

> a few days we have been in much fear, by reason of the sudden and severe illness of our second child. He has had a fever; and, though still confined to his bed, is greatly mended. Let the God of our salvation be exalted.
>
> How much, in time of sickening fears, we are made to feel our need of a *direct* and *immediate* Divine influence; and how gracious is the hand which so often gives it to us! Our reasonings, even on the basis of the word, do not reach the case in such a time.
>
> The healings, and manifold compassionate acts of our Lord, while on earth, as given in the simple narrative of the gospels, have been an unspeakable comfort to me, in days of despondency. "When my foot slipped, thy mercy, O Lord, held me up."[57]

A letter written a few months later in early May 1846 illustrates the ongoing counsel Alexander sought to provide Hall with regard to the matters that troubled him. Alexander encouraged his friend to deepen his personal dependence on Christ through prayer. Personal experience in one's relationship with Christ, Alexander advised, is crucial.

> I lately preached on Mark ix.19; a subject which I felt a good deal myself, in reference to some former domestic experiences, and which seemed to affect my people more than usual. Direct bringing of our cares to Christ, is a duty or privilege less practiced than is thought. If we ventured more on Him, (unless the very term savours of unbelief,) we should doubtless have more to praise for. See Psalm xxxiv. 4–6. Is not our Christianity derived too much from report, from a sort of average, from common experience of those about us, and not from the simple Word?[58]

On Reading the Best Books

As the nineteenth century progressed, a number of new publishing houses were established for the printing of Christian literature. Books, periodicals, journals, magazines, and tracts were soon to play an important role in shaping the thought of American Christianity in a manner unprecedented to previous centuries. But the benefits that accompanied cheaper publishing costs quickly gave way to popular religious magazines that

---

57. Hall, *Letters*, 2:48.
58. Hall, *Letters*, 2:51.

lacked substantive theological content.[59] Prized by the reading public, they served to undermine the level of biblical literacy among the church's congregants. Although different from the secular magazines and novels for which Alexander had earlier expressed concern, the effect was similar in poisoning the spiritual appetite for literature useful in the cultivation of the life of piety.

Alexander was deeply distressed by these developments. As he observed the change in spiritual culture taking place, he saw fewer and fewer people—especially the younger generation—interested in reading works of a substantive spiritual nature.[60] "Some notions have lately struck me more than ever before; such as these: In proportion as cheap publication goes on, *books* become more and more like *conversation*; and the attributes and laws of the latter belong to the former: this admits of being carried out to wonderful particulars."[61] Nurtured on a diet of spiritual froth, Alexander realized the immediate danger to the church's future if congregants, as well as ministers, do not develop a spiritual appetite for solid works of practical theology marked by experiential application to the conscience and heart.[62]

In an attempt to address this emerging crisis, Alexander devoted several sermons to the topic in January 1846.[63] A brief reference in one of his letters highlights the balanced reading diet Alexander recommended to his congregation:

---

59. For a helpful essay on the changes, see David Paul Nord, "Systematic Benevolence: Religious Publishing and the Marketplace in Early Nineteenth-Century America," in *Communication & Change in American Religious History*, ed. Leonard I. Sweet (Grand Rapids: Eerdmans, 1993), 239–69.

60. "Cheap literature blasts religious reading. I seldom see a young professor with a spiritual book." Hall, *Letters*, 2:37.

61. Hall, *Letters*, 2:41.

62. Alexander's publications during his time at the Duane Street Church were intended to offset this problem. Titles included "'A Manual of Devotion for Soldiers and Sailors;' 'Prayers and Hymns, &c. for the Blind;' 'Frank Harper; or the Country-boy in town;' 'Thoughts on Family Worship.' Among his multifarious subjects in the Repertory was, 'Poverty and Crime in cities.' He wrote for the American Tract Society, and the Presbyterian Board of Publication, as well as for the Sunday-school Union, and for the weekly religious papers." "James Waddell Alexander," 75.

63. Alexander had earlier addressed these concerns in an article published in the *Biblical Repertory*: James W. Alexander, "The Evils of an Unsanctified Literature," *The Biblical Repertory and Princeton Review* 15, no. 1 (January 1843): 65–77.

The evils of indiscriminate reading, even of religious books, has so weighed with me, that on Sunday I devoted both sermons to "Christian Reading." Inter alia, I gave a list of books, under these heads: 1. Explanatory of the Bible; 2. Awakening and Inviting; 3. Experimental Religion; 4. Theology; 5. History; 6. Biography; 7. Poetry; 8. Miscellaneous, including Periodical.[64]

Ultimately, Alexander urged his congregation to immerse themselves in the reading of Scripture. While Christian books have their place, the Scriptures must remain preeminent in their reading priorities. "Again, the more we are flooded with bad books, the more should we read the bible—I mean the simple text; even of ministers, few do what they ought of this."[65]

In a related context, Alexander argued the benefit of psalmody in the public worship of the church. While he supported the use of uninspired hymnody, he also urged the incorporation of the psalms in the weekly worship of his congregation set to tunes that can be easily sung. He viewed the singing of inspired Scripture a corollary for spiritual growth and edification to that of his recommendations for the reading of the Bible. Correspondence from September 1847 details the approach he recommended:

> My idea of psalmodic service is, that it should be: (1) universal; (2) vocal; (3) slow, (in general;) (4) without complication of parts; (5) simple; (6) little varied; *i.e.* a few tunes well learnt; (7) with no prominence of individual voices, (duets or solos;) (8) without fugue; (9) without frequent repetition of words; (10) depending on volume of many voices, rather than brilliant execution of one or two. It is plain as A B C, that whole masses cannot sing, unless the tunes be familiar to a high degree. This ideal I never expect to see realized. The nearest approach is in the large Lutheran congregations, barring their harshness; but better the harshness, than the feeble warble of twenty percent. *in vacuo.*[66]

Reflections of a Father

A family man at heart, Alexander often commented on the affection he felt for his loved ones. His earlier counsel to Hall upon the death of his

---

64. Hall, *Letters*, 2:46.
65. Hall, *Letters*, 2:41.
66. Hall, *Letters*, 2:72–73.

sister and related family concerns no doubt weighed heavily on his mind as he reflected on the mercies he had received from the Lord in provision of his own wife and children. In a letter dated August 25, 1846, Alexander contrasts one of the great natural wonders that the Lord had created with the even greater glory of God's handiwork to be found in the faces of one's children:

> I will not inquire how you were affected by a sight of the "Falls," [Niagara]. I remember the great object, with a sort of religious awe. None of our Heavenly Father's works seems more expressive of his sublime, incomprehensible greatness. Yet, I dare say, so far as pleasure in concerned, you more value the moment in which you met with your children. There is a depth of joy in such affections, which no external objects can produce.
>
> I am writing in my solitary house; having returned to the city without my family. We were afraid to bring our infant back too suddenly from the purer air of the country. Of my season of holidays I spent ten days at Saratoga, with much advantage, and four or five at Long Branch, with none at all: for I took a cold and cough, under which I am still laboring.
>
> The place of our daily duties, with all its cares, is, after all, the place where we are usually most happy. This I feel very sensibly on my return to New York. Though almost overwhelmed with the press of matters which have been waiting for me, I am nevertheless rejoiced to be at home.
>
> Let us be instructed by the many mercies which we receive, to trust our God and Saviour more implicitly, and to yield ourselves to his service with more entire resignation of all that we have and are. To write and to say such things is easy, but we need special grace to enable us in any degree to realize such a character of mind and life. A cheerful reliance on God, and a firm hope in his promises, are great part of our duty; and these tempers should be encouraged in us, by every new instance of Divine compassion.
>
> You will understand me when I say, that home is not home without my children. I am more dependent than most men, for personal comfort, on the presence of my immediate family circle. I pray for the hour when, by God's favour, we may be gathered once more.[67]

---

67. Hall, *Letters*, 2:55–56.

Yet the comfort Alexander found in the company of his wife and children was to be broken again in the loss of a third son, John Alexander.[68] Writing to Hall the following year on April 5, 1847, Alexander spoke of the sorrow he and Elizabeth felt over the death of another of their boys.

> Your kind letter of the 2d was received on the 4th, and you will accept my thanks. Our little one was a very lovely object in our eyes; and our remembrance of him is peculiarly free from all that could give pain. He faded away exactly like a slowly-dying flower. Partly to avoid funeral mockeries, and partly to have the three little graves together, for the moral influence on my other children, I removed the remains to Princeton, to "the plot of ground" where I shall probably lie myself.[69]

The emotions Alexander felt over the death of his son come to expression in a letter from June 15, 1847. While the Alexanders had just lost a child, the Hall's had recently gained one and wished to give him the name *John* in respect of their friendship and show of support in their mourning. Moreover, Hall had invited Alexander to baptize their son at an upcoming service—an invitation that Alexander had tremendous emotion over. Alexander feared that returning to his former congregation in the midst of the grief he was now passing through would make it difficult to officiate at the service without loss of composure:

> I have been waiting for time to fill a sheet, but cannot any longer hope for it. Till my Princeton Discourse it is utterly out of my power to do any thing out of New York and Princeton, great or small. This must be my reply to your invitation, which I fully estimate, to baptize your child. There is, however, another thing: though not often moved, I am sometimes very weak, and I do not think I *could*, publicly in Trenton, pronounce the name you have given your boy without a degree of pain, which I am perfectly sure you would not allow me to incur, even for the pleasure which the solemn service, thus administered, might afford your friendly minds.[70]

The tragedies that would on occasion break the joy of the Alexander home did not diminish the bond of love by which the family was marked. Bitterness at God's providence did not impair Alexander's commitment

---

68. Born October 23, 1845, John died March 31, 1847.
69. Hall, *Letters*, 2:67.
70. Hall, *Letters*, 2:72.

to continue to love his family in the nurture and fear of the Lord. The daily worship for which the family gathered no doubt helped the Alexanders pass through such difficult seasons of life in a spirit of adoration and submission.[71] Having been raised in a home that engaged in daily worship, Alexander continued the practice in his own household throughout the years of his marriage.

The importance that Alexander attached to family worship is evident in a book first published on this topic in 1847. Drawing upon the rich heritage of catechetical training and daily family worship common to the various ecclesiastical formularies emerging at the time of the Protestant Reformation, Alexander sought to give stimulus to its continuance in his day.[72]

> Although this is but a small book, there may be some by whom it will be thought too large for its subject. Such persons must differ in their estimate of domestic religion from the writer, who has been impelled to study the institution by a profound conviction in its value. In a period when the world is every day making new inroads into the church, it has especially invaded the household. Our church cannot compare with that of the seventeenth century in this regard. Along with Sabbath observance and the catechizing of children, family worship has lost ground. There are many heads of families, communicants in our churches, and (according to a scarcely credible report) some ruling elders and deacons who maintain no stated daily service of God in their dwellings. It is to awaken such to their duty that this volume has been prepared.[73]

---

71. A rare glimpse of unedited parental emotion is found in a letter in May 1847: "I thank you for reminding me of the date of our correspondence. I feel it somewhat tenderly in connexion with the kindness you intend for us, in the naming of your boy. My tears (I seldom shed tears) flow profusely while I think that in a sort he takes the place of our sweet translated child. Forgive this burst (unusual in our long correspondence, and proving, perhaps, that I grow weaker as I grow older,) and accept my prayers for the little one's eternal good." Hall, *Letters*, 2:69.

72. For a valuable historical overview of catechetical practice, see James W. Alexander, "The History of Catechizing," *The Biblical Repertory and Princeton Review* 21, no. 1 (January 1849): 59–81. Alexander's article can also be found in Garretson, *Princeton and the Work of the Christian Ministry*, 2:75–98.

73. James W. Alexander, *Thoughts on Family-Worship* (Philadelphia: Presbyterian Board of Publication, 1847; repr., Morgan, Pa.: Soli Deo Gloria Publications, 1998), 1–2.

The goal of Alexander's book is summarized in his chapter "The Influence of Family Worship on Children."[74] The directives that he provided are as much a summary of its historical practice as an indication of the ways in which he led his own home in family worship.[75]

> The simple fact, that parents and offspring meet together every morning and evening for the word of God and prayer, is a great fact in household annals. It is the inscribing of God's name over the lintel of the door. It is the setting up of God's altar. The dwelling is marked as a house of prayer. Religion is thus made a substantive and prominent part of the domestic plan. The day is opened and closed in the name of the Lord. From the very dawn of reason, each little one grows up with a feeling that God must be honoured in everything; that no business of life can proceed without Him; and that the day's work, or study, would be unsheltered, disorderly, and in a manner profane but for this consideration.[76]

Of all the books that Alexander published, his volume on family worship is one of his most important. Alexander recognized the crucial role that family worship serves in the cultivation of a life of piety and the strengthening of a nation's moral fiber.[77] His work remains one of the finest treatments of its subject ever published.[78]

---

74. A title page devotes the book to his parents in gratitude for the profound influence family worship had upon his life: "TO MY FATHER AND MY MOTHER; BY WHOSE HANDS I WAS FIRST LED TO FAMILY-WORSHIP, AND FOR WHOSE CONTINUANCE IN LIFE AND HEALTH AT A PERIOD IN WHICH MOST SONS ARE BEREFT OF THIS BLESSING I AM BOUND TO GIVE THANKS, THIS VOLUME, WITH HUMBLE PRAYERS FOR EVERY DIVINE FAVOUR TO REST ON THEM AND THEIRS, IS, IN LOVE AND DUTY, RESPECTFULLY INSCRIBED." Alexander, *Thoughts on Family-Worship*, viii (no pagination).

75. Alexander had earlier promoted the Bible reading plan of Robert Murray M'Cheyne: "I am about to get Carter to print McCheyne's scheme for reading through the Old Testament once, and the New Testament twice in the year. It includes family worship as well as private reading, and the table will do to hang up, or paste in a book; though as he issued it, it is a pamphlet, with remarks." Hall, *Letters*, 2:26.

76. Alexander, *Thoughts on Family-Worship*, 58–59.

77. For a comprehensive study on the role of family worship during the middle and latter half of the nineteenth century, see Colleen McDannell, *The Christian Home in Victorian America, 1840–1900* (Bloomington: Indiana University Press, 1986).

78. For a helpful review of Alexander's volume, see John William Yeomans, "Thoughts on Family Worship," *The Biblical Repertory and Princeton Review* 20, no. 1 (January 1848): 57–74.

On Slavery

The subject of slavery continued to be a topic of interest in Alexander's correspondence during his time at the Duane Street Church. A letter written at the end of January 1845 highlights the hope he had for its gradual dissolution on American soil.[79] While Alexander's letters do not address in detail the role of the church in the eradication of slavery, it should not be assumed that Alexander held to the doctrine of the "spirituality of the church" later advocated by Presbyterian congregations in the South at the time of the American Civil War. Instead, his remarks often anticipate its dissolution through legislative actions enacted by the state or federal government.

It is also important to recognize Alexander's advocacy for the humane and intelligent treatment of the slave population and freed slaves living in Northern states. His compassion and concern for Northern and Southern African Americans is evident throughout the entire corpus of his correspondence with Hall. His interest in African Americans, whether in the North or the South, bespeaks a genuine love and care for their spiritual and physical needs. Accordingly, his graphic observations on the "free blacks" who lived in Northern cities should be viewed as descriptive and not racist in nature.[80] Hygiene and matters of sanitation were problems endemic to modern urban life with which freed slaves and immigrants alike were plagued. The squalor of mid-nineteenth century city life is well documented and led to the extensive social activism for which the Christian churches took a leading role. Alexander's comments expose the inequity former slaves experienced as "free" men in a country that still refused to recognize their full humanity and treat them with a dignity appropriate to their membership in society. He did not excuse himself from the circumstances that fostered the social conditions that

---

79. Sweeney summarizes the magnitude of the problem: "Roughly eleven million Africans were coerced into bondage during the transatlantic slave trade. Half a million slaves were imported into the United States, but because American slave owners also owned their slaves' children, four million slaves were toiling here by 1860. In addition, half a million free blacks were eking out a meager living. Most of the slaves were grown men, but many, of course were women and children. In fact, by the nineteenth century, 46 percent of them were children." Douglas A. Sweeney, *The American Evangelical Story: A History of the Movement* (Grand Rapids: Baker, 2005), 108.

80. While mildly sarcastic, Alexander's remarks are not condescending. Rather, his remarks caricature the prejudice by which the African Americans were treated and often belittled. The mistreatment of the African Americans weighed heavily on Alexander's conscience and proved influential in shaping his ministry emphases.

confronted African Americans in antebellum culture, but, like many in his generation, Alexander found it difficult to determine the best remedy to alleviate the mistreatment of the African Americans from choices that were all less than ideal.[81] He writes:

> You see that Texas is all but annexed and the "area of *freedom*" widened: N. B. *area* is the Latin for "threshing-floor." I am heretic enough to believe, in very earnest, that this very enormity will be overruled to the good of the negro. It will drain Maryland, Virginia, Kentucky, and Tennessee of their slaves. It will push the slave-mass towards the tropics. There they may physically thrive; there they are always happiest. There they will outgrow their white holders. There they will be in the region which is exempt from the real hinderance to their freedom, the prejudice of colour and caste. In Mexico, Central America, and Colombia, black is almost as good as white. Half the Mexican officers of the two steamers whom I saw, were one-half or two-thirds Africans. Amalgamation, say what they please, can go on, does go on, and will go on. The longer we put off the national break the greater will be the Free America. All this, I think, leaves the emancipation question just where it was. But leave this out of view, and what becomes of our negroes, slave or free? Those called by mockery free people, are a race of Helots or Yahoos, in our estimation. We do not give them our dinners, or our daughters; we debar them from pulpits, pews, and omnibuses; we deny them actual citizenship. We smell their rancid odours, and hustle them off our streets more vehemently now that they are free, than when they were slaves. Educate them, and this prejudice makes them miserable.[82]

While Alexander did not believe that the Bible condemned the institution of slavery, he felt various elements of its practice in American society immoral and injurious to the slave population. A letter dated May 28, 1846, explains Alexander's rationale for why he thought the institution fraught with problems, but also why he was convinced that immediate emancipation would not be in the best interests of the slaves or the country. He was especially troubled with recent laws in the South that prevented the slaves from learning how to read and the effect this would have on their ability to learn the Scriptures. His observations betray the duplicity of a culture

---

81. For related observations on the frustrations Alexander felt in addressing issues related to the eradication of slavery, see Hall, *Letters*, 2:19.
82. Hall, *Letters*, 2:18.

that prided itself on Christian values while blind to its own hypocrisy in the damage caused to human life by "man-stealing" and the moral deterioration it cultivated in a country that embraced its practice.[83]

> I see no proof that Onesimus ever ran away, in the technical sense, at all. I can go a peg higher than you about slavery, and fail to see the scripturalness of much that is postulated now-a-days, respecting the popular idol, liberty. As existing slavery is fraught with moral evil; the want of marriage, and of the Bible, and the separation of families, &c., &c., are crying sins; but I am totally unable to see the relation to be necessarily unjust. The moral questions are so various from the circumstances, that each must be decided apart, *e.g.*, "Is A justifiable in holding B to service?" Our church, I am clear, ought to protest against the laws about reading, &c. As clear am I, that our States should regard slavery as transition-state, to be terminated as soon as possible, and that they should enact laws about the *post-nati*. That the most miserable portion, physically and morally, of the black race in the United States, is the portion which is free, I am as well assured as I can be of any similar proposition. That immediate emancipation would be a crime, I have no doubt; and therefore believe there are cases in which there is neither injustice nor inhumanity in holding.[84]

Recognizing the manner in which slavery had deliberately incapacitated the African American slave population to take upon themselves the liberties and responsibilities that freedom would provide, Alexander uses provocative language when he asserts "that immediate emancipation would be a crime." Speaking as a contemporary and knowledgeable of the seemingly insurmountable cultural, relational, and employment obstacles that would be foisted upon a people unprepared to enter, or likely be received as, a free population with equal rights as whites without suitable preparations having been made by federal and state

---

83. "The evangelical movement has suffered from the sins of racial prejudice ever since it first emerged from the eighteenth-century Great Awakening. While evangelicals did not invent the sins of racism or ethnocentrism, the slave trade, segregation, discrimination, or racial hate groups, literally millions of white evangelicals have either participated in or sanctioned one or more of these things, distorting their common witness to the gospel." Sweeney, *American Evangelical Story*, 108. Sweeney's chapter in the same volume titled "Crossing the Color Line without Working to Erase It" is an excellent introduction to the way in which American churches have addressed the issues of slavery and race relations from the early colonial period into the twentieth century. The chapter also includes a valuable bibliography of related works for further study.

84. Hall, *Letters*, 2:52.

governments, local communities, and churches, Alexander feared more harm than good would come to the African American population than the present circumstances in which they found themselves if they were freed prematurely. For Alexander and others of his time who longed for the dissolution of slavery, it was a matter of choosing between the lesser of two evils in seeking both the short- and long-term best interests of a people whom he knew were being treated immorally, but would likely find themselves worse off if released without a collective commitment on the part of American society for their full integration and incorporation into American culture and citizenry.

Alexander revisited the topic of slavery in a letter written the following year on February 22, 1847. While readers today may find the comparison invalid, Alexander thought the condition of slaves better than that of some of the free immigrants who had arrived on American soil. His time in Virginia and related experience in states such as New Jersey and New York convinced him that the "freedom" former slaves now enjoyed in the urban areas in which he labored was in fact a new kind of bondage for which their former life had not prepared them to live wisely and responsibly. While he looked forward to the day when the institution of slavery would no longer be part of American society, he felt the best assistance he could provide to the slaves during this interim period was instruction in the Bible.[85] Although Alexander may be criticized for his tolerance of the institution, he had the foresight to recognize the character formation that embrace of the gospel message brings as a preparative to the lifestyle commitments that must be made among a free citizenry for their lives and communities to flourish. He recognized the slaves' receptivity to the gospel message as a kind providence uniquely positioning them for a future as free citizens whose character and convictions would ideally be rooted in the teaching of the Word of God. It

---

85. For an important review of efforts made to instruct the Southern slave population by former Princeton Theological Seminary student Charles Colcock Jones, see "Suggestions on the Religious Instruction of the Negroes in the Southern States, together with an appendix, containing forms of Church Registers, form of a constitution and plans of different denominations," *The Biblical Repertory and Princeton Review* 20, no. 1 (January 1848): 1–30. Both Jones and Alexander believed education critical for exercise of the free citizenship which they anticipated would one day be available for the slaves.

was to this end that he devoted his ministerial labors on their behalf throughout the years of his public ministry.[86]

> I can't help thinking how much better off the Southern slaves are, physically and morally, than the Irish. Who ever heard of slaves starving until the master starved? I see no trace of the modern dogmas about absolute freedom in the Bible. The wretchedest portion, by far, of the black race, is the free portion. Our New York negroes are lower than savages in many respects. I believe slavery will be abolished; and will be abolished in Mexican lands, and parts adjacent, where the climate suits, and where the taint of colour is less felt; and that all attempts to wall slavery within its present bounds, only hurts the negro and procrastinates the grand result. I am more and more convinced that our endeavours to do at a blow, what Providence does by degrees, is disastrous to those whom we would benefit. To give the gospel to the slaves, is a duty pressing above all others; and my painful and mortifying endeavours for two years to build up a black church here, and my previous preaching for six years to free people in Jersey, convince me that it is easier to give the gospel to the slaves.[87]

Missions

The topic of Christian missions also remained close to Alexander's heart. He had been taught its importance as a child and was committed to its support as a pastor.[88] Among the stimuli on international missions at this time in Alexander's thinking was the war in which the United States had recently engaged with the neighboring country of Mexico. While Alexander viewed it as a form of illegitimate national expansion at great cost to human life, he also recognized the missionary outreach that could take place in its aftermath if the church would awaken to the opportunity now afforded.

As he reflected on the deaths of soldiers in the recent war with Mexico, a letter from early March 1848 ruminated on the benefits that might come

---

86. For a valuable summary of Alexander's views on American slavery, see Gary Steward, "Old Princeton and American Culture: Insights from J. W. Alexander," *The Confessional Presbyterian* 8 (2012): 59–63.

87. Hall, *Letters*, 2:65.

88. A passing reference from a letter on April 5, 1847, provides a glimpse of his missionary mindedness: "I have this morning been furnishing New Testaments (they cannot carry large-print Bibles) to a company of the 10th regiment. I have been stimulated by the war to prepare a manual of devotions for sailors and soldiers, which is now complete." Hall, *Letters*, 2:67.

to the people of that land if the church would be as zealous to evangelize its population as the government had been to engage in war to achieve its goals.[89] His theme verse for the year was from Hebrews 13:8—"Jesus Christ the same yesterday, and to day, and for ever." It likely gave impetus to the confidence Alexander expressed for the way in which the preaching of Christ could transform Mexican culture as it had European civilization in a previous generation:

> O how desirous one feels that the Gospel might pour in through these channels! What a glorious thing if the ambition of war could only be emulated by any analogous zeal for the introduction of the Gospel! I do not perceive why these poor, simple, brave, perfidious, paganized people might not be plied by thousands of books and tracts. They are not more hopeless than were the boors of Bohemia and Germany, when the tracts of Wiclif and the Lollards came among them, or than the Swiss mountaineers when the writings of Zuingle and Calvin roused them. Further, I soberly think some daring young ministers (if any such are left in these days of literary clerical *petit-maitres* [literally: "a small master," meaning a dandy or a person only concerned about appearances]) ought to dash into Vera Cruz, Perote, Puebla, and Mexico, and blow at least a long loud blast of defiance, where Satan's seat is. In 1555, men were found to go to torrid Brazil, from Geneva; and several died martyrs there. I have expressed this opinion in my official capacity; but my brethren think me flighty. Would God my boys might preach Christ in that, or any other foreign land; so only they be faithful! Amen.[90]

Interest in international missions was accompanied by an equal passion for domestic missionary outreach to the urban communities along America's eastern seaboard. In the midst of the burgeoning population among whom he ministered, Alexander was increasingly convinced of the need to be actively engaged in missionary outreach to the many different nationalities who called New York City home.[91] The practice of paying for pews to provide revenue for the church's budget prohibited

---

89. In a separate context Alexander observed: "God reigns, even in wars, and truth has made its way very often through the breaches opened by conquest." Hall, *Letters*, 2:175.
90. Hall, *Letters*, 2:80–81.
91. Alexander devoted time to a number of missionary organizations while a pastor in New York City: "One of the most agreeable hours I spend in the week, contrary to all my expectations, is on Monday morning at the Foreign Missionary Executive Board." Hall, *Letters*, 2:41.

access to services that people may wish to attend. Formal attire and the stilted atmosphere that can accompany worldly wealth when it makes inroads into a church's values also served to misdirect the missionary nature of the church's calling.[92] Alexander was convinced that his congregation had fallen victim to these deceptive influences and become blinded to the real purposes for which they were called to exist as a church. He writes:

> One of the great Christian problems of the age seems to me to be how to carry the gospel to the thousands, in cities, who will not enter any church. Pews are high. Or they are not dressed well enough. An effort is making to establish minor religious meetings, for such purposes, here and there, all over the city. It is a fine scheme, though not a new one, being that of the old Evangelical Society of our boyhood. But its simplicity and homeliness gives it a Bible-look. When shall we come down from our stilts, and be in earnest with a perishing world? Decorum and conservatism do not rank as the most needed virtues just now.[93]

As Alexander came to realize, wealthy churches can be indifferent to the needs of the very community in which they reside. They then often have no bigger vision than celebrating their own existence. The accumulated comforts that wealth affords may leave little interest in sacrifice for the sake of others. In comparison to other cities in which Presbyterian churches were established, interest in the planting of new works to reach the rapidly growing population of New York City left much to be desired. "Church extension goes on coldly," Alexander noted. "We are not quite as far behindhand, as to new churches, as Philadelphia, but we add them by threes and fours, when we should by twenties and thirties." Gone

---

92. "In every direction he saw opportunities of doing the work of Christ for the bodies, minds, and souls of a vast neglected population. Above the lowest strata of these, he saw enough in the condition of strangers, emigrants, young men, children, the respectable poor and aged, the sick and disabled, that called for more personal benevolence than the existing institutions could, or ought to be required to supply, independent of more strictly Christian effort. On the other hand, he believed that the church-system restricted itself too much to church-limits, leaned to conservatism rather than to aggression; that the humbler classes were almost excluded from worship, and consequent access of the best of friends, by the worldly show of the houses of worship and the cost of sittings; and that there was a growing spirit of worldliness and 'moderation' in the church itself, which suppressed the evangelical zeal and earnestness that constitute the life of practical religion." "James Waddell Alexander," 74.

93. Hall, *Letters*, 2:38.

were the days when mission-minded Presbyterian pastors braved the dangers and challenges of the colonial frontier: "Vacant ministers swarm in our cities, beseeching one for places, instead of rushing into the wild West and South, as was done by the Mckennies, Henrys, Blairs, Todds, Grahams, and Davieses, who founded our church."[94]

> There is a congestion of candidates about our cities, while at the extremities and frontiers, all is chill and suffering. Unless we all get awakened, in some extraordinary degree, I don't see how we are to fail sinking into Moderatism. Some people absurdly ascribe the diminished zeal of ministers to Seminaries. This is much as if I should ascribe our poor beef to the change of market-house. Those who never saw a college or seminary are as low as we. It lies deeper, and affects the whole church, I verily believe. It means just this, want of zeal for the salvation of souls.[95]

Compassion for the spiritually lost and zeal in evangelistic outreach are essential for a church to maintain its spiritual vitality. Its absence inevitably leads to a moribund and spiritually constricted church life.

As Alexander recognized, spiritual deterioration in a denomination's or congregation's evangelistic interest may be traced to any number of causes (failure of seminaries and pulpits to explain its centrality to the Christian mission, personal indifference, obstacles to its advance in society, etc.); but the remedy is the same: namely, a renewed commitment to the evangelistic charge that Christ has given to His church to carry out on behalf of all the nations. Without such personal commitment, the church will fail in its calling.[96] Programs and services are no substitute for the personal offering up of oneself in the service of Christ in one's daily vocation.[97] "All our missionary gifts will fall short," Alexander

---

94. Hall, *Letters*, 2:37–38.
95. Hall, *Letters*, 2:77.
96. Alexander was invited to deliver the General Assembly's sermon on Missions during its annual gathering in 1847.
97. "He took special pleasure in his class on the catechism, in conversing with and in other ways benefitting young men, in the weekday services, in promoting through the agency of his congregation and otherwise, city missions, Sunday-schools, churches for the poor and for the coloured people, and in the duties of his position on the Executive Committee of Foreign Missions, Tract Society, and several organizations for evangelical efforts in the city alone. His visits and gifts to the poor and neglected, and the influence he exerted to procure help for them in every way, constituted an important department of his efficiency, not only as a pastor, but as a minister at large." "James Waddell Alexander," 75.

said, "unless people come to give their own selves first unto the Lord; in some such sense."[98]

The Duane Street congregation also found itself in the swirl of rapid population growth and changing demographics that were emerging. As the city's population enlarged, a number of Alexander's congregation migrated "uptown" to neighborhoods more family friendly than the industrialized development encroaching on residential living that the south side of the city was experiencing.

While Alexander was optimistic about the prospects for growth with the Duane Street Church when he first arrived in 1844, letter entries throughout his time there indicate a growing despair with the direction that the church was taking.[99] A letter dated May 11, 1848, expresses the gloom Alexander felt for what the future held:

> At no time have things looked duller in my charge. Additions very few, and a general fluctuation, which makes me doubt whether our church, like so many others, will not be swept away before the surge of commerce. About twelve families leave us. Of nine persons dismissed by us since last communion, all but one were dismissed to us within five years. If my powers were of the arousing sort, I might hope for more in a mission-church, but all the little I can attempt is in the way of gradual training; and this requires people to stay with you. Our Sunday services are as full as ever, but our other indications are all bad.[100]

In a letter written three weeks later, Alexander acknowledged that his gifts were not the best match for his congregation's present needs as the nature of the community in which the church resided had changed. Still, he was not interested in moving the location of his ministry for the material sustenance from which he might benefit if the church relocated "uptown." His pastoral commitment was as a servant of Christ on behalf of the congregation's spiritual good. The status that could result from a change of location, or even congregation, was of no appeal to Alexander. What he desired most was his congregation's spiritual vitality:

---

98. Hall, *Letters*, 2:31.
99. "Long before leaving New York, Dr. Alexander had foreseen that the tide of business would soon place the Duane-street church beyond convenient reach of the congregation." "James Waddell Alexander," 76.
100. Hall, *Letters*, 2:82.

I see, beyond denial, that my congregation is suffering from its site. Though we have tens of thousands downtown, they are mission folks, and increasingly foreigners, if not papists. The talent they require is not mine. I say truly, when I add, that I have not even a momentary hankering for uptown: my leading members feel otherwise; so should I, were I they. We have sent away about fifteen families this spring, thither and out of town.[101]

1849

Alexander's letters at the beginning of 1849 are filled with newsy commentary on national figures and local events.[102] A cholera outbreak which occurred the previous December seems to have passed without the large number of infections doctors feared.

"Hope Thou in God"
Interest in German hymnology marks correspondence from early February. "The German method of singing is the true one," Alexander said, "in these respects: 1. The harmony is confined to the organ. 2. The choir, which is small, sings the *air*. 3. They introduce no new tunes. 4. The *chorals*, which they sing, (Old Hundred being one,) are slow and familiar. 5. Consequently the people all sing; and all sing the *air*, except as individual fancy may vary to suit the voice."[103]

Correspondence from the following month speaks of the frustration Alexander felt with the sale of the property he was renting. "This perpetual moving is a plague to a family situated as mine is," he said. "The house I occupy has just been sold over my head, and the new landlord raises the rent from $700 to $800."[104]

Alexander's congregation was on the move as well.[105] Matters related to their permanent location remained unsettled, and this was becoming a source of increasing frustration to a number of his congregants:

---

101. Hall, *Letters*, 2:83.
102. Comparing the piety of Presidents Madison and Washington, Alexander remarked: "It just occurs to me, that in his earlier life Madison used to have family-worship. Afterwards his religion assumed a Washingtonian invisibility." Hall, *Letters*, 2:91.
103. Hall, *Letters*, 2:92.
104. Hall, *Letters*, 2:93. Alexander could not afford the increase in rent and by May had relocated to a new rental at 10 Beach Street.
105. The church expected to lose at least twenty families from relocation by early May.

My congregation is going down, by going up (town). We dismiss two for one we receive. Though the house continues full, it is of transient people; no pews are sold, though all are hired for short terms. About nine-tenths of the property-holders want to sell and go up town; they would do so in a moment if I should say the word; and with every probability of a new and full church there: but that word I dare not say, nor have ever given any countenance to the proposal. Two of my elders move uptown in May. If you want a colleague you had better strike while the iron is hot, and call me now.[106]

A letter from this time comments on Alexander's new reading interests. He found special delight in the reading of authors whose style was the opposite of his own:

> My taste increases for books which flow straight on, as from an inner source; little erudition, no quotation, no heads or divisions, growing, swelling, &c.: not the less because I am individually of the opposite sort, and tend to mince things up, and put them into patty-pans, with numbers. I got a shove for weeks from reading "Foster's Estimate of R. Hall, as a Preacher." Don't fail to read it, especially what he says about Hall's faults. John Howe is the only Puritan writer of the sort I mean. Addison, in one or two of his best sermons, exemplifies my meaning.[107]

The same letter also mentions Alexander's feeling of loneliness in the ministry setting in which he served. Repeated efforts to gather fellow Presbyterian clergy together for prayer had failed for lack of interest. Alexander believed in the importance of prayer and was frustrated by his colleagues' apparent indifference to meet for such purposes. "I wonder if every other Presbyterian minister in New York feels (in secret) the same want of brotherly support and communion that I do. Four distinct times I have essayed a weekly ministerial meeting, chiefly for prayer. All other sects but ours, I believe, maintain such a service here."[108]

Call to Serve at the Seminary
Advanced in years and incapable of continuing his classroom responsibilities, Samuel Miller's active tenure at Princeton Theological Seminary

---

106. Hall, *Letters*, 2:93–94.
107. Hall, *Letters*, 2:95.
108. Hall, *Letters*, 2:95.

concluded in May of 1849.[109] Miller had served with distinction for thirty-six years as the seminary's first Professor of Ecclesiastical History and Church Government. As the board of directors and denomination prayed for guidance in selection of his successor, their thoughts turned to the native talents and spiritual orientation of Alexander as the man most suited to fill Miller's vacated chair.

Having acted on Miller's resignation, the General Assembly proceeded to vote on Alexander's nomination to the seminary faculty. "On the 26th of May, a telegraphic dispatch informed Dr. James Alexander that he was that day elected by the General Assembly at Pittsburg to succeed Dr. Miller."[110] Alexander's reflections on the appointment can be found in a letter penned to Hall on May 31, 1849:

> Just at this time, as you may suppose, I am in much heaviness. Only a day or two had I any warning of what was impending, as it did not spring from my Princeton friends. At this moment I am absolutely void of all information except the telegraphic vote. The thing gives me unspeakable pain. To you I will say, believing you can understand it, that any little unction of flattery in the appointment is instantly more than absorbed by the greatness of the question, and the anguish of a separation from my charge, if I accept. They (with no syllable from me) seem to give up at once, and think I have no option. *This* I do not think: but, at the same time, the judgment of our highest court is very grave, in a case where all previous plans seemed to fail. There is no need of saying so to the public, but to *know* that I might remain here would be a joy unspeakable. No dreams of mine respecting the social happiness of the pastoral relation have failed to be realized: in this I compare it to marriage. I have tried academic and Princeton life, and was less happy. Every thing makes me feel solemn, and I am (not metaphorically, but literally) sick. All my ministerial friends, to a man, say *Go*. Seldom have I more deeply felt my utter insignificance—the blindness of fellow-creatures, who

---

109. "In the General Assembly, at Pittsburg, May 21, 1849, the Report of the Directors of the Princeton Seminary was received, in which it was announced that the venerable Professor Miller, on account of bodily infirmities, wished to resign his office. The Assembly resolved to continue Dr. Miller's connexion with the institution, under the title of Emeritus Professor, with its salary and all other rights during his life, and to elect a new professor for the active duties of instruction. On the 26th May, the Assembly proceeded to the election, and Dr. Alexander received a majority of the votes. The professorship was that of Ecclesiastical History and Church Government." Hall, *Letters*, 2:97.

110. Alexander, *Life of Joseph Addison Alexander*, 2:665.

from some view of outside think me of any value in such a matter—and the unimportance of the question, in all but a religious and eternal view. Life is very short: *Dirigat Deus* [May God direct]![111]

The Alexanders had barely moved into their new rental home when they received word of the Assembly's action. While Alexander was not prepared to make the move from New York City back to Princeton so soon, he recognized the timeliness of the offer. After a period of prayer and consideration, he accepted the call of his denomination to serve at the seminary.

His farewell sermon to his congregation was preached on June 10, 1849. Alexander chose as his text 1 Corinthians 3:21–23: "Therefore let no man glory in men. For all things are yours; Whether Paul, or Apollos, or Cephas, or the world, or life, or death, or things present, or things to come; all are yours; And ye are Christ's; and Christ is God's." While the parting was painful, both pastor and people accepted the will of God in Alexander's removal to Princeton.[112] Little did either party realize how much their lives would remain intertwined in the years following Alexander's resignation from his ministry at Duane Street Church.

---

111. Hall, *Letters*, 2:97.
112. "And on Sunday, June the 10th, at the close of the service in the morning, he announced to his congregation that he must leave them. There was much weeping. Pastor and people were both greatly overcome. Soon after he removed to Princeton." Alexander, *Life of Joseph Addison Alexander*, 2:665.

I am giving you a very grave letter. Sometimes one reads that men may be known by their letters, and biographies go upon this postulate. Certainly it fails sometimes as to habitual moods. E.g. In my private hours, nine out of ten, I am grave even to a fault. In my letters I am apt to seek recreation; they are a sort of conversation. I never saw it alluded to, except by Boz, (frequently by him,) but the funniest things that ever come to my tongue's end, are in seasons of deep affliction, so that repression is needed, to save appearances.

—JAMES W. ALEXANDER
November 14, 1849

Chapter 10

SEMINARY PROFESSOR: 1849–1851

In June of 1849, Alexander and his family relocated to Princeton, New Jersey, to begin his new position at the seminary.[1] The town was familiar and home to many fond memories from his youth and early manhood. While the change in position was sudden and somewhat unexpected, Alexander's letters express relief in how God's providence had "ordered all things well." Sensitive to the call that he had been given from his denomination to assume Miller's chair, Alexander was encouraged by the support he had received from family, friends, and fellow clergy.

A letter written a few days after his resignation from the Duane Street Church describes the peace that he now felt in having made the decision to resign his congregational charge. "My anxious suspense is so far relieved that I have determined to remove hither. The voice of the Assembly seemed to leave me little option, except in points of which they could not be cognizant. The voice of my clerical brethren, in and out of New York, so far as known to me, has been in favour of my translation." Earlier concerns about the opposition he might incur from clergy in Philadelphia proved unfounded: "Jones informs me that this is the unanimous wish in Philadelphia; and a number of my own people have reluctantly owned that they think it my duty to go. I have been somewhat moved by this singular concurrence; but more by the unexpected Providence which has secured such a result, by the frustration of all preceding plans."[2]

Although the voice of the General Assembly had spoken and countless friends concurred in the call, Alexander still had reservations about his personal qualifications for the position. "As to competency I cannot judge

---

1. "Again our relation is changed, and you are once more the city, and I the country mouse." Hall, *Letters*, 2:99.
2. Hall, *Letters*, 2:99.

of that," he said. But as to the strategic significance of the chair to which he had been called, he had no doubt: "As to the comparative importance of the two posts, I have never had any question, that (to one competent) the teaching-place was equal in importance to any ten of the other."[3]

Alexander thought the move a timely one—neither he nor his congregation could have continued going forward together upon their present course. For the church to survive, it needed to move to a more receptive neighborhood before the loss of further members would force it to close. At the time, Alexander did not wish to move with the congregation to a wealthier neighborhood. "I have seen clearly that the Duane Street Church could live only by moving up-town, and thither I wished not to move." But the six years of ministry with the Duane Street congregation had also broken Alexander's health and raised questions in his own mind as to whether he was fitted for the kind of neighborhood ministry the church now required.[4] In the end, Alexander concluded that the life of a scholar-educator would be in the best interests of his personal health: "I have seen as clearly that my powers were tasked to a tension which must soon be fatal; while, in the steadier routine of teaching, I might last a season, with ordinary favour of Providence."[5]

By early September, Alexander had recovered his health. Although he had "passed through a thicket of thoughts and cares," he felt "blessed with unusual health."[6] Alexander's son Henry summarizes Alexander's first week as a professor:

> Dr. James Alexander delivered his introductory lecture at the Seminary on the 4th of September. It was to the second or middle class. He also attended his first preaching exercise, which was with the seniors; and chatted with them about the Chironomian society of former days, and its champions, "Kirk, Bethune, Vermilye, Collins, Benedict, Lansing, Christmas, Waterbury, and Alexander." He strongly urged the young men not to use notes.[7]

---

3. Hall, *Letters*, 2:99.
4. "In any other light the election by the General Assembly, which summoned him to the Theological Seminary at Princeton, would have met with serious objection, but under the circumstances there could be no resistance." "James Waddell Alexander," 75–76.
5. Hall, *Letters*, 2:99.
6. Hall, *Letters*, 2:103.
7. Alexander, *Life of Joseph Addison Alexander*, 2:66.

Alexander shared in the pulpit ministry of the seminary chapel and preached his first sermon as a professor to the students and faculty on September 16. "After it was over his father told him that he spoke too loud."[8]

Alexander found his position quite demanding.[9] While the field of church history was familiar, Alexander lacked the specialization of Miller's expertise. The resettlement of his family into new quarters also required attention. "My new business involves more pressing study than I had thought," Alexander wrote to Hall, "and in a new habitation there are daily wants emergent which take time and money. Then the pleasing-painful care of other people's cares has been daily."[10]

While Alexander was busy with the demands of his professorship, the ongoing needs of the Duane Street Church remained a source of prayerful concern and found mention in his letters to Hall:

> My poor congregation in New York is in a bad way. The two or three old-hunkers, who can't see that the earth has gone round any since Dr. Romeyn's day, would never believe (what is undeniable) that the Church cannot be maintained where it is, except as a free church. This I perceived two years ago, and discovered six months ago that five-sixths of the people were ready to move. But the plan was quashed by the conservatives, and I fear they will be left alone, unless they in stanter remove. The house is almost embedded in sugar-refineries and other stews. Its real supporters live far above it. Drs. Spring and McElroy will soon go up, and the sense of being a preacher to a fluent crowd was what chiefly discouraged me, and hindered my labours. I say these things to them freely now, because they cannot charge me with any worldly lust of a better *locale*, which they constructively did while I was with them. I have said to Mr. Auchincloss that two years hence there cannot by possibility be a Presbyterian church at that corner. They must choose between scattering (already repeated till the identity is gone) and removal. The

---

8. Alexander, *Life of Joseph Addison Alexander*, 2:66.
9. Although occupied with his professorial obligations, Alexander continued to write and publish during his time at the seminary: "The preparation of lectures occupied many of the hours he had been accustomed to give to miscellaneous writing, but he contributed to every new number of the *Repertory*, and supplied an article for each of the twelve numbers of the 'Princeton Magazine' published in 1850. In that year he gave one of the lectures, in the University of Virginia, of a course on the 'Evidences of Christianity,' which has been published in a volume with the rest of the series." "James Waddell Alexander," 76.
10. Hall, *Letters*, 2:103.

greater the man they get, the sooner will he translate the Church. Lower New York is in no proper sense other than as a *warehouse*, compared with a *dwelling*.[11]

As Alexander settled into his new responsibilities, he found delight in ministering to his students.[12] He equated the satisfaction he experienced in working with his students to the pastoral involvement he had enjoyed with his former congregation. Both were close to his heart and likened to the "fireside" pleasures of family life enjoyed in the early nineteenth century. "In the sore loss of my parochial comforts, which were always delightful to me, in the net result, and which are to a sincere man a sort of expansion of his fireside pleasures, I try to comfort myself by looking with new eyes on my pupils," he mused. "We matriculated fifty-three, and 'still they come.'"[13]

Although Alexander was already widely read when he assumed his position on the faculty, he worked hard to familiarize himself with the field of church history.[14] He read historical summaries as well as a number of the primary sources in preparation for his classes.[15] He found contemporary German historical scholarship valuable and commended it to Hall in one of his letters. "I should like to give you Milman's History of Christianity, volume by volume, for though it is written with an

---

11. Hall, *Letters*, 2:103–4.
12. Words that Alexander once wrote about his father likely influenced the pastoral approach he took toward his students: "I know not a busier man in the world than my old father. And half of every day is spent in talking with students privately. True, he does not chase them from room to room, or run through the roll, but he never chains up his gate, or pleads any business to exclude any one, at any hour." Hall, *Letters*, 2:228.
13. Hall, *Letters*, 2:104.
14. For earlier reviews demonstrating Alexander's proficiency in European and American church history, see James W. Alexander, "History of the Planting and Training of the Christian Church by the Apostles," *The Biblical Repertory and Princeton Review* 16, no. 2 (April 1844): 155–83; James W. Alexander, "Religion in America; or an account of the Origin, Progress, Relation to the State, and Present Condition of the Evangelical Churches in the United States. With notices of the Unevangelical Denominations," *The Biblical Repertory and Princeton Review* 17, no. 1 (January 1845): 17–43. Baird's work was enlarged and reviewed again in 1856: James W. Alexander, "Religion in America; or an account of the Origin, Progress, Relation to the State, and Present Condition of the Evangelical Churches in the United States. With notices of the Unevangelical Denominations," *The Biblical Repertory and Princeton Review* 28, no. 4 (October 1856): 642–54.
15. "The new professor's reading lay much in the Augustinian field, and especially the part pertaining to the controversy with Pelagius." Alexander, *Life of Joseph Addison Alexander*, 2:670.

almost infidel coolness, it is the only English work that gives the distilled essence of the Germanic researches into out-of-the-way antiquities of early mother church." A conscientious scholar, Alexander was committed to the study necessary to master his field of instruction. "If I live, I must be some years familiarizing myself with the original documents of the former ages," he told Hall.[16]

In his conversations with Hall, Alexander sometimes lampooned contemporary church practice.[17] His familiarity with divisions in the history of the church no doubt provided a backdrop to his observations on current matters of conflict. In a letter on September 19, 1849, Alexander bemoaned the failure of his denomination to deal with the disorderly and divisive conduct found within its membership which precipitated congregational splits and the subsequent ridicule which the church incurred for its behavior:

> Great evils arise in the United States from the ease with which new congregations, churches, and even sects are formed. Ex. gr.: suppose a minority in Smithville choose to do wrong. Presbytery animadverts. Minority turns on heel; "who cares!" Presbytery more stringent. Minority turns on heel; new church; two steeples; two miserable handfuls; two starving preachers; perhaps one independent society. There is no disgrace, and little difficulty, in rearing a new sect. Hence an ecclesiastical censure is *brutum fulmen* [an irrational thunderbolt]; and hence church courts shrink from uttering their thunders. Our practice is a century or more below our book of discipline, in all courts but the highest; and nobody abides by acts of General Assembly, whether anent sitting in prayer, or reading in preaching. A vermilion edict.[18]

---

16. Hall, *Letters*, 2:105.

17. An earlier letter speaks of the benefit he had received from the reading of Philip Schaff's works on church history: "I wish you would read *Schaff's* famous book. Cry out as we may, he tells us some plain truth, and reveals things which none but a transatlantic eye could discern. It is a most exciting and suggestive volume, with a figment for the hypothesis, but great genius, learning, and truth in many of the details. I have always felt the force of what he says about the Puritans having cut to the quick, in regard to externals; about the charity we should have for Papists; and about the evils of innumerable sects. But he goes fearfully far, about visible unity." Hall, *Letters*, 2:54.

18. Hall, *Letters*, 2:105–6.

Like his father before him, Alexander continued to maintain an active preaching schedule in conjunction with his work as a professor.[19] A note from Hall provides record of Alexander's pulpit ministrations. "The number of his sermons in 1844 was 97; 1845, 117; 1846, 120; 1847, 107; 1848, 109."[20] "In 1849 Alexander preached 80 times; in 1850, 49 times."[21]

Although he delighted to preach, the combination of duties soon took a toll on Alexander's health. A letter dated October 15, 1849, describes the exhaustion he felt as he tried to balance classroom obligations and pulpit opportunities. Noticeable, too, are his longings for the work of the pastoral ministry. Although called to serve as a professor, his heart remained with the pastorate.[22] He writes:

> I feel the week's *ideology* does not fit me bodily for Sunday-ism: I came flagged to the "desk:" yesterday two sermons: this morning nervous. I did not leave pastoral life willingly; I foresaw the very evils I begin to feel; but they distress me more than I reckoned for. I miss my old women; and especially my weekly catechumens, my sick-rooms, my rapid walks, and my nights of right-down fatigue.[23]

Illness and Death in the Seminary Community

One of Alexander's letters from November 1849 records the deathbed exercises of seminary student James Montgomery Candor. Candor, like several young men before him, died while enrolled as a student at the seminary. The frequency of such events in the lives of young men preparing for the pastoral office no doubt served to impress upon their consciences the things of time and eternity as they gathered around their friend in the closing days of his life:

> My mind does not easily leave the death-bed scene of our dear young friend Candor, with whom I have spent many hours of the last few days. I went from his speechless countenance to marry ——, and hurried back to find him just gone. He was ill six weeks, and

---

19. "I have preached as much as usual ever since I left New York, besides the tough work of getting ready for classes." Hall, *Letters*, 2:106.
20. Hall, *Letters*, 2:106.
21. Hall, *Letters*, 2:129.
22. "The transition from the city to the village, from the active pastorate to the sedentary school, was too great and sudden to be entirely satisfactory. Besides, he was conscious that his aptitude lay in preaching rather than teaching." "James Waddell Alexander," 76.
23. Hall, *Letters*, 2:107.

never seemed to me to suffer much more in mind or body than you or I probably this moment. It was a most natural death-bed, if I may say so of what was so gracious. Perhaps a dozen hymns were sung around him yesterday up to the very cessation of his utterance: there was no loquacity or tendency to talk of his exercises, but an uncontrollable thirst for prayers, hymns, and Scriptures. I preached from I Thess. iv. 14, on "sleep in Jesus." His friends admitted with surprise that his fellow-students nursed him with a skill, devotion, and gentleness, that scarcely a father's house could have afforded, for so long an illness. He was one of the first minds of our house, as formerly of the college.[24]

Alexander's letters from this period also reference Dr. Miller's rapid decline in health. Having preached his last public sermon in August 1849, Samuel Miller's health deteriorated in the months that followed to the point of being housebound, though he was still able to receive visitors. Alexander visited with Miller on the morning of November 14, 1849:

This morning Dr. Miller sent for me, and for the first time in his life did not rise when I entered. He then formally made over to me the charge of the instruction, and said, inter alia: "No, sir, my time is come. I must go to the grave; no skill of man can do me any good." He no longer drives out. Every expression connects itself with his departure. In all my life I never saw a gentler decline, or a more serene, collected, looking into eternity. Our numerous cases of illness in the Seminary have kept me in parochial service, and our pot has been constantly over the fire with beef-tea, broth, &c.[25]

Alexander had hoped that Miller would be able to attend his inauguration the following week, but Miller was too weak to leave his home. The festivities which were held on November 20 included a sermon by Dr. William S. Plumer at half-past two in the afternoon and the inauguration services in the evening held at the Presbyterian Church in downtown Princeton. Following a charge by Dr. William W. Phillips, Alexander delivered his inaugural lecture, "The Value of Church History to the Theologian of Our Day."[26]

---

24. Hall, *Letters*, 2:108.
25. Hall, *Letters*, 2:108–9.
26. The sermon, charge, and inaugural discourse were published shortly afterward: *Discourses at the Inauguration of the Rev. James W. Alexander, D.D. As Professor of Ecclesiastical History and Church Government in the Theological Seminary at Princeton. Delivered at*

The Task of the Christian Historian

In the opening remarks of his inaugural discourse, Alexander paid homage to Miller's life and influence upon the Seminary. More importantly, Alexander turned his audience's attention to Christ who provides ministerial gifts to edify His church and in whose care the future of the seminary must be entrusted. Alexander's observations draw attention to Miller's legacy while pointing his audience to trust in the Lord's providence for directing the seminary's ongoing service in the training of future generations of ministers. Miller would have approved of Alexander's interest in glorifying Christ's role in the lives of his servants and work of the seminary:

> I should meet you with less of sadness, were it not for the absence of that venerable man, whose induction to this chair I distinctly remember six-and-thirty years ago, whose paternal guidance many of us have since enjoyed, and whose useful and eminent discharge of this function might well cause trembling in his successor. Let us therefore, hasten to look away from men, even the best, to the Great Head of the Church, who will bless both his aged servant and this school to which his life has been devoted.[27]

Alexander introduced his topic by looking first at what he called the "general contents" of church history. In this section, Alexander enumerated a biblical framework for interpreting the working of divine activity in the history of the church and humankind.

> There is in the matter of Church History an intrinsic value, which is the basis of all its importance to any class of minds. As a record of facts, history is a record of what God our Creator and Redeemer has seen fit to bring into existence in the course of his providence; and therefore a record, in part, of God's manifest glory, in his conduct of human affairs: this indeed is the truest notion of all history. For it is this reference of all that takes place in time to the will of God, which gives unity to the otherwise disjointed annals of our race. More specially, Church History is the record of God our Saviour, in the unfolding of the method of grace; and is thus a history dear to Christ himself, as being that of the Church, which is his body, to which he is united, and also the history of what the adorable Spirit of

---

Princeton, November 20, 1849, Before the Directors of the Seminary (New York: Robert Carter & Brothers, 1850).
27. Alexander, *Discourses*, 69.

Christ is doing, in regenerating and compacting and glorifying the elect people. It may even be called the history of mankind, as it is the history of that portion of mankind, from the beginning to the end of the world, which God has chosen to be the depositary of his grace, together with all that portion, adjacent to every part of the series, which has a visible though imperfect connection with the development of the spiritual work.[28]

Following treatments of how the truth of God serves to expose theological error and determine the nature of the church's polity, Alexander devoted a section of his address to an examination of the way in which "Church History is valuable to the Christian minister, for the CULTURE IT AFFORDS TO HIS INWARD PIETY." Alexander's presentation provides important observations on how piety shaped the history of the church and the role it must have in the life of the Christian historian for how he reflects upon its outworking through the centuries:

> It is true, Christian history may be so studied as to deaden all religion within us. Of the histories in use among us, nothing is so characteristic as their coldness. One might read them carefully without ever finding the principal thing. For what is the intimate and essential treasure of Christian history, and of the Church, if it is not Christ's religion, or the life of God among men? Leave this out, and you may have prosperous and adverse events, creeds and canons, developments of dogma, and suppression of heresy, but these are as cheerless as Egyptian temples, or sculptured cenotaphs. No wonder men have grown chilly in such chambers of the dead, among Church annals which give them only sepulchral inscriptions. It is the life which once dwelt in these piles after which we are seeking; and the search cannot be unedifying, for this is God's work among men. If the work of the Spirit in a single soul is lovely, wonderful, more worthy of profound study than the marvels of material planets and suns, how much more the work of the same Spirit in thousands, in systems of souls, in the body of Christ! What a partial view of Christ's work among men it would be to judge only those histories of grace worth knowing which occurred before the close of the canon! Each individual's spiritual life is a microcosm, and the operations of God are as varied in different souls as in different crystals, flowers, or worlds. Every conversion is a part of Church History. Every revival is a little system of God's working. The whole organism of

---

28. Alexander, *Discourses*, 70.

Divine operations from beginning to end, in all lands, can be studied only in the next world; but there is reason to believe it will be a chief study, since it is by the Church that principalities and powers in heavenly places know the manifold wisdom of God. To pursue this study now is only to learn more of that effusion which is the fruit of Christ's death, the work of Christ's Spirit, which is going on in us, and in all the family in heaven and in earth.[29]

Alexander's approach places special emphasis on the study of Christian biography for comprehending the spiritual dispositions that shaped the development of church history in both its personal and public dimensions. He writes:

> The glory of Christ shines with boundless variety and riches in the experience of the church; always the same, always different; and this is to be studied in the rich coloured texture of multiform piety, in all its individual traits; not the diaries of people of our own canton or century, but the widely differing yet brotherly experience of Polycarps, Wiclifs, Melancthons, Knoxes, and Simeons, formed by the same Spirit in circumstances remote from ours. The growing persuasion of this has given a biographical character to the Church History of our age, and there is no history which admits of being presented in biographical portraits so much as that of the Church.... And as Christ deals with the individual soul, his new creature, watching over its birth and growth with matchless love, so Christ's ministers will love the work of their Lord in the graces of all times, and hang over a single instance, as of Augustine in his Confessions, or of Chalmers in his Sabbath hours, as fondly as the botanist over a new species, or the chemist over a new metal. It is Christ's handiwork; surely we shall love and study the marks of his fingers.[30]

The address also identified the balance that must be maintained between outward activism and the intentional cultivation of an inner piety for the church to fulfill its calling in the proper manner and spirit. In an age in which Protestant activism was predominant, Alexander's cautionary observations evidence the practical application which as a professor he intended to demonstrate from study of the annals of church history.

---

29. Alexander, *Discourses*, 80–81.
30. Alexander, *Discourses*, 81–82.

The experimental Christianity of past ages will sometimes bring strongly before us a phase of piety which looks strange in modern eyes, as contemplative, nay mystical; yet is it not without instruction to the teachers of a generation who are exposed to the danger not only of measuring all religion by the quantity of motion, but of making its very essence reside in outward acts. God teaches us the evil of two extremes, of the active and the contemplative life, in events of unsurpassed greatness and vivid hues, and this teaching is Church History.[31]

Alexander's concluding sections examine the value of church history in relation to evangelical missions and "the study of the future." Rich in treatment and broad in perspective, Alexander's lecture models an approach to the study of the church's development sensitive to the spiritual dimensions and purposes by which its history is characterized and can only be properly understood.

Forging a Sacred Succession

Alexander would meet again with Miller shortly after his inauguration. Henry Carrington Alexander's account records what took place on that day:

[Miller's] colleague and successor in the Seminary called upon him about this time, and found him in his study, a room which he seemed greatly to love. He was reclining on an easy chair, with his person half extended. His visitor could not perceive the slightest decay of feeling and intellect, or even of hearing and sight. "If this continues," he records, (*quod concedat Deus*! [should God permit]) "is it not Euthanasia?" The aged Christian talked some time about the state of the church, and deplored the absence of religious revival in the country. When his friend arose, the old man asked him to lead in prayer; and, as he closed, said, "Remain on your knees, my dear friend!" He then offered a most touching prayer, thanking God for giving him a colleague, or "more properly a successor;" spoke of himself as God's "departing servant;" prayed that God would not forsake him in his old age; and made earnest request for blessings on me. I regarded it as in some sort his parting benediction. He said, "Lord, now lettest thou thy servant depart in peace, for mine eyes have seen

---

31. Alexander, *Discourses*, 83–84.

thy salvation!" The prayer was deliberate, and the words well chosen; in two instances he seemed to hesitate about an expression.[32]

Writing to Hall in December 1849, Alexander chronicles the continuing physical decline of Miller even as he catalogues the strength of his ripening piety. It is likely that Alexander's choice of an annual new year's text was made in relation to Miller's imminent parting and the hope that the message of the book of Hebrews provides for all who die in Christ.

> Dr. Miller has declined very gradually even till now. His greeting to my brother Samuel was, "Almost home." Take it altogether I never knew such a euthanasy. All the decorum of his long life kept up *"duntaxat ad imum"* [to this extent to the end]. Never one intrusion of doubt. Heaven has seemed just as much a-jar, as his next-door bedroom. Still in his study, among his life-long things, and still in a sort of chair, not bed. It is not four days since he ceased going to the table. He forbids prayer for recovery; longs to depart: has not seemed to have any anxiety but about the church, for a long time. Often has wept, more than of old, on spiritual matters. Greatly revived at hearing of conversions, &c. Our year's text is Looking unto Jesus.[33]

Alexander visited with Miller for the final time on Monday, December 31. Miller's health had declined since they last met, but his spirit remained strong.[34] Notes from Alexander's journals allow the reader to be present at a moment in time never to be forgotten by Miller's young successor:

> He was greatly enfeebled and attenuated. The princely carriage had been broken by a slight paralysis. The power of articulation had also been much impaired. The younger minister had been called in suddenly, and was sensible of having a cold hand at the time he greeted the dying saint, and apologized for it. Dr. Miller said, "how do you do? how is your family?" Then, alluding to my momentary apology for my hand, "Christ's hand is never cold! He has propped me up and led me and comforted me, more than I am able to express, and I wish you affectionately to thank Him for it in my name." His visitor knelt down and prayed with him; on which the feelings of the courtly gentleman, by which he had always been distinguished

---

32. Alexander, *Life of Joseph Addison Alexander*, 2:670–71.
33. Hall, *Letters*, 2:110.
34. "But the time was now approaching when this great light of the intellectual firmament of Princeton was to be extinguished, or rather, let us say, hidden from the view of mortal sin and ignorance." Alexander, *Life of Joseph Addison Alexander*, 2:671.

among his contemporaries, seemed to work strongly within him, and he said, as if he feared he might have been misunderstood in what he had uttered respecting the cold hand, "Your hand has never been inconveniently cold to me; but the hand of Christ is always warm." Thereupon his visitor withdrew.[35]

Miller died on Monday evening, January 7, 1850. Alexander eulogizes his memory in a brief paragraph from a letter on January 8, 1850:

> When I heard last night, Dr. Miller was almost gone; like a sleeping child, but knew my father. One of the boys came in as I had penned this, to say that Dr. Miller died last night about 11, a few hours after my father saw him; without any struggle, oppression, or seeming pain. The funeral is to be from the church, on Thursday, (January 10,) at 2 o'clock. It has been a great comfort to the Doctor to have his medical son with him so many weeks. The Doctor was in his 81st year. Of all the deaths I ever knew, this is the most surrounded by all the things one could desire.[36]

Alexander's grief at the death of Miller is likely understated. Miller had been a regular part of his family's life from shortly after his parents removed from Philadelphia to Princeton in the summer of 1812. Miller was not only a close personal friend of the family, but also one of the professors whom Alexander had studied under as a student. Memories of his days as a student in Miller's classes would have come to mind.[37] Miller's paternal care for his students was legendary, and Alexander was one of the many recipients of Miller's affection while a student and in the years that followed. Miller's example had surely become the model to which Alexander would now aspire as his mentor's successor.[38]

---

35. Alexander, *Life of Joseph Addison Alexander*, 2:671–72.
36. Hall, *Letters*, 2:110–11.
37. In his review of Sprague's volumes, Alexander remarked on Miller's theological tenacity: "A more staunch and loyal Presbyterian Calvinist never lived. The warfare which he waged against high-church assumption was prompted by pious conviction of the truth; its fruits are still held in honour as well by our brethren in Scotland as by ourselves." James W. Alexander, "Annals of the American Pulpit; or Commemorative Notices of distinguished American Clergymen of various Denominations. With Historical Introductions," *The Biblical Repertory and Princeton Review* 30, no. 3 (July 1858): 411.
38. Alexander would write of Miller: "He was by nature fearless, we may even say polemic; yet a more melting forgiveness, or a larger charity, we do not hope to find. In all our knowledge of ministers, we never knew one who was so ready to own himself in the wrong, or so unfeignedly lowly in regard to his own attainments; nor one more conscientious in self-denial and special prayer. Those who judge him only by his books,

Revival at the College of New Jersey

As the cold winter months gave way to the warmth of springtime, Alexander's letters describe his growing appreciation for the writings of Martin Luther.[39] "I don't know on whose side the shuttlecock has fallen," he said, "but I have had my hands very full of writing, having worked along to the Reformation-period, as good Mr. Pollock might say. Renewed studies of Luther have made me admire and love him more than ever."[40]

In a communication on March 5, 1850, Alexander reports on a revival that was taking place among the students at the College of New Jersey. As a consequence, the local Presbyterian pastor found himself busy counseling large numbers of students coming under spiritual conviction at this time:

> You will have heard that Mr. Schenck is having daily meetings. I fail to perceive a very deep stirring of the people's mind, or special tenderness under the Word; but thirty to forty have been to talk with the pastor, and a number are reported to be in a state of hope. It is certainly something to get large numbers willing to be approached, and anxious to hear truth; and I believe this is so.[41]

Two weeks later, Alexander reported that the majority of the students at the college—close to two hundred—were believed to be actively engaged in seeking God. In a separate correspondence, Alexander commented on the growing influence of the revival: "There is no abatement of the stir. About thirty-seven additional in college are serious. I observe that our butchers, bakers, and *id genus* [others of the sort], flock to meetings, and talk of little else."[42]

---

can have but a remote conception of what Dr. Miller was, either as the vivifying spirit of delighted groups, or as the spiritual and tender Christian friend." Alexander, "Annals of the American Pulpit," 412.

39. Coincident with his readings in Lutheran theology, Alexander was also busy preparing a tract to reach German immigrants with the gospel message: "I am slowly and feebly working on a tract, long on hand, for incoming German emigrants. I desire to have it published in German, say by the American Tract Society. I have tried in vain to get something of the kind. It contemplates temporals as well as spirituals." Hall, *Letters*, 2:113.

40. Hall, *Letters*, 2:112.

41. Hall, *Letters*, 2:112.

42. Hall, *Letters*, 2:114.

Growing Criticism of the Seminary's Academic Program

But while a revival was sweeping the college campus, the seminary was finding itself a source of denominational criticism for the quality of students it was graduating. By the late 1840s, the school began receiving criticism for having overweighted the program with academic learning and failing to produce competent preachers.[43] Acquisition of faculty with limited pastoral experience lent validity to the criticism.

Among critics of the school's program was the Rev. Dr. Gardiner Spring, pastor of the famous Brick Street Presbyterian Church in New York City. Spring had served for a number of years on the seminary's board of trustees and was a longtime friend to the institution, but over time he had become increasingly troubled by the quality of the graduates, especially in relation to their ability to preach. Spring's criticism of the institutional model of ministerial training which the seminary had come to represent found expression in sections of his influential book *The Power of the Pulpit*, first published in 1848.[44]

Spring believed that the institutional development of the school had resulted in a focus on academic acquirements in place of the pastoral training emphases for which the seminary had been founded. Preparation for the needs of the church had given way to the preferences of the academy. Scholars with minimal pastoral background, Spring was convinced, would be incapable of providing the orientation essential to ministerial training. He advocated a return to the earlier pastor-mentor model once dominant in American clerical culture as a corrective to the ministerial declension that had occurred through the academy model that the seminary represented.

The faculty at the seminary responded to Spring's concerns in a somewhat biting review in the July 1848 issue of the *Biblical Repertory*. Spring's criticisms were addressed, and a defense of the school's current program was presented.[45]

---

43. The challenge of finding qualified faculty with experience in pastoral ministry was a source of ongoing concern beginning in the 1840s. For a brief overview of the issues involved, see Calhoun, *Faith and Learning*, 1:371–74; Garretson, *Princeton and Preaching*, 260–64.

44. Gardiner Spring, *The Power of the Pulpit; or, Thoughts Addressed to Christian Ministers and Those Who Hear Them* (New York: Baker and Scribner, 1848; repr., Edinburgh: Banner of Truth, 1986).

45. James W. Alexander, "The Power of the Pulpit By Gardiner Spring, D.D., a review," *The Biblical Repertory and Princeton Review* 20, no. 3 (July 1848): 463–89.

Alexander had arrived at the seminary shortly after the issues became a source of published debate. The matters were important to Hall as well and were introduced into their correspondence during Alexander's time as a professor. Apparently, Hall agreed with some of Spring's concerns and directed them to Alexander.

Responding to Hall's observations from one of their recent letter exchanges, Alexander expressed his disapprobation of Hall's criticisms toward the model of education the seminary provided. Alexander defended the school's program, pointing out the strong emphases on practical theology included in the required curriculum.[46] Writing to his friend in a letter on June 30, 1850, he remarked:

> You are too severe in your stricture on seminary teaching. I never heard the methods complained of as failing to make ministerial practice the daily end. Whole portions of the course have no other ingredient; as Dr. Miller's lectures on Sermons and Discipline, and the long series of teachings in pastoral theology. Other portions daily include the same, at proper places. The separate teaching of experimental religion, would be finely illustrated by our Presbyterial examinations thereanent.[47]

Observations on Preaching

On various occasions in his letters, Alexander would comment on the ongoing influence of Charles Finney's preaching. Alexander, like the Princeton faculty in general, was troubled by Finney's New Measures revivalism and semi-Pelagian theology.[48] Although Finney was lauded by the press for the large crowds that attended his preaching, Alexander and his fellow Princeton faculty were deeply disturbed by the after-effects of his revival campaigns and views on sin and perfectionism.[49]

---

46. The controversy had not affected student enrollment. A letter from early September 1850 reports: "Thus far, our accession to the Seminary is about 46. They are still coming in." Hall, *Letters*, 2:123.

47. Hall, *Letters*, 2:116.

48. For a collection of articles republished from the *Biblical Repertory* addressing these issues, see *Princeton Versus the New Divinity: The Meaning of Sin, Grace, Salvation, Revival: Articles from the Princeton Review* (Edinburgh: Banner of Truth, 2001).

49. Alexander contrasts the interest in reporting on numbers that characterized Charles Finney's ministry with that of his father, Archibald Alexander: "My good old father has not been less than 60 years a preacher; but I have never heard him preach any autobiography, self-statistics, or census of successes." Hall, *Letters*, 2:124.

Alexander's letter dated September 5, 1850, warns of how the public press may misrepresent the true impact of a popular man's ministry:

> The London papers give flaming accounts of Finney's sermons and audiences. There is no allusion to his later doctrines of perfectionism. I wonder if a day will not come, when the immense increase of printed matter will cause a reaction in favour of old-time methods, oral learning, discoursing sub dio, like that of the Athenians and the New Testament. Even in Plato's day, he was led to fear the ill consequences to human powers from overmuch reading. News is a very different affair, in daily papers and word of mouth.[50]

As a preacher turned church historian, it is not unexpected to find Alexander stressing the importance of history for the subject matter of pulpit proclamation. Observations made in his inaugural address find frequent mention in his correspondence with Hall. "Variety in sermons might be helped by an occasional history, with free bursts of remark, whenever suggested; it is remarkable how much of the Bible is history," he said. Bible biographies were especially recommended: "I think Elijah and Elisha a good topic. The argument of the book of Job would make a good sermon. In general, the argument of a Sunday School book might be occasionally preached with advantage."[51]

Alexander observes that biographical preaching is an effective means of teaching spiritual principles for Christian living. Biography can touch the human heart in ways that other forms of preaching may not:

> How much of the Bible is history; and how much of the history is biography. No other reading so much shows me to myself, or so much stimulates me. As we grow older, do we not find a pleasure in the lesser lines of character? seeing differences which formerly did not strike us; just as we learn to detect handwritings, which to children are all alike, and to *idiota* are unmeaning. If a botanist loves to collate flowers, how much more, &c., &c. I will borrow for you the Life of good old Bengel, which will much please you. N. B. To introduce into our sermons more biography; I mean detailed pictures of character; not for ornament, but for searching—to hold the mirror up to nature. Models in Bible, Prov. xxxi. The Hireling. Several sketchy portraits in the Psalms.[52]

---

50. Hall, *Letters*, 2:124.
51. Hall, *Letters*, 2:125.
52. Hall, *Letters*, 2:130–31.

Alexander took particular pleasure in familiarizing himself with the sermons of Martin Luther. With the exception of Lutheran pietist theologian August Tholuck, he found Luther's sermons more spiritually edifying than anything coming from the German pulpits of his day.

> I have been acquainting myself with Luther's sermons. Nothing can be more natural, simple, earnest, downright, practical, pungent, or affectionate. They are models of the plainest, liveliest sort; the very opposite of modern German sermons, which are as constrained in their elegant partition as a sonnet or an acrostic. I have had to look into some of these professionally; and I declare I am unable to find one, which is worthy of reperusal, except some of Tholuck's, which are beautiful warm rhapsodies.[53]

Lecturer at the University of Virginia

Although the focus of Alexander's labors at the seminary was directed to the subjects of ecclesiastical history, church government, and sermon composition and delivery,[54] earlier studies delivered to his former congregation on the life of Christ found expression in an important contribution Alexander made to a series of lectures delivered at the University of Virginia during the 1850–1851 academic year on the topic "Evidences of Christianity."[55]

Leaving Princeton on December 2, Alexander traveled to the University of Virginia where he delivered a lecture entitled "The Character of Jesus Christ, an Argument for the Divine Origin of Christianity." As might be expected, Alexander's lecture provides a rich overview of biblical testimony to Christ's character and mission, interspersed with numerous historical analogies and related practical observations for

---

53. Hall, *Letters*, 2:125.
54. "During 1850 he lectured on homiletics—the only year he taught this course—and James P. Boyce, who entered Princeton in 1849, said that in the area of 'sacred rhetoric' Dr. J. W. Alexander was 'the most delightful lecturer' he had ever heard." Cited in Calhoun, *Faith and Learning*, 1:287. While incomplete, a small selection of Alexander's lectures on style, elocution, and composition and delivery of a sermon can be found in The James Waddell Alexander Manuscript Collection at Princeton Theological Seminary Library. The collection also includes undated lectures on style, questions on rhetoric, and practice of composition.
55. Hall notes: "He had begun such a course, and given sixteen lectures, at the close of his ministry in Duane street, (October 31, 1848, to May 29, 1849.) He began it anew with the Fifth Avenue congregation January 27, 1852, and continued it at the Tuesday meetings until February 27, 1855." Hall, *Letters*, 1:338.

what it now means to live a life of obedient faith in response to the scriptural evidence for the divine origin of Christianity.[56]

Duane Street Church Revisited

A passing reference in a letter on October 7, 1850, mentions Alexander's continuing concern for his former congregation. Apparently, the church had entered into a holding pattern after his departure with little progress having been made on acquiring a new site for their congregation. "My poor Duane Street folks make no progress. I look confidently for the stronger portion of them to go up-town, at whatever loss of property in the present building."[57]

Developments at the congregation in the ensuing weeks proved otherwise and soon took Alexander by surprise. Not only did the majority of the congregation agree to make the move uptown and build a new facility, but they also solicited Alexander's interest in returning to New York City to serve as their pastor! Alexander's thoughts about their inquiry can be found in a letter penned to Hall on December 13, 1850:

> I am struck all of a heap by the news from New York. What Providence means I am at a loss to say. Surely I have done nothing I know of, to invite a re-call to Duane Street. What moves me somewhat is, (1,) I do not feel a special quality for teaching: (2,) I greatly miss pulpit and pastoral work. Yet when I think of tearing up again—it seems next to impossible. I am much concerned, and in real trouble of mind, and shall profit by any unprejudiced thoughts you have.[58]

Alexander missed pastoral work and considered his efforts as a seminary professor somewhat of a failure. For reasons that are not specified, Alexander felt more aptitude for the pulpit than that of the seminary classroom. Yet Alexander was hesitant to uproot his family and return to New York. He had barely been in Princeton three years, and he fretted

---

56. James W. Alexander, "The Character of Jesus Christ, an Argument for the Divine Origin of Christianity," in *Lectures on the Evidences of Christianity, Delivered at the University of Virginia During the Session of 1850–1*, ed. W. H. Ruffner (New York: Robert Carter & Brothers, 1859), 193–211.
57. Hall, *Letters*, 2:125.
58. Hall, *Letters*, 2:128.

about the criticism he would receive if he resigned his professorship for a popular pulpit location in one of America's most influential cities.[59]

As he prayed and reflected on the invitation, he began to feel at peace with the prospect of a return to pastoral ministry. Apparently, his health began to deteriorate from the pressures of his professorship. Ironically, he now felt a return to the pastorate would bring about the needed rejuvenation in health he so desired![60]

Consultation with his family confirmed the wisdom of returning to his former congregation. Even Archibald Alexander agreed that his son's gifts were more suited to the pulpit than the lecture room. Personal preferences aside, what Alexander wanted most of all was to honor his Lord with the ministerial gifts with which he had been entrusted. He set aside December 24 as a day of prayer and fasting to seek God's will in the matter. Spiritual considerations, rather than worldly motives, were uppermost in his mind.

In an extended letter penned on Christmas 1850, Alexander unburdened his heart to Hall. His reflections demonstrate the humility that characterized his sense of calling to the gospel ministry:

> I wish you as many Christmases and as happy, for you and yours, as the Divine Disposer shall give in token of love; for as I grow older, I trust I sometimes look forward to something better than the years of this world. The *number* of persons subscribing for the new church is rather favourable. The place talked of is Fifth Avenue and Nineteenth street. I am puzzled and darkened by conflicting opinions. There are some who will charge me with great fickleness, if I leave Princeton so soon. The Philadelphia men will generally think it a wild and wrong move. My father and family think I had better go, on the score of health; and it is especially my father's opinion, that the measure of talent I have is for preaching. It would not be exactly like a new experiment. The people calling know me, and are known by me. The recent move reveals an amount of influence on the New York mind,

---

59. "It was a struggle for him to leave Princeton in the first instance. It was a greater struggle to return to it. He was soon to be called to make up his mind to leave it. This last step was not taken without a violent shock to all his newly rooted affections; but was no doubt ordered in mercy and wisdom." Alexander, *Life of Joseph Addison Alexander*, 2:680–81.

60. "He knew care and sorrow and perplexity, and has covered the pages of his diaries for this period with confessions, thanksgivings, and supplications, written partly in English, partly in Latin, and partly in stenography." Alexander, *Life of Joseph Addison Alexander*, 2:680.

which (however unmerited) deserves to be considered. I was very happy in my work, and (if I may presume to say so) was improving in it, more than I feel myself to be doing in my teaching-function. These are things I cannot say abroad, but they affect my mind not a little. *Per contra*, I have the New York hum and interruption; New York summers; leaving a delightful home and rural quietude, and academic regularity, and above all my dear old father and mother, whose decline I should covet to wait upon. These, however, are, for the most part, *worldly* considerations; while I am impressed by the thought, that many of the reasons for return are *spiritual* in their nature. People say, "You can preach every Sunday in Princeton." So I can—but what a different thing it is! I feel lifeless in comparison. I make no new sermons. Indeed, I hardly can take my present preaching into the account. The true comparison must be between *teaching* here, and *preaching* there. Looking as modestly and honestly at it as I can, I feel (comparatively) some aptitude for preaching; at least, I have most undeserved acceptance—and that particularly in New York: I feel no special aptitude for teaching. In the city I drew young men around me: here, all my efforts have failed with the students, privately and socially: the difference I cannot express to you; nor is it a matter I can discuss with people generally. I know the matter of health is very uncertain, and the causes of health and disease are obscure: but I think the four to five years in New York were of as much health, certainly they were of as much working-strength, as any similar portion of my life. As you might suppose, the matter is constantly in my thoughts, and I earnestly seek Divine leading; for I know that my decision must be reviewed in the Judgment, and that if I determine on worldly and selfish grounds, I must expect a blight if not a curse. I wish to settle this question before many days.[61]

By December 29, Alexander had decided to return to the pastorate on condition that the new building which was to be built would not incur debt. A statement from a letter on January 6, 1851, signals the enthusiasm he had for his future pulpit ministry.[62] "The impulse to write sermons

---

61. Hall, *Letters*, 2:128–29.
62. Alexander's awareness of the weightiness of the pulpit ministry to which he intended a return can be found in remarks made to Hall a few weeks later on January 23, 1851: "I hardly know how to speak of —'s death. It came on us like a thunderbolt. The agonizing thought, when such an event occurs, is, *Perhaps I might have saved a soul from death!* What plainness, labour, and earnestness it ought to give us in preaching!" Hall, *Letters*, 2:130.

has come over me very strong, and I have two half done. There is no employment I ever found so uniformly agreeable."[63]

He "resigned his professorship in February, but continued to act until April 30th."[64] A final letter written at the end of his professorship hints at the sadness he felt in leaving his position. "I heard this day my last recitation," he reported in a letter written to Hall on April 30, 1851. "There is something sad in these 'Last Things.'"[65] Yet for all the sadness he felt at leaving the seminary, the letter expresses Alexander's plans for a pulpit ministry addressed to the various "states and stages" of his future congregation:

> A hint towards sermons: make a sermon, one for each, on the different states and stages of mind and character among people not converted, yet not altogether hardened. E.g. 1. The occasionally awakened. 2. Those who are already somewhat thoughtful. 3. Those who have gone back. 4. Those who are deeply concerned. 5. Those who are so for the first time. 6. Those who see obstacles to coming to Christ. 7. Those who occasionally hope. 8. Those who are overwhelmed with a sense of sin, &c., &c. [66]

Alexander's desire to be a parish minister wholly and with all his soul was about to be realized afresh in his return to the city that he had left just three years earlier.[67]

---

63. Hall, *Letters*, 2:129.
64. Hall, *Letters*, 2:129.
65. Hall, *Letters*, 2:132–33.
66. Hall, *Letters*, 2:132–33.
67. "Here the rejoicing, anxious, fearing, troubled, jaded, broken pastor spent the remainder of his life." Alexander, *Life of Joseph Addison Alexander*, 2:683.

No duty is plainer than that of standing out firmly for the encouragement of a MASCULINE LITERATURE, EMBODYING AND DEFENDING THE PRECIOUS TRUTHS OF THE REFORMATION. We want MEN; and they must be trained in hardy methods. The three years which, as military authorities declare, are required for transforming the raw recruit into the disciplined soldier, are not spent in light or easy exercises. Mighty Christian muscle will not be produced by catching up and devouring whatsoever floats by on the surface of the current authorship. Let us run all the risk of being judged censorious, we nevertheless affirm that the predominant trait of the now popular religious press is lightness. In proportion as fancy has been amused, the understanding has been famished; every addition to imagery has tended to defraud the heart. Sermons and volumes have been constrained to become picture-galleries of illustration and series of metaphor and similitude gay as the slides of the magic-lantern. Even this were tolerable if truth and reason had held their place; we could love and embrace divine truth even in a suit of motley: but distinct vision of gospel verity has been impaired. The system of lenses has become more entertaining but less achromatic. Readers and hearers grow less and less able to define with exactness the doctrines of grace. Doctrine itself—the very name of what disciples covet—has become with certain schools a term of disparagement. Let us be fully understood: the books which we need are not vague, compromising, latitudinarian, all-comprehensive rhapsodies or strains of sentimentality, however tinted with the rainbow, but undeniable statements of Reformation Truth. *Of making many books there may be no end; but there will be a speedy end of all sound theology unless we can make some which shall utter a bold, intelligible language in regard to the points for which Huss died and Luther labored. Many are so lulled into sweet slumbers by the siren voice of mock-charity as not to know that there is any controversy. And no marvel; "for if the trumpet give an uncertain sound, who shall prepare himself to battle?" (1 Cor. xiv. 8).*

—J. W. ALEXANDER
November 1856
(From *The American Sunday-School and Its Adjuncts*)

Chapter 11

EUROPEAN VOYAGE: MAY–OCTOBER 1851

Having completed his service at Princeton Theological Seminary, Alexander embarked on a six-month tour of Europe in May 1851. It was Alexander's first trip abroad, and he eagerly looked forward to the places that he planned to visit. The trip was also intended as a time of respite for recuperation of his health in preparation for his return to the rigors of pastoral ministry.

Writing from off Cape Clear on June 3, 1851, Alexander spoke briefly of his traveling companions and the opportunities for public worship that he enjoyed during his transatlantic crossing. "Through God's mercy," he wrote to Hall, "I am here on the Irish coast, in our eleventh day. It has been a perpetual delight, without accident, hinderance, or 'evil occurrent;' without pain, alarm, sea-sickness, languor, low spirits, or weariness; with as delightful a company as ever was thrown together, with sumptuous entertainment in a floating palace." He was particularly struck by the spirit of his fellow travelers and their enthusiasm for daily worship. "Will you believe it—our 141 passengers have been like a loving family. Since the 25th we have had solemn and delightful worship every night, and services both Sabbaths. On each I preached once. I suppose we sang forty complete hymns on Sunday night."[1]

Alexander was delighted with the opportunities the Lord gave him for religious exhortation during the voyage, but he was embarrassed by the notoriety he gained for his efforts: "I have had frequent opportunities of religious exhortation, and was never more blessed, than on this voyage, with willing ears. I am sorry to say my health was publicly drunk at

---

1. Hall, *Letters*, 2:134.

the closing dinner on board, 'for his services as chaplain.' Tupper made a speech, and various poems were recited."[2]

Alexander arrived in Liverpool, England, on June 4, and from there he traveled to London where he spent the next two weeks seeing the major sites in the city. From London, he journeyed to Paris, France, where he also enjoyed a few weeks of sightseeing and meetings with influential Christian leaders. "Paris is more like an American city than London," he wrote in an entry for June 24. "It is filthy and has abominable stenches. But there are thousands of flowers and birds here, which cannot be said of any American city." He was especially elated with a worship service he attended where the famous French preacher Adolphe Monod spoke. "O what a meeting, Sunday evening, in the little chapel Oratoire! Adolphe Monod—'God is Love.' Huguenot women in caps. Old Psalm (103d)—old tunes. It was an hour to be remembered for life."[3]

In addition to the public worship service that he attended, Alexander enjoyed a time of tea at Monod's home later in the day. While there, he was invited to conduct evening prayers and expound a passage of Scripture. "We ran together like two drops," he remarked.[4] Another entry comments on the piety that marked Monod and his extended family: "Mr. A. Monod is the most remarkable mixture of sweetness with intense solemnity I ever saw. Three months ago his mother died leaving twelve living sons. All the connexion seem to be in the fear of the Lord."[5]

In a country characterized by cultural elitism, Alexander was impressed by the way in which Christians from different levels of French society interacted with one another. "All ranks of evangelical people meet here like brothers. All ranks are equally polite," he noted.[6]

Visits to various cathedrals and churches provided fodder for Alexander's distaste of Roman Catholicism even as he found satisfaction with the devotional exercises of Parisian Christians. A letter on June 27 describes his forays into French worship services:

---

2. Hall, *Letters*, 2:135. A later entry from 1854 records the mixed response to one of his messages: "I have a sermon which I preached on board that vessel [May 25, 1851], on the text, 'And the sea gave up the dead,' &c.; in which is a description of just such a mode of death. It was much censured at the time, as alarming and unseasonable." Hall, *Letters*, 2:203.
3. Hall, *Letters*, 2:143.
4. Hall, *Letters*, 2:144.
5. Hall, *Letters*, 2:146.
6. Hall, *Letters*, 2:144.

My days are spent in rambling,: for the things I want to see differ from the common sights. I have been in the principal churches, have heard masses enough to keep my soul in repose (if they have any such virtue) a thousand years, have seen paintings till I weary of them, have sought out the burial-places of some great men, some Protestant antiquities not commonly visited, and have learned to hate Popery more intensely than ever. At two soriees I have good opportunity to scan the customs of Parisian Christians. I have never seen any thing more simply elegant or affectionate. In both instances we had prayers before tea. Last evening a company of about thirty united in singing a hymn, hearing chapter, and offering a prayer—all in French.[7]

The grandeur of worship in the French cathedrals was overwhelming to Alexander. He had never experienced anything like it before and found that it had no equivalent among even the most polished of American churches. As one conscientious of the elements appropriate to the order of public worship, Alexander was almost beside himself in describing the atmosphere of the spectacle that he witnessed:

> Yesterday was the Lord's day, the octave of Fete Dieu, (Corpus Christi,) a day specially devoted to the idolatry of the wafer. I felt it my duty to go to the Madeleine before worship. How can I make you conceive the worldly grandeur and beauty! It is the greatest of modern churches. It is more beautiful outside than St. Peter's. Conceive of a Greek temple of massy marble: images on images by the greatest sculptors, many times as large as life, all outside. Hangings of velvet, purple, and gold between the columns. Ancient tapestries hung outside the walls, within the vast pillars. Inside, the smell of millions of flowers. It is called the *fete des fleurs*. If I saw one bouquet I saw ten thousand. You cannot imagine the art in their disposition. The high altar was so backed by a forest of flowers, that the singers were perfectly concealed. Scores of priests, deacons, boys in graceful albs with pink girdles; scores of girls all veiled, all white for their first communion, as they went in procession, and carried a rich bouquet. The nuns and girls had bouquets wholly of lilies and other white buds of flowers. The music was such as I am sure I shall never hear the like of in this world. The vast area within was filled with people.[8]

---

7. Hall, *Letters*, 2:144.
8. Hall, *Letters*, 2:145.

Having attended worship at the local cathedral, Alexander afterward visited "the poor little English Wesleyan chapel." The contrast in atmosphere could not have been more striking. About one hundred fifty were present. A Dr. Richie delivered the message. It was a "good sermon," Alexander said, on "'Behold the Lamb.'" Ritchie's sermon had a powerful effect on Alexander. "The application of it was such gospel, gospel, gospel, that I laid my head down and almost dissolved."[9]

In his reflections on the difference in worship practice that he had experienced, Alexander commented on the dangers to which piety is subjected when the senses are overwhelmed with visual pageantry. For all the outward religiosity that he had witnessed, he doubted whether it was rooted in genuine piety. While he felt American worship services paled in comparison to the size and visual splendor of French cathedral worship, he believed faithful exposition of the Word of God remained central to the public worship of the churches in America in a way that was not true of the cathedrals in France:

> These things which are daily bread in blessed America, are here like God's manna. The beauty, the grace, the extent, the glory of these illuminated forests, these spacious *places*, these statues, buildings, orderly crowds, this music—a hundred orchestras and concerts every night in open air—these things pass description, and steal the soul of the people from God. Since the cities of the plain, vice has never had such blandishment. Most, even of religious Americans, forget all restraint. Not that I have seen drunkenness or heard one profane word. All is courtesy and *bienseance* [propriety]. The common people have a grace which reproves me every instant. Around a puppet-show or dancing dogs, the folk in blouses are so polite and still; they do not even rub against you without a "Pardon, monsieur," the tone of which is more than the words. But they are Godless, and at one rap of the drum (especially just now) are ready to become *simiotigres*.[10]

Alexander left France and traveled on to Geneva, Switzerland. Home to Calvin's ministry in the sixteenth century, Geneva played a strategic role in the success of the Protestant Reformation during Calvin's time and afterward. As he journeyed to Geneva, Alexander, like many visitors before him, was awed by the majesty of the Swiss Alps. His first sighting

---

9. Hall, *Letters*, 2:145.
10. Hall, *Letters*, 2:145.

of the Alps evoked in him a spirit of worship and thoughtful reflection on the glory of God's handiwork. An entry for July 12, 1851, captures the enraptured moments Alexander experienced:

> All this day we have been in mountain-raptures; but when suddenly, through a near gap, the Alps burst on us, it was so different from any forethought of mine that I was relieved from swooning only by tears. I am thankful to say all my thought at the moment was of God, of Christ, and of heaven. Though a hundred miles off in many parts, they were clear as diamond. I was absolutely speechless. I had dreamed of vast dimensions, and of big mountains and chains, but this was mother-of-pearl, azure, agate, all colours, more solid than granite, and looking among the clouds, heavenly. We all sank under the religious impressions. The impression of death, heaven, and eternity is unavoidable. It has been a means of grace on the blessed, quiet Sabbath in the city of Bernard, Calvin, Farel, Vinet, Knox, Beza, and the Turretines. Yet around this lake lived Voltaire, Rousseau, and Gibbon. "The entrance of *thy words* giveth light."[11]

While in Geneva, he visited the St. Antoine quarter and the church building in which Calvin once preached. "We visited the Cathedral; a very old church, like St. Denis in some points. Here the Byzantine arch is seen growing into the early Gothic. The old stalls from before the Reformation remain, with figures of apostles and prophets in wood, and blazonry indicating the alliance between Geneva and Florence, as republics," he noted. "The pulpit is modern, but the sounding board is the same as when Calvin preached here." "This was his favourite place," Alexander remarked.[12]

A letter from Chamonix on July 17, 1851, records Alexander's delight in the mountains and glaciers he encountered. Once again, he was striken by the beauty of God's creation:

> The Alp-horn was sounded for us and we listened to its echoes. I did not properly understand a glacier, before I came here. It is most like a mighty river, tossed into fury, and then turned to ice. Glaciers have a constant, though imperceptible motion. They look like frozen cataracts, coming down the hollows of the mountain-sides. They give origin to rivers. The air is very rare, cool, and clear, so

---

11. Hall, *Letters*, 2:148.
12. Hall, *Letters*, 2:148.

that objects seem greatly nearer than the reality. The clouds, and fogs, and snows, which play fantastically about the mountains, keep the great peaks most of the time concealed; but enough is visible to make us adore Him "who setteth fast the mountains."[13]

As Alexander journeyed from Geneva to Cologne, he found himself in an environment far removed from the culture and mannerisms he had recently experienced. Even the wines were different. "The Rhine-wines, which everybody drinks, are acid though lively, and require a training to endure." Public etiquette, at least as Alexander preferred it, was all but absent from what he encountered. "I confess, the peasantry look happy, dwell cosily, and enjoy a merriment unknown with us. The instances of personal and table filthiness, common in German inns, would nauseate you if described. At Basel, a German gentleman, at the table d'hote, dinner going on, cleaned his teeth with his brush, and spat into a glass." Alexander was disenchanted at the women he encountered during this portion of his trip. "The female sex, generally, tends to a masculine coarseness," he told Hall. In a further comment—one that his wife would no doubt have found special pleasure in reading—he remarked, "I have learned to prize an American woman."[14]

His visit to Cologne also provided opportunity for further reflection on the way in which architectural splendor can misdirect the spiritual priorities for which worship in public facilities is intended. Alexander's burden for the spiritual welfare of the people he observed is evident in an entry for August 2, 1851:

> Of Cathedrals, I have now seen the greatest, Freiburg, Strasburg, and Cologne. Next to God's works, no work has ever amazed me. In the gorgeous temple, amidst painted windows and music that made me tremble and sink, my soul was oppressed at the heathenism to which Christianity is here reduced. And then to think what the Protestantism is, which is to oppose it! I deeply fear some judicial dealing with this whole continent. Unless Christ work some Pentecostal miracle, where is the hope?[15]

Writing from his steamboat while near Rubens on August 4, 1851, Alexander spoke appreciatively of the piety he had witnessed among the

---

13. Hall, *Letters*, 2:149–50.
14. Hall, *Letters*, 2:150–51.
15. Hall, *Letters*, 2:150–51.

churches in Holland.[16] While he was hopeful that the Dutch churches would remain faithful to the rich confessional heritage from which they had been birthed during the Protestant Reformation of the sixteenth century, he recognized the slippery doctrinal slope upon which they had already embarked:

> I observed signs of strong drink in Holland. Schiedam has 300 gin distilleries. The house in which Erasmus was born, is a gin-place. I observed, for the first time in Europe, pallor among the children; yet the people look healthy. The working-women are as neat at their work, as ours on Sundays. The churches are full. My general conclusion is, that the impulse of the Reformation, and its traditionary customs, abide very strong, and that, while they are on the descent towards German rationalism, they are not so far down as we think in America. They are dead and formal, but not universally erroneous. In the country places, I am assured, people read the old books and cling to the old doctrine. Catechizing and pastoral visiting are kept up. Country pastors are "orthodox," but I failed to learn precisely what that term imports in Holland. Two educated and sensible men agreed in declaring that Utrecht is still orthodox, and that the body of the churches hold the divinity of our Lord and the atonement.[17]

His travels eventually led him to Scotland—a country that was home to the beginnings of Presbyterianism, the theological heritage in which he had been raised and the denominational convictions to which as a minister he now subscribed.

While visiting Edinburgh in late August 1851, Alexander preached "for the Rev. C. J. Brown, in the Free New North Church." He was pleased by the congregation's interest in his ministry among them. "I will only say," he remarked to Hall, "I was never so *helped* by a congregation. Imagine me in the Geneva cloak; five hundred Bibles rustling at once; such deep, penetrative, animated looks from whole rows of people, all seeming fired with zeal, and all singing without an exception that I could note. I thought it far better than the Madeleine or Cologne." Committed as he was to the catechetical instruction of his own congregation, Alexander

---

16. Alexander's interest in the development of Christianity in Holland found earlier expression in a review published in the *Biblical Repertory* during 1833: James W. Alexander, "The Religious Condition of Holland," *The Biblical Repertory and Theological Review* 5, no. 1 (January 1833): 19–33.

17. Hall, *Letters*, 2:152.

was greatly encouraged by what he witnessed in the Scottish congregation through the labors of a certain Mr. Dickson:

> Mr. Dickson edits a youth's paper. He teaches two Bible classes. I preached to one of them. It contains 70–80 girls. An hour was spent studying rather than saying the lesson. I should have thought the examination a good one for the first [the youngest] class in the Seminary. They answered the questions with a pertinence, knowledge of Scripture, and exactness which amazed me.[18]

Of all the places on his European journey, Scotland found a treasured spot in Alexander's heart. Familiar with the country's rich history of Calvinistic piety, preaching, confessional convictions, and church reform, Alexander counted it a special privilege to visit and worship among the Scottish congregations.[19] While some of their doctrinal exactness exasperated his patience, he could not help but glory in the church that God had established.[20] Although it was a wish unable to be fulfilled, Alexander relished the spiritual joy his father would have if given the opportunity to experience what he had witnessed during his time in Scotland. Alexander recorded his impressions in a letter on September 9, 1851, while in the city of Glasgow:

---

18. Hall, *Letters*, 2:156–57.

19. For an appreciative history of the Scottish Reformation, see James W. Alexander, "The Life and Times of Alexander Henderson, giving a History of the Second Reformation of the Church of Scotland, and the Covenanters, during the reign of Charles I," *The Biblical Repertory and Princeton Review* 12, no. 4 (October 1840): 481–515. For a related study on an influential Scottish minister greatly used during a time of revival, see James W. Alexander, "The Life and Times of John Livingston," *The Biblical Repertory and Princeton Review* 4, no. 3 (October 1832): 428–50.

20. A letter in September 1851 provides a vivid description of nineteenth-century Scottish Presbyterian church life: "All the Scottish churches have vestries and all the ministers wear the Geneva gown or cloak, which has come down from the days of Knox. In some churches the preacher pronounces the Lord's Prayer immediately before the sermon. The old version of the Psalms is universal. The prayer after sermon is uniformly longer than with us, and the service varies from an hour and three-quarters to two hours. At this season the usual hours in town are eleven and two. The custom of 'turning up' the passage remains in all its strength, and hundreds of Bibles are rustling at once. So far as I can learn, the topics which fill the pulpits are just those which fill the Catechism; and the general strain of preaching is not so much alarming as persuasive. The person and work of our Lord form a prominent part of public discourses. Great diversities, of course, obtain among men of various gifts and temper, but in general there is much earnestness in public addresses. In the cities many sermons are read from the manuscripts, but the country parishes scarcely tolerate this." Hall, *Letters*, 2:351.

That my journeying has done any good to my body, I am not sure. I am sure it has been good for my soul. And especially these few days in Scotland have shown me a permanent revival of religion, such as proves to me that God has a favour to his covenanting people. The preciousness of it is, that religion is founded on chapter and verse; free from outcry and sanctimony, and even talk about personal feelings, but is so courageous, active, and tender, that I am as certain as that I am writing these lines, that I am among the best people on earth. A thousand times have I said to myself, "O if my father could just for one hour hear these prayers, and observe these fruits of unadulterated Calvinistic seed!" Here is the fruit of prayers sent up by Rutherfords and Bostons. Don't think all are such, or that these people are faultless. Their faults are as prominent as their good qualities. They have the bad points belonging to strong, sanguineous, choleric, fearless, outspoken people. Their quarrels about hairsbreadths (for they are all agreed about doctrine and order) are inexplicable.[21]

Having returned to England in September, a final letter written from Oxford on September 26, 1851, captures Alexander's reflections on his trip. His observations report on the intersection between "Old World" Christian practice and the advance in scientific technology that he had witnessed (especially in Britain), and what these developments portend for the church and the future of civilization.[22] Although troubled by the spiritual darkness that enshrouded much of the culture and church life that he observed in the countries he visited, Alexander was optimistic about the advance of God's kingdom and the spiritual benefits that would ensue on the benighted people among whom he had spent the past six months. He writes:

My hopes rise beyond what I am able to report during this rapid tour, that God is working by new agencies, and a new *zeitgeist*, and our new world, to bring in a new kingdom. So far from letting my intense and scarce excusable fondness for the relics of darker ages tempt me to wish them back again, or try to imitate them, I am even more filled with a sense of the gigantic progress of the modern arts

---

21. Hall, *Letters*, 2:157.
22. Alexander sometimes castigated himself for living too much "in the past": "I find myself to be an undeniable antiquary. My portrait ought to be taken, as Savigny is caricatured in Germany, with eyes at the back of the head. I have been such a miserable book-worm for forty years, that I live almost in the past." Hall, *Letters*, 2:154.

and civilization. One day at the Exhibition, one day at Birmingham and Manchester, or one day on any one trunk of English railways, is worth volumes to awaken expectation. I have meditated, I trust not unusefully, amidst objects which have the odour of past ages. My reigning sentiment, after hurrying and exciting travel among the thousands of this unspeakably teeming population of Europe, is an impression that men and generations pass away like the herb of the field, but the Word of the Lord abideth forever; his kingdom is coming; his house is going up; his plan is unfolding; old traditionary things which vain man calls eternal, are crumbling; new things predicted, but not expected, are rolling in like a flood; our life and that of our children, is but a link in the great chain. I trust I can sometimes add, "Thy kingdom come: Thy will be done."[23]

---

23. Hall, *Letters*, 2:161–62.

I know no experience which has grown on me more, within a few years, than the impression of nearness of the other world. I have not a corresponding temper; but I certainly realize this as never before. Concerning the future, I do not see things so distinctly and definitely as some; for example, Baxter, in the "Saints' Rest." Howe's "Blessedness of the Righteous," comes nearer my views. But my persuasions of this seem natural, rather than religious. They do often, however, furnish me a motive. Poor unlettered saints (I am now caring for one on his death-bed) unquestionably have more comfort of their faith than we. Books, disquisition, analysis, habits of objection, looking at difficulties, hearkening to latitudinary talk, all tend to break the charm of childlike faith. Would we were more like children!

—J. W. ALEXANDER
November 12, 1855

Chapter 12

FIFTH AVENUE PRESBYTERIAN CHURCH: 1851–1857

Alexander's European tour was a welcome relief from the physical exhaustion he developed while serving at the seminary. His travels and conversation with influential political and church leaders proved to be the right combination of intellectual and spiritual refreshment needed in preparation for his new ministerial responsibilities.

But his joy in returning to pastoral ministry was quickly tempered by learning of the death of his only daughter, Jessie, and declining health of his father.[1] Not only had his daughter passed away unexpectedly while he was in Europe, but Archibald Alexander's health had rapidly deteriorated in the weeks prior to his return. Learning of the seriousness of his father's condition, he journeyed to Princeton to be with his parents and siblings as well as to visit the graveside of his daughter.

By the time James reached Princeton, Archibald Alexander was in the process of making final preparations for care of his family upon his death. Known for his strong piety, Archibald Alexander's conversations during his final days were marked by the same spiritual fortitude and intimate fellowship with God that he had enjoyed throughout the majority of his long life. J. W. Alexander provides a glimpse of his father's final days in a letter penned to Hall on October 18, 1851:

> I write more to stay my mind during hours of waiting than to communicate much. My father seems to grow weaker. He believes himself to be on his death-bed, and this more than any symptoms of a grave

---

1. "During his absence, a member of his own family had been removed by death. He records, 'What a dream of pleasure in being in the bosom of my family! One is not; but Jessie is with the Lord.'" Alexander, *Life of Joseph Addison Alexander*, 2:685. Alexander's daughter, Janetta ("Jessie"), was born June 18, 1850, and died the following summer, August 24, 1851.

character makes us apprehend the same. I think his perception and judgment greater than in any moment of his life. An endless train of minute arrangements have occupied his mind, each of which he has settled in the most summary way. He says his views are what they have always been; that he has never feared to die; that he has never seen so proper a time to die; that all his prayers have been answered; that he has no ecstasy but assured belief; and that no one should pray for his recovery. He says his views of God's goodness are expressed by "How MARVELLOUS is thy loving-kindness, &c." Every one of us, even my dear mother, feels most calm when nearest to the scene of suffering. The affairs of the Church employ far more of my father's words than any family concerns. He talked an hour with me on the prospects of the truth in Scotland. The whole tone of his discourse is free from what John Livingston calls "shows," being precisely what it always was—passing with childlike ease from the settling of a bill to the grace and glory of the gospel. He said, "I have this morning been reviewing the plan of salvation, and assuring myself of my acceptance of it. I am in peace. The transition from this world to another, so utterly unknown, is certainly awful, and would be destructive, were it not guarded by Christ: I know he will do all well."[2]

Alexander's father even found time to send a special care package of books to a needy minister serving on the frontier. "He yesterday ordered a ten-dollar library to be sent to a minister in the West," Alexander reported. Appropriately, Archibald Alexander's final publication in the November issue of the American Messenger was on the topic "A Disciple." As he reflected on his father's impending death and ripening piety, J. W. Alexander remarked, "I am naturally led to think of unseen things, and am strangely beset with mercies, chastenings, and lessons."[3]

Archibald Alexander died a few days later on October 22, 1851. His funeral was held on Friday, October 24, with internment in the cemetery at Princeton in the same section where "little Jessie's...grave was still fresh."[4] Archibald Alexander's death left the school without its founding faculty member and created new questions for how the seminary would maintain the pastoral emphases that he had established.

---

2. Hall, *Letters*, 2:163.
3. Hall, *Letters*, 2:164.
4. Alexander, *Life of Joseph Addison Alexander*, 2:687.

J. W. Alexander hoped that the seminary would keep its pastoral priorities properly aligned. A letter written the following month on November 26, 1851, expresses his concern:

> What they will do in Princeton I know not. Whatever changes may supervene, I earnestly hope there will be none to lower the general standard of our theological training. There is a view of it in which one minister might teach every thing; but if we would maintain that high ground which I solemnly believe American ministers now have in comparison with those of other countries, we must have at least one well-sustained Seminary. This was my father's great desire, which gained strength in his more sober hours, and formed part of his dying conversations with me.[5]

The same letter speaks of Alexander's intention to produce a biography of his father. "Note any thing you can remember or hear, about my father's Philadelphia labours," he remarked. Alexander invited Hall to speak with as many people as he could who had known Archibald Alexander. "Do try and see any old people who know. Could not you find old Mr. Nassau?" he asked. "Addison and I, or one of us, will, *Deo adjuvante* [God willing], write a life." In contrast to the few papers left behind to Samuel Miller's biographer, Alexander was encouraged by the material available on his father.[6] "The MS. autobiography is voluminous, but only for material. How strangely we misjudge often. Dr. Miller left not one line of diary!"[7]

Once back in New York, Alexander took up the responsibilities involved in the pastoral care of his new congregation.[8] He preached to his congregation for the first time following his return from Europe on October 26. Although he had only been abroad for a half year, he found the changes that had taken place in the city during that time "surprising." "Sabbath-traffic" and "grog-drinking," he observed, had both increased.

---

5. Hall, *Letters*, 2:164.
6. A letter from the following May requested that Hall "do any thing you deem discreet, even by placard or advertisement, to get *letters* of my father; this is like to be the desideratum; especially letters before 1812." Hall, *Letters*, 2:175.
7. Hall, *Letters*, 2:165.
8. "The November of 1851 found him at his new home in New York. Duane-street was abandoned and the congregation worshipped in the chapel of the University while the church was in progress in Fifth Avenue." "James Waddell Alexander," 77.

Besides the dangers that these developments posed to the life of piety, Alexander was soon troubled by his congregation's apparent indifference to the city's destitute citizens. The combination of material wealth and interest in building a magnificent edifice had blinded their eyes to the pressing poverty and spiritual needs of their urban neighbors.[9] Memories of the lavish grandeur and empty religiosity of the French cathedrals he had recently observed likely came to mind. In a letter written just a month after his return from Europe, Alexander bared his concerns to Hall:

> I am troubled in my mind at the sort of church I am coming to. I certainly should never have accepted the call if I had dreamt of such outlay. I fear the total exclusion of the poor, and the insufficiency of my voice. As I had no hand in it, and know myself to be crossed rather than gratified by it, I hope God will turn it to some good. On Sunday I urged the destitutions of New York, and proposed the erection of a free church down town. On Monday a man whom I never knew before came and offered me $1,000 towards it.[10]

By early December, Alexander's frustration with his congregation's indifference to the pressing spiritual and social needs of the city was reaching a fever pitch. A letter on December 2, 1851, details his concerns while shedding valuable light on the ministry challenges that confronted churches in the growing urban setting of cities such as New York in mid-nineteenth-century America:

> We are among a good many open lots and much rubbish; and to feeling, as far from the New York I knew, as if in another city. I find a good smart walk from here to Trinity Church quite tonical. My mind works incessantly on such themes as these:—the abounding misery; the unreached masses; the waste of church energy on the rich; its small operation on the poor; emigrant wretchedness; our boy-population; our hopeless prostitutes; our 4000 grog-shops; the absence of poor from Presbyterian churches; the farce of our

---

9. Alexander's congregation was extremely wealthy: "From the day of its opening (December 19, 1852) everything in the secularities of the church was highly prosperous. In less than a month the whole cost of the ground and building (more than one hundred thousand dollars) was paid, and all the pews (204) sold or rented. In the same month the annual contribution for Foreign Missions amounted to $3,300; in the next month that for Domestic Missions to $3,750; in the next, for the Board of Education, $3,500." "James Waddell Alexander," 77.

10. Hall, *Letters*, 2:164.

church-alms; confinement of our church-efforts to pew-holders; the do-nothing life of our Christian professors, in regard to the masses; our copying the Priest and Levite in the parable; our need of a Christian Lord Bacon, to produce a Novum Organon of philanthropy; our dread of innovation; our luxury and pride. I have preached twice on some of these things; but I work at the lever very feebly. Since I saw the drinking customs of Britain, I am almost a tee-totaler, and half-disposed to go for a Maine law against venders of drink.[11]

Troubled by the insularity of his congregation's outlook, Alexander's personal understanding of the global horizons of God's kingdom had broadened in recent months. In particular, his European trip had forever changed his awareness of the international dimension of God's kingdom advance. Parochial narrowness had given way to a more comprehensive embrace of the ecclesiological diversity that can properly exist among the body of Christ in the countries and cultures in which the church is rooted. Strong denominational convictions were now softened a bit as Alexander pondered the recent split that took place within American Presbyterianism in 1837. "After settling a little from the shocks of late events, and looking back on my tour," he commented to Hall, "I find my judgment of differences among Christians somewhat modified. Surely our battle is too momentous, to leave much time or zeal to spend on niceties of old school and new."[12]

In addition to the pastoral frustrations Alexander notes, his letter on December 2 also includes thoughtful reflections on how God uses pain in the maturation of the Christian life.[13] His observations contrast Protestant and Roman Catholic teaching on the topic and the practical benefits that accompany the presence of pain in the ripening of biblical piety:

> Surely there are divine uses of pain which we cannot fully understand. Nor can we reason much about the rules of its mission to individuals. The amount of suffering such persons as — — and — — have endured often amazes and puzzles me. Yet in — —'s case the

---

11. Hall, *Letters*, 2:165–66.
12. Hall, *Letters*, 2:166.
13. Thoughtful meditations on pain and patience, "written as a pastoral gift to an esteemed friend, who had been more than two years confined to her dwelling by a dangerous, lingering, and sometimes exceedingly painful malady," can be found in a biblically rich treatment of the topic Alexander published the following year: James W. Alexander, *Patience* (Philadelphia: Presbyterian Board of Publication, 1852).

spiritual joy resulting is almost as specific as of a medicine. I have thought much of this as a point in divinity. The Papists have missed the right doctrine of pain; but have we made enough of it? Some day we shall see what it was sent on good people for. I have known moments when it has seemed to me a great boon to have the will broken, and self-pleasing mortified."[14]

But of all the things mentioned in his letter to Hall, it was the recent death of his father which most captured his emotions. Alexander missed his father's wise counsel in his life and felt at a loss in his father's absence. "Ah! How I daily feel 'I have lost my adviser!' How often, 'I must tell this to my father,' and then I awake to the reality. But there is no bitterness in the reflection." Memory of his father's wise instruction gave Alexander hope as he pondered the impact of his own life upon his children. "If it please God to touch our sons," he said, "our work will seem more clearly less needed here."[15]

1852

As he settled back into the responsibilities of pastoral ministry after the Christmas season, memories of his recent trip to Europe still captured Alexander's imagination. His European tour had clearly broadened his thinking on the catholicity of the church. He even found reasons in one of his letters to celebrate the leavening influence of Roman Catholic teaching on French national life despite its various doctrinal deviations.[16] "When we consider that France was all but atheistic, we must regard even the acquisitions of Popery as conversions to a sort of Christianity. I find it very hard to swallow the tenent, that the existing church of Rome is incapable of being improved, and is to be looked at only as for hell-fire." But,

---

14. Hall, *Letters*, 2:165.
15. Hall, *Letters*, 2:166.
16. While Alexander saw elements of truth in Roman Catholic doctrine, he believed Roman Catholicism fraught with theological error and a dangerous distortion of the Bible's teaching on salvation. Remarks made at an earlier stage of life during an outbreak of disease remained true in his thinking on the Roman Catholic Church in later years: "Popery is a delusion greatly destructive to souls. If these thousand Papists were to die next week with Cholera, I have every reason to think that not one of them would have a conception of any preparation beyond the *opus operatum* [the work performed] of ceremonies. This is my conclusion from personal conversation, and various reports of credible members of my church. O that the Bible and the accompanying Spirit of God might rid the world of blindness and impenitence!" Hall, *Letters*, 1:192.

for all his optimism in this regard, he was careful to qualify his enthusiasm, noting, "My prophetic specs are very dim."[17]

His recent trip to Europe likely gave impetus to an important message he preached on February 8, 1852, titled "Our Modern Unbelief." Providing an impressive overview of ancient and modern unbelief, Alexander's printed sermon includes insightful observations on how the life of piety is nurtured and matured in the context of radical unbelief and opposition to the gospel message. His message draws attention to the important role that revival, spiritual renewal, and prayer have played in pushing back the tides of unbelief.

> Yet, churches and Bibles depend for their efficacy on the direct influences of the Holy Spirit, an agency which it is part of the reigning infidelity to disbelieve, but for which we will pray, as the chief hope of our salvation. Who can tell how far the revolutionary atheism of France might have become the established irreligion of America, if it had not pleased God to make our country the theatre of mighty and extensive revivals? Perhaps I address some who love to recall these awakenings, as the scenes in which they were made to know Christ. Such will join in testifying, that the progress of convincing and converting grace did not wait for the tedious preparative of philosophic reply and formal argument, but went forth to consume at once and forever the difficulties of the sceptic and the cavils of the deist, as the flame of a conflagration reduces combustible obstacles in its rapid and blazing career. All other means together will not do so much to rid our land of antichristian scoffing, as would one general communication of power from on high. Increased prayer for this fresh dispensation is the duty of the Church. This is the defensive means which Satan and his hosts dread, while they cannot emulate. They can blaspheme, they can argue, they can fight, they can write books, and, if need be, quote Scripture for their purpose; but pray they cannot.[18]

As he reflected upon the effects of his ministry, Alexander was encouraged by the impact he had on a young man who once sat in his catechism class. "A youth died the other day, at 19, who said he had used every day for eleven years a prayer I gave him on a card, when my catechumen,"

---

17. Hall, *Letters*, 2:168.
18. Alexander's message was included in a volume of sermons first published in 1858: James W. Alexander, *Discourses on Common Topics of Christian Faith and Practice* (New York: Charles Scribner, 1858; repr., Birmingham, Ala.: Solid Ground Christian Books, 2004), 46–47.

he reported. His ruminations led to thoughts on the role of the church's educational ministry. He wrote:

> I am getting to think professing religion much less presumptive of grace, than once I did. Nor do I see that any strictness at the door helps the matter. Have we not added to the New Testament notion of communicating in the Lord's Supper? The anabaptist essays at a church of pure regenerate believers have not worked well. I used the word "catechumen" in the vulgar sense; but the κατηχουμενοχ was as such unbaptized—under schooling—long watched—slowly indoctrinated. The Church *as a school* has declined; hence the Sunday School has been built up alongside.[19]

A letter from early February expresses Alexander's concern at the popularity of Valentine's Day cards! A growing phenomenon in American culture, Alexander believed the cards were a form of commercialization injurious to the nature of true love while also lending themselves to aberrant expressions of sexuality.

> I don't know how it is so elsewhere, but here the Valentines have become a plague. As the day approaches, whole rows of shops of every sort fill their windows with valentines, from a penny up, which from having been amatory have become cynical and opprobrius, affording boobies and snobs an opportunity of venting cheap gall on a neighbour. For the first time I find some tending to irreligion. You have seen the account of the perfectionism and promiscuous abomination. How few cards after all the devil has in his pack; this is only the "Brethren and Sisters of the Free Spirit" over again. It more than fulfils predictions made by Nettleton, which at the time I thought absurd.[20]

Alexander's concern for the spiritual welfare of his denomination found expression in observations he penned in late February 1852 on the vitality of contemporary pulpit ministry and the role that public worship serves in the strengthening of the church's witness.[21] While he

---

19. Hall, *Letters*, 2:169–70.

20. Hall, *Letters*, 2:169. Hall notes in a footnote that Alexander's remarks were in reference to "Public assemblies held in Broadway of the advocates of 'Free Love'—eventually suppressed by the police."

21. Alexander's letter also commented on the status of Irish and Scotch preaching: "I observe an absence of all 'onction' in all Irish Presbyterian preachers. It is very different with the modern Scotch school. Guthrie of Edinburgh talks of coming hither for a jaunt.

recognized the importance of preaching in the church's public ministry, he was also convinced of the critical role that worship is to have in the maturation of biblical piety:

> I admit that our period is singularly barren of great divines and great preachers. Yet the average working talent, I apprehend, was never greater. As to what is called pulpit eloquence, I grow in disbelief of its importance. The gaping multitudes who fill churches are little reached, as to the main matter. *Worship* is certainly overshadowed by our sermons. How few quoters of our Directory ever quote p. 497, where the sermon is compared with "the *more important* duties of prayer and praise."[22]

A man-centered approach to church growth was also of concern. Alexander queried whether too much had been made about men's gifts, planning, and money when it came to the ordinary and often uneventful daily discipleship that God uses to grow believers into the likeness of His Son. He also raised concerns as to whether or not the church had begun to distrust God's Word as the foundation for its spiritual vitality.[23] The natural tendency to count numbers and identify material affluence as a sign of spiritual success was misguided at best and a form of worldliness at worst when it came to assessing what matters most in relation to the church's real purpose in the eyes of God. A number of questions framed his thinking on these matters:

> Whether we do not err in ciphering so much about the time, men, and money it will take to convert the world? Whether God's plan is not to work upon, in, and by a peculiar people, elect and called; εκλεκτôι? "little flock"? Whether the other world is not the great collection of saints? Whether God is not taking out of this world a constant select addition to that? And whether, consequently, both hopes and fears do not mislead us, as to the extensiveness of visible success?[24]

Guthrie draws more crowds than anybody since Chalmers. He has both poetry and wit, with plenty of fire." Hall, *Letters*, 2:173–74.

22. Hall, *Letters*, 2:171.

23. For an important treatment of this topic, see J. W. Alexander, "Distrust of the Word," in *The Living Pulpit, or Eighteen Sermons by Eminent Living Divines of The Presbyterian Church*, ed. Rev. Elijah Wilson (Philadelphia: C. Sherman & Son, Printers, 1857), 109–28.

24. Hall, *Letters*, 2:171.

Alexander's letter also notes the increasing phenomena of "spiritual-knocking" occurring in the city. Concurrent with the growth in church attendance was a simultaneous growth in occult spirituality gaining widespread acceptance among the city's population:

> Absurd as it sounds, the spiritual-knocking business is like to be really alarming. If Satan ever interferes, one might think it would be in such mesmeric and analogous delusions. I am told there are scores of distinct and stated meetings in town, for these spiritual investigations. Miss Martineau, in her late book, avows high-mesmerism and utter atheism.[25]

By early spring, a religious stirring began to take place among Alexander's congregation. His prayers for spiritual renewal were beginning to find fruition and would portend an even greater awakening that would take place in his congregation and throughout the city in 1857 to 1858. A letter dated April 3, 1852, highlights the religious impressions that were forming among his people:

> We have not the least stir in our congregation; but at no time have I known so many persons under a deep religious concern. I have perceived something unusual in the manner of hearers, for some weeks. The proportion of non-professors in our assembly is small. In every place where I have been, I have observed that I never have marked increase of hearers, but always a striking adhesiveness in those who come. We are suffering greatly for want of a good place for meeting; it is most obvious in our weekly lecture. A lady came to me under great convictions, produced by the funeral services of E. B.[26]

While Alexander rejoiced at these developments, he soon found his health weakening in response to the increased ministry demands that accompanied the religious stirring. "My health has not been improving lately," he told Hall. "Constant pastoral visits and anxieties, and mental work without relaxation, have run me down exceedingly, so that I am sleepless in a good many nights, and quite nervous by day."[27]

Although he was busy with pastoral labors, Alexander found time to prepare his father's writings on moral philosophy for publication. "It will

---

25. Hall, *Letters*, 2:171.
26. Hall, *Letters*, 2:172.
27. Hall, *Letters*, 2:173.

rank with his Evidences," he said, "but will awaken more opposition. He wrote nothing more simple, clear, or convincing. It is the only work which he left ready."[28]

Alexander's letter on April 3 also expresses concern regarding the infidelity of recent German immigrants.[29] The majority of German immigrants who came to America in the eighteenth century were pious Christians committed to Protestant catechisms and confessions. But the present influx of German nationals flooding New York City ports was marked by a pronounced hostility to the teachings of Christianity:

> Does any one properly estimate the approaching certain influence of the Germans, as a power in our country? I often hear as much German as English in my day's walk. Of all the Protestant portion, nine-tenths are infidel. All I meet with are radical. Most of the German newspapers are infidel, and some blasphemous. A friend of mine heard some talking yesterday; one said, "Our grand error in Germany was not using the guillotine; let them employ it freely, and let them begin with the *Pietisten*." The second Psalm comes to my mind as affording the only hope.[30]

As the months passed, Alexander continued to struggle with the disparity between the splendor of the church building in which he served and the obvious needs of the city's population who could not afford the cost of pew rentals. The problem that Alexander confronted with regard to the seating arrangements within his sanctuary had to do with nineteenth-century church practice for raising funds to pay for the church's expenses. The system made provision for the costs involved in building and operating churches by charging prices for "rental" of pews. While the practice was effective in securing funds for the operational costs of the church, it excluded large numbers of people who otherwise would benefit from the church's ministry but could not afford (or find room!) to be present if they so desired.

---

28. Hall, *Letters*, 2:173.
29. Alexander's experience with German immigrants may have varied from that of other parts of the country where German nationals settled. A number of the new immigrants had strong ties to the Lutheran Church. Orr notes: "Between 1830 and 1860, close to one and a half million Germans migrated to the United States, hence Lutheran growth was three times that of the general population." J. Edwin Orr, *The Event of the Century: The 1857–1858 Awakening* (Wheaton: International Awakening Press, 1989), 5.
30. Hall, *Letters*, 2:173.

Although the system was not changed during Alexander's tenure, he believed that once the church's operational debt was canceled a number of pews should be left open and rented at a low rate in order that the poor could attend services. In correspondence at the end of December 1852, he remarked: "I wish I could turn out about twenty pews of rich folks and fill them with poor. But this is one of those dreams not to be realized." "I never was stronger in my opinion, that all church-sittings ought to be free. Yet we can't reach this without establishments, endowment, and all that," he wrote.[31]

Despite the frustration he had with the pew rental system, he recognized that his preaching gifts were a good fit for the congregation that he served. He knew that God's gifting is matched with the proper positioning of a man's talents to a specific ministry location. The congregation at the Fifth Avenue Presbyterian Church placed a premium on its pulpit ministry, and Alexander's preaching style fit well with their expectations. Even though some of the interest in his ministry was due to his oratorical eloquence, Alexander knew that God could still bring spiritual blessing into the lives of people who come to church for the wrong reasons. He was careful not to allow the interests of his hearers, however appropriate or misguided, to determine how he exercised his pulpit ministry to his congregation. A letter on June 21, 1852, explains his reasoning:

> I am in a very false position as to my edifice [its costliness], while I never saw a *congregation* so suited to me. They are all drawn around me, by partiality for my explanatory and uncoloured ministrations. For years I have seen people who want to hear oratory, &c., come once or twice, and then depart. Elderly and afflicted persons, of the plainer sort, are chiefly those who drop in. Once I scuffled to be other than I am; now I see a providence in it, and even rejoice. I look back, and see that I have often erred by trying to be (1) more original than I am, (2) more animated; especially No. 2. No man can be anybody else. Don't you, as you go on, feel increasing complacency in variety of gifts? We could not miss a —— , or a —— , little as you or I fancy them. I was pleased when a friend of McNeile's said: "He is a *teacher*." That we can all be. If tears break out—well; but the teaching is effective, sans halloo and spasm. I have lately had unusual comfort in my lectures, by omitting my little notes of one or two pages; and, after hard study of the context and more of the words, going

---

31. Hall, *Letters*, 2:183.

on without any sort of MS. The briefest notes ripple and detain the current. This method I seldom venture on, on Sundays; for in the morning I read every word—usually.[32]

During the month of July, Alexander traveled to Princeton for a meeting with his mother and siblings. Apparently, he had little idea of the purpose for which he had been requested to return to his family home when he first left New York City.

> On the 6th, Dr. James Alexander was called to Princeton, "little knowing," as he says himself, "what he was sent for." On getting out of the carriage he found the house still, and entering the study he was shocked to see his mother lying in a state of alarming weakness on the same sofa from which his father had been carried the previous October. She looked pale and haggard, but rose on her son's entrance, and during the afternoon sat with the family, drank tea, and engaged in conversation. That evening she was forced to go to bed. In the morning she dressed herself and walked across the passage up stairs to the room over her son Addison's study. This was her last effort. She sank rapidly during the day, and at noon fell into a gentle sleep from which she was never aroused. She breathed away her spirit at five minutes before nine P.M. Several members of her family were standing by, and one of her sons was kneeling in prayer. There was no convulsion of her person, and there has seldom been an instance of a more tranquil or painless death.[33]

The emotions surrounding his mother's death weighed heavily on Alexander's heart as he returned to his pastoral duties in New York City. The coming months were exceedingly busy, and by early summer of the following year Alexander had once again experienced a collapse in health. Fatigue had set in, and Alexander was paying the price for the unselfish devotion that he demonstrated to his pastoral calling. Correspondence from June details the problem:

> The past winter has been one of too unremitted labour; I am conscious of having had a pride which made me do double duty, to prepare for the incapacities of summer. The consequence is, that my nervous system is very much shattered. I do not feel it *inter loquendum* [in conversation], but afterwards and in any excitement which

---

32. Hall, *Letters*, 2:176.
33. Alexander, *Life of Joseph Addison Alexander*, 2:697–98.

unmans me. God rules—but I have serious apprehensions about being able to bear up. I find my four-mile heat, walking to the University, quite disabling.[34]

Alexander's annual summer vacation did little to rejuvenate his flagging health. Writing from Newport on August 26, 1852, he stated that he had not found his "health much benefited, except by the repose." "Within a fortnight," he remarked, "I have had a bad turn of disabling rheumatism."[35]

While Alexander's health might not have improved, his time in Newport reoriented his thinking regarding the spiritual emphases that should characterize his preaching. Although his church building was not yet completed by the conclusion of his summer vacation, his understanding of the priorities that should mark his return to pulpit ministry had been refocused in a way commensurate with his developing spiritual maturity.[36]

> I have this day brought home my little flock from Newport; thanking God that we have been kept in life, and that some of the number have derived such benefit. Our church still lingers. The pews are in, but not the pulpit. I am less and less elated with the magnificence of this pile. I feel however, a growing desire to spend what is left of me, in plainer, simpler, more instructive preaching.[37]

The "plainer, simpler, more instructive preaching" to which Alexander aspired is well captured in his enthusiasm for Cecil's remark: "Eloquence is vehement simplicity."[38]

As he reflected upon his own pulpit inadequacies, Alexander's vacation provided opportunity for further reflection on how many of the once strong pulpit ministries found within the churches of New England had declined in recent years. Literary emphases, Alexander noted, were predominant. Elegant rhetorical productions had replaced biblically grounded messages delivered "in power and demonstration of the

---

34. Hall, *Letters*, 2:176–77.
35. Hall, *Letters*, 2:178.
36. Eloquence without emphasis is of little value. Alexander came to value the focused preaching approach that characterized the best preachers in the Reformed experimental preaching heritage: "But you carry away no *one* deep impression, as from Chalmers, Edwards, or Nettleton." Hall, *Letters*, 2:217.
37. Hall, *Letters*, 2:179.
38. Hall, *Letters*, 1:165.

Spirit." Its effect was chilling, and a spiritual stupor had now shrouded their public gatherings:

> I am in low spirits about the condition of the New England churches. The whole feeling, in their assemblies, is different from that of ours—bad as we are. The choirs carry matters clear away from the congregation, who in very numerous instances stand during singing, gazing up into the singers' gallery. The sermons are never expository; and those which are reputed the best are extensively on general topics of national law, ethics, and philanthropy. A sort of cold revival is superinduced in many of them, which adds communicants, but does not help the matter much. An ordinary laying open of a large context, especially with any stress laid on particular pregnant expressions, would, I am sure, be received with surprise in most places. They admit themselves, that the new generation of preachers is giving all its zeal to the construction of rhetorical specimens.[39]

Despite his misgivings over the decline of the New England pulpit ministry, Alexander was encouraged to learn that Hall had been invited to teach some of his father's courses at the seminary while the school sought his replacement. Alexander provided Hall counsel on his new assignment while highlighting the approach that his father had taken to the teaching of pastoral theology. Alexander's thoughts can be found in a letter on September 23, 1852:

> I am glad you are willing to do the service in Princeton. Young men need and desire the very plainest directions how to go about their work. Religious biographies will furnish many suggestions.... My father used to go largely into ministerial life and ways, marriage, economy, choice of a field, principles about settlement and removal, and a great deal concerning preaching, that is commonly left to Homiletics, or, more properly speaking, omitted. I mean all that considers preaching in regard to the private religion, &c., of the minister. I know he also lectured fully and frankly on revivals; on missions; on call to foreign work. Be advised not to withhold facts and deductions from your own ministry.[40]

By late October, Alexander's latest collection of sermons titled *Consolation: In Discourses on Select Topics, Addressed to the Suffering People of God*

---

39. Hall, *Letters*, 2:179.
40. Hall, *Letters*, 2:179.

had been published.[41] The sermons model the compassionate pastoral care that Alexander provided through his weekly pulpit ministry at the Fifth Avenue Presbyterian Church as he sought to comfort his congregation in the trials and tragedies of daily life.

Alexander's final letter of the year speaks of the various pastoral challenges he now faced with the growing size of his congregation. An opening paragraph in his letter on December 31, 1852, details the matters he was addressing:

> Here is my last letter of the old year, with my best wishes for you and yours, for the new. This has been a period of events and mercies for me. Some of the things, which I dare say people think tend to elate me, have a quite contrary effect; especially the worldly increase of my cure. Seldom, if ever, have I had any private exercise more solemn, than in the whole progress of this matter. And I never more felt the necessity of dealing plainly with my people. My congregation is fearfully large. Every pew which was not sold, is rented, except about two and a half. One of my responsibilities is that of begging and dispensing large alms. Yesterday I had to raise some money for poor members of a German congregation. I went nowhere for this purpose, but mentioned it in calls, and received $68. On the first Sunday we collect for our Foreign Missions, and I hope we shall do better than ever.[42]

The letter also includes Alexander's discussion on the application of Sabbath principles to matters of public transit within the city. Like his fellow pastors throughout the centuries, Alexander was called upon to give guidance in the contextual application of biblical principles of Sabbath-keeping to the new circumstances modern technology created for the emerging urban life of nineteenth-century American cities. It is not surprising that Alexander's observations on a conscientious keeping of the Sabbath principle should conclude with a reminder of the way in which New Testament teaching on God's grace is to be determinative for defining the details of how each believer lives out "the obedience of faith." He writes:

---

41. James W. Alexander, *Consolation: In Discourses on Select Topics, Addressed to the Suffering People of God* (New York: Charles Scribner, 1852; repr., Morgan, Pa.: Soli Deo Gloria Publications, 1992).

42. Hall, *Letters*, 2:183.

The question of riding in our street cars on Sunday, is agitating our community. I have not been able to decide it. The poor go in cars; the rich in coaches. The number of horses and men employed is less than if there were no cars. It is a query whether as many cars as these would not be demanded by those (among half a million) who have lawful occasion to journey. If so, the question of duty would be reduced to one of individual vocation to this amount of locomotion. The whole matter of the Christian Sabbath is a little perplexed in my mind. 1. All that our Lord says on it, is *prima facie* [at first appearance] on the side of relaxation. 2. The apostles, who enforce, and as it were re-enact every other command of the ten, never advert to this. 3. Even to Gentile converts, they lay no stress on this, which might be expected to come first, among externals. 4. According to the letter, Paul teaches the Colossians (ii.16) not to be scrupulous about Sabbaths. I am not therefore surprised, that Calvin had doubts on this subject. The very strict views of the Sabbath have prevailed in no part of Christendom unconnected with the British Isles. I must wait for more light. I admit the fact, that spiritual religion has most flourished where the strict opinions have prevailed. My good father used to say: "Be very strict yourself; be very lenient in judging your neighbour." I have always taken milk, without scruple; which is an offence to hundreds of good people among us. Some began to have qualms about Sunday gas; but on inquiry they found that the labour which produced it fell on Thursday or Friday. As I always give my people a motto for the year, and preach on it, I have chosen "My Grace is sufficient for thee."[43]

1853—"My Grace Is Sufficient for Thee"

Although the problem of "pew holding" would remain a source of constant irritation to Alexander, his congregation continued to prosper and grow under his ministry. A letter on March 9, 1853, describes his growing responsibilities: "With more than two hundred pew-holders, I find my circuit wide enough. In regard to visiting, I am forced to seek how to please God and not man. Cases of illness, &c., break in very much on what I have heard called a 'routine of rounds.'"[44]

The letter also includes additional observations on Alexander's emotions and valuable information on the weekly ministry in which he was

---

43. Hall, *Letters*, 2:183–84.
44. Hall, *Letters*, 2:184.

engaged. The increasing burden of the ministry weighed heavily upon his conscience while at the same time continuing to take a toll on his health:

> Our congregations are full to a degree which oppresses me. I believe only half a pew is unlet. Our collection for Education Board, on Sunday, was $3,510. Our weekly lecture is crowded. With much external attention there is little proportionable coming out by profession. Next Sunday we shall admit about twenty on certificate, and six on examination. Of the whole twenty-six, about twenty are made up of husband and wife. I am very soberly apprehensive of failing under my burden, and that before long. I generally lose my rest on Sunday night, and on the last had the addition of a vomiting. In no winter have I had more of nervous tremor. But I try to disregard these symptoms, as I see no way out of my present duties.[45]

While the demands of his ministry were increasingly fatiguing, his reading of Christian ministerial biography provided inspiration for pursuing his daily round of duties. "Bickersteth's life [by Birks]," he said, "is a plain book but O how full of healthy, ardent piety! I think him one of the loveliest ministerial models." He felt differently about a recent biography on Thomas Chalmers, one of the great Scottish theologians of his time.[46] "Chalmers's 'Life' [by Hanna] contains an extraordinary amount of trifling matter. The plan seems to have been to publish all that could be raked and scraped. It is, however, a wonderful monument to his frankness of nature."[47]

In a letter written one month later, his correspondence brims with optimism regarding the spiritual awakening taking root among his flock. He was especially elated by the congregation's interest in establishing a mission church among the poor. "I think there is more stir among our good people than I ever knew, about the condition of the poor, ragged boys, &c." Sensitive to the changing demographics among the various neighborhoods of the city, he was eager to move quickly in establishing

---

45. Hall, *Letters*, 2:185.
46. Alexander's interest in Chalmers's life and ministry can also be found in an earlier review contributed to the *Biblical Repertory* in 1842: James W. Alexander, "The Works of Thomas Chalmers, D.D., and L.L.D., Professor of Theology in the University of Edinburgh, and Corresponding Member of the Royal Institute of France," *The Biblical Repertory and Princeton Review* 14, no. 4 (October 1842): 562–83. Chalmers's experiential preaching and active social philanthropy were of special interest to Alexander in the urban ministry settings where he labored.
47. Hall, *Letters*, 2:184.

Protestant mission works in each of the districts. Although few of his fellow clergy shared in his vision for outreach, he was undeterred in his missionary enthusiasm on behalf of his fellow citizens:

> I cannot get any other churches to agree with me in a favourite scheme, to have a great and inviting building erected, far down town, with a striking preacher, seats free, and no proximate regard to what is called a church-organization. Our folks are nearly ripe for a mission church; but I do not mean it shall be down town. The churches left in that quarter are nearly empty, as for example the spacious North Dutch. Soon every thing below will be warehouses, &c. The teeming population of the upper wards are falling a prey to the Catholics. O that our sect-divisions did not make territorial operation impracticable! How much more we could do, if we could only mark off nine squares, as our own field—for schools, church, charity, care of poor, &c. I sometimes scruple whether a uniformity, like Sweden, properly worked, would not overbalance the advantages of our ultra free inquiry and individual judgment.[48]

Although interest in city missions was increasing among Alexander's congregation, the same could not be said of the Presbyterian Church.[49] A letter written to Hall in late April 1853 expresses the frustration Alexander felt toward his denomination for not being more aggressive in church planting and ministry to the city's poor. Tragically, the denominational bureaucracy of the Presbyterian Church had failed to keep pace with the increase in population and growing ministry needs of the city. Ultimately, Alexander came to realize that the outreach he envisioned would have to begin at the congregational level and not wait upon denominational initiative.[50]

> We spent hours in Presbytery, upon city destitution and church extension. I came away with a heavy heart, persuaded that as a

---

48. Hall, *Letters*, 2:187–88.
49. A statement from the following November balances Alexander's criticism: "Our whole system of modern means works slowly, and seems often to work backward. And yet, as to the influence on the world at large, it has not been ever greater, in my opinion, since the Reformation, than at this moment. I do not see that Christianity was ever more enlarging itself." Hall, *Letters*, 2:192.
50. For a powerful but unpublished sermon on the life of radical discipleship to which every Christian is called, see James W. Alexander, "Festus and Paul," The James Waddell Manuscript Collection. Special Collections. Princeton Theological Seminary Library, 1853.

Presbytery we shall do nothing. Whatever is effected must be done congregationally. Just think—our great and wealthy Presbytery has not one preaching station for the poor and wicked. As it is, the only work that is doing, is by the irresponsible City Tract Society, under A. R. Wetmore. The plea of some is, that the only mode is to set off colonies from large churches. But how can we get our members to leave us? And the worst necessities are just where self-supporting churches can never exist. I would rejoice from the bottom of my heart if the twenty best families in my charge would leave me to found a new church. But this would by no means reach the layer of population that I have in view. We opened a mission—school last Sunday: five in the morning, twenty-two in the afternoon.[51]

As spring turned into summer, Alexander's letters comment on aspects of his vacation and travel. The letters of this period also record some of the continuing health concerns with which he struggled. A letter dated June 24, 1853, sent from Sharon Springs, New York, states he felt "refreshed and rested by being here, but not well."[52] Writing once again from Newport on July 26, 1853, he notes, "I was very poorly, with choleroid affections, in New York, but have rallied."[53]

Alexander "returned to New York early in September, and was soon busy over the pages of Montaigne, Fenelon, Quintilian, and Plato—also in his wonted laborious pastoral duties."[54] While illness had plagued his summer months, Alexander was eager to resume ministering to his congregation.

Congregational Worship

Upon his return to pastoral ministry in 1851 with the newly established Fifth Avenue Presbyterian Church, Alexander had implemented changes in the worship style of the congregation so as to avoid incorporation of external means common in New Measures evangelism which were used to manipulate the emotions of their auditors.[55] As one writer observes, "The popular devices for effect through externals he despised, and one

---

51. Hall, *Letters*, 2:188.
52. Hall, *Letters*, 2:189.
53. Hall, *Letters*, 2:190.
54. Alexander, *Life of Joseph Addison Alexander*, 2:731.
55. For an important study examining the history of American Presbyterian worship practice, see Julius Melton, *Presbyterian Worship in America: Changing Patterns Since 1787* (Richmond: John Knox Press, 1967).

of his first successes in the Fifth Avenue church worship was to restore congregational singing under the lead of a single precentor, standing, as in old time, near the pulpit, and only *assisted* by the organ."[56]

While worship practice was important to Alexander, references to how it was conducted at the Fifth Avenue Presbyterian Church are infrequent in his communications with Hall. Observations found in his correspondence from early November 1853 provide additional insight on his approach to the practice of public worship in his congregation:

> We are in an odd state as to music. Lowell Mason is our leader; but since his return from Europe he is so bent on severe, plain tunes, and congregational signing, that while I am tickled amazingly, the people are disappointed. His success in making the people sing has been marvelous. I enter no house where so many join. But I fear we cannot hold it against such odds.[57]

In an extended footnote on this topic, Hall provides portions of a letter written to him from Alexander's leader of congregational worship, Lowell Mason. Alexander was intimately involved in preparation of the worship format to insure a biblical focus was maintained in the elements and order of service. Mason's remarks provide a window into Alexander's interest in ordering the worship services of his congregation.

> During the four years or more that I had the privilege of leading the singing exercises in Dr. Alexander's church, he often spoke to me on the subject. Indeed, I did not often meet him when this was not a leading topic of remark. He always spoke with great decision, and once certainly he told me, when it was suggested that there might be danger of a return to choir-singing, that he would not remain pastor of a church where the singing was exclusively in the hands of a choir. He often spoke to me after the public service, of the gratification he experienced from the psalmody, and I well remember on one occasion he told me he had never before enjoyed so much the exercise of song in the house of the Lord. He spoke to me also of the growing importance of the singing service in his own estimation. He used to attend our little preparatory meeting, often making remarks, suggesting topics, &c., and always closing with prayer.[58]

---

56. "James Waddell Alexander," 78.
57. Hall, *Letters*, 2:191.
58. Hall, *Letters*, 2:191.

Pastoral Reflections

A sensitive and thoughtful man, Alexander continually reflected on his growth in pastoral understanding.[59] A notable entry on this topic can be found in a letter dated November 11, 1853. With the hindsight of age, Alexander came to place new emphasis on the depth of his congregation's piety in ways that he had not in the earlier years of his ministry. The spiritual growth of his congregation became a primary focus of his ministerial labor. "I find this great change in my pastoral experience: I am more concerned about the *quality* of religion in my flock, than when I was young. Sometimes I am almost as glad to observe a ripening, as once to observe a conversion," he said. "A few instances, very striking, have come under my knowledge."[60]

His letter continues with reflections on his preaching style. Unlike his father, Archibald Alexander, Alexander's preaching seemed better suited to the instruction of the saints than that of delivering hortatory messages to the unsaved. He grieved over this perceived inadequacy in his preaching, wishing that he had been more effective in delivering messages "alarming" and "pungent." He writes:

> Doubtless from some grand defect in my preaching its influence has been most on professors; this beyond any hopes of mine. Awakenings are rare with me. My father long ago pointed out this evil in my sermons, and it has caused me many a pang. The invitatory part, I am always free to hold forth; but in every instance when I have tried the alarming and more pungent, I have been like David in Saul's harness. I am often depressed beyond expression at the apparent waste of my exertions. Private addresses and expository lectures have done most of the little good that appears. Sad, sad, to think how nearly the glass is run out![61]

While Alexander may have been frustrated at certain aspects of his preaching style, he was not without some encouragement from that which he knew he could do well. He drew particular satisfaction from a series of recent lectures that he had delivered to his congregation. "I have arrived at

---

59. "The interruptions of a city pastor are sometimes the occasions of his chief usefulness. I have had three to-day, all beyond my church pale." Hall, *Letters*, 2:191.
60. Hall, *Letters*, 2:192.
61. Hall, *Letters*, 2:192–93.

the last Feast of Tabernacles, in lecturing on the Life of Christ. It has been by far the most delightful homiletical exercise I ever tried," he stated.[62]

1854

Alexander's introductory letter to Hall at the beginning of January 1854 describes his ongoing struggle with the presence of remaining sin in his life. Like many Christians before him, his growing maturity in the Christian life made him increasingly sensitive to areas where sin found opportunity for manifestation. He writes:

> I wish you and yours a happy New Year. The last has been to us a year of mercies. As years roll on, the most despondent thought I have is a fear of never being much better in this world; I am glad there is another. I used to make resolutions at the new year; but now I am disheartened. The same habits, the same tendencies, the same selfishness, the same "old man," the warring sarx.[63]

Although Alexander was discouraged with the progress that he had made in his personal piety, he was heartened by completion of the biography on his father titled *The Life of Archibald Alexander, D. D.* "I expect to go to press this week," he told Hall. "No one knows the anxiety I have had in preparing this work, chiefly from the absence of diaries and letters for the last forty years. I think I have benefited, however," he said, "by conversing with so many of my father's best thoughts."[64]

Congregational Life

Alexander's letter also notes that two hundred twenty children were enrolled in the mission "ragged school." Alexander's fervor for the poor led him to exclaim, "Daily do I grow more opposed to pews. I honour Popery and Puseyism for this point." Although committed to Presbyterian denominational outreach to the city's growing population, Alexander saw warrant for the opening of more "free churches" whose ministries could reach those outside his own denominational orbit. In a playful moment, he pointed out what he and Hall might be able to accomplish if

---

62. Hall, *Letters*, 2:193.
63. Hall, *Letters*, 2:193.
64. First published in 1854, J. W. Alexander's biography of Archibald Alexander remains the only complete treatment of his life and influence.

they left the security of their present ministries and served an inner-city free church pulpit:

> Free churches are unanimously voted a nuisance by New York Christians; but my mind is unchanged. They have, with us, always been undertaken by poor preachers. If such Chrysostoms as you and I wot of were to open a free church, it would tell another story; and I am persuaded the only way to effect it will be for individual preachers to lead the way. I have not the spirit of a reformer, or I know what I would do. My Tuesday lecture is the only service in which I feel at all apostolical.[65]

Reports from Alexander's congregational life continue to surface in letters from March and May of 1854. Although the majority of his parishioners appreciated his public ministry, not everyone was equally enamored. "My sermon on the prayers of the unconverted was not so pleasing to one hearer, who sent me eight pages of confutations—said she uttered the 'voice of God,' that she hardly refrained 'from rising in the church and uttering the true doctrine,' &c."[66] On the other hand, he notes, "More young persons are serious among us than I have known before." He was also encouraged by the church's effort to engage in outreach. "Our Mission-school does well," he said. "We have set up another down town, in which is a class of adult Germans."[67]

He was particularly pleased to observe the growing interest among his congregational attendants for establishing equitable labor relationships between employers and employees. Life in a city could be harsh. The land of promise to which many had emigrated was often met with unscrupulous employment relationships that disadvantaged working men, women, and children whose labor did not receive fair compensation or sanitary work conditions in which to perform their service.[68]

---

65. Hall, *Letters*, 2:194.

66. Yet Alexander knew that God can overrule for spiritual good even the poorest of sermons. An earlier letter from January 1847 speaks to the topic of public criticism: "I sensibly feel what you say about reports of sermons. Some months ago I was shocked at the inane stupidity of a report of one of mine. A few days after, a poor mantuamaker, not of my parish, read it in the newspaper, and found something in it the means of bringing her to Christ, after two years bondage. I wonder whether our meanest sermons are not our best." Hall, *Letters*, 2:63.

67. Hall, *Letters*, 2:195.

68. Upwards of eighteen hundred new immigrants arrived daily at New York City ports.

As the problem mushroomed with growth in population and industry, Christians began to seek creative ways to address the inequity:

> A plain but pious man of our church lately made a suggestion to me, which indicates Christian labour in a right direction. He is a clothier, employing five hundred hands. He is impressed with the fact that in our efforts to do good the relation of *employer and employed* is ignored. He proposes that every Christian employer should seek the benefit of his employees. He points out methods. He suggests associations of employers for mutual illumination and incitement, and to accomplish jointly through visitors, Bible-readers, &c., what cannot be done so well singly. He has a number warmly engaged with him. The scheme contemplates the Germans chiefly. He astonished me by saying that the calculated number of hands engaged by wholesale clothiers in New York is 25,000, of whom two-thirds are Germans. There is so much real working-spirit among these pious clothiers, that I can't help hoping it is of God.[69]

By May 1854, Alexander informed Hall, "At no time in my ministry have so many been coming to me to talk of their souls. These are not known to one another."[70] In an additional entry, he remarks, "There continues to be much quiet seriousness among my hearers. Yesterday I heard of five cases unknown to me before; but this concurrence is very extraordinary." Interest in inquiry was also reflected in attendance at his weekly lecture. "My lecture is very full and serious. I have arrived, in the Life of Christ, at the last Passover."[71]

Although eager to do all that he could to care for his flock, Alexander found some ministerial duties taxing. This was especially true of the monthly prayer meeting he superintended. "I find no meeting so hard to conduct as the Monthly Concert, so called." On other occasions he was fearful that he had overlooked some pressing pastoral needs. "Now and then I have some keen chagrins at finding, from imperfect lists, &c., that I have neglected some worthy family for several years." "Such things," he

---

69. Hall, *Letters*, 2:196.
70. In an effort to educate new members regarding their participation in the Lord's Supper, Alexander published a valuable introduction to the topic: James W. Alexander, *Plain Words to a Young Communicant* (New York: Anson D. F. Randolph & Co., 1854).
71. Hall, *Letters*, 2:197.

told Hall, "plague me more than greater trials, and not always in a warrantable way."[72]

National Matters
Alexander's letter also comments on the tensions that were developing over slavery.[73] "The Nebraska bill has passed. I have never opposed it, but feel very sad at the prospect of increased slavery. As to what would be the fact, I suppose this rests on causes which will not be affected one way or the other by this bill. The marshalling of South against North is more open and violent than I remember."[74]

The difficulties facing the nation are well captured in additional remarks Alexander made on this topic. His observations express the moral incongruity of the period in which he lived with regard to the institution of slavery and its potential future eradication:

> I have often tended to your opinion on the fugitive business; but these things make me pause, viz.: if the slaves are not sent back, the peril of their other suffering will be much increased: again, we shall be flooded with runaways, and our free negroes are burden enough already: lastly, I don't see how such a state of things can continue long, without war *ad internecionem* [to extermination] upon the borders. Yet I believe that the Fugitive Slave Law will be repealed, and that the Union will be dissolved on this question, sooner or later. The second Psalm is my chief comfort in politics.[75]

Vacation
As in previous years, Alexander's family left the city during the summertime for a break from the rigors of pastoral ministry. A letter written from

---

72. Hall, *Letters*, 2:198.
73. Fortson's summary captures the political climate of the period: "This was a time of increased strain between slave and free states as vocal antislavery men continued their unabated attack upon the South, while Southerners pushed back with hardened proslavery positions. The Fugitive Slave Act of 1850, the publishing of Uncle Tom's Cabin in 1851 by Harriet Beecher Stowe (daughter of New School Minister, Lyman Beecher), and the 1857 Dred Scott decision each added to the swelling tide. The 1850's mayhem in 'bleeding Kansas' became an armed contest between proslavery and antislavery settlers. Militant abolitionist John Brown and six comrades executed five proslavery Kansas settlers in 1856. In 1859, Brown tried to initiate a slave insurrection at Harper's Ferry but was stopped by soldiers under Colonel Robert E. Lee." Fortson III, *The Presbyterian Story*, 158.
74. Hall, *Letters*, 2:197.
75. Hall, *Letters*, 2:197–98.

Newport while on vacation in the summer of 1854 provided opportunity for further reflection on the state of the pulpit ministry in New England.[76] Alexander was saddened by what he observed in the piety, preaching, and worship of New England congregations. His annual summer visit served to confirm the continuing deterioration in spiritual vitality noted in letters from previous years. Revival influences had passed, and the decline in personal piety found expression in the formal elegance of literary-inspired sermons that lacked the strong biblically grounded exposition once characteristic of the colonial churches in New England. Portions of a letter written in August 1854 detail his concerns:

> With no disposition to judge harshly, but all the reverse, I am led to think that what we regard as experimental piety is at a low ebb in New England. The revival day has gone by. I hear of no savoury old-time Christians. Of Unitarians, I find many more than I expected. The absence of a spirit of worship, in assemblies, is very striking. Communion-seasons are brief and perfunctory, and the ordinance is just an addition, as when we baptize a child. The New England clergy seem to me a highly cultivated class; but the elegant or ingenious essay-style gains ground in sermons. Expository preaching is absolutely unknown, so far as I can learn. I have seen a number of young—preachers. They are scholarly, but somehow impress me as totally devoid of ministerial zeal. The intellectual and tasteful in —— appears to have a forming influence on all the new race of preachers. I own my survey has been somewhat narrow, but I should have expected an exception here and there.[77]

The Cost of Pastoral Ministry

Upon his return to New York, Alexander immersed himself in pastoral ministry. Unfortunately, his health soon collapsed. By early October, he had become quite ill. For several weeks, he suffered severe physical pain

---

76. Alexander also published an important historical overview of preaching in the July 1854 issue of the *Biblical Repertory*. His article examines the decline in pulpit influence which takes place when the expository method is abandoned: James W. Alexander, "Sketches of the Pulpit, in Ancient and Modern Times," *The Biblical Repertory and Princeton Review* 26, no. 3 (July 1854): 454–83. Intended as a corrective to the decline in pulpit power that had taken place among American churches, Alexander published a related article in early 1855 urging disciplined habits in the preparation of sermons properly grounded in biblical texts: James W. Alexander, "Remarks on the Studies and Discipline of the Preacher," *The Biblical Repertory and Princeton Review* 27, no. 1 (January 1855): 1–24.

77. Hall, *Letters*, 2:200.

and loss of energy. After preaching on October 8, he would not preach again until November 10. Although his body was in a weakened state, his faith continued strong in the midst of the maladies with which he was afflicted. A letter written to Hall on October 21, 1854, describes the nature of his condition:

> This is the fourteenth day of my illness, and I am still in my room, though dressed and sitting up a good deal. My disease has been obscure. It has given me more severe pain than all my previous sicknesses put together; but it has been *clean* pain, without nausea or depletory processes. It has been a series of dreadful paroxysms, averaging about eight hours each; of these I have had about five. In their acme, the pain was all but intolerable. One night I took what would equal 480 drops of lauda num, without effect. My doctor (Delafield) is a very Napoleon in decision; but his methods are mild, and he exactly resembles Dr. Belleville [vol. i., 125] in his expectant practice. I have from the beginning supposed that the root of the evil was calculus. Spasmodic colic co-exists. In the intervals I am wonderfully smart. I ought to say that Divine considerations have been of great support to me, especially when I was almost gone with pain.[78]

By the end of October, his condition had improved but remained delicate. The intensity of his illness caused Alexander to reflect on Scripture promises and draw strength from "the great truths" upon which he had built his life and proclaimed in his preaching. The illness was alarming, but Alexander rested quietly on the promises of the Word of God for his present circumstances, hoped-for healing, and security of his salvation in the finished work of Christ.

Having recovered some of his strength, he wrote to Hall on October 29, 1854, to inform him of his ordeal:

> Since the 20th I have been free from the peculiar pain, the very remembrance of which makes me shudder. At present I am suffering chiefly from the impression on my nervous system of so much severe pain. I have appetite, take a glass of port and gentian bitters, drive out for an hour, and walk fifteen to twenty minutes. You may imagine I have a great feeling of worthlessness. I ought ever to be thankful, that in my most painful moment, the great truths, which I trust I have believed, were not less clear or less precious than usual,

---

78. Hall, *Letters*, 2:201–2.

but unspeakably more so. I wish to make record of this. I did not find that intense and wasting pain took away the power of thinking, but all the other way. While it is fresh I wish to write down, that in, with, and under all the very poignant distress, there was an under-current of peace and religious satisfaction, which now comes up associated with the pain—but more abiding in my mind than the pain. These are new experiences for me. In former illnesses, my head was always cloudy; in this, I had pure, unadulterate pain.[79]

As Alexander's health recovered, he turned his attention to the ministry setting in which he served. The urban conditions in which Alexander ministered continued to be an ongoing source of pastoral concern. A letter written in early November 1854 helps explain the sense of responsibility that rested upon his conscience for reaching out to the crime-ridden city in which he lived: "The crimes of our city are horrid, but they are committed chiefly by foreigners. Of the 1,500 who daily land here from Europe, the worst, for various reasons, never get beyond New York, except to go to the State's Prison. Balloons go up every few days in our neighborhood; one to-day with four inmates."[80]

While the troubles of the city remained constant, Alexander's correspondence from November spoke appreciatively of the help he had received for preparation of sermons from the writings of Richard Trench. "I like an expression of Trench, in his book on Bible synonyms: 'to awaken in our scholars an enthusiasm for the grammar and lexicon.' This has been my great 'Help to Preaching,' and more and more so. Nothing has so suggested not only meanings, but parallels, illustrations, divisions, and inferences."[81] Alexander also recommended the works of Bengel for the biblical insights they provide. "If you have not been familiar with Bengel, [Gnomon], you will be struck with his pith, and the unexpectedness of his remarks."[82]

Besides the encouragement that he found in these authors for sermon preparation, Alexander's family was also appreciative for the financial support that the congregation provided for his pastoral services. On two occasions, Alexander had received a raise in salary but declined it. The leadership was undeterred and found a way to provide the assistance they

---

79. Hall, *Letters*, 2:202.
80. Hall, *Letters*, 2:203.
81. Hall, *Letters*, 2:204.
82. Hall, *Letters*, 2:203.

intended. "As I twice declined the augmentation of stipend, our trustees have insured my life; payable to relict. It is indeed a Godsend," Alexander said, "to one who never would lay up, if his salary were $20,000."[83]

Although the Alexander family was well provided for, the comforts of their income never precluded Alexander's passion for the extension of Christian missions both at home and abroad. Even with a shift in American foreign policy, he remained committed to the global expansion of the gospel message:

> As we are cutting ourselves off more and more from the old world, and likely to carry out the Monroe doctrine, it seems to me that Christians in the United States are proportionally more bound to devise means of sending the gospel to Spanish America. Brazil is quite open, and New Grenada nearly so. It seems to me that this, along with the black and red man, falls more justly to our share, than Hindoos, Nestorians, Druzes, Arabs, or Turks.[84]

Reflections on the elements of the order of worship close out Alexander's final letter of the year. A liturgist at heart, he was constantly thinking of the ways in which the worship of his congregation could be enriched. He found, however, that not everyone in his congregation was as enthusiastic as himself about the selections he included!

> If I could have one sufficient *ex tempore* prayer in each diet, I should be glad to have a prescribed form for those things which we ought *always* to pray for: *e.g.* government, general thanksgiving, &c. I would have the Lord's Prayer, Creed, *Te Deum, Gloria in Excelsis*, and a few more ancient portions. Our church singing is of the very plainest sort, and the people join pretty generally. This has been the result of (1) a limited list of tunes, and (2) these very easy, with no repeats, and scarcely any slurs or dividing of syllables. But the protest of our young people has been formidable.[85]

1855

As a new year dawned, a letter on January 23, 1855, records the problem Alexander was now experiencing when attempting to write. As he aged, his hand had begun to shake, making use of his pen difficult. A prolific

---

83. Hall, *Letters*, 2:204.
84. Hall, *Letters*, 2:204.
85. Hall, *Letters*, 2:204–5.

Engraving of J. W. Alexander, age fifty (1855), during his pastorate at Fifth Avenue Presbyterian Church.

ENGRAVING BY A. H. RITCHIE.

writer, Alexander was no doubt troubled by how it might affect his work as an author. It was an inherited condition, he believed, passed down through his family ancestry. "The trembling of my hand, which I inherit from mother and grandfather, makes me try first one hand-(writing) and then another—as I can go steadiest."[86]

Alexander's letters at this time again address his concern to preach to the masses in a more humble setting.[87] "I think *if I could support myself*, I would leave my charge any day, and begin down town; I ought to add— if I had any prospect of life. This is not a new 'spirit;' I never, in all our correspondence, said any thing more seriously. I perfectly *long* to preach daily in our now finished chapel."[88] "If I were ten years younger," he assured Hall, "I would have a building erected to hold 2,000, and would preach to free seats; not that I think the existing plan ought to be abandoned, but because I think we ought to have several, yea many plans, yea many sorts of preachers, 'unlearned deacons' and all."[89] Unfortunately, his wishes were never fulfilled. While he often felt most "apostolical" in the freedom that he experienced when preaching in the missionary chapels and outreach settings of his community, his primary pulpit labors would remain at the main facility with all its lavish accoutrements.[90]

Although Alexander would not be set free from the large edifice that his congregation had built, he did find satisfaction in the numerous ministry opportunities involved in pastoral visitation. A poignant moment is recorded in a letter dated March 14, 1855, following a visit to the home of an ill man whose son had once attended Alexander's Sunday schools. The pathos of the father's pain is evident in Alexander's description of the visit and the reflections it prompted with regard to God's fatherly care for His children:

---

86. Hall, *Letters*, 2:205.
87. Alexander's letters frequently mention the addition of new members. An entry for January 1855 mentions "nine on examination, and three on certificate. Several of the cases very interesting." Hall, *Letters*, 2:205.
88. Hall, *Letters*, 2:205.
89. Hall, *Letters*, 2:206.
90. Alexander's public lectures were equally valued: "I find Dr. James Alexander lecturing one Sabbath night early in February to his young men on Augustin, one of his prime favourites among saints and authors, and one among whose writings he was thoroughly at home. Those scholarlike addresses were often indescribably fascinating. No one had a better idea of Augustin's biography and opinions, and few could tell the sweet story of Monica more effectively." Alexander, *Life of Joseph Addison Alexander*, 2:750.

> I visited a bon vivant very ill, whose only tie to church or religion seems to be the memory of a little boy who was several years in our Sunday school. The father repeated whole hymns which his boy used to say at night; the child's portrait hanging all the while in sight by the bed. The intensity of paternal affection led me to dwell on that particular view of God's love in Scripture.[91]

While the contrast in ministry to the destitute of the city and the members of his congregation was profound, Alexander never withdrew affection for his church—although he could at times find humor in what his congregants had built for themselves in the construction of their new facility. Commenting on the ongoing renovation taking place during the 1850s, a letter from early October 1855 reveals Alexander's feelings about the remodeling that the church had undertaken so soon after its initial construction. Alexander was encouraged by the changes to the sanctuary. He was also pleased with the spirit of worship that marked the congregational singing in the absence of a choir. But he found, for the first time in his life, that his pulpit ministry would now forever be carried out in the shadow of the organ that had been installed. His bemusement with his preaching circumstances finds humorous expression in his closing remarks regarding the size of the organ that the congregation had purchased.

> Yesterday we entered again our remodeled church. My feelings are complex in regard to it. Some things are beyond my hopes: 1, the acoustical trouble seems thoroughly cured: I could not wish it better for speaking and hearing; 2, the lowering of the west gallery is altogether pleasing; 3, the singing led by a precentor, and no consolidated choir or band, pleases me; the people joined heartily. On the other hand, my pride suffers at being made, with my pulpit, sermon, &c., a mere appendage to a great big organ. A savage, on entering, would certainly take the instrument for the divinity of the shrine.[92]

A series of scattered reflections from correspondence written in late October 1855 includes Alexander's Scripture ruminations and their application to the life of faith. Portions of a letter follow:

---

91. Hall, *Letters*, 2:206.
92. Hall, *Letters*, 2:214.

Bible instances show us that God is concerned in our private sorrows. The Psalms especially appear more divine to me every day. What a body of experience! How they have formed the character and devotions of the Church! How remarkable, to have issued from such a land and age!

In regard to the future state, continual, earnest, and I believe reverent reading of God's Word, has produced in me some persuasions and hopes, which I should not like to be called on to prove in mood and figure. It is my belief, that many things are made true to us, and from Scripture too, for which we cannot cite a particular prooftext. The general result is, that I look on the world of disembodied saints as nearer to us than is usually held, and on the future glory as less unlike the good things of the militant church, than many teach. Holiness here is found not in abstractions, but in the concrete feelings, words, and acts of human creatures. Some good people talk of holiness in heaven, as if they must secure it from carnality by making it vague, dreamy, and metaphysical. Though "equal to angels," Luke xx. 36, the blessed are not dehumanized. All New Testament allusions show them as *ours* still.[93]

Commenting on the hope he had for his children, Alexander's letter also sheds light on his fatherly aspirations. His remarks bear witness to the deep burden he carried for their spiritual welfare and the importance of prioritizing the life of faith in the midst of worldly success and academic advancement. "The anxiety I feel for my children, oppresses me at times very much. It is hardly at all about their temporal advancement—even their learning; but I am deeply solicitous that they should be truly religious, and more painfully alive to their perils in this respect than once I was."[94]

His letter from late October also expresses his concern to preach naturally and "in power and demonstration of the Spirit." The use of God-given gifts in a manner true to one's personality—rather than the practice of artifice to gain public renown in pulpit eloquence—was his goal for the model of preaching he wished to embody. His letter again notes his felt inability to preach by "pungent method":

We are hardly yet arranged in our habitation. It is eminently commodious, clean, and spacious. Church continues surprisingly full;

---

93. Hall, *Letters*, 2:215.
94. Hall, *Letters*, 2:215.

with very little token of awakening. I fear I entertain rather than impress my hearers; this has long been a sore place within me. Yet when sometimes I have for a little attempted the pungent method, it has been Saul's armour to me, and I have been fain to come back to my natural way.[95]

In a letter on November 1855, Alexander revisited concerns he felt for his family's future. Sensitive to the calamities that may occur on any given day, he commented on the importance of sanctified affections for giving balance to the concerns a father will feel for his family's temporal and spiritual needs. He writes, "How gravely things look in our families, when we project our thoughts into the future! My yearnings about my house-hold are sometimes very affecting. 'The fondness of a creature's love,' &c." "To have these affections sanctified," he informed Hall, "is greatly desirable, but how little realized! Some parents seem to be cheered with a continual confidence in regard to the salvation of their offspring; and I own this comes over me too, in my best hours. Happy, happy are they who are safely landed on Canaan's shore."[96]

As he continued his observations to Hall, Alexander lamented how his broodings on the subjects of time and eternity had given a "somber cast" to his outlook. Ideally, he felt a balanced approach to the Christian life should also be marked by an attractive optimism rooted in the promises of God. Perhaps the time he recently spent with a dying woman gave impetus to Alexander's pensive reflections on balancing these emphases in his walk as a Christian:

> Some of the most serious reflections I ever have, are connected with the lapse of time and nearness of eternity, as viewed along with my small attainments hitherto; especially with the thought that these are not likely to be greater. I am deeply sensible that these and the like thoughts give a somber cast to my manner, of late, which is by no means fitted to make religion attractive. The normal or ideal sort of Christianity would be beautifully cheerful.... I have been part of the day with a dying woman, who has neglected religion, and is in terror of death. Such cases (I mean the terror) are less common than I expected to meet when I began my ministry.[97]

---

95. Hall, *Letters*, 2:215.
96. Hall, *Letters*, 2:216.
97. Hall, *Letters*, 2:216.

A final entry for the year written on December 25, 1855, announces Alexander's theme verse for the coming year and his rational for this annual tradition in his public ministry: "For the coming year I have fixed on the year-word, 'God with us.' This method of year-motto I have pursued now for about fifteen years, with much comfort to my own heart, and I believe to others; especially as I have preached on the text whenever I had a congregation."[98]

1856—"God with Us"

New York City was especially cold during January 1856. Alexander notes that his thermometer reading had dropped to five below zero Fahrenheit. "Unless Providence interpose frequent frosts our formidable force of snow-banks will furnish a fresh," he said.[99]

Correspondence from early January 1856 records Alexander's continuing optimism for the abolition of slavery. With abolitionist sentiments on the rise, sectional tensions within the country were also accelerating. He hoped that legislative action would resolve the impending crisis to which the nation was headed.[100] The biblical institutions of marriage and family had been rent asunder in the treatment of the slaves, portending, Alexander believed, a far greater national division soon to take place if not reversed.

> I am deeply convinced that a majority of the South will one day come to the point of mitigating slavery so far as to make it a sort of feudal apprenticeship; and that it will be abolished. Every year—even in the face of Northern rebuke—hundreds of new voices are raised in behalf of marriage, integrity of families, and license to read. To a practical mind it is striking that Abolitionism has abolished no slavery.[101]

---

98. Hall, *Letters*, 2:218.
99. Hall, *Letters*, 2:218.
100. Alexander thought Charles Hodge's commentary on Ephesians highlighted the moral incongruity of its practice in the United States: "Dr. Hodge has most admirably stated the slavery doctrine, in his Ephesians. *Inter alia*: 'It is just as great a sin to deprive a slave of the just recompense for his labour, or to keep him in ignorance, or to take from him his wife or child, as it is to act thus towards a free man;' p. 369. How nobly this clear enunciation of a scriptural principle towers above all the extravagancies of both sides!" Hall, *Letters*, 2:225.
101. Hall, *Letters*, 2:218.

Thinking Biblically about Worship and Congregational Growth

Alexander's communication also contains a passing reference to the theology of worship that characterized the Fifth Avenue Presbyterian Church during the 1850s. Fashionable settings and a service that was entertaining were far removed from Alexander's approach to public worship.[102] A recent comment in a local paper on his congregation's worship style provoked Alexander's ire: "I have seldom been more provoked [than by a newspaper notice laudatory of the singing in his church]. Earnest endeavour on my part to make *worship* supersede *music* is disturbed by these newsmakers."[103]

Besides the problem of churches that turn worship of God into a form of entertainment, the congregations of his day were being confronted by a form of teaching that undermined the lordship of Christ by an undue emphasis on His office as Savior. Hall notes that in certain preaching, "Christ is not held forth in his Divine authority as Lord, in due proportion with his gracious office as Saviour." Apparently, Alexander had not personally encountered the teaching even though Hall was aware of it: "I have no fears of any one's dwelling unduly on Christ as a Saviour, and know none who have the fault you seem to apprehend," he responded.[104]

An unusually disheartened entry is recorded in a letter dated March 26, 1856. Troubled by the absence of conversions from his pulpit ministry, Alexander castigated himself for his failure, viewing the issue as a divine "chastening for sin."

> I am unfeignedly humbled, though not a whit surprised, that people are not converted under my teaching; and it is always far from me to lay the blame on "the church," and scold my communicants for the default. I should wonder if any good number should ever be

---

102. Alexander understood the importance of Divine worship in the economy of God's grace and sought to protect it from subversion by human manipulation. An observation found in his correspondence sheds light on the importance he attached to the purposes of public worship: "Dr. B. used to read Voltaire as the best Christians read the Bible. Mrs. B. often said to me that the only comfort she had was in going to church, and that she looked forward to this all the week. I have often pondered on this and hoped it might prove to be the case with many whom we overlook in estimating the value of Divine service." Hall, *Letters*, 2:236.
103. Hall, *Letters*, 2:218–19.
104. Hall, *Letters*, 2:221.

awakened by me; and as a personal matter, own with abasement that I accept unfruitful ministry as an intelligible chastening for sin.[105]

His remarks continue by pointing out that this perceived weakness in his preaching would not lead him to embrace a "New Measures" approach to attracting crowds and manipulating results in order to achieve larger measurable statistics for enhancing his pulpit reputation. His opposition to manipulative invitation practices is also accompanied by his ongoing frustration with the "pew-system." He writes:

> Let me add—none of these things give me any freedom to press measures. I have no doubt, either you or I could get up a stir in one week, which would fill a column of tabulated statistics. Ah me! I am sadly and increasingly unfit to work in the conventional traces. I utterly reject the entire pew-system—I speak of cities—as against the spirit of Christianity. But all my opinions are held too tremblingly for me ever to be a reformer. So I quietly and sorrowfully go on expounding those things I am sure about.[106]

Three weeks later, Alexander reported on a spiritual stirring within his congregation. His explanation for what was occurring at his church is careful to differentiate its effects from any man-made measures used for inducing emotional response:

> I shall not be surprised if you hear there is some awakening among my people. And so there unquestionably is—but only in one corner. The "Church," to use the Yankee phrase, is not awakened at all. There are, all since I last wrote to you, appearances of converting influence in about seventeen persons. These have all been gradually led on for months, and some for years. Except where they are in the same households, they are almost all unknown to one another. I have not had any inquiry-meeting. Once I have met "those willing to be guided about seeking their salvation," (writing down this form of notice, and reading it,) and thus have drawn to my house yesterday more than forty. With these I had no private talk, *then*, but expounded a Chapter. I am troubled as to whether I shall repeat even this. I have no additional meeting, as yet, and have not departed from my routine of lectures on Acts. It is a remarkable coincidence, that the meeting of Presbytery was almost a Bochim, and from beginning

---

105. Hall, *Letters*, 2:223.
106. Hall, *Letters*, 2:223.

to end exhibited tenderness, humility, and affection on the part of ministers. I am dreading, beyond expression, the rise of a fanatical breeze among my church-members, and shall humbly endeavour to suppress rather than arouse human passions. You will understand me, better than anybody, when I say, I will, as at present advised, continue private address, but use no precipitating means. I even deprecate them. And so I feel about the whole affair. The way I am taking would be deemed a quenching of the spirit by sundry of my brethren. But I distrust every thing in revivalism, which is not common to it with the stated, continued, persistent presentation of the gospel.[107]

In the interchange of conversation that took place between Hall and Alexander over the New Measures, Hall expressed concern about Alexander's openness to the use of private meetings to assist in a work of grace. What role do inquiry meetings and personal conversations have in the public ministry of the church during seasons of spiritual outpouring? Hall writes:

The trouble I have about the private meetings is the apparent admission that all the directions for "guiding those that are seeking salvation," are not given in the pulpit, and so countenancing the notion of some that there are esoteric instructions which they must get in some other than the ordinary way. Would it not be well to hold the inquiry-meeting in the church? I mean, to make the regular services take the direction of the simplest colloquial advice.[108]

In a follow-up letter dated April 23, 1856, Alexander elaborates on his opposition to the use of New Measure tactics for effecting conversions. He thought the real issue a doctrinal one. He believed that a grasp of sound doctrine was essential for understanding the presence, power, and guilt of sin, and that it was only through an apprehension of biblical teaching on such topics as sin, conversion, and genuine faith that an unbeliever would be given the proper framework for seeking salvation in Christ. His observations warn against "premature birthing" into the Christian life as counterproductive to the purposes and means of grace in bringing about the regeneration of a person's soul. However, similarity in outward means, Alexander points out, should not be mistaken for an identity of

---

107. Hall, *Letters*, 2:223.
108. Hall, *Letters*, 2:224.

theological conviction in the conversational involvement of a pastor with inquiring souls during times of spiritual refreshing. He writes:

> I have nothing to change my opinion, that the inquiry among our people is lately discovered, but not lately produced. It was not an inquiry-meeting I held—but an exposition, and I had no private talk. I never met with the misapprehension you surmise. On that ground, we should never have a Bible Class, or a Young Men's Meeting. Above all, the objection would lie against your taking a child into your study for advice and prayer which would yet more suggest the esoteric scruple. Though I have no "inquiry-meeting," I should make the having one a simple question of degree. If a pastor cannot conveniently see them apart, I think it would be prudery not to see them together. As an instrument of excitement I have always feared them. I add but a few to the cases first known. But a very large proportion of my flock appears in the very state you mention, "in the place of the bringing forth of children." All this winter I have preached doctrinally—in a disguised series—and chiefly about conviction, conversion, faith, &c. I generally conclude, after interviews, that this reluctancy (in truly serious persons) arises from dim views of doctrine, feeble grasp of the truth, legal notions of the preparation which they must see in themselves. New-measure people undertake to use instruments, and often kill the child. In spiritual as in natural travail, I suppose there must be much waiting.[109]

Family Travails

By late summer, Hall's mother had fallen ill. Having learned of the illness, Alexander wrote a letter of encouragement. His communication dated September 1856 is filled with fond observations on the important role mothers play in the shaping of a child's character. Alexander's and Hall's mothers were lifelong friends, and both men were recipients of their love and affection. In Alexander's case, his parents were committed Christians known for their piety. The rich spiritual heritage that the Alexander home bequeathed to their children found legacy in Alexander and his siblings. His remarks honor their mothers for the way in which each cared for their families.[110]

---

109. Hall, *Letters*, 2:224.
110. In the biography of his father, J. W. Alexander spoke in glowing terms of his parents' marriage and the role model that his mother provided: "It may be safely said that no man was ever more blessed in such a connection. If the uncommon beauty and

There is no harm in repeating, what I said in my last, how seriously I feel the tidings you give respecting your mother. It brings my own warmly before me. Not only were they mutual friends, but they were lovely persons, long permitted to escape the uncomely accidents of old age, and carrying much of the sweet natural interest of girlhood into later years. Where shall we ever find such sympathy with us—especially in the minor trials of life? Who will ever so understand the little weaknesses of our character? If I go on much in this strain, I shall lose my composure; especially if I touch on other associations, more equal, and as strong. Let us bless God for such relations and affections.[111]

Observations on his family heritage continue in a letter written a few weeks later. Memories of his parents and influential figures from the days of his youth filled his mind with gratitude for all the ways in which he had benefited from their lives and instruction. He writes:

> How natural it is for our minds to go back to those who are gone! Where are our parents, and the religious teachers of our youth? Where are our own companions? Well do I remember Mr. Hall, with that spare, and dignified, and gentle form which belonged to him. My dear friend, "The fashion of this world passeth away." May we find grace to appear clad in the righteousness of Christ at his coming![112]

Alexander's pensive reflections surface again in a letter of the following week. His at times brooding personality finds explanation in memories of his childhood. The frank and open conversation which he often shared with Hall provided a means of healing through "disclosure" he had not known as a child.

> A letter of my father (1809) has turned up, in which he states that I had been at school a week. I remember it well; it was to "Madam Thomson," in Lombard street, [Philadelphia]. A sort of self-pity always comes over me when I think of my days of childhood; I do

---

artless grace of this lady were strong attractions in the days of youth, there were higher qualities which made the union inexpressibly felicitous during almost half a century. For domestic wisdom, self-sacrificing affection, humble piety, industry, inexhaustible stores of vivacious conversation, hospitality to his friends, sympathy with his cares, and love to their children, she was such a gift as God bestows only on the most favoured." Alexander, *The Life of Archibald Alexander*, 272.
   111. Hall, *Letters*, 2:224.
   112. Hall, *Letters*, 2:230.

not detect it so much in others. It seems to me I had more unuttered distresses than most children. How long a poor child will harbor an afflictive scruple about religion, which would have been instantly dissipated by disclosure![113]

Student and Author
Always the biblicist at heart, Alexander would often comment on points of theological difference he discovered through study of a biblical text with that of the ecclesiastical heritage in which he shared. His study of the book of Acts raised fresh questions in his mind regarding the relationship between pastors and congregations in the era in which the New Testament was being written and the contrast with current denominational practice. He writes:

> Lecturing on Acts xv. 1—35 I find it very tough to make that Council at Jerusalem a college of Bishops, or a General Assembly, or a Synod, or a Presbytery, or a Kirk-session, or an independent congregation. The common fiction of the Church having been organized on the plan of the Synagogue is "revolting" to me: *incredulous odi* [being incredulous, I cannot bear it]. While the Apostles lived, they clearly had supreme authority, and they as clearly had no successors. Where they were not, Elders ordained by them had local and temporary rule. I have searched in vain for a single instance of *one* pastor tied to *one* congregation, or of the call of *one* congregation as necessary to order. All the ministry, for what appears, was *ministerium vagum* [a roaming service], which the impugners of ordaining *sine titulo* [without title] do so eschew.[114]

In early October, his completed manuscript *The American Sunday-School and Its Adjuncts* went to press.[115] A volume of 342 pages, the work was written "to prove the necessity and duty of providing for general religious education, and to show how this end is promoted by Sunday schools and religious reading." Alexander was a childhood beneficiary of the Sunday-school movement, and throughout his lifetime sought to

---

113. Hall, *Letters*, 2:230.
114. Hall, *Letters*, 2:231.
115. James W. Alexander, *The American Sunday-School and Its Adjuncts* (Philadelphia: American Sunday-School Union, 1856). The volume addresses such matters as the importance of a religious education, spiritual instruction of youth, cultivation of Christian reading habits, the "age of preparation," "the collateral influence of Sunday schools upon the social condition of the poor," and "the teacher's incitement."

extend its influence through the many publications he contributed to the American Sunday-School Union press. A statement found in the preface explains his interest: "More than forty years ago it was my lot to sit on an humble form in one of the earliest Sunday schools set up in America. In process of time I became a teacher in similar institutions; and ever since my entrance upon the Gospel ministry I have counted it an honor to work collaterally in the same cause."[116]

The fall of 1856 was notable for its "fine weather." Alexander enjoyed the beauty of its colors despite the sprained foot he was nursing. His Thanksgiving sermon for that year was to be from Deuteronomy 32:8, a message in which he planned "to touch on the importance of our being united in peace with all English-speaking people."[117]

Volumes one and two of Sprague's monumental work *Annals of the American Pulpit* were published in 1856 as well. Alexander thought them "both valuable and entertaining."[118] In addition to his various literary contributions for the year, he was considering another volume of collected sermons for publication. "Some sermons, which I have on hand, (having preached about eight), will perhaps grow into a book on Faith," he reported.[119]

---

116. Hall, *Letters*, 2:231–32.
117. Hall, *Letters*, 2:231–32.
118. The series would eventually total nine volumes. Encyclopedic in nature and comprehensive in coverage, Sprague's work is a near exhaustive biographical history of the Christian clergy in the United States from the colonial period through the mid-nineteenth century: William B. Sprague, *Annals of the American Pulpit or Commemorative Notices of Distinguished American Clergyman of Various Denominations, from the Early Settlement of the Country to the Close of the Year 1855. With Historical Introductions*, 9 vols. (New York: Robert Carter and Brothers, 1856–1869; repr., New York: Arno Press, 1969). A review of Sprague's volumes appeared a few years later: James W. Alexander, "Annals of the American Pulpit; or Commemorative Notices of distinguished American Clergymen of various Denominations. With Historical Introductions," *The Biblical Repertory and Princeton Review* 30, no. 3 (July 1858): 401–19.
119. Hall, *Letters*, 2:232. A volume of 444 pages containing 16 sermons was published posthumously in 1862: James W. Alexander, *Faith: Treated in A Series of Discourses*, ed. S. D. Alexander (New York: Charles Scribner, 1862). For a perceptive analysis of their content and representative nature of nineteenth-century Old School preaching model which Alexander embodied, see Old, *The Reading and Preaching of the Christian Scriptures in the Worship of the Christian Church, Volume 6, The Modern Age*, 248–71.

1857—"Rejoice Evermore"

Alexander's first sermon of the new year emphasized the joy inherent to the life of faith. In his work as a pastor, he wanted to help his congregation learn to live in the most spiritually profitable way in the coming year.[120] As with previous New Year's days, Alexander was busy with calls and visiting. "We had 175 calls," he told Hall. "I am told Dr. Spring sometimes has 300."[121]

Solicitation for a soon to be published biographical work on well-known preachers found little interest from Alexander. Although considered one of the top preachers of his time, Alexander had no relish for the notoriety that accompanied his ministry. "An odd fish has applied to me for my life towards his 'Eloquent Divines,' about to appear. I have refused and derided, but experiences teach that this is no protection."[122]

A letter on March 9, 1857, includes an extended Latin quote from a prayer that the fourth century bishop Augustine often used to close his sermons. "It is beautiful Latin," Alexander observed. He found Augustine's writings a valuable companion throughout his life. "Augustine is the only father of whom I read much," he told Hall, "and the more I read, the more I perceive that if you leave out predestination and justification by faith, his scheme, and that of the Catholic Church of his day, was just that which Pusey would restore."[123]

While the weather became more temperate with the arrival of spring, Alexander was again experiencing problems with his health, forcing him to forgo his weekly pulpit ministry on occasion. A note written April 9, 1857, states, "I am laboring under a very painful irritation of throat and fauces." The problem worsened with the passing of the weeks. Alexander's symptoms are described in his correspondence of April 27, 1857: "Addison preached for me yesterday, though I think I could have preached once

---

120. Hall's comments on the sermon and the annual offerings that were taken for that day shed light on the budget of Alexander's congregation: "His sermon of the year-text was usually preached at the afternoon service of the first Sunday in the year. The morning service of that day had usually a reference to the annual collection made at that time for Foreign Missions. The collection on Jan. 2, 1857, amounted to $7,600. In the preceding month, the collection for Domestic Missions had been nearly $4,000. In February 1857, the collection for the Board of Education was $4,600; in May, for Sunday schools, $1,300; in November, for the Bible Society, $2,600." Hall, *Letters*, 2:233.
121. Hall, *Letters*, 2:233.
122. Hall, *Letters*, 2:233.
123. Hall, *Letters*, 2:234.

myself. My chief annoyance is a difficulty of breathing, oppression, or strangling sensation, which comes on at times, and especially at night."[124]

It soon became obvious that Alexander was in need of a break from the burdensome schedule of his pastoral ministry. Hall notes, "He was able to preach but twice in April, and four times in May. His cough had then become so threatening, that a voyage seemed to be the only resort that promised permanent relief."[125]

His congregation agreed and supported their pastor's departure for a period of recuperation in Europe.[126] For a second time, but now with his wife and smallest child, Alexander would again make the trek across the Atlantic seeking a recovery of his health.

The solemnity of his circumstances was often on Alexander's mind. In a final note to Hall, penned before boarding for passage, Alexander wrote: "There is something serious in such separations, which I feel just now; in better moments we will remember one another."[127]

---

124. Hall, *Letters*, 2:235.
125. Hall, *Letters*, 2:235.
126. "His consent to the arrangement was after all a reluctant one. He did not like the thought of intermitting his labours for any but the most serious cause, and his sensitive spirit shrank from the generosity of his friends and parishioners. He nevertheless fell in with the wishes of his best advisers." Alexander, *Life of Joseph Addison Alexander*, 2:80.
127. Hall, *Letters*, 2:236.

Each messenger has some peculiarity in his way of influence. Every man who thinks long and deeply upon the plan of grace has certain favourite views, which have cost him something, which he cherishes with delight, and in which he strongly desires that others may participate. Even truths as old as Christianity itself strike him in such a way that he flatters himself he can bring them home with a kindred freshness to his neighbours and brethren. Let me avow that there are doctrinal statements in the following pages, which, though in no sense novel, are such as conduce to the very life of my soul, and such therefore as I am exceedingly desirous, in my humble measure, to rescue from misapprehension and inculcate on my children and friends. No speaker or writer is likely to leave a deep mark upon other minds, or in any degree to mould the thinking of his contemporaries, except by the utterance of principles, which not only are held by him in sincerity of belief, but are dear to his heart and operative on his character, as being inseparable from the current of his daily and nightly thinking. They may be true, or they may be false; but of him who holds them they are the weapons of warfare. Hence we are sometimes fain to do homage to the earnestness of a man, whose reasonings do not bring us over. For the doctrines here set forth, I claim only this: whether with or without reason, they are my belief. Years fly apace, natural vigour wanes, and opportunities of personal influence become fewer; but my profound conviction of the verities here proposed waxes stronger and stronger, with a corresponding earnestness to diffuse and impress them. No concealment or compromise has been attempted as to the tenets; which belong to a scheme of belief, ancient, intelligibly distinct, even singular, long contested, read and known of all men. Yet if there is aught here which shall disturb any evangelical mind, it has crept in without a polemical purpose. The field is immeasurably large, in which we may expatiate, without setting foot upon the minor controversies of the schools; and some who are immovably attached to certain theological distinctions, would be the last to lay them among the foundations, or erect them into terms of communion, or set them forth as tests of grace. It is hoped, meanwhile, that humble experienced believers will find here in due prominence those central truths concerning Jesus Christ and Him crucified, by which all theology and all sermons must stand or fall.

—J. W. ALEXANDER
November 1858
(From *Discourses on Common Topics of Christian Faith and Practice*)

Chapter 13

EUROPE AGAIN: MAY–OCTOBER 1857

Alexander and his family arrived safely at Liverpool, England, on June 7, 1857. The passage was calm, and the family enjoyed their voyage by steamer together in the company of good friends.

Alexander wrote to Hall shortly after they had docked, commenting on the friendships they formed while traveling and were greeted by upon their return to England. "We found valuable friends on board, and have also found numerous acquaintances of ourselves or our friends, in this town." "I had really forgotten how cool the weather is here," Alexander wrote. "We have been under the necessity of having fires every evening, and I shudder with cold most of the time. Though my cough is less, it has not left me."[1]

Filled with numerous observations on British life and culture, Alexander's letters from this period speak of visiting the exhibition of the "Art Treasures" at Manchester, the beauty of the English countryside, and neatness of the towns. He also often notes the green value of the land.

While in England, Alexander attended an "Anniversary soiree of the Regent Square and Somerstown Sunday Schools." Recognized internationally for his support of Sunday schools, the presiding chair—a Dr. Hamilton—requested Alexander to address the meeting. Following his address, the assembly applauded Alexander's contributions to the Sunday-school movement. "Hamilton's gifted vocabulary flowed in my behalf," Alexander reported. "The cheers and 'hears' were a little appalling to me; but good nature and a disposition to be pleased marked everything. I thought the talent displayed by these teachers very remarkable. The

---

1. Hall, *Letters*, 2:238.

heartiness and almost convivial glee of the meeting were unlike what we have at such times."[2]

As he traveled throughout the English countryside, Alexander was impressed by the strictness of Sabbath observance. In his judgment, British practice far outweighed the importance attached to it by even the strictest of American churches. "In no New England town have I ever remarked a more exact and still observance of the Sabbath," he observed.[3]

As on his previous trip, he visited worship services of various denominational persuasions. One of the more interesting stops he made was at an Irvingite congregation in London where he "heard one pray in the spirit, one prophesy, and three give the word of exhortation."[4]

Perhaps the most fascinating experience occurred when he sat under the preaching of the young C. H. Spurgeon. At the time, Spurgeon was just in the opening years of his London ministry but was already renowned for his winsome and powerful preaching. A letter on June 29, 1857, provides an extended commentary on Spurgeon's pulpit ministry:

> I have heard the wonderful Spurgeon. I am told the effort was feeble, for him. He has none of those captivating intonations which we remember in Summerfield and others; neither should I judge him to have any pathos. His voice is incomparable, and perfect for immense power, sweetness, and naturalness. His pronunciation is admirable, with the never-failing English eyther, knowledge, wroth, &c. Though very like his likenesses, he becomes almost handsome when animated. His gesture is paring and gentlemanlike. I detect no affectation. The tremendous virtue of his elocution is in outcry, sarcasm, and menace, and his voice improves as it grows louder. I seriously think his voice the great attraction. His prayers were concise and solemn; a shade too metaphoric. His short exposition was so-so in matter, but well-delivered.... He requested the people in the gallery (there are three one over another,) not to lean forward. He said you could tell a Dissenter in church, by his sitting down before the hymn was over.[5]

---

2. Hall, *Letters*, 2:240–41.
3. Hall, *Letters*, 2:239.
4. "A sermon of an hour was preached by Mr. John Wells, on the 'procession of the Holy Ghost.' It was read, was well-delivered, and very theological and orthodox, until near the close he declared that the day of miracles and prophecy had returned." Hall, *Letters*, 2:241.
5. Hall, *Letters*, 2:242–43.

At some point during the delivery of his message, Spurgeon offended Alexander by his remarks about sickly ministers taking advantage of their parishioners' tithing for trips abroad! "During the sermon he described broken-down preachers, spitting blood, going to the continent and travelling at other people's expenses. This did not please me, for 'Who e'er felt the halter draw, With good opinion of the law?'"[6] Made in the flush of youthful health and success, Spurgeon's criticism was tempered by Alexander's maturity of judgment and personal experience of the debilitating effects of disease and age that as an older man Spurgeon would one day know all too well himself.

Alexander's description of Spurgeon's ministry continues with further observations on his sermon, church service, and the impact of his preaching style on the masses in attendance:

> He told a very funny story of a minister with a rich wife. He was very severe on the establishment, and rather intimated that the gospel was very little preached. In this part of the discourse, he preached himself. Notwithstanding all this and his dreadful onslaught on written sermons, I think his work here matter of the greatest thankfulness. He preaches a pure gospel, in the most uncompromising manner, with directness, power, and faithfulness; and he preaches it to hundreds of thousands, to beggars and princes. I am at a loss to say what they come for. They seem to be led of God. All strangers go. Some of the nobility are always there. Church ministers abound in every assembly. I ought to have said there is nothing that savours of the rude or illiterate. Such a building I would beg a year to have in New York, for some stentor. It is the beau-ideal, being the theatre of Surrey Gardens, where Jullien has his concerts. It will hold ten thousand seated. Every aisle and corner was filled by a dense mass of standing persons numbering perhaps a thousand. The attention was unbroken. What struck me, was the total absence of the ill-dressed classes. A person behind me pointed out actors, Waterloo officers, noble-men, &c. Old Hundred by about ten thousand voices was really congregational singing. His sermon was fifty minutes, Ezek. xxxvi. 37—on the connexion of prayer with blessings. 1. Fact. 2. Reasons. The first head was admirable; as scriptural, simple, chaste, direct, winning, and full of Christ, as one could wish. Only I wondered all the while why it drew the masses so. Then he began to suffer with the terrible heat; said so; and evidently lost his strength of body and mind. The

---

6. Hall, *Letters*, 2:243.

application was common-place, but his felicitous language and glorious voice will carry along any thing. I am persuaded he seeks to save souls, and believe that he is as much blessed to that end, as any man of our day. My childish recollections of Larned, represent him as much such a speaker. Spurgeon is a blended likeness of Prof. Atwater, and Mr. Bartine, the Methodist. His eyes are disproportionally small. In many points of assurance, dogmatism, conceit, and sarcasm, he reminds one of ——, to whom he is greatly superior in gentlemanlike bearing and absence of nasal twang, while he falls far below him in learning, original illustration, and I think inventive genius. But Spurgeon preaches the blessed gospel of the grace of God.[7]

During his time in London, Alexander also notes that he "heard Dean Trench read prayers at Westminster Abbey, and *saw* him preach in a surplice and scarlet hood." "He is a robust, hale, good-looking Englishman, with much of that 'holy-tone' which belongs to all readers here," Alexander said.[8] Besides the church services he attended, he was also able to visit the House of Commons and the House of Lords. From London, he traveled to Brighton, the Isle of Wight, and eventually Paris, France.

By late July, Alexander had arrived in Geneva. While there, he had opportunity to renew his friendships with Dr. Tyng and Dr. Cesar Malan. A letter written from Geneva expresses his delight in the famed city: "Delightful place; one can't help breathing the air of Protestantism and freedom.... There are few places I ever saw in which I could more willingly reside."[9]

Following his time in Geneva, he journeyed to Berne, Interlaken, and Baden-Baden. By early September, he had reached Frankfort on the Main, with additional visits to Wiesenbaden, Coblenz, and Cologne. A route through Belgium provided opportunity to visit the cities of Antwerp, Bruges, and Brussels.

He returned to England in mid-September. A letter written from London describes the prayer posture of the congregations he had visited and his personal preference for what he believed was the most honoring practice:

---

7. Hall, *Letters*, 2:243–44.
8. Hall, *Letters*, 2:242.
9. Hall, *Letters*, 2:252.

> The Dissenters in England have universally abandoned standing in prayers, so far as I see. As I cannot consent to irreverence in worshipping God, I am as frequently an object of note as in our prayer-meetings at home, where grown men pray sitting, and sometimes staring. Two-thirds of the Episcopalians also sit. The Germans and Scotch all stand. To such as kneel I feel much respect.[10]

A final visit to Scotland at the end of September concluded Alexander's European trip. While in Edinburgh, he was delighted to sit under the ministry of two of Scotland's finest preachers.

> On the Sabbath I heard Dr. Bruce at Free St. Andrew's Sermon on Christ's two quellings of storms in Matt. viii. and xiv. General doctrine, that afflictions are ordered not only to try our faith, but to try our utmost faith; in the second case, Jesus let them go alone. It was a profound piece of experience, viewed philosophically; strong meat; dense, witty at times, unexpected turns like Foster; no elegance of manner, but immense impression. The prayers were almost inspired. Ah here is the true *Eutaxia*, without printed worship![11]

Having heard John Bruce preach in the morning, Alexander attended an afternoon service to hear the preaching of another leading Scottish minister, the Rev. Dr. Thomas Guthrie.

> At 2 I went to Free St. John's. Strangers (how truly I comprehend the term!) are admitted only after the first singing. I found myself waiting in a basement with about 500 others. At length I was dragged through a narrow passage, and found myself in a very hot, over-crowded house, near the pulpit. Dr. Guthrie was praying. He preached from Isai. xliv. 22, "Return unto me, for I have redeemed thee." It was fifty minutes, but they passed like nothing. I was instantly struck by his strong likeness to Dr. John H. Rice. If you remember him you have perfectly the type of man he is; but then it is Dr. Rice with an impetuous freedom of motion, a play of ductile and speaking features, and an over-flowing unction of passion and compassion, which would carry home even one of my sermons; conceive what it is with his exuberant diction and poetic imagery. The best of all is, it was honey from the comb, dropping, dropping, in effusive gospel beseeching. I cannot think Whitefield surpassed him in *this*.

---

10. Hall, *Letters*, 2:264.
11. Hall, *Letters*, 2:266.

You know while you listen to his mighty voice, broken with sorrow, that he is overwhelmed with the "love of the Spirit."[12]

Alexander appreciated Guthrie's preaching, but was not as impressed with aspects of the worship service in which he participated. Surprised by what he encountered, he thought the worship practice of Guthrie's congregation on the same downward spiral that he believed was also taking place back in New England. "I disliked the singing at Dr. Guthrie's; a choir, with twiddling tunes; a clear retrocession towards the way which is becoming unsavoury even to New England. The singers were in pews near the pulpit, and I saw an advertisement in the lobby for a tenor singer."[13]

An entry in one of Alexander's letters of this period speaks of the appreciation he felt for being able to sit under the pulpit ministries of these two able expositors. A descriptive paragraph captures the power of Bruce's pulpit effusions:

In reflecting on the two great and precious sermons of yesterday, I wonder at the beautiful diversity of gifts. They were as unlike as an apple and a pine-apple. I have no remembrance of any preaching so analytically experimental as Dr. B.'s, except my own dear blessed father's. At each step he seemed to *assume* all that an ordinary preacher would have preached, and to go on beyond that. His prayers were the same; so searching in confession that I winced, and so paternal and pastoral in intercession, that I could not but fancy his hand feeling all around and gathering sorrows out of every heart to bring before God. His sternness in no degree modified the graciousness of his gospel freedom, as I have too often seen to be the case with rigorous casuists in America.[14]

Alexander regarded "Scotland as the flower and crown of all our tour." "It is worth while to come here to learn how a Sabbath may be kept," he told Hall. He hoped that his son Henry could "spend some months in Scotland to learn how to preach, catechize, and do pastoral duty." "Gladly," Alexander said, "would I forego for him all that the continent has to offer, for the sake of this."[15]

---

12. Hall, *Letters*, 2:266.
13. Hall, *Letters*, 2:267–68.
14. Hall, *Letters*, 2:267–68.
15. Hall, *Letters*, 2:268.

A concluding observation from one of Alexander's letters while in Edinburgh provides not only a fine summary of Scottish piety, but also good insight into the biblical principles underlying the Protestant heritage which shaped Scotland's identity. He writes:

> Both Guthrie and Lee (before the Committee of the House of Lords) have formally ascribed the "canny" character of the Scotch, not simply to their being trained on the Scriptures, and to their reading of Solomon, but particularly to the custom of using the book of Proverbs as a reading-book. The Anglo-Saxon words and short sentences, where books are rare, made it the thing for the children. There is a pious weaver mentioned in Guthrie's "Gospel in Ezekiel" as a man of prayer. The Doctor said to us "this man prayed, not as one going to heaven, but as one just come out of heaven. He would sit in his loom and superintend our education." And what we read was such pith as "he that hateth suretyship is sure," &c.[16]

As he reflected on his travels, Alexander remarked, "The thoughts are very serious which one has amidst the most favourable circumstances, in a foreign land." "I trust," he said, "they are not without spiritual profit."[17]

---

16. Hall, *Letters*, 2:270.
17. Hall, *Letters*, 2:244.

When the writer of these lines—before any tokens of our American awakening had appeared—was in Great Britain, he was made aware of a most remarkable movement in the religious world. The increase of endeavors to carry the Gospel to the poor, in their most abject retreats—the continual use of open-air preaching—the rise of several evangelical ministers upon whose words the multitude were disposed to hang—the services in Exeter Hall, and even the opening of Westminster Abbey, spoke of zeal on one hand, and roused attention on the other. And when he surveyed an assembly of ten thousand souls giving rapt attention, at the Surrey Gardens, to the great evangelist of our age, and discerned evidence that these multitudes, continually filling anew that vast receptacle, were drawn together, not more by the remarkable gifts of that young man, than by the fearlessness with which he declares the vengeance of God against sin, and the freshness and fullness with which he offers an accomplished salvation through Jesus Christ—the conclusion was irresistible, and was repeatedly expressed, that England also was enjoying a Revival of Religion. Accidents may vary, but the essence is the same. And, all the world over, whenever God chooses to smile upon his work, instruments will be forthcoming, in free abundance and beautiful diversity. Enlarged prayer for the spread of the Gospel among the whole human family is especially demanded at the present time, when God has touched so many hearts with desire, and manifested so great a readiness to answer.

—JAMES W. ALEXANDER
1859

Chapter 14

THE FINAL YEARS: 1857–1859

Alexander and his family returned from their European trip on October 25, 1857. On the day before they docked, he preached on board the ship from 1 Peter 4:3. It was the first time he had preached since the previous May.

Alexander was delighted with the time he spent in Europe and was grateful for the respite that his family enjoyed during their travels. He was especially pleased to be home among his family and friends.[1] "How deeply grateful we ought to be, that during six months' absence, no case of indisposition has occurred in our circle here; all alive and all well; let the God of our salvation be exalted!" "I was everywhere a most reluctant traveler," he informed Hall, "and drew a lengthening chain." "My own general heath is almost robust; and yet I have the same catch in my throat."[2] Even though some symptoms of his earlier duress remained, Alexander was pleased by the progress he had made in the restoration of his health.

As he rejoined his congregation, he was equally encouraged by the number of people who were in attendance at public worship services on the Sabbath. While it was common for the numbers to dwindle during the summer months, by early fall the crowds were back. More importantly, an outbreak of revival in New York City had affected the religious consciousness of Alexander's congregation.[3] "The people have generally

---

1. "It was," records the happy traveler, "almost like a foretaste of heavenly rest, when from the dark and dingy and uneasy ship I came to our sweet, clean, light, cheerful home, and after six months' absence sat down among the beaming faces of those who love us." Alexander, *Life of Joseph Addison Alexander*, 2:815.
2. Hall, *Letters*, 2:271.
3. For valuable treatments of the New York revival of 1857 to 1858, see especially Kathryn T. Long, "The Power of Interpretation: The Revival of 1857–58 and the Historiography of Revivalism in America," *Religion and American Culture* 4 (Winter 1994): 77–105;

returned, and are in a promising state, as to attendance," he remarked. "I even hope for more," he said, "as there is a marked reviving of religious interest during the six months of our absence."[4]

Alexander found himself quite busy upon his return as he sought to catch up on his pastoral duties. "After fast-day, preparatory lecture and communion, (next Sabbath,) I shall feel a little more ease of mind than now," he told Hall in a letter dated November 3. "I hitched at once into the old rut, wrote two full sermons last week and have been hard at visiting ever since my return."[5]

Apparently, Alexander had put on weight during his travels. Earlier optimism about his recovery in health appears more tempered as he began to preach and teach regularly. "I am fleshier than need be, borne twice as much fatigue as in '51; but the ring of irritation, phlegm, and strangle in my pipes remains much as before; I mean D.v. to speak, &c., exactly as if it wasn't there, till something stops me."[6]

Despite the ongoing health issues with his throat, Alexander maintained an active visitation schedule. A letter dated November 16, 1857, describes the loneliness he felt while his family was away and the problem that the weather was causing for "sore throat folks" such as him. "Lonesome, indeed, is this habitation, as my wife and children are in the Jerseys, and the dreary easterly rain makes egress undesirable for sore throat folks. Natheless, I have spent most of the day abroad, as the arrears of visits (occasioned by my absence) to cases of trouble are very large."[7]

Making light of his health concerns, he joked about the options that lay before him with his increased corpulence: "I continue to cough, and begin to think I shall as long as I preach, yet I am well up in colour, fat and paunch, eat well, drink kindly, sleep so-so, and altogether am in good case to retire on a pension, turn president, go to Congress, or negotiate a loan in Europe."[8]

Kathryn T. Long, *The Revival of 1857–58: Interpreting an American Religious Awakening* (New York: Oxford University Press, 1998). For a comprehensive analysis of the revival's origin and its national and international effects, see Orr, *The Event of the Century: The 1857–1858 Awakening*. For an earlier treatment of the same period, see J. Edwin Orr, *The Fervent Prayer: The Worldwide Impact of the Great Awakening* (Chicago: Moody Press, 1974).

4. Hall, *Letters*, 2:272.
5. Hall, *Letters*, 2:272.
6. Hall, *Letters*, 2:272.
7. Hall, *Letters*, 2:273.
8. Hall, *Letters*, 2:274.

1858—"Thy Kingdom Come"

In a short letter addressed to Hall on January 1, 1858, Alexander notes that "sixty murders and one hanging" took place in New York City during 1857. Commenting on the city's moral fiber, he stated, "Lying, stealing and bribery, perjury, covetousness and rapine, make things sometimes look to me like some prophetic tableaux."[9]

A passing remark also hints at the manipulative techniques of the New Measures revivalism being used among some of the churches in the city for effecting man-made "spiritual" results. Alexander viewed the practice as spiritually misguided and incapable of producing the inner spiritual renewal that the Holy Spirit alone can provide for true transformation of the heart at a motivational level. "I know twenty young people, whom I could foment into any given amount of excitement in two weeks. What amazes me is, that the men who apply these methods, at set times, are at other times as little raised above worldly thoughts and deeds as common folks."[10]

Correspondence from early March 1858 speaks of a recovery in health while mentioning Alexander's ongoing struggle to mortify the presence of remaining sin in his life. "I record with a sense of dependence that the last sigh of my cough has left me for about three weeks, and that I am more fleshy. An undue and irregular beating of the heart, though lessened, remains. I am nearly fifty-four years old, (March 13.)" "In the serious retrospect of life," he observed, "I see nothing so dark as my sins; nor did they ever seem more hateful."[11]

His letter notes that seven people were admitted "on examination, and eight on certificate" into the membership of his congregation. Preaching, he pointed out, "is assuming a more prominent place than heretofore." While the pulpit ministry was prospering, Alexander expressed concern for the direction that some of the prayer meetings in the city had taken. Indiscriminate involvement by laypeople had led to a loss of decorum in how the meetings were being conducted. "A great danger is lest a go-ahead, joyous, auction-like, unreverent elation take possession of the [daily] prayer-meetings," he said. "Up town this has been very much avoided by the lead which ministers have taken."[12]

---

9. Hall, *Letters*, 2:275.
10. Hall, *Letters*, 2:275.
11. Hall, *Letters*, 2:276.
12. Hall, *Letters*, 2:276.

An extended paragraph comments on the pastoral involvement that Alexander had with his congregation and the effect that the revival was having upon the city's population.[13] Because of the increased interest in seeking God, he wanted to address only "the most important class of subjects" in his pulpit ministrations.[14]

> Did I write of visits I am paying every day or two to the Roman Catholic Hospital of St. Vincent de Paul? A young medical student, a pay-patient, is there recovering from typhoid fever, and was baptized by me. There are twelve sisters of charity, and 120 beds. This young man has been nursed in the best manner conceivable. I have seen five or six of the ladies, including the superior. They have treated me with a very graceful courtesy, and are altogether a winning generation. The tidings of the revival on every side certainly tends to set people a-thinking about their souls; which is a point gained. I feel it overshadowing my own mind, and opening ways of address to the careless, as well as shutting me up to the most important class of subjects.[15]

The pastoral context in which Alexander labored at this time is aptly described in an important sermon preached in early 1858.[16] First published in *The New York Pulpit in the Revival of 1858*, Alexander's sermon "The Holy Flock" is a stirring indictment of the contemporary religious atmosphere found among churches in New York City as well as an impassioned invitation to return to the older doctrinal paths for understanding the origins and progress of genuine Spirit-wrought revival. The enthusiasm that marked interest in revival "techniques" was not matched with a corresponding interest in the teaching of Scripture for learning how to assess and critique revival phenomena. Alexander believed that a loss of appreciation for biblical truth lay at the heart of the doctrinal indifference now common to many in attendance at the city's churches. A failure

---

13. By the beginning of 1858, the estimated population of New York City was near 800,000.

14. For a representative collection of sermons delivered by ministers in the city of New York during the revival of 1858, see Samuel I. Prime, ed., *The New York Pulpit in the Revival of 1858: A Memorial Volume of Sermons* (New York: Sheldon, Blakeman & Company, 1858; repr., Laurel, Mass.: Audubon Press, 2008).

15. Hall, *Letters*, 2:276.

16. Alexander's text came from Ezekiel 36:37–38: "Thus saith the Lord GOD: I will yet for this be enquired of by the house of Israel, to do it for them: I will increase them with me like a flock. As the holy flock, as the flock of Jerusalem in her solemn feasts."

by the churches to pass on "the treasure in earthen vessels," Alexander warned, would be sure to compromise future generations' ability to distinguish truth from error. Spiritual ignorance would result, and the integrity of the church's testimony collapse.

> We have not been faithful to the deposit with which we are intrusted. From the absurd attempt to keep up religion without doctrine, a large part of the present generation has grown up already, with no proper safeguard against soul-destroying error. Not only have they no tests to distinguish Pelagianism from Gospel grace, but they even learn to treat with indifference the heresies which deny the atonement and the godhead of Jesus. That charity which believeth all things but God's truth, opens the doors to a fatal religious literature; in which, by a sort of universal solvent, all the doctrinal bones of theology are reduced to a gelatinous mass of ambiguous sentiment. The consequence is easily predicted. In stupid dread of the catechism, and the definitions of the church, these people and their children lose all sense of the diversities of creeds, become looser and more ignorant as falsehood grows familiar, and are led off to universalism on one side, and popery on the other; or, more degrading and ruinous still, to Socinus, Swedenborg, familiar spirits, or the Mormons. We have not been laborious and careful for the perpetuity of the truth. We have multitudes among us who are losing every impression of their infancy, becoming latitudinarian in their creed, relaxed in their morals, and tending towards the world from whom their fathers came out. We have a mixed multitude without the camp, accompanying our march, who ever and anon fall a lusting after some error or some wickedness. Time was, when the population of many regions of America was almost entirely religious; it is not so now. Thousands there are, even of those who regularly attend public worship, who have no theology, no family prayer, no catechizing, who care for no differences of doctrine, and whose children grow up even more ignorant than themselves. By unavoidable mixtures and alliances, the parents have learned a new dialect, and "the children speak half in the speech of Ashdod."[17]

As Alexander's message is careful to point out, an erosion of the church's doctrinal foundations will inevitably be accompanied by a decline in piety. Deterioration in doctrinal orthodoxy will always result in an overshadowing of the agency of the Holy Spirit in salvation as

---

17. Prime, *New York Pulpit*, 26–27.

knowledge of the divine origin of grace is replaced by man-centered initiatives and "measures" believed essential for effecting or securing the regeneration necessary for salvation. Alexander's earlier tolerance for New Measures revivalism first discussed in his letters of the 1830s had given way to principled opposition as he came to recognize the doctrinal damage it had caused in the intervening years to the spiritual life of the churches that had embraced and propagated its false theology. He writes:

> The nature of genuine piety is less weighed, less understood. The agency of the Holy Spirit has been cast into the shade; new and dangerous views of regeneration have become common; while the tendency has been away from dependence on God, and towards a religion of human fabrication. Even the traditional reverence of our people for revivals has been played upon by the adversary, and we have had the name, without the reality, and have been called upon to wink hard at error, lest we should fight against the God of truth. Thus, when the king of Egypt took away from the temple the shields of gold which Solomon had made, King Rehoboam made in their stead brazen shields. The name was as before. At the same time that we were doing away with the true glory of revivals, even the sovereign agency of the Holy Spirit in changing the depraved nature, we were in some places laying mighty stress upon certain external means and measures, which are questionable at best, but which, when erected into sacraments, are like the brazen serpent Nehushtan which Hezekiah destroyed, when the children of Israel burned incense to it. So that even if our population were not to increase, we should need the reviving influences of God.[18]

Alexander's April letters continue with news of the revival that was taking place in the city and among his congregation. While the spiritual obstacles he had described in "The Holy Flock" were real, they were not the final word on what God was doing through revival grace. The Spirit of God was at work bringing new birth and spiritual renewal in an unprecedented manner among the city's population and churches. Alexander's pastoral workload increased exponentially. Opportunity for writing gave way to the increased demands of pastoral ministry as worship services, lectures, and prayer meetings were thronged by numbers of people new and old alike. A letter written on April 3, 1858, provides

---

18. Prime, *New York Pulpit*, 27–28.

a vivid description of the developing ministry circumstances in which Alexander was engaged:

> I have generally discredited people who say they have no time to write, but lately I have been tempted to plead that excuse. Though I have aimed to keep down and regulate excitement among us, and have had no additional service but an exhortation on Monday to such as seek instruction on points connected with conversion, I perceive such a degree of inquiry as has never met me in my ministry. The number of declared inquirers is not more than twenty-five, and most of these have dates a good way back; but the feelings of communicants and the indescribable tone of assemblies, are new to me. From the start I have held myself ready to adapt measures to emerging demands; I however feel glad I have pursued the repressive method; which, by the way, has lost me sundry good opinions even among my own flock. Study I cannot, being run down by persons, many of whom I never knew, in search of counsel. The uptown prayer-meetings are very sober and edifying. I am told that the general tendency in all is to increased decorum. The openness of thousands to doctrine, reproof, &c., is undeniable. Our lecture is crowded unendurably—many going away. The publisher of Spurgeon's sermons, says he has sold a hundred thousand. All booksellers agree, that while the general trade is down, they never sold so many religious books. You may rest assured that there is a great awakening among us, of which not one word gets into the papers; and that there are meetings of great size, as free from irreverence as any you ever saw. I have never seen sacramental seasons more tender and still than some meetings held daily in churches in our part of town. The best token I have seen of revival was our meeting of Presbytery. I never was at such a one. Brethren seemed flowing together in love, and reported a great increase of attention in all their churches—and this within a very few days. The inquiring condition among ourselves is strange, and all but universal; God grant it may be continued, or exchanged for true grace in them all.[19]

Alexander's letter proceeds to describe the additional services and prayer meetings that his congregation was establishing in response to the increased demand from inquiring souls.[20] It is notable that while Alex-

---

19. Hall, *Letters*, 2:276–77.
20. Alexander's letter also expresses concern regarding the indiscriminate public speaking and prayer occurring at the various "union" meetings being held among the city's congregations: "The attendance on the union meetings here is not lessened. Last

ander was eager to report all that the Lord was doing, he was hesitant to boast about the numbers that could be recorded.[21] His familiarity with seasons of revival helped him realize that not every blossom found on a fruit tree in spring will form as a bud—or even that it would ultimately mature into a harvestable fruit. Regardless of the eventual outcome, he took time to talk with everyone making inquiry of him. He found "plain, elementary instruction" the most important doctrinal need for the people to whom he was ministering.[22] As he recognized, proper emotional "excitement" must be in response to biblical truth. The fact that an emotional response has occurred to the preaching of biblical truth is not necessarily an indication that the effect is divine in origin.

> We are just setting up a daily (nightly) prayer-meeting in our Mission Chapel for the poor, (really not nominally.) It is superintended by a Committee of about ten leading gentlemen, under sanction of the session. Among the numerous cases of persons seeking me as pastor, most of the inquirers have been inquiring long. Numbers are often given rashly; no man knows how many are convinced; perhaps thirty such are known to me; I lay little stress on registration in this matter, and deprecate publicity. I have found it a good way to appoint a certain hour *every day*, for persons willing to be talked with. Never have I felt so much the need of plain elementary instruction as to the simplest matters in religion. The greater the excitements around us, the more I see the absolute necessity of knowledge. People come to me, who have not even the meaning of justification.[23]

---

week the meeting, which embraces Potts, Van Zandt, Hutton, Prentice, A.D. Smith, &c., was at our church. The house was filled. Every day but one it was as solemn and tender as most communion seasons. Constant attendance for weeks leaves my judgment unaltered, that it is bad to throw the meeting open for whomsoever to speak and pray." Hall, *Letters*, 2:277.

21. "The statistics of conversion are sometimes unsafe; where there is so much room for mistake and exaggeration, it may by wisest to venture no figures." J. W. Alexander, *The Revival and Its Lessons: A Collection of Fugitive Papers, Having Reference To The Great Awakening* (New York: Anson D. F. Randolph, 1859), 8–9.

22. Archibald Alexander found similar doctrinal ignorance during his ministry in Philadelphia: "There is a very wrong opinion frequently entertained of congregations in such a place as this; as if all the members were well informed people. The truth is, there is much less religious knowledge among the bulk of the people here than in the country. Multitudes grow up with very little knowledge of the doctrines of religion, and many after they are grown join themselves to a congregation by taking pews, who were never instructed at all. These require very plain preaching, and when they become serious need to be taught the very first principles of the doctrine of Christ." Alexander, *The Life of Archibald Alexander*, 283.

23. Hall, *Letters*, 2:277.

His correspondence from April also provides detailed commentary on the preaching of Charles Finney. The famed evangelist visited New York during the spring of 1858. Although no longer at the height of his earlier career as a revivalist, Finney still commanded audiences wherever he spoke. Alexander had opportunity to sit under Finney's ministry on April 28. A letter written the following day on April 29 records his impressions of Finney's message.

> While it is in my mind I will jot down something about Finney, whom I heard last night at Cheever's. Assembly middling. F. looks sound and well, but, of course, older. He preaches in spectacles, and with a "brief," which he mentions: "my little brief, here." Manner much subdued. Voice ringing and capital, but with Yankee twang and nasality. Perfectly colloquial and lawyerlike; avoiding every big word, and as plain as any one could be talking to children. Says the same thing over and over and over, sometimes pausing between, with a singular effect on attention and memory. Doctrinal and argumentative, but hortatory; with numerous anecdotes and illustrations. Text was: "This is the record," &c. His sermon (*exceptis excipiendis* [with necessary exceptions]) might have been preached by the Erskines or McCheyne. It was all about Christ and believing. *E.g.*, "All you have to do is to *believe.*" "There is the *record*: God has *given his Son.*" "He says not 'I will give so and so, *if* you do so, &c.,' but *God hath given.*" "You are all looking inward for feelings and experience, before believing. Believe first. Believe the record. Then you will have feelings." Figure: A New York beggar. Steamer bring news of a great donation in his hands. But he does not believe it. "I am no rich man; rich men have fine clothes, money, coach and horses, my experience is all the other way." "Belief of the record brings soul into union with Christ, and experience ensues." He was able and tremendous against infidels. The interest, though intellectual, was intense. I find his plan and all the details graven in my memory. He keeps up the obsolete custom of an Inquiry Meeting, after sermon.[24]

Alexander's letter on April 29 includes additional observations on the progress of the revival among the clergy and laity of New York. "Seriousness prevails among us," he told Hall. "I have had no extra meetings, except four exhortations on doctrines connected with conversion, &c. The best means I have alighted on is an hour given out to receive persons

---

24. Hall, *Letters*, 2:278.

seeking direction every day. This has brought many, and some very often; and the interviews have been sometimes long and always private." "I expect to take in on examination more than thirty-five, and less than fifty."[25] His hesitation regarding indiscriminate speaking and prayer at the public gatherings remained a concern. "The daily prayer-meetings are unabated in interest. Long attendance in no degree reconciles me to the license given to A B or C, to teach or pray; nor to the advertisements requesting prayer."[26] Most of all, he was encouraged by the ministerial fellowship the revival engendered. "The presence of numerous ministers in fraternity, and their frequent remarks and expositions, produce a good impression," he assured Hall.[27]

Writing about an upcoming trip to Princeton, Alexander shared his hope of visiting with Hall while in the area.[28] The busyness of the preceding weeks had sapped much of his energy. "I feel it almost necessary to interrupt the tension of thought and feeling," he said. On a positive note, he remarked on the growth of his congregation. "Our Session has admitted fifty-seven on examination, and four on certificate. The majority are persons with whom I have been dealing for years." He was happy to report that he knew "of no abatement in religious interest."[29] Prayer remained a priority in the gatherings. "The noon-day prayer meeting (this week in the 1st Church) was crowded. There must have been twenty

---

25. One biographer notes: "Fifty-seven persons made their first profession in the April (1858) communion, and many subsequently; so that the year's report of the session in April 1859—the last one he lived to present to the General Assembly—gave a total of one hundred and twenty-five additions on examination. This number included some who worshipped statedly in the Mission Chapel, which then was still under the care of the one session. The whole number of communicants at that time was 711." "James Waddell Alexander," 78–79.

26. In a letter written six months later, Alexander remarked: "I most earnestly wish that these frequent prayer meetings, which have now grown into regular feasts and fasts, could have infused into them some scriptural instruction." Hall, *Letters*, 2:283.

27. Hall, *Letters*, 2:278.

28. Hall notes that Alexander was elected a trustee of the College of New Jersey in 1851. His involvement with the school included enrollment as a student, and subsequent service as a tutor, professor, and trustee. At the time of his anticipated visit, Alexander was involved with the Committee of Examination of the Senior Class.

29. In a footnote Hall states, "The whole number of new communicants received in the years 1858–'9, was 125 in examination; 32 on certificate. These numbers include those who worshipped at the Mission Chapel." Hall, *Letters*, 2:279.

ministers yesterday; still, solemn, and tender; more like a communion than a prayer-meeting."[30]

In addition to the remarkable events taking place in the city at this time, one of the great preacher-theologians in nineteenth-century American Presbyterianism filled the pulpit at the Fifth Avenue Presbyterian Church during late spring. On May 10, "by appointment of the Board of Foreign Missions," the Rev. R. L. Dabney preached before Alexander's congregation during a season of communion. "Dabney's sermon," Alexander remarked, "was a marvelous one, for logic, weight, and scholarship."[31] The entire lower floor of the church was filled with communicants about to receive their first communion meal, among whom was one of Alexander's sons.

Alexander concluded his extended series on the book of Acts during the month of May—a total of sixty-eight lectures in all. He was grateful for the series, acknowledging the help that his brother's recent commentary on Acts had been to him.[32] "I have never put any one in my place, and never substituted any other passage. The attendance has constantly increased." "In no instance," he informed Hall, "have I ever penned a line in preparation for them."[33]

The busyness of the preceding months had physically fatigued Alexander's frail constitution. He admitted how tired he was from his labors. "I have no plans for summer," he wrote. "My brain needs rest."[34] A letter from June 1858 mentions a deterioration of health. "Having passed through a winter of unexampled employment with perfect health, I am seized with a severe cough upon the accession of summer."[35]

Alexander continued his pastoral work through the summer months, with only a few short letters written to Hall. Travel to Saratoga is mentioned along with some other communities, but remarks on summer vacation are largely absent as described in earlier years. A passing reference describes his frustration with the debates on church government taking place at a recent General Assembly. "Weary, weary, am I of these

---

30. Hall, *Letters*, 2:279.
31. Hall, *Letters*, 2:279.
32. J. A. Alexander, *The Acts of the Apostles Explained*, 2 vols. (New York: Scribner, 1857; repr., Minneapolis: Klock & Klock, 1980).
33. Hall, *Letters*, 2:279.
34. Hall, *Letters*, 2:279.
35. Hall, *Letters*, 2:280.

[theological] controversies *de lana caprina* [concerning unproductive trifles]. I have a peculiar position; being in favour of strict subscription, but to a very short creed."[36] By September, he was again able to report on improvement to his health. "I have been very well," he told Hall.

While the preceding months had been filled with a flurry of pastoral activity, he found time to attend public lectures delivered by visiting speakers. He was especially pleased with speeches that he had heard delivered in New York City by "Jno. McGregor, Esq., of London, on the Open-air preaching, ragged schools, and other philanthropies of England." "He is a barrister of the Middle Temple, a downright, rapid, witty, merry speaker, whose description of low life in London and the means of dealing with it, was sometimes almost in the Dickens vein," Alexander observed. Alexander appreciated his interest in alleviating the needs of the poor and preaching open-air discourses. The latter was particularly impressive to Alexander because of the pew-letting with which he had to battle throughout his ministerial life among American Presbyterian churches. Alexander remained optimistic that the practice would eventually be discontinued. "After I am dead and gone, I feel sure our cities will have large and elegant free churches." "I would not object to sumptuousness," he quipped, "if it went to elevate, solace, and enrich the poor."[37]

Publications

Despite the increased ministry demands that accompanied the outbreak of revival, Alexander continued to work on various manuscripts for publication. A new collection of sermons which he had compiled titled *Discourses on Common Topics of Christian Faith and Practice* was about to go to press in early fall of 1858.[38] A volume of 463 pages in length, the collection dealt with a variety of subjects related to the Christian life.[39] Although filled

---

36. Hall, *Letters*, 2:281.
37. Hall, *Letters*, 2:282.
38. James W. Alexander, *Discourses on Common Topics of Christian Faith and Practice* (New York: Charles Scribner, 1858; repr., Birmingham, Ala.: Solid Ground Christian Books, 2004).
39. "The affectionate and often fondly partial hearers of any preacher, are apt to desire the publication of what has been blessed to their spiritual strength and comfort; and such derive a profit from the printed book which cannot be measured by its intrinsic quality. It is with this view that these pages are more particularly dedicated to the beloved people of my charge." Alexander, *Discourses*, 4.

with much valuable material, Alexander considered it the least favorite of the sermon collections he had published from his pulpit ministry.[40]

A related collection of revival tracts written and distributed during the previous months was also soon to be published under the title *The Revival and Its Lessons*.[41] Authored primarily by Alexander and an anonymous contributor, the little volume was intended to help ordinary people assess their spiritual state and interest in the work of grace that was taking place in the city.[42] While modest in size, the volume provides an important introduction to the distinguishing characteristics of the revival and theological emphases that undergirded Alexander's ministry to his church and community.[43] Chapter titles include: "The Revival; Seek to Save Souls; Pray for the Spirit; The Unawakened; Harden not your Hearts; Varieties in Anxious Inquiry; Looking unto Jesus; God be merciful to me a Sinner!; O for more Feeling!; Have I come to Christ?; My Teacher—My Master; My Brother; Sing Praises; The Harvest of New York; Compel them to Come In; Help the Seaman; To Firemen."[44]

Alexander provided a brief preface to his work, highlighting key aspects of the phenomenon. As he observes, the revival followed upon what was arguably the worst financial crisis ever experienced in American history. In the summer and fall of 1857, America's banking industry collapsed, and countless numbers of investors lost their financial assets overnight. Alexander writes:

---

40. "I have never sent a book to press with as little self-gratulation." Hall, *Letters*, 2:282.

41. The work was entered according to Act of Congress in 1858 but not published until 1859.

42. "The short papers here for the first time gathered, had a certain measure of acceptance, less from their own merit, than from their having been struck off during the prevalence of an unusual interest in divine things. For the most part they were penned in the intervals of a hurried life, with the hope that scriptural instruction of the simplest kind might gain a hearing, at a time when every one's attention was drawn to the work of God in the land." Alexander, *Revival and Its Lessons*, 5.

43. "The very titles of these seventeen tracts (one of them written by an intimate fellow-labourer in the ministry) show their high evangelical character and aim, and the wide range of usefulness to which they are adapted, and in which they will doubtless long continue to give what may be almost regarded as their author's dying testimony to the truth and excellency of the gospel of Christ." Hall, *Letters*, 2:237.

44. As individual tracts, Hall notes that "a large number of these were distributed at the police stations. The one addressed to firemen was sent to each of the engine houses in sufficient number to furnish a copy to each member of the department." Hall, *Letters*, 2:276.

Besides the great number who were utterly ruined, there were ten times as many whose earthly destinies seemed to be in libration. If we were to look no further than to the wear and tear of mind and brain, caused by pecuniary apprehensions and troubles in business, such as drove some to despair and madness, the evil could not be reckoned at the rate of millions of gold and silver.[45]

In God's providence, what often hardens men to spiritual realities was used on this occasion to make them hunger and thirst after that which remains and abides.

In the present instance, it pleased God, in his marvelous loving-kindness, by the ploughshare of his judgments to furrow the ground for precious seed of salvation, and to make distresses touching worldly estate to awaken desire for durable riches and righteousness. Out of the eater came forth meat and out of the strong came forth sweetness. From the very heart of these trials emerged spiritual yearnings, thirsting, and supplications after the fountain of living waters.[46]

One of the notable characteristics of the revival was a strong emphasis on prayer.[47] Its origins can be found in the consistory room of the North Dutch Church at the Corner of William and Fulton Streets. It was here that Jeremiah Lanphier and a few others gathered with a handful of businessmen during the noon hour "to confer, to read the Word, to sing, and to cry unto God for the outpouring of his Holy Spirit."[48] The numbers in attendance quickly outgrew the facilities and spread across the city. As Alexander notes, the "great attraction was Prayer."

The great business was intercession. This, as springing from the "love of the Spirit" seems especially pleasing to God, who answers us more signally when we seek the good of others. As the meeting went on, solicitude for the conversion of sinners unto God became more apparent. Requests bearing this character were greatly multiplied. From curiosity, from inward anguish, from vague alarm, from

---

45. Alexander, *Revival and Its Lessons*, 5.
46. Alexander, *Revival and Its Lessons*, 6.
47. For important firsthand accounts of the phenomena, see Samuel I. Prime, *The Power of Prayer: Illustrated in the Wonderful Displays of Divine Grace at the Fulton Street and Other Meetings in New York and Elsewhere, in 1857 and 1858* (New York: Charles Scribner, 1859; repr., Edinburgh: Banner of Truth, 1991).
48. Alexander, *Revival and Its Lessons*, 6.

the mingled motives in which religious concern has its beginnings, numbers of worldly visitors entered the doors. Conversion after conversion was reported.[49]

The awakening first began among churchgoers and then quickly spread among nonbelievers. As the revival spread, interest in prayer continued. Prayer was as formative for its development as it was for its origin. "It was eminently, a revival of Prayer. Desires to approach God, jointly, in importunate supplication, were awakened. This was perhaps the leading characteristic. It was repeatedly noticed, that assemblies were more interested in the prayers than the addresses."[50]

> Never was this so strikingly the case. Never have we known such honor conferred upon God's ordinance of prayer. And the mode of prayer which prevailed, as has already been hinted, was Intercession. Every relation of life has appeared in tender, touching request. The applications for such intercessory address have been numberless; and if not always seasonable or judicious, they have generally been affecting. They have been transmitted hundreds of miles, and from all parts of the land.[51]

Alexander is careful to point out that every work of revival has its own "peculiarities…arising from acknowledged diversities in the sovereign dispensation of the Spirit." In the case of the revival that took place in New York, it "was not the result of human project, concerted arrangement, or prescribed plan. It was not an excitement foreseen, predicted, and made to order."

> Equally incontestable is it, that this great interest in things divine and eternal, did not "come with observation." There had been no pomp of preparation. Indeed the foregoing season was one of remarkable aridity and dearth; so that multitudes of the younger professing Christians had never seen what is called a Revival. And even when the holy elevation of feeling was at its height, it was, in the circle open to our survey, entirely free, on one hand from the machinery of religious maneuver, and, on the other hand, from manifestations of an unruly enthusiasm. An exception here and there, out of thousands, lamented, suppressed, and never propagating itself, in no degree

---

49. Alexander, *Revival and Its Lessons*, 7–8.
50. Alexander, *Revival and Its Lessons*, 10.
51. Alexander, *Revival and Its Lessons*, 11.

impairs the force of the assertion just made. Decorous stillness, reverent waiting upon God, and a tender sense of the heavenly presence, have marked many of these delightful assemblages.[52]

A prominent feature of the revival in New York City that Alexander comments on is the visible unity it created among Christians of different denominational persuasions:

> That fraternity which had been sought with less success by separate means, was here seen to flow naturally from concert in prayer; under the influences of the Holy Spirit; thus indicating it may be the source from which we are to expect the sublime unity of a coming day. Except where some unscriptural and exclusive pretensions have been trampled on, it has not been heard that any branch of the Christian Church has uttered complaint. There has been no compromise of tenets, except as to the utterance of disputed points upon the common ground. In our country at least there has never been so open an acknowledgment of varying Christians by one another.[53]

Another unique feature of the revival was that it had not originated with any one individual's ministry. "The observation has been often made, and with the greatest truth, that among the instruments of this awakening no prominence has been given to particular men, or distinguished gifts of learning and eloquence." It originated with laypeople, and never had any kind of clerical dominance directing its course. "But there has not been the slightest tendency, so far as appears, to magnify any special human agency, or to lean upon what is often alleged to be the inordinate strength of public exhortation."[54]

"Two great truths have been made exceedingly prominent, in every stage of the revival," Alexander said, "the influence of the Holy Spirit, and free salvation through the righteousness of the Lord Jesus Christ."[55] Alexander proceeds to compare and contrast the characteristics of revivals that have taken place throughout the history of the Christian church; while each had distinct features, all were equally a work of the Spirit of God:

---

52. Alexander, *Revival and Its Lessons*, 9–10.
53. Alexander, *Revival and Its Lessons*, 11.
54. Alexander, *Revival and Its Lessons*, 12.
55. Alexander, *Revival and Its Lessons*, 13.

The rumor of what God has done for us has gone into other lands, and believers there have inquired with eagerness into the state of the facts, the means which have been used, and the likelihood of benefit from adapting our means to their condition. Our brethren abroad have probably been prone to ascribe to our churches an absolute advancement in piety much beyond the truth. The principles should never be forgotten, that while the great laws of the divine government and the dispensation of grace remain the same, the Supreme Giver varies his modes of bounty, with reference to differences of country and period. Apostolic awakenings were in some things unlike those of the Reformation day. The quiet, spring-like renewal of vital godliness, under Spener, Francke, and the Pietists, bore little external resemblance to the prodigious revolution under the Wesleys, Whitefield, Edwards, the Tennents and the Blairs. The very remarkable awakenings in which Dr. Nettleton and his friends were instrumental differ again from the times of refreshing in which we live. Let us not limit the Holy One of Israel.[56]

For Such a Time as This

On Sunday, November 21, 1858, Alexander had the privilege of preaching the opening message for a series of religious services to be held at "The Academy of Music" in downtown New York. The special location was chosen to accommodate the large number of people expected to attend. Interest in religious assemblies was strong, and love for the preaching of the Word of God was evident among the city's population. He preached from Revelation 22:17. Although the weather was "dismal," the crowd in attendance was estimated to be near three thousand. "Numbers sat in the lobbies and saloons, of the very class who are never seen in church. I wish I could see a free church to hold just as many, and as easy to speak in," he commented in a letter on November 23. Apparently, not everyone in Alexander's circles felt such a meeting was appropriate. "Our faultfinders, however, who spy the evil in all plans of others, and suggest none of their own, find objection to this night-meeting also."[57]

Alexander also reported to Hall about developments in the prayer meetings being held throughout the city. "The daily prayer-meetings down town keep up with great spirit, having an influx of strangers; our

---

56. Alexander, *Revival and Its Lessons*, 14.
57. Hall, *Letters*, 2:283.

uptown ones have no revival character, but simply the grave and occasionally tender character of an ordinary large meeting of Christians."[58]

In his letter to Hall, Alexander again opined on the struggle he had in stimulating interest among his congregation for sending out individuals and families to help build up struggling works in the city. Presbyterians were not the only denomination facing the closing of churches in areas where the population demographics had changed. Despite the spiritual awakening that had taken place, interest in outreach had not developed in the ways Alexander had hoped. He wrote:

> I have never succeeded in getting a single man to leave us, for the purpose of building up weak churches, and I have had every occasion to ask it and press it. As population moves up, each of the lower churches in its turn dwindles. It is just the same with the Baptists and Methodists. The Episcopalians are the principal free-churches, since the Methodists went over so largely to pewsyism.[59]

1859—"God, My Exceeding Joy"

Alexander wrote to Hall and his family on January 4, 1859, wishing them all a happy New Year. The year, he said, was off to a busy start because New Year's day had fallen on a Saturday. The customary round of pastoral visitation on the first day of a new year kept Alexander occupied. "There was not much rest," he told his friend, before he began his Sabbath ministrations.

Various physical maladies still plagued Alexander. His letter also expresses concern for what the ailments indicated. "My reins, by occasional suffering, instruct me, with regard to weakness and mortality; and at this moment I am ailing—though unusually well in general health."[60]

Two weeks later, the Alexander brothers (James, Addison, and Samuel) enjoyed the rare privilege of sharing in one another's pulpit ministries on the Lord's Day.[61] It was a special moment not soon forgotten by brothers whose hearts had been knit together through birth and, even more profoundly, a common salvation in Christ in whose service they had each

---

58. Hall, *Letters*, 2:283–84.
59. Hall, *Letters*, 2:284.
60. Hall, *Letters*, 2:284.
61. Samuel Alexander, a lesser-known brother to James and Addison, served a congregation in nearby Freehold, New Jersey.

devoted their lives and professional careers. Henry Carrington Alexander's account illumines the deep spiritual emotions that the day evoked:

> On the 17th of January, Dr. Addison Alexander preached for his brother James in the morning, and Dr. James Alexander for his brother Samuel in the afternoon. The brothers James and Addison sat together in the Nineteenth street pulpit. The former of these records that he felt the solemnity of sitting in the pulpit with one brother in the morning and with the other in the afternoon. He also gave vent to a wish or sigh, that he could preach with more simplicity and nature—less of the conventional, less regard for rule, less care for criticism, more as Calvin, as Luther, as Paul preached. "As life runs on," he says, "I feel the seriousness of my situation as a minister, but oh, how little improvement! Oh, my ascended Lord and Master! Be pleased to anoint me afresh for my ministry, send me some new and special grace, and cast me not aside as a useless instrument: for Christ's sake. Amen."[62]

Henry Carrington Alexander also notes J. W. Alexander's growing despondency over his feeling of pastoral inadequacy. The fatigue of public ministry, increasing physical frailty, and sense of failure in having fallen short in pursuit of the life of faith all coalesced in Alexander's sense of debilitation. "This fear," Henry Alexander said, "was becoming an increasing anxiety to him. He had a dread of growing old and worthless, and of being incapacitated for the service of his Master."[63]

Despite his deepening depression, Alexander was heartened by a growth in mission outreach sponsored by his congregation to the destitute and unchurched. Writing in early February, he remarks on the encouragement he found in the progress of their Mission Chapel. "Nineteen," he said, "have been admitted on examination, making nearly 70 in the Chapel, during the year."[64]

An unusual entry can be found in a letter dated April 4, 1859. In addition to making note of a prolonged irritation in his larynx and a bout of indisposition that prevented him from preaching the previous day, the letter describes an unusual encounter with "spiritualism." While various forms of spiritualism and "door-knocking" were mentioned in earlier letters, this is the fullest account we have of Alexander's exposure to the

---

62. Alexander, *Life of Joseph Addison Alexander*, 2:825–26.
63. Alexander, *Life of Joseph Addison Alexander*, 2:826.
64. Hall, *Letters*, 2:285.

phenomena. Although "spiritualism" was increasingly common in mid-nineteenth-century America, it was not a pastoral matter Alexander had been called upon to address before.[65] "I have, for the first time, to treat a case of spiritualism," he wrote to Hall. He summarizes the man's case:

> A man, well educated, sound health, good habits, strong mind in every other direction; but perfectly hag-ridden by spirits of his wife, his father, and Robert Hall. He sits up sometimes whole nights, writing; or rather his hand is used by the spirits; the character varying with the spirit. He himself is willing to believe it demonical possession; but I have not felt clear to take this ground with him.[66]

Writing a few weeks later on April 19, Alexander comments on what he considered to be a "Divine monition." New ailments afflicted him, and he believed them to be precursors of greater trouble to come.[67] He writes:

> For the first time in my life I have been attacked with something like chills—now about a fortnight. The beginning was a tremendous shake, which made all quake again; since then, crawls, or whatever be the name of those simulations. During these the feeling of "misery" has been very great. I have spoken to very few persons of it, but since the beginning of the year, I have lost all power in the middle-finger of my right hand. The finger *stutters* in writing; indeed, I cannot use it at all. Whether this is paralysis I know not, but I regard it as a Divine monition. I am under regular and active treatment. Writing, which was a solace, has become a very burdensome task.[68]

In the weeks that followed, Alexander's health fluctuated but continued on a downward spiral. On May 1, he preached a Sunday-school sermon with what Hall described "as an unusual and unnecessary power of voice." The following week, Alexander preached at a communion service on May 8 from 1 Peter 2:24. It would be his last sermon.

On May 9, Alexander wrote to Hall, saying, "My health has steadily gone down: yet, through mercy, I was enabled to get through the

---

65. For a valuable study on the phenomena, see Bret E. Carroll, *Spiritualism in Antebellum America* (Bloomington: Indiana University Press, 1997).
66. Hall, *Letters*, 2:286.
67. "The diary of the elder brother for the spring months is a reflex of his feelings during a season of profound nervous and mental depression, connected no doubt with the gradual decay of his physical powers." Alexander, *Life of Joseph Addison Alexander*, 2:868.
68. Hall, *Letters*, 2:286–87.

communion services." Initially, Alexander hoped to find respite by sailing to Richmond, then traveling on to Drake's Branch, Charlotte County, and afterward visiting the University of Virginia. By May 10, however, he was forced to change his itinerary. "A change in the signs of Providence has changed my plans. So obviously my cough has increased, and my flesh has decreased, that Session and Trustees, *motu proprio* [on his own impulse], last night ordered me to vacate from now till October 1. I propose to go to Virginia in about a fortnight. Don't stay at home an hour; but if it be fair I will try to drop in *chez vous* [your house] some day this week."[69]

Alexander wrote to Hall again on May 25 to update him on his condition. Although packed and ready to leave, Alexander's doctor forbade him travel. "We are forbidden by the doctor to go, in consequence of my severe cough, but more particularly a fever which comes on at night." At the time, he had night sweats and a pulse of 120. "Plans uncertain," he told Hall. "I have not gained any. I endeavour to cast my burden on the Lord."[70]

In a brief letter to Hall at the end of May, Alexander said that he was "ready to catch at any little straw of amendment." "I feel cheered by being very slightly better to-day," he remarked, "though after a bad night of vexing dreams and waking. My cough is in abeyance; the disguised chill and consequent fever return every evening. I have taken a refreshing drive for three successive days."[71]

By early June, Alexander was well enough to travel. The Alexander family journeyed by train, their route taking them through the state of New Jersey, home to so many memories of their life together. As Alexander's train passed through Princeton, Hall notes that "his emotions gave unequivocal signs of his reflecting that it was likely to be the last view he should have of that endeared place."[72]

Writing from the University of Virginia on June 7, 1859, Alexander spoke of the pleasantness of his surroundings. "In Virginia I have mountains, numerous friends, at whose houses (as here) I can be sheltered, with sweet, rural quiet, and daily horse-exercise." "The journey has done me good, though I have very bad nights."[73]

---

69. Hall, *Letters*, 2:287.
70. Hall, *Letters*, 2:287.
71. Hall, *Letters*, 2:288.
72. Hall, *Letters*, 2:288.
73. Hall, *Letters*, 2:288.

As Alexander reflected on his condition, he shared with Hall the lessons that he was learning in relation to the living out of God's will in one's life during a time of sickness. He writes:

> After having written and printed a good deal about sickness, health, &c., I find there are pages of experience to turn over, which are quite new. Especially do I see that we may be brought into stumbling and stripping dispensations, of which during their continuance we cannot comprehend the nature. I never felt more perfectly resigned to God's will, or more disposed to justify all his dealings, be it life or death, or disability. This is my strong permanent feeling. Nevertheless, with this, and perhaps from physical depression, all things seem sad. The chords are unstrung, and the instrument relaxed. Give my love to all yours, and to inquisitive friends.[74]

A letter that Alexander penned on June 9 to James M. Halsted speaks optimistically about a recovery in health, though it is guarded in its realism:

> Since our arrival here, I have on the whole been a gainer. While I cannot say that my cough is gone, it is wonderfully lessened, and quite suspended for long periods. My nights are bad, and I suffer from a dyspeptic collie, which makes very strict diet necessary. My appetite is good, and I am riding on horseback every day. My friends think I shall recover, against the fall. That is as God pleases, unto whom I desire to submit myself.[75]

During his stay at the University of Virginia, Alexander lodged "with his wife's brother, Dr. James L. Cabell, Professor of Comparative Anatomy and Physiology." Cabell records Alexander's distress during the first few days of his visit over the complications his illness was causing for his congregation back in New York. Letters from his elders assuring him of their support and desire for him to take whatever time would be necessary to recover his health helped set his mind at ease. "The remainder of his days," Cabell notes, "was spent in tranquil enjoyment, evidently at peace with God through faith in Christ, and in love and charity with all men."[76]

Housebound and unable to attend public worship, Alexander composed prayers to quiet his soul. "On the 12th he was again kept from

---

74. Hall, *Letters*, 2:288–89.
75. Hall, *Letters*, 2:289.
76. Hall, *Letters*, 2:291–92.

the sanctuary, and took the opportunity of writing out a most heart-searching prayer for help and comfort." Just as he had as a young pastor found comfort in the reading of published prayers, he now found spiritual solace in their composition as a statement of his faith. The closing portion of an extended prayer follows:

> And oh! for Jesus's sake make me sweetly submissive to all thy holy will; cheerful in hope; perfect in acquiescence; setting an example of Christian peace and patience. Oh! that my discourse may be always with grace, seasoned with salt, that it may be for the edification of the hearers. And, O my ever glorious God! Condescend to lift up thy poor, sunken creature from the earth, and deliver him from those subduing influences which oppress both body and soul. *Jehovah Rophi*, stretch out thy mighty arm for cure. *Jesu Rophi*, vouchsafe to heal, as of old. And oh! graciously pardon for Christ's sake. Amen.[77]

Faced with Alexander's declining health, the family determined to make the trip to the mountains where he could enjoy the benefits of the Warm Springs baths. The Alexanders left the university at noon on July 12, eventually taking "a chartered coach for the Warm Springs." Alexander's delight in the mountain scenery during their journey "was almost rapturous."[78] "He would repeatedly say that he had no language of his own adequate to the expression of his feelings, and could only exclaim with the Psalmist: 'Oh that men would praise the Lord for His goodness and for His wonderful works to the children of men.'"[79]

The family enjoyed a week of respite at the Warm Springs.[80] Alexander's appearance improved, and Cabell and others hoped it was a sign of

---

77. Alexander, *Life of Joseph Addison Alexander*, 2:869.
78. A diary entry for Sunday, July 17 captures the essence of Alexander's delight: "A Sabbath quiet in this lovely spot. Though my health is less encouraging, I thank God that I have so lively a sensibility to the beauties and glories of his creation. The sights, sounds, and odours are all rural, all mountainous. Every bird and flower and tree, and the variety is great, seems placed aright in a beautiful harmony with the whole. Gentle ascents of mountains on several sides, enclosing this happy valley; grassy up to a certain point of their smooth sides, then merging into thick forests, the line of junction being marked with beautiful shades; herds and flocks ever and anon emerging into the light. It is a country of springs, and the sound of water is much in our ears." Alexander, *Life of Joseph Addison Alexander*, 2:870.
79. Hall, *Letters*, 2:293.
80. "One day the sunrise, out of creamy mountain mists, was transcendent. It was almost celestial. The patient sufferer read the 104th Psalm, and looking abroad over the

recovery. Alexander felt otherwise. "I have a strange feeling of increasing debility," he remarked.

At Alexander's encouragement, the family set out for the Red Sweet Springs. Cabell's narrative continues the story of Alexander's final journey:

> He was impatient to go on to the Red Sweet Springs, (Alleghany county,) his favourite resort in these mountains. Waiting for a rain to lay the dust and cool the air, we left the Warm Springs on the 20th July, the day after a heavy shower had produced this twofold change, on a bright and beautiful morning. But we had not gone many miles before we found, to our great regret, that the clouds of the preceding day had not extended far in the direction of our road, and we were greatly oppressed by the heat and dust. Towards noon he requested me to stop the coach at the nearest house as he was suffering extreme pain. In about a quarter of an hour we reached an obscure country tavern, where we remained four or five hours, and then proceeded eight miles further to a more comfortable house, where well-ventilated rooms and good bedding could be obtained. Here, during the night, symptoms of dysentery appeared, but were relieved by prompt remedies to such an extent as to admit of his travelling the next morning over the remaining eighteen miles of his journey, which brought us to the Red Sweet Springs. Having here more comforts, conveniences, and appliances for gratifying his tastes, than could have been brought together elsewhere, both he and my sister made it a subject of thanksgiving that he was permitted to reach a spot endeared to him by its rural and quiet charms and many pleasant associations.[81]

The location, while scenic, was far too busy with traffic for the rest Alexander needed. The family decided to move on to the White Sulphur Springs. The journey, however, proved too much for Alexander's flagging health.

> Our determination to continue our journey was based upon the fact that the tavern at which we lodged, though in many other respects quite comfortable, was rendered unfit for invalids by reason of its being the night-stand for the enormous travel to the White Sulphur

---

enchanting pinnacles cried out, 'Oh, how it lifts the soul!'" Alexander, *Life of Joseph Addison Alexander*, 2:870.

81. Hall, *Letters*, 2:293–94.

Springs. The stages were coming in or going out nearly all night, and there were not two hours of quiet during the entire night. He passed over the eighteen miles with no little discomfort, and with so frequent manifestations of delight as he recalled the familiar objects along the road, that I really thought the disease must have been extinguished. The symptoms returned, however, after our arrival at the Springs, but with so moderate a degree of intensity as to awaken no alarm. The immediate cause of death was an uncontrollable diarrhea supervening upon an attack of dysentery. His system responded readily enough to the remedies employed, and this circumstance induced to indulge very sanguine hopes of his recovery until a few days before the termination; but his physical constitution had been so completely wrecked that he had no recuperative power in reserve for such exigencies. On Wednesday morning, July 27th, after a night of fever, I sent telegraphic communications to his friends respecting his condition. From this time till his death I did not leave his bedside, except to take my meals. Wednesday night the fever was scarcely perceptible, and his sleep was so refreshing that on awaking at dawn of day, he said to me: "I slept delightfully and am much refreshed." An hour or two later he said to my sister: "I must be better—I feel entirely comfortable." This delusive appearance of amendment continued all the day, and slightly revived our hopes. But Thursday night the fever recurred, and again on Friday night. On the latter occasion a collapse ensued on the subsidence of the fever, which looked like the final shaking. He rallied, however, but the fever recurred early Saturday night, and by midnight he was evidently and unquestionably sinking, though he continued to breathe till about five o'clock on the Sabbath morn.[82]

****

In the days leading up to his death, Alexander spent his time preparing farewell messages to friends and family. Cabell's account includes a stirring statement by Alexander regarding his personal trust in the promises of God's Word and the consolation Scripture provided in anticipation of his impending departure:

> Much of the time before his strength entirely failed, was spent in sending messages of farewell and comfort to his congregation and the absent members of his family. He said: "I have not been in the

---

82. Hall, *Letters*, 2:294–95.

habit of talking much on the subject of my own spiritual states of feeling. With respect to my subjective religion, I have often disappointed people who look for manifestations of a certain kind. But I have frequently made known to Elizabeth [his wife] the grounds of my hope." It was now suggested to him that he was exhausting himself, and needed rest, but he added, "Let me say one word more with respect to the solemn event to which you have called my attention. If the curtain were to drop now, and I were this moment ushered into the presence of my Maker, what would be my feelings? They would be these: first, I would prostrate myself in an unutterable sense of my nothingness and guilt; but, secondly, I would look upon my Redeemer with an inexpressible assurance of faith and love. A passage of Scripture which expresses my present feeling is this: 'I know WHOM' (with great emphasis) 'I have believed, and am assured that he is able to keep that which I have committed to him against that day.'" In quoting this sentence he remarked, "some persons read it '*in* whom I have believed,' but there is no preposition. Christ himself was the direct object of the Apostle's faith." This took place about twenty hours before his departure, after which he fell into a sweet sleep, which continued till the last.[83]

While issues of melancholy had plagued Alexander throughout his lifetime, his final days were remarkably free from affliction.[84] He approached death with a confidence founded on the finished work of Christ on his behalf. The sting of death had already been removed in the victory of Christ's cross and triumphant resurrection from the grave. Cabell's closing observations capture the strong faith in which Alexander lived and by which he died back home in the mountains of the state that meant so much to him and his family:

> It increases our cause of thankfulness for the perfect peacefulness and serenity of this passage through the valley of the shadow of death, to know that Dr. Alexander expected to suffer some severe spiritual conflicts before his release. In view of such a trial he had deliberately prepared the minds of those who might be expected to be most

---

83. Hall, *Letters*, 2:295.
84. "His warfare was now almost accomplished; but the declining slopes of the hill were at length irradiated with heavenly sunshine. If his sun went down while it was yet day, it sank in the spotless heavens. The cloud which had so long hung over his prospects and happiness was now forever rolled away, and the remaining weeks and days of his life were a serene contemplation of the glory of nature and the more resplendent 'glory that was to be revealed in him.'" Alexander, *Life of Joseph Addison Alexander*, 2:868.

deeply moved by it; reminding them of the nature of such temporary temptations of faith, as sometimes occur in Christian experience before the final triumph, and bidding them not to be disturbed by what might take place in his own instance. But no such darkness, doubt, or trouble came, even for a moment. His countenance, even in silence and sleep, bore such a happy and transported expression, that it was remarked by one who witnessed it that he was already looking into heaven. In this respect, those prayers appear to be answered, which were intimated by his speaking of the comfort he found in his death-bed in such stanzas as these, (translated from German:)

> Forsake me not, my God,
> Thou God of my salvation!
> Give me thy light, to be
> My sure illumination.
> My soul to folly turns,
> Seeking she knows not what:
> Oh! lead her to thyself—
> My God, forsake me not!
>
> Forsake me not, my God!
> Take not thy Spirit from me;
> And suffer not the might
> Of sin to overcome me.
> A father pitieth
> The children he begot;
> My Father, pity me;
> My God, forsake me not!
>
> Forsake me not, my God!
> Thou God of life and power,
> Enliven, strengthen me,
> In every evil hour;
> And when the sinful fire
> Within my heart is hot,
> Be not thou far from me;
> My God, forsake me not!
> Forsake me not, my God!

Uphold me in my going;
That evermore I may
Please thee in all well-doing;
And that thy will, O Lord,
May never be forgot
In all my works and ways—
My God, forsake me not!

Forsake me not, my God!
I would be thine forever.
Confirm me mightily
In every right endeavour.
And when my hour is come,
Cleansed from all stain and spot
Of sin, receive my soul;
My God, forsake me not![85]

---

85. Hall, *Letters*, 2:295–97.

IN MEMORY OF
JAMES WADDELL ALEXANDER
FOR THIRTEEN YEARS THE BELOVED
AND REVERED PASTOR OF THIS CHURCH;
WHOSE SINGULAR NATURAL GIFTS,
RIPENED BY GENEROUS CULTURE,
WERE SUCCESSFULLY GIVEN TO HIS SACRED WORK;
AND WHO, BY HIS FERVENT PIETY,
PURE LIFE, TENDER AFFECTIONS,
LARGE BENEVOLENCE, AND UNSPARING LABOUR,
SO ENDEARED HIMSELF TO
HIS PEOPLE, THAT THEY MOURN
AS FOR A DEAR BROTHER AND BELOVED FRIEND.
HE WAS BORN MARCH 13, 1804,
HE DIED JULY 31, 1859, DECLARING, AS THE
SUM OF HIS FAITH AND HOPE,

"I know whom I have believed, and am persuaded that he is able to keep that which I have committed to him against that day."

Chapter 15

GOD, MY EXCEEDING JOY

As a man whose life was marked by delight in the public worship of God, it is fitting that Alexander's death in the early morning hours of July 31, 1859, took place on the Sabbath. Following his passing, Alexander's body was removed to Princeton to be buried alongside his parents. His burial on August 3 was accompanied by religious services held at the First Presbyterian Church, Princeton. Speakers at the service included "the Rev. Dr. Thompson of New York, Dr. Magie of Elizabeth, Professor Hope, (since deceased,) of the College, and Dr. Hodge, the last of whom preached a discourse from the words in Matthew xxv. 34, 'Then shall the King say unto them on his right hand, Come ye blessed of my Father, inherit the kingdom prepared for you from the foundation of the world.'"[1]

The impact of Alexander's ministry went beyond his denominational affiliation. Hall notes, "The sympathy felt by Christians of all branches of the church, in the removal of Dr. Alexander from their communion, was strikingly displayed in a meeting which took place on the 5th of August, at the most largely frequented of American summer-resorts—Saratoga." Interdenominational in attendance, representatives from a variety of church backgrounds gave common testimony to the respect in which Alexander was held. "At this assembly clergymen of the Episcopal, Congregational, Baptist, Methodist, and Reformed-Dutch, as well as the Presbyterian churches, expressed a common sentiment of brotherly affection and high esteem."[2]

In early October 1859, memorial services were held at Alexander's former church in New York City in commemoration of their late pastor's life

---

1. Hall, *Letters*, 2:299.
2. Hall, *Letters*, 2:299.

and ministry.³ The services took place on the second Sabbath of October, the date having been reserved in anticipation of Alexander's return from Virginia and for celebration of renovations that were to be undertaken to improve the sanctuary's acoustics in order "to assist the voice of the pastor." In place of the renovations and service of dedication, the congregation was presented with a marble tablet commemorating Alexander's ministry. "Inserted in the wall near the pulpit," the tablet served as a public testimony on behalf of Alexander's pastoral labors to the congregation.[4]

During the services of public worship held on that day, commemorative sermons in Alexander's honor were delivered by Professor Charles Hodge and the Rev. Dr. John Hall, Alexander's lifelong friend and correspondent.[5] At the morning service, Hodge spoke from Acts 9:20 on the topic "He Preached Christ." Hall's afternoon message was based on 2 Peter 1:15, "Moreover, I will endeavor that ye may be able, after my decease, to have these things always in remembrance."

Celebrated by his congregation, community, and fellow clergy, J. W. Alexander was particularly missed by his immediate family. A note written by Addison Alexander a month after James's death expresses the emptiness he now felt in his brother's absence.[6] He believed a combi-

---

3. In honor of her late husband, Elizabeth Cabell Alexander published before year's end one of Alexander's final sermons, "Bring Me Up Samuel," dedicating it to the congregation "as a memento of their pastor and an expression of the abiding affection of E.C.A." James W. Alexander, *Bring Me Up Samuel* (New York: Anson D. F. Randolph, 1959).

4. For the tablet's inscription, see the beginning page of this chapter.

5. In his opening remarks, Hall commented on the propriety of holding commemorative services for a deceased minister on the Lord's Day: "Whatever helped to make a minister efficient whilst living, will contribute to enforce and prolong his influence after his decease. The remembrance of the truth he ministered will be assisted by the remembrance of all that qualified him for his usefulness and characterized it; by all that marked him as designed and authorized to be an ambassador of Christ. We may hope, therefore, to aid the practical and permanent objects before us this day and not depart from their legitimate connection with the Lord's day and the Lord's house, by adverting to some of those particulars in which we may discern the arrangements of Providence to qualify our deceased brother for the work assigned him, and which were completed and crowned in his ministry with this congregation." Hall, *Sermons*, 30–31.

6. The two brothers were bound by a lifelong affection for one another. Henry Carrington Alexander comments on the delight Addison felt at his brother's return to the seminary in 1849: "Of course there was much to please the younger brother in the thought of 'James's' return to his old haunts in Steadman street. They were as unlike in many things, and yet as necessary to each other, as two complementary colours. The younger leaned on the intellect and good taste of the elder brother, while the latter felt himself supported by the strong sense and resolute temper of Addison. The mutual admiration and love was truly extraordinary." Alexander, *Life of Joseph Addison Alexander*, 2:670.

nation of "morbid anxieties" and overwork contributed to his brother's premature decline.[7] It is reported that Addison was never the same following James's passing.[8]

> I have no doubt you have often turned in thought to our departed "son of consolation," as if he were still living. With a strange but not unnatural forgetfulness, I find myself looking to him for support even under the irreparable stroke of his own death. I had no conception of my intellectual dependence upon James, until I caught myself continually laying things aside to tell him as the person who could best appreciate and enjoy them. All this says very loudly "cease ye from man whose breath is in his nostrils," and shows the grace and wisdom of that constitution which reserves the office of comforter for a divine person. The circumstances which you mention certainly go far to reconcile us to his death at this time; but I feel now and then a disposition to repine at the circumstances themselves. I have no doubt that he shortened his own life by morbid anxieties, connected not merely with his health, but with his duties. I find it hard to acquiesce without a murmur in the loss of such a man from such a cause, or to reflect, without a momentary pang of discontent, that he might have preached for many years with ease and pleasure, but sunk under the weight of other cares.[9]

The Making of a Pastoral Leader

Every man who is called by the risen Christ to serve in pastoral ministry will be enabled for the responsibilities of the office to which he has been appointed. While the calling is divine in origin, the means by which a man is prepared and shaped to serve as Christ's representative take place in the ordinary circumstances of life as his character is formed and piety matured. In this respect, a number of factors stand out in Alexander's preparation for his work as a gospel minister.

---

7. In a footnote, Hall commented on Addison Alexander's observations: "The writer alludes to his brother's extreme, almost morbid conscientiousness, which led him to attempt an amount of labour beyond his physical ability, and which oppressed his mind when he found he could not overtake his work." Hall, *Letters*, 2:298.

8. "The tidings of his brother's death gave him a shock from which he never recovered. The only indication of his feelings at the time he received the dreadful news, which is presented in his journal, is the heavy black line which he drew under the bare record of the fact. But the grief inwardly consumed him. The iron had entered his soul." Alexander, *Life of Joseph Addison Alexander*, 2:871.

9. Hall, *Letters*, 2:298.

Family

An obvious factor in the shaping of Alexander's character was the family into which he was born and raised. As Hall recounts, "The beginnings of these Providential designs are to be traced to his pious ancestry, and above all, to his immediate parentage." Archibald and Janetta Alexander each came from godly homes and valued the cultivation of piety in their children's lives.[10] Their example of Bible reading, prayer, church attendance, and catechetical instruction bore spiritual fruit in the lives of their children with the passing of the years. While neither James nor his younger brother Addison became Christians until their teenage years and after, both men were given a godly foundation upon which their subsequent conversions were rooted.

Hall properly notes these factors in his observations on Alexander's life and how they contributed to the work of grace that took place in Alexander's heart during his teenage years. Alexander would himself acknowledge the important influence of his mother's and father's piety in the shaping of his character, and he often drew attention to it in his personal correspondence.

College

While a college education may not always be conducive to a young man's spiritual health, the educational opportunities that Alexander received while studying at the College of New Jersey would help shape his character and hone the scholarly skills which in coming years would be put into the service of Christ and His church. Although Alexander's boyish immaturity and spiritual indifference limited the advantages he enjoyed while a student at college, grace overcame the spiritual liabilities of his personality and redirected his affections in the use of the scholarly training he received for his later work as a pastor, author, and professor. The lessons of these years were not lost to Alexander in his subsequent service as a professor at the college and seminary in the manner in which he sought to minister to the spiritual needs and developing personalities of the students he taught.

---

10. "Inheriting the Christian birthright through both lines of descent, grandson of the country pastor whose name he bore, and whose venerable person is an historical portrait in our literature—it is as the son of Archibald and Janetta Alexander, that we of this day are assured that it was his lot not only to be baptized in the name, but raised in the nurture and admonition of the Lord Jesus." Hall, *Sermons*, 31.

Seminary Training

Although Alexander did not complete the three-year program that the seminary curriculum prescribed, his time as a student at Princeton Theological Seminary left an indelible impression upon his character of the high calling and weighty responsibilities inherent to the Christian ministry. Having entered "the third class of the theological school" in the autumn of 1822, he was privileged to enjoy one of the finest ministerial training environments then available to students interested in preparing for the work of Christian ministry. Senior faculty such as Archibald Alexander and Samuel Miller brought a wealth of ministerial wisdom into their classroom instruction from the many years spent in pastoral ministry before becoming professors at the seminary.

While at seminary, Alexander's theological acumen was refined, as was his understanding of the purpose and practice of preaching in the economy of God's salvation. In combination with the instruction he received from his father and others, Alexander's theology of experiential preaching and pastoral care began to take shape in ways that would only be expanded and deepened in the coming years. The combination of campus life, classroom instruction, personal devotions, and developing skill in the art of writing would all prove instrumental in his preparation for the years of pastoral ministry in which he would engage.[11]

Tutor

Alexander's early labors as a tutor at the College of New Jersey not only refined his teaching skills but also provided opportunity for concentrated study in the humanities and the reading of theology in its biblical, theological, historical, and practical divisions. In addition to cultivating the life of the mind, Alexander's responsibilities as resident staff taught him the obligation of addressing logistical and relational problems that he otherwise, by temperament, would have avoided. The experience proved

---

11. "The letters of his years in the Seminary are eloquent with description of his enjoyment of the studies and of the companionship of the band of congenial minds, with whom the topics of the classroom were subjects of animated discussion in their more private and social encounters. Those unrestrained communications also reveal the discipline by which the heart of the future preacher, pastor, and consoler, was learning how to speak to multitudes from the resources of a deep personal experience." Hall, *Sermons*, 34.

salutary in forging his identity and sense of resolve when matters of principled difference are at stake.[12]

Pastoral Service

While Alexander's apprehension of the work and responsibilities of pastoral ministry would continue to grow and develop over the course of his lifetime, his early experiences in ministry would prove influential in shaping his expectation for what the pastoral office entails. The cross-cultural experience he encountered while ministering in Virginia would reshape his approach to extemporaneous preaching and forever change his outlook on the subject of slavery. Likewise, the years spent in Trenton would not only provide ministry experience in an urban setting but would also recalibrate his interest in reaching out to the poor and downtrodden members of society often ostracized by fashionable congregations whose ability to purchase seating in the pew-renting system of churches precluded less fortunate members of the community from joining with them in public worship.

Editor

Alexander's work as an editor may also be viewed as a contributing factor in the shaping of his personality and gifts. His skill as an author had already been proven before assuming the responsibilities of the editorship of *The Presbyterian*, but the experience served to further enhance his literary acumen for the extensive writing ministry to which he devoted himself during his later years as a professor and pastor. The turbulent period in which he worked as editor of *The Presbyterian* helped prepare him to handle the even more contentious strife soon to burst upon his denomination between New School and Old School adherents. Alexander's balance in adjudicating matters of dispute between dissenting brethren in the debates that took place within the Presbyterian Church during the 1830s was as much a trait of his personality as it was a learned skill gained from the equitable obligations inherent to good editorial practice.

---

12. "Here is another item not insignificant to be regarded in the work of his preparation for the life of a pastor; that of counteracting his natural tendency to shrink from everything like authority or discipline over others." Hall, *Sermons*, 37.

With Christ in the School of Faith

By the time Alexander began his eleven-year tenure at the College of New Jersey as Professor of Rhetoric and Belles Lettres, his life had been forever changed through marriage, parenthood, and the various employments and experience in ministry of the preceding years. But God's grace was still at work in Alexander's life, refining his piety, increasing his devotion, and developing his gifts for preaching and pastoral ministry in ways that he could not have anticipated.

As Professor of Rhetoric and Belles Lettres, Alexander was privileged to instruct his students on the great themes and characteristics of classical literature—material that had played an important role in the shaping of Western culture. In his funeral address on behalf of Alexander, Hodge eulogized his friend's academic accomplishments:

> Dr. Alexander united in himself gifts and graces rarely found in combination. God had endowed him with a retentive memory and a perspicacious intellect, with great power of application and acquirement, with singular delicacy of taste, with a musical ear, and a resonant voice. These gifts were all cultivated and turned to the best account. Probably no minister in our church was a more accomplished scholar. He was familiar with English literature in all periods of its history. He cultivated the Greek and Latin, French, German, Italian, and Spanish languages, not merely as a philologist, but for the treasures of knowledge and of taste which they contain. To this wide compass of his studies is in good measure to be referred many of his characteristics as a writer, the abundance of his literary allusions, his curious felicity of expression, and the variety of his imagery. Many of his productions are like strings of pearls; each sentence complete in its own beauty, and all connected by an invisible thread. His facility of production was wonderful. He would often accomplish in days what few men could accomplish in as many weeks. He used his pen as if it were a living member of his body, and found a positive pleasure in its exercise.[13]

Alexander also became an accomplished theologian. His position at the college not only allowed him time for original research among the classic orators and great thinkers of Western civilization, but also provided opportunity for concentrated study in the history of the church and theology. Additional studies while in the pastorate further strengthened

---

13. Hall, *Sermons*, 15–16.

his theological acumen and competency in both didactic and practical theology. Hodge writes of him:

> It was, however, not only in the department of literature that Dr. Alexander was thus distinguished. He was an erudite theologian. Few men were more conversant with the writings of the early fathers, or more familiar with Christian doctrine in all its places. He embraced the faith of the Reformed churches in its integrity with a strength of conviction which nothing but the accordance of that system with his religious experience could produce. A faith founded on argument may be shaken by argument; but a conviction arising from religious experience, that is, from a state of consciousness produced by the Spirit of God, is not to be moved. Theology and philosophy are so related, that devotion to the former involves of necessity the cultivation of the latter. Dr. Alexander was therefore at home in the whole department of philosophical speculation. His last publication was an able exposition of the views of the metaphysicians of the middle ages on one of the most important questions in mental science.[14]

Never content to be only a professional educator, Alexander preached regularly for seven of his eleven years as a college professor to the African American congregation that met on Witherspoon Street in Princeton. It was here Alexander honed simplicity in his preaching skills, having delivered what he considered some of his best sermons.

In addition to regular pastoral visitation in his community, he frequently served as a guest preacher in outlying congregations. An active speaking schedule and experience during seasons of revival taking place at this time in churches along the eastern seaboard matured his thinking on a biblical theology of preaching and the practical effects it will have on the life of piety in individuals, congregations, and communities when the Spirit of God comes in power. Having learned the difference between a nominal religiosity and Holy Spirit—wrought renewal and revival, Alexander prayed and longed for further outpourings of divine grace among the churches and American society.

The labors of his professorship and pastoral activity during these years were offset by the delight he found in his wife and children. But,

---

14. Hall, *Sermons*, 16–17. Alexander's final contribution to the *Biblical Repertory* evidences his familiarity with the complex field of "mental science": James W. Alexander, "The Doctrine of Perception, as held by Doctor Arnauld, Doctor Reid, and Sir William Hamilton," *The Biblical Repertory and Princeton Review* 31, no. 2 (April 1859): 177–206.

as with many families of his time, the joys of parenthood were blighted by the untimely deaths of several of his children to disease. Seasons of bereavement as well as diminishing health were used by God for maturing Alexander's faith in the midst of the loss his family felt at their children's graveside.

Likewise, Alexander's pastoral experience in New York City provided opportunity for the maturing of his gifts and expansion of his awareness of the horizons of ministry to which the Christian church is called. Preaching, pastoral visitation, prayer, and outreach to the poor and downtrodden all found home in Alexander's heart in the ways in which he sought to minister to his church and community.[15] Increasing national influence and public acclaim for pulpit eloquence did little to inflate Alexander's personal pride. Earlier reticence with regard to pastoral visitation had given way to a relentless energy of compassion and outreach to the multitudes around him. Like his Lord before him, Alexander wept over the spiritual condition of Christ's churches and the spiritual ignorance of the communities in which they were situated.

Finally, while sandwiched between his two pastorates in New York City, Alexander's labors as a professor at Princeton Theological Seminary provided further opportunity for the maturation of his thoughts on preaching and pastoral ministry in various articles and journal publications. These were later brought together in published form a few years after his death. His research into the interrelationship between rhetoric and gospel preaching would find fruition in an important and still valuable work titled *Thoughts on Preaching*, published posthumously in 1860 and in revised form in 1864.[16] A volume of 318 pages, Alexander's work became one of the standard texts of its time in the field of pastoral theology.

While it is true that Alexander never produced any major works in the fields of ecclesiastical history and church government during his brief time as a professor at the seminary, over a hundred articles and reviews were contributed to the *Biblical Repertory* during his lifetime, providing

---

15. "Irenaeus Prime, editor of the *New York Observer*, praised Dr. Alexander as a 'model preacher' and a faithful pastor. 'How fond he was of the daily prayer-meetings,' Prime wrote, 'how his soul longed for a revival of religion and the conversion of sinners!'" Cited in Calhoun, *Faith and Learning*, 1:380.

16. J. W. Alexander, *Thoughts on Preaching: Being Contributions to Homiletics*, ed. S. D. Alexander (Edinburgh: Banner of Truth, 1975). Several chapters were first published in the *Biblical Repertory* during 1838, 1854, and 1855.

rich and nuanced historical treatments of their topics. Besides his more formal academic contributions, his published collections of sermons often contain important historical observations reflecting his mastery of ancient and modern sources related to secular and church history.[17]

Although Alexander felt his labors as a seminary professor unsuccessful, this is more likely a statement of his self-effacing nature than a record of the rich pastoral emphases he brought to his classroom lectures—the substance of which can be found in *Thoughts on Preaching*. Among all his published works, Alexander's collected writings on the work of pastoral ministry most clearly represent the model he embraced and propagated among his contemporaries. To grasp the thrust of Alexander's life is to learn the theology of pastoral ministry by which he lived.

Thinking Pastorally about the Work of the Pastor

While many of Alexander's observations on the work of preaching and pastoral ministry can also be found scattered throughout his correspondence with Hall, *Thoughts on Preaching* contains his most organized presentation of the subject matter.[18] Among nineteenth-century treatments of pastoral theology, Alexander's material contains a masterful collection of wise observations, aphorisms, and instructive counsel for men called to serve in pastoral ministry.

A series of random "Homiletical Paragraphs" form the first third of the book. Approximately 168 in number, the subject matter is selective without any apparent order provided by the editor. Dates are omitted, as well as sources; but the arbitrariness of selection betrays an intentionality of focus in surfacing some of Alexander's wisest pastoral insights and counsel. While some selections are extremely brief, others run to a few pages in length. Biblically grounded, historically nuanced, and often

---

17. Alexander's sermons include topical, textual, and expository treatments of biblical passages and subjects. The majority of Alexander's published sermons are from his ministry in New York City and reflect the constituency to which he preached at the Fifth Avenue Presbyterian Church. Alexander's varied sermonic style no doubt reflects his interest in connecting with the diverse population and educational backgrounds of those who attended upon his public ministry.

18. There is occasional overlap of material due to the extraneous nature of the selections having been written over several decades. Individual entries vary in perspective, suggestive of Alexander's personal development and experience in ministry.

biographical or autobiographical in focus, readers will find suggestive material brimming with practical pastoral wisdom.

The heart of the volume consists of a series of ten "Letters to Young Ministers," which were first published in the *Presbyterian*, along with chapters addressing the studies and discipline of the preacher, the matter of preaching, expository preaching, the pulpit in ancient and modern times, and the eloquence of the French pulpit.[19]

Designed as a "serial" treatment examining key issues of the ministerial calling and commission, Alexander's opening letters address the crucial topics of devotion to the work of the ministry, the cultivation of personal piety for ministerial effectiveness, and the delights of ministerial happiness. At the time Alexander's letters were published, it had become a common criticism that devotion to the work of the ministry had declined among young men of the time in comparison to twenty or thirty years earlier. Alexander felt the problem originated in the heart of the men involved, not in the schooling they may have received. He writes:

> It is vain to attribute the alleged change to any particular mode of education. In this there has been no such alteration as will account for the loss of zeal. The cause must be sought in something more widely operative. The effect, if really existing, is visible beyond the circle of candidates and probationers. Nor need we go further for an explanation, than to the almost universal declension of vital piety in our Churches, which will abide under every form of training, until the Spirit be poured out from on high.[20]

Additional remarks elaborate on the problem as Alexander diagnosed it:

---

19. "It had long been the cherished wish of Dr Alexander to prepare a volume on Homiletics, for the use of young ministers and students; and with this object in view, he was in the habit of jotting down, in his private journals, in the form of paragraphs, such thought as occurred to him on the subject. In one of his later journals I find the following entry: 'If the Lord should spare me below, it will be well for me some day to look over all my dailies, and collect what I have written from time to time on Ministerial Work. It is already enough for a volume. It might do good when I am gone.' But death defeated his plans." Alexander, *Thoughts on Preaching*, v. In addition to the letters written for the *Presbyterian*, the remaining chapters first appeared as articles in the *Biblical Repertory and Princeton Review*.

20. Alexander, *Thoughts on Preaching*, 101–2.

Here and there are young ministers, visiting among vacancies, and ready to be employed in any promising place, who are often well educated persons, of good manners, and irreproachable character: but what a want of fire! There can be no remedy for this evil, but a spiritual one; yet it is of high importance that the young man should know what it is he needs. He has perhaps come lately from his studies, in the solitude of country parish, or from some school in the mountains; or from some sound but frigid preceptor, who, amidst parochial cares, has afforded him few means of stimulation. His thoughts are more about the heads of divinity, the partitions of a discourse, the polish of style, the newest publications, or even the gathering of a library, than about the great, unspeakable, impending work of saving souls. He has no consuming zeal with regard to the conversion of men, as an immediate business. Let us not be too severe in our judgments. It cannot well be otherwise. None but a visionary would expect the enthusiasm of the battle in the soldier who, as yet, has seen nothing but the drill. Yet this enthusiasm there must be, in order to any greatness of ministerial character, and any success; and he is most likely to attain it, who is earliest persuaded that he is nothing without it. It is encouraging to observe, that some of the most useful and energetic preachers are the very men whose youthful zeal was chiefly for learning, but who, under providential guidance, were brought at once into positions where they were called upon to grapple with difficulties, and exert all their strength in the main work.[21]

Alexander considered education critical for ministerial usefulness, but not exclusively so. "Some who have been most successful in winning souls have been men of learning; Augustine, Calvin, Baxter, Doddridge, Martyn; but they laid all their attainments at the foot of the cross." Alexander quotes with enthusiasm one of his favorite Puritan authors on this point: "As Leighton said, to a friend who admired his books, 'One devout thought outweighs them all.'"[22]

Key to the issue of ministerial effectiveness is devotion to the calling. Without undivided concentration to that for which the minister is set apart, his energies will be defused and his time, misdirected. "No man can reach the highest degrees in any calling or profession, who does not admire and love it, and give himself to it—have his mind full of it, day by

---

21. Alexander, *Thoughts on Preaching*, 102.
22. Alexander, *Thoughts on Preaching*, 102–3.

day. No great painter ever became such, who had it only as a collateral pursuit, or who did not reckon it the greatest of arts, or who did not sacrifice everything else to it. Great commanders have not risen from among *dilettante* soldiers, who only amused themselves with the art of war."[23]

Writing in a somewhat pensive spirit, Alexander recalls the loss men have felt who have divided their energies upon too many fields of interest in contrast to those who gave themselves wholeheartedly to the work to which they had been called:

> It is a source of deep regret to many in review of life, that they have scattered themselves over too many fields; let me entreat of you to spend your strength on one. When we call up in memory the men whose ministerial image is most lovely, and whom we should resemble, they are such as have been true to their profession, and who have lived for nothing else. Some there are, indeed, who have had a clear vocation to the work of teaching, which is really a branch of the ministry, and one of its most indispensable branches, and who have served Christ as faithfully in the school-room or the university, as in the pulpit; such were Melancthon, Turrettine, Witsius, Witherspoon, Dwight, Livingston, Rice, and Graham. But our concern is with ordinary ministers, called to no other public station; and of these it is unquestionable, that the most successful are those who have lived in and for their spiritual work. Call to mind the chief Nonconformists; also of later date, Newton, Cecil, Brown, Waugh, Simeon; the Tennants, Rodgers, M'Millan, M'Cheyne, and our own acquaintance the "greatly beloved" William Nevins. In these men, the prominent purpose was ministerial work. If at any time they wrote and published, it was on matters subservient to the gospel. This accounts for the holy glow which, even amidst human imperfections, was manifest in their daily conversations. They might have been eminent in other pursuits, but they had given themselves to the work of Christ.[24]

Ministerial vigor, as Alexander notes, is found in direct proportion to a man's piety and understanding of the grand calling of the pastoral office. "No wonder," Alexander quipped, "we preach so coldly on the Sabbath, when we are so little moved on week-days, about what we preach."

> You have perhaps met two or three clergymen lately; what did their conversation turn upon? The coming glory of the Church? the power

---

23. Alexander, *Thoughts on Preaching*, 103.
24. Alexander, *Thoughts on Preaching*, 103–4.

of the Word? the best means of arousing sinners? even the most desirable method of preparation? or some high point of doctrine? Or were they upon the last election, the last land speculation, the last poem, or the price of cotton and tobacco? According to your answer, will be the conclusion as to the temperature of their preaching. There is indeed a sort of pulpit fire which is rhetorical—proceeds from no warmth within, and diffuses no warmth without; the less of it the better. But genuine ardour must arise from the habitual thought and temper of the life. He with whom the ministry is a secondary thing may be a correct, a learned, an elegant, even an oratorical, but will never be a powerful preacher.[25]

Having given prominence "to this devotion of heart to your work," Alexander charged his readers "to hold all [their] studies as only means to this end, the glory of God in the salvation of souls." "The day is near," he said, "when your whole ministerial life will seem to you very short in retrospect." "That which we all need," he observed in a further comment, "is to magnify our office, to recognize the sublimity of our work. There would be more Brainerds, and more Whitefields, if such views were more common; and there would be more instances of great men struggling on for years in narrow, remote situations, but with mighty effects."[26]

Alexander's remarks become more impassioned as he further elaborates on the glory of the ministerial office:

> My dear young friend, if there is anything you would rather be than a preacher of the gospel; if you regard it as a ladder to something else; if you do not consider all your powers as too little for the work; be assured you have no right to hope for any usefulness or even eminence. To declare God's truth so as to save souls, is a business which angels might covet: acquire the habit of regarding your work in this light. Such views will be a source of legitimate excitement; they will lighten the severest burden, and dignify the humblest labour, in the narrowest valley among the mountains. They will confer that mysterious strength on your plainest sermons, which has sometimes made men of small genius and no eloquence to be the instrument of converting hundreds. Think more of the treasure you carry, the message you proclaim, and the heaven to which you invite, than of your locality, your supporters, or your popularity.[27]

---

25. Alexander, *Thoughts on Preaching*, 104.
26. Alexander, *Thoughts on Preaching*, 104–5.
27. Alexander, *Thoughts on Preaching*, 105–6.

For Alexander, impassioned piety is foundational for giving oneself wholeheartedly to the ministerial calling. While an all-encompassing vision of the work is essential in order to fulfill its responsibilities, piety is the fuel that fires the godly ambition that is to motivate the minister in his work. But can a minister preach beyond his "own experience" in the manner in which he seeks to instruct others for walking in a life of holiness? Alexander believes he can and must do this in respect to the responsibilities of his office. As he observes, "He is commissioned to preach, not himself, or his experience, but Christ Jesus, the Lord, and his salvation; he is a messenger, and his message is laid before him in the Scriptures; it is at his peril, that he suppresses aught, whether he has experienced it or not."

> He is, for example, not to withhold consolation to God's deeply afflicted ones, till he has experienced deep affliction himself. Yet every preacher of the gospel should earnestly strive to attain the experience of the truths which he communicates, and to have every doctrine which he utters turned into vital exercises of his heart; so that when he stands up to speak in the name of God, there may be that indescribable freshness and penetrativeness, which arise from individual and present interest in what is declared.[28]

Genuine piety is nurtured and matured over the course of a lifetime. Accordingly, Alexander urges his readers to an intentionality of devotional exercise each day of their life.[29] Mindful of the ministerial hypocrisy that can accompany a calling honored for its public piety but which may be nothing more than notional religiosity, Alexander is equally hesitant to prescribe specific "rules" for its practice lest they encumber the heartfelt love for Christ that must underlie all personal and public expressions of piety.

> Of all people on earth, ministers most need the constant impressions derived from closet piety. If once they listen to the flattering voice of their admirers, and think they are actually holy because others treat

---

28. Alexander, *Thoughts on Preaching*, 108.
29. "Our age is disposed to sneer at high religious passions: it is perhaps the reason why the pathos of the pulpit has to such a degree departed. It is not, however, as a homiletic instrumentality that I would urge you to grow in grace, but far more momentous reasons, which as a preacher, you have long since learned." Alexander, *Thoughts on Preaching*, 115.

> them as such; if they dream of going to heaven *ex officio*; if, weary of public exercises, they neglect those which are private; or if they acquire the destructive habit of preaching and praying about Christ without any faith or emotion; then their course is likely to be downward. Far short, however, a minister of Christ may be of so dreadful doom, and yet be almost useless. To prevent such declension, the best advice I know of, is to be much in secret devotion; including in this term the reflective reading of Scripture, meditation, self-examination, prayer and praise. And here you must not expect from me any *recipe* for the conduct of such exercises, or rules for the times, length, posture, place, and so forth; for I rejoice in it as the glory of the Church to which we both belong, that it is so little rubrical. How often you shall fast or sing or pray, must be left to be settled between God and your conscience; only fix in mind and heart the necessity of much devotion.[30]

Genuine piety not only sustains the minister in his walk with God but empowers him to press forward in a life of holiness and ministerial diligence during seasons of spiritual warfare and pastoral fatigue.

> The truth is, such are the discouragements of genuine cross-bearing ministry, and so repugnant to the flesh are many of its duties, that nothing but true piety will hold a man up under the burden; he will sooner or later throw it off, and begin to seek his ease, or preach for "itching ears," or phonographic reporters. It is an easy thing to go through a routine, to "do duty," as the phrase of the Anglican establishment is; but it is hard to the flesh, to denounce error in high places, to preach unpopular doctrine, to labour week after week in assemblies of a dozen or twenty, to spend weary hours among the diseased and dying, and to watch over the discipline of Christ's house. Nothing but an inward enjoyment of divine truth, and a reference to the final award, will stimulate a man to constancy in such labours.[31]

While conflict and tribulation are part of the Christian life and especially pronounced in the work of Christian ministry, Alexander remained confident "that the life of a faithful minister is the happiest on earth." Once again, perspective is key to enjoying its blessedness:

> In seeking the constituents of this happiness, you should not look at the accidents of the ministry, but at its substance; not at the quietude,

---

30. Alexander, *Thoughts on Preaching*, 111.
31. Alexander, *Thoughts on Preaching*, 109.

respectability, emolument, or refining culture, but at the life-long embassy from the Redeemer to lost men. The truest, safest, most abiding ministerial pleasures are those which come from delight in the genuine object of the ministry, the salvation of men. But there is a collateral blessedness, which we may not despise, since God has designed to bestow it on his servants. Even this you will be most sure of attaining, if you have much love of Christ, love of the gospel, and love of souls.[32]

In addition to the personal pleasures that accompany a life devoted to the study of God's Word, times of personal and corporate prayer, and the satisfaction that comes from ministering to people's spiritual and physical needs, Alexander places particular emphasis on the happiness experienced in the act of preaching.[33] "There is happiness in preaching," he remarked:

> It may be so performed as to be as dull to the speaker, as it is to the hearers; but in favoured instances it furnishes the purest and noblest excitements, and in these is happiness. Nowhere are experienced, more than in the pulpit, the clear, heavenward soaring of the intellect, the daring flight of imagination, or the sweet agitations of holy passion. The declaration of what one believes, and the praise of what one loves, always give delight: and what but this is the minister's work? He is called to converse with the highest truths of which humanity can be cognizant, and, if God so favour him, to experience the noblest emotions; and this most, while he is standing "in Christ's stead."[34]

An extended paragraph elaborates Alexander's perspective while providing one of the finest short summaries of the beauty and glory of preaching found in all of his published writings.

> I am persuaded, that previously to trial, no young man can duly estimate the glow of public discourse as a source of pleasure. When

---

32. Alexander, *Thoughts on Preaching*, 116.
33. "The private life of a Christian minister ought to be a happy one. The apostle informs us in what it should be spent, to wit, the word of God and prayer. Acts vi. 4. I should account it lost time to go about persuading you, that there is a happiness in the study of great moral and religious subjects, especially of the word of God. To have this made the business of your days; to find your chosen solace enjoined as your duty to be shut up for life with prophets and apostles, nay, with Jesus Christ himself, speaking in the 'living oracles,' to be perpetually drawing water from the wells of salvation; this is but a part of the minister's joy." Alexander, *Thoughts on Preaching*, 116.
34. Alexander, *Thoughts on Preaching*, 117.

the soul is carried by the greatness of the subject, and the solemnity of the occasion, above its ordinary tracts, so as to be at once heated and enlarged by passion, while the kindled countenances of the hearers, and the reflected ardour of their glance, carry a repercussive influence to the speaker; or when the tear twinkles in the eye of penitence, and weeping throngs attest the power of truth and affection; then it is that preaching becomes its own reward. This is more than rhetorical excitement and stage-heat; it is caused by Christian emotion. Call it sympathy, if you please; I am yet to learn what harm there is in this: it is legitimate sympathy. If a Christian minister ever has deep impressions of truth, we may expect it to be in the pulpit; there, if anywhere, we may hope for special gifts from above; and these gifts are dispensed for the sake of the hearer, and are reckoned on, as graces, or tokens of individual piety. Yet they constitute a great part of the preacher's happiness. They are not dependent on eloquence, in its common meaning; for they fall equally to the share of the humblest, rudest preacher, provided he be all on fire with his subject, and bursting with love to his people. No scholarship, filing, or varnish, can compass this; it comes from the heart: and many a minister has chipped at the edges of his sermon, and veneered it with nice bits of extract, only to find that its strength had been whittled away. There may be more awakening or melting, in a backwoodman's improvisation, than in all the climacteric periods of Melville, or all the balanced splendor of Macaulay. Certainly the delight of soul is on the side of him who is most in earnest. It is especially love that moves the souls of hearers, and love, in its very nature, gives happiness. It cannot be, that a man can be frequently the subject of those feelings which belong to evangelical preaching, without being for that very reason a happier man.[35]

Mindful of the modest circumstances in which most ministers labor, Alexander was careful to remind his readers that the true splendor of preaching is unrelated to the edifice or time in which it occurs. It is the same Spirit who blesses the preached word at both large assemblies and at smaller gatherings of those who meet in Christ's name. Christ meets with His people equally everywhere His Word is preached faithfully in power and demonstration of His Spirit.

The better moments of Andrew Gray, Hall, and Chalmers, must have been snatches of heaven. But be not discouraged when I mention

---

35. Alexander, *Thoughts on Preaching*, 118.

these great names: the more you refer the joy of preaching to its legitimate and gracious causes, the more you will see that it may exist independently of what the world calls eloquence. It is not only in the vast assemblies of Chrysostom, a Bridaine, or a Whitefield, that the service of Christ brings its sacred pleasures, but in Philip Henry's little parish of Worthenbury, which never numbered eighty communicants; or in the early morning-lectures of Romaine, when two candles lighted all the house. Nor is this happiness restricted to great and decorated edifices; it belongs to the itinerant missionary, who dismounts from his tired horse and gains refreshment by dispensing the word to the gathering under the ancient oaks; or who meets his circuit of appointments in regions where the truth has scarcely ever been heard.[36]

Ultimately, ministerial happiness finds consummation in the spiritually transformed lives of the people among whom the minister labors. The reward of ministry is neither in reportable numbers or public reputation. "After all," Alexander asks, "what is the scriptural statement of ministerial happiness?" "'What is our hope, or joy, or crown or rejoicing?' asks Paul; and answers, 'Ye are our glory and joy!' 1 Thess. ii. 19, 20." Therefore, Alexander said, "Seek happiness, my dear young friend, in contemplation of this reward. That moment will indemnify the minister for the losses of a whole life." A quote from an unidentified volume of Hall's *Works* concludes his paragraph:

> "And is this the end," he will exclaim, "of all my labours, my toils, and watching; my expostulations with sinners, and my efforts to console the faithful! And is this the issue of the ministry under which I was often ready to sink! And this the glory of which I heard so much, understood so little, and announced to my hearers with lisping accents and a stammering tongue! Well might it be styled *the glory to be revealed*. Auspicious day! On which I embarked in this undertaking, on which the love of Christ, with a sweet and sacred violence, impelled me to feed his sheep and to feed his lambs. With what emotion shall we, who, being intrusted with so holy a ministry, shall find mercy to be faithful, hear that voice from heaven, 'Rejoice and be glad, and give honour to him; for the marriage of the Lamb is come, and his wife hath made herself ready!' With what rapture shall we

---

36. Alexander, *Thoughts on Preaching*, 118–19.

recognize, amid an innumerable multitude, the seals of our ministry, the persons whom we have been the means of conducting to glory!"[37]

Letters four through six focus on the topics of clerical studies, how to find time for learning, and the need for learned pastors. While the Presbyterian Church valued an educated ministry, not every denomination or Christian group in Alexander's time was equally committed to the extensive theological training modeled by such institutions as Princeton Theological Seminary.

Although Alexander was widely read, he did not hold this as the standard for every man seeking ordination. While ministers might become men of "distinction in science or letters," the learning which he recommended was "none of these," but "solely the discipline and accomplishments whereby you shall be better fitted for your appropriate work, and is therefore subordinated to your professional activity." While many ministers enjoyed the privileges of formal education and continued study in their capacity as clergy, their personal goals in learning must be focused primarily on augmenting their skills for service in ministry. "The study is not a place for lettered luxury, nor for ambitious lucubration, with views fixed on secular authorship or academical promotion; but the sacred palaestra [ancient Greek wrestling school] in which Christ's soldier is supposed to be forging his armour, and hardening his muscle, and training his agility, for the actual combat of the ministry."[38] Although he did not expect all ministers to become scholars, Alexander was adamant in affirming the number of scholarly ministers whom God had blessed the church with and whose labors successive generations were the beneficiaries of their scholarship.

In this respect, Alexander argued for what he called *habitual* preparation alongside *actual* preparation. An approach modeled by his father Archibald Alexander, J. W. Alexander believed it the best strategy for becoming an effective preacher. While specialized study is essential, a vast proportion of the preparation necessary for effective, extemporaneous preaching is of the habitual preparation kind. "The great point is this; there must be perpetual acquisition." "This," Alexander is careful to observe, "is the secret of preaching. What theologians say of preparation for death, may be said of preparation for preaching; there is *habitual*, and

---

37. Alexander, *Thoughts on Preaching*, 121.
38. Alexander, *Thoughts on Preaching*, 123.

there is *actual* preparation: the current of daily study, and the gathering of material for a given task." Just as a lawyer engages in both general and specialized preparation to argue a case, so too the minister must engage in general and specialized study in order to be adequately prepared to fulfill the duties of his office as a preacher. Thus:

> The clerical scholar, however diligent, punctual, and persistent, who throws his whole strength into the preparation of sermons, and who never rises to higher views, or takes a larger career through the wide expanse of scientific and methodized truth, must infallibly grow up stiff, cramped, lopsided, and defective. His scheme of preaching may never take him through the entire curve of theology and Scripture; or the providential leading of his ministry may bring him again and again over the same portions. These are evils which can be prevented only by the resolute pursuit of general studies, irrespectively of special pulpit performance. Such habits will tend to keep a man always prepared; and instead of getting to the bottom of his barrel as he grows older, he will be more and more prepared, as long as his faculties last.[39]

Of the various problems peculiar to preaching in his time was the absence of substantive biblical content.[40] Hortatory harangues were common to the exclusion of more studied material for sermon subjects. While exhortation is an appropriate form of pulpit discourse, it must be grounded in biblical exegesis and responsible exposition of Scripture. "The crying evil of our sermons is *want of matter*; we try to remedy this evil, and that evil, when the thing we should do is to get something to say: and the laborious devotion of some young clergymen to rhetoric and style, instead of theology, is as if one should study a cookery-book when he should be going to market."[41]

---

39. Alexander, *Thoughts on Preaching*, 128.

40. "With all their blindness in certain matters, the public are very sagacious in discovering when the minister gives them that which costs him nothing." Alexander, *Thoughts on Preaching*, 242.

41. Alexander, *Thoughts on Preaching*, 129. A subsequent chapter is devoted entirely to the topic, "The Matter of Preaching." Originally believed to have been written by J. W. Alexander, an editorial note clarifies its inclusion in the book although the result of a case of mistaken identity: "The above article, by Professor Atwater, of Princeton, was inadvertently inserted; but as it so admirably complements the matter of this work, with the consent of the author it is retained." Alexander, *Thoughts on Preaching*, 227.

Among the remedies Alexander proposed for this pulpit deficiency was a return to an expository preaching model. An extended chapter, "Expository Preaching," provides persuasive argument for its benefits and historical precedence.[42] In a series of learned historical observations, Alexander notes that "the expository method of preaching is the most obvious and natural way of conveying to the hearers the import of the sacred volume." It "has the sanction of primitive and ancient usage"; "is adapted to secure the greatest amount of scriptural knowledge to both preacher and hearers"; "is best fitted to communicate the knowledge of scriptural truth in its connection"; "affords inducement and occasion to the preacher to declare the whole counsel of God"; "admits of being made generally interesting to Christian assemblies"; and "has a direct tendency to correct, if not to preclude, the evils incident to the common textual mode of preaching."[43]

Alexander draws upon the history of Scottish Presbyterianism as representative of the spiritual progress that can be made when Christians sit under sustained expository preaching.

> The mental habits of any Christian community are mainly derived from the preaching which they hear. It is fair to ask, therefore, from what source can the Christians of our day be expected to gain a taste and ability for interpreting the Scripture in its connection? Certainly not from the pulpit. Among the ancient Scottish Presbyterians the case was different. Every man and every woman, nay, almost every child, carried his pocket-Bible to church, and not only looked out the text, but verified each citation; and as the preaching was in great part of the expository kind, the necessary consequence was, that the whole population became intimately acquainted with the structure of every book in the Bible, and were able to recall every passage with its appropriate accompanying truths. The genius of Protestantism demands that something of this kind should be attempted.

---

42. Alexander notes that the strength of the Christian pulpit was often in proportion to the practice of expository preaching and particularly pronounced at the time of the Protestant Reformation: "When the light of divine truth began to emerge from its long eclipse, at the Reformation, there were few things more remarkable than the universal return of evangelical preachers to the expository method. Book after book of the Scriptures was publicly expounded by Luther, and the almost daily sermons of Calvin were, with scarcely any exceptions, founded on passages taken in regular course as he proceeded through the sacred canon. The same is true of the other reformers, particularly in England and Scotland." Alexander, *Thoughts on Preaching*, 233.

43. Alexander, *Thoughts on Preaching*, 229–44.

> Where the laity are not expected to search the Scriptures, or in any degree to exercise private judgment, it may answer every purpose to give them from the pulpit the mere *results* of exposition; but more is needed where we claim for all the privilege of trying every doctrine by the word of God; and sermons should therefore be auxiliaries to the hearers in their investigation of the record. And we earnestly desire a general return on the part of our preachers to a method which will necessarily tend, from week to week, to open the Scriptures, and display what is by no means their least excellency, the harmonious relation of their several portions.[44]

In addition to the study of the Scriptures for doctrinal substance, Alexander encouraged familiarity with the confessional standards of his church—the Westminster Confession of Faith and Larger and Shorter Catechisms—as primary resources replete with a lifetime of preaching topics addressing the totality of divine revelation.[45]

Having emphasized the importance of diligence in ministerial preparation and development, a further letter provides practical counsel on "How to Find Time for Learning." Alexander knew well the pressures of ministerial life from the various charges he served; once again, a proper perspective on one's pastoral priorities is essential for making the most of a minister's study time.

> First of all, if you would make the most of your scanty hours, keep the one sacred object in view in every study you undertake. This is the way to secure unity of plan. You bear in mind the twentieth proposition of Euclid's first book: the straighter your line, the shorter.

---

44. Alexander, *Thoughts on Preaching*, 240.
45. Alexander's tenth letter, "On Diligence in Study," especially emphasizes lifelong reading of theology to maintain freshness and vitality in preaching and pastoral ministry: "Besides all your sermon making, *Theology, as a system, must be your regular study.* Neglect this, and your pulpit theology will be one-sided; many topics will never have due consideration. I shall augur badly for your career, if you are found uninterested in great theological questions. Some established works should be daily in your hands; and of such works a few should be often re-perused. Find a clergyman who knows nothing of such pursuits, and you will observe his preaching to be unmethodical, and little fitted to awaken inquiry among deep thinkers in his flock. He will soon attain his acme, and will continue to dispense milk where he should give strong meat. The analogy of other professions will occur to you; the lawyer or physician who reads law or physics only for this or that case, can never take high rank." Alexander, *Thoughts on Preaching*, 168.

I trust it is no wresting of the apostle's words to say, *One thing I do*; or more laconically still, in the four letters of the original, εν δέ.[46]

Speaking as much from personal experience as personal love for the humanities and classics, Alexander is quick to caution learning that is too diffuse. "Let your intentions branch out in every direction, undetermined whether you mean to be a great linguist, or an elegant classic, or a mathematician, or peradventure, a botanist, or a master of English literature, and it is plain enough that you will find all your time too little. There is such a thing as being very idly and unprofitably engaged in one's study."

> Far from loving restriction, or from wishing to coerce the mind in pursuing its bent, I would, nevertheless, beseech you, when you go among your books, to know what you are after. Your end in life is sufficiently obvious; and the studies by which it is to be attained are enough to occupy your time, if you are but faithful. It is of deliberate and stated application that I now speak: you certainly will not expect me to plan ways and means of gaining time for the annuals, monthlies, or weeklies. In your regular professional studies, you will find the whole field brought more clearly under survey, and the whole process simplified, by looking on every part of it with reference to your main work of expounding the Scriptures and preaching the gospel.[47]

Alexander urged his readers to keep the study of Scripture the primary focus of their intellectual labors; related studies were viewed as complementary to how a minister must use his preparation time for sermons and lectures. He considered both essential for maintaining long-term balance in one's pulpit ministry.[48] An extended paragraph graphically illustrates his point:

> This leads to a second suggestion of a particular under this general head. Form the habit of contemplating all your study as the study of the word of God. In a large, but just sense, it is undoubtedly so. All

---

46. Alexander, *Thoughts on Preaching*, 130.
47. Alexander, *Thoughts on Preaching*, 130–31.
48. "The man who grows old with no studies but those which terminate upon the several demands of the pulpit, becomes a mannerist, falls into monotony of thought, and ends stiffly, drily, and wearisomely. At the same time, he wants that enlargement and enriching of mind derived from wide excursion, into collateral studies, of which all the world recognizes the fruits in such preachers as Owen, Mason, Chalmers, and Hall." Alexander, *Thoughts on Preaching*, 167.

your discipline and all your acquisition, all your reasoning power and all your taste, all your library and all your eloquence, are only so many means for learning God's word, and for teaching it. Exegesis, theology, controversy, church history, are only portions of the apparatus for learning and teaching. With this in mind, you may go much further than many think, and yet return safe. As Scott, the commentator, used to say, "The bee may range widely, so that it brings all to the hive." Say to yourself daily, *En codicem sacrum* [Behold the sacred book]! "Here is my hive; higher all my gatherings must be brought." The range of some men has been wonderful, and their powers of assimilation have been so great, that they have laid every department under contribution, and filled their discourses with the digested results of multifarious and almost incongruous reading: take, as instances, Baxter, Saurin, and Chalmers. But common minds need a strong centripetal force, and this is to be found in reverential love for Holy Scripture. No method known to me is so likely to keep you in the right state of mind, in this respect, as the practice of devoting the first and best part of every day to the perusal of the Bible in the original tongues. Few will the days be, in which you will not discern the directive influence of this on the researches of the subsequent hours; and the influence will be there, even when not discerned.[49]

By narrowing the focus of one's studies, more concentrated learning is to be acquired. "The all-important rule," Alexander states, is "to lop off all irrelevant studies." "Observe," he said, "we are not talking now of amusement, but of dogged labour."

And if you mean to succeed, and to save precious time, see to it, that you rid yourself of all impertinent matters. In this age of books, tempting studies will grow rank around you, and creep into your windows, as a great vine has been doing into the chamber where I write; but you must be unrelenting, and make short work with their pretensions. The blue and yellow flowers among the corn must be plucked out, and you must be doing it every day. It is not a bad remark of Helvetius, though a bad man, that in our day the secret of being learned, is heroically to determine to be ignorant of many things in which men take pride.[50]

---

49. Alexander, *Thoughts on Preaching*, 131.
50. Alexander, *Thoughts on Preaching*, 132.

"While in nothing is it more important for a man to open his own path, than in habits of study,"[51] Alexander urged his readers to make effective use of whatever area they have set aside for prayer and sermon preparation. Today the word *office* is commonly associated with the room in the church building where the pastor labors; in Alexander's time, most churches did not have this area as parsonages were typically equipped with rooms set aside for pastoral ministrations and study of the Scriptures. An extended comment extols the glory of the space set aside for the pastor's study:

> The clergyman's study, which some people regard as they would a pantry, or a genteel appendage to housekeeping, is the main room in the house, and (if consistent with Heb. xiii. 2) ought to be the best. It is the place where you speak to God, and where God speaks to you; where the oil is beaten for the sanctuary; where you sit between the two olive-trees, Zech. iv. 3; where you wear the linen ephod, and consult Urim and Thummim. As you are there, so will you be in the house of the Lord. A prevalent sense of this will do more than anything to procure and redeem time for research, and will cause you to learn more in an hour, than otherwise in a day. That upper-chamber is also the spot where you will enjoy one of the most valuable means of learning and preparation, which we too much neglect—I mean conference with brethren about your work, and especially your preaching. And it will be your duty to impress on your people the truth, that you are as really serving them, when you are in your study, as when you are in their houses. But to render these views efficacious, you must, from the beginning, look on all your meditation, reading and writing, as a tribute to God, and a free-will offering in his holy temple. This will lead you to pray over your researches, and to handle every topic as in the presence of Christ. It will tend to prevent your lucubrations from lapsing into a selfish, solitary, anchoretic abstraction from your charge. The more you are occupied upon the simple text of Scripture, the more remarkably will this temper prevail in you.[52]

Of special interest is the amount of attention Alexander gives to the topic of extemporaneous preaching. While later chapters look specifically at the history of preaching as it came to expression in different churches,

---

51. Alexander, *Thoughts on Preaching*, 136.
52. Alexander, *Thoughts on Preaching*, 134.

cultures, and styles, Alexander was interested in its virtues and wished to extol its practice among his fellow preachers. In letters seven through nine, Alexander presents his case for the benefits of an extemporaneous style of preaching.[53]

It is important to recognize that Alexander's recommendations in no way suggest the need for little or no preparation if one were to choose to embrace an extemporaneous model of preaching.[54] Quite the contrary, for, as Alexander is at pains to point out, habitual preparation, along with specialized study, is essential to have thought oneself clear on a topic in order to present the subject in a cogent, coherent, and applicatory manner to the consciences and hearts of one's hearers.[55] He explains:

> As I am perfectly convinced that any man can learn to preach extempore who can talk extempore, always provided he has somewhat to say, my earnest advice to you is that you never make the attempt without being sure of your matter. Of all the defects of utterance I have ever known the most serious is having nothing to utter. You will say that is not extemporaneous which is prepared, and, etymologically, you are doubtless right. But the purely *impromptu* method, or the taking of a text *ad aperturam libri* [literally: "to the opening of a book," or opening a book at random], is that towards which I shall give you no help, as believing it to be the worst method possible; for however suddenly you may ever be called upon to preach, you will choose to fall back to a certain extent upon some train of thought which you have previously matured. In all your experiments, therefore, secure by premeditation a good amount of material, and let it be digested and arranged in your head, according to an exact partition and a logical

---

53. As noted elsewhere, Alexander employed a variety of approaches to sermon composition ranging from written manuscripts, brief notes, and purely extemporaneous delivery. Both textual and expository approaches were incorporated into the style of preaching Alexander modeled notwithstanding his criticism of the "insular" use of texts characteristic of the "textual" preaching common to his time.

54. "*Ministerial study* is a *sine qua non* [literally: without which not] of success. It is absurdly useless to talk of methods of preaching, where there is no method of preparation." Alexander, *Thoughts on Preaching*, 167.

55. Alexander's chapter, "Remarks on the Studies and Discipline of the Preacher," also addresses the impress of one's life in the making of a sermon: "The average of any man's sermons will be as the character of his general thinking. A good discourse is not so much the product of the week's preparation, as of the whole antecedent studies and discipline; it flows not from the pitcher, but the deep well. Hence that celebrated preacher spake a weighty thing, who, on being asked how long it took him to make a certain sermon, replied, 'About twenty years.'" Alexander, *Thoughts on Preaching*, 190.

concatenation. The more completely this latter provision is attended to, the less will be the danger of losing your self-possession or your chain of ideas. I lay the more stress on this because it must commend itself to you as having a just and rational basis. Common sense must admit that the great thing is to have the matter. All speaking which does not presuppose this is a sham. And of method, the same may be observed with regard to the speaker which is enjoined by all judicious teachers with regard to the hearer, namely, that even if divisions and subdivisions are not formally announced, they should be clearly before the mind, as affording a most important clue in the remembrance of what has been prepared.[56]

Although Alexander's personal preaching practice varied in relation to location and congregational expectation, his preference was clearly that of an extemporaneous expository model.[57] He advised that it was best learned in a live setting removed from the "unnatural" atmosphere found in schools and societies for public speech—one "must begin *ex abrupto* [literally: "from haste" or without preparation] and develop naturally through repeated experience, avoid use of a written manuscript or exercise of the memoriter style, and remain free of notes."[58] "Carry no scrap of writing into the pulpit. Let your scheme, with all its branches, be written on your mental tablet." "The practice," he said, "will be invaluable."[59]

For Alexander, ideas may be formulated in advance, but the exact phrases a minister uses during the delivery of his message were best left to the guidance of the Spirit and circumstances of the moment whose kinetic energy instinctively aids in the selection of the words most beneficial to the audience throughout the development of the message. To preach in the fear of God means allowing the sovereign Lord free exercise of His

---

56. Alexander, *Thoughts on Preaching*, 149.
57. In a related context, Alexander observed: "If Apostolical preaching could reappear, while it would be mighty in its effects upon the assembly and on multitudes, it would probably answer no demands of the schools or the stage; but would be unartificial, expository, simple, paternal, brief, natural, varied, gushing, and eminently spiritual." Alexander, *Thoughts on Preaching*, 31–32.
58. "It is hardly possible for any man to produce valuable matter in a purely academical exercise. Hence it is all-important to practice *bona fide* preaching before a real audience. All pretences there vanish; there is an object to be gained; and the true springs of preaching are unsealed. This is the discipline by which all great extemporaneous speakers have reached facility and eminence." Alexander, *Thoughts on Preaching*, 150.
59. Alexander, *Thoughts on Preaching*, 151.

discretionary will during the preaching of the Word.[60] While the subject is to be premeditated, a certain amount of freedom must be left to the Spirit's leading during the delivery of a sermon in order that the message He wants heard is in fact the one which the preacher delivers.[61]

While argumentative discourse lends itself to a natural freedom of expression and thought, purposeful reflection on a sermon's content is essential for extemporaneous preaching to be successful. It is why Alexander is insistent "that everything in a sermon is secondary to its *contents*."[62] Rhetorical form is subordinate "to the great earnest business of conveying God's message to the soul; being convinced," Alexander insisted, "that here as elsewhere the seeking of God's kingdom and righteousness will best secure subordinate matters."[63]

As noted elsewhere in Alexander's writings, each man must be true to his nature and the gifts with which God has equipped him.[64] The fusion of what is nature by birth and grace by divine endowment must be both honored and acknowledged even if indistinguishable to the human eye. Some men are gifted linguistically, whose written sermons are blessed with great power and effect by the Spirit; others may find equal blessing in their public preaching but who lack, by talent or training, the qualities that would make them writers of great sermons or authors whose messages merit publication. Alexander quotes with effect the thoughts of Cicero on this topic:

---

60. In his counsel to young preachers, Alexander assured them "that the true way of being raised above the fear of man in your early services is to be much filled with the fear of God; and that the only just confidence of the preacher is confidence in the promised assistance of God. Until you cease to regard the preaching of the word as in any sense a rhetorical exercise, it matters little whether you read or speak, or what method of preparation is adopted; you will be 'as sounding brass or a tinkling cymbal.'" Alexander, *Thoughts on Preaching*, 153.

61. "Generally speaking, the best possible word is the one which is born of the thought in the presence of the assembly. And the less you think about words as a separate affair, the better they will be." Alexander, *Thoughts on Preaching*, 152.

62. Alexander, *Thoughts on Preaching*, 155.

63. Alexander, *Thoughts on Preaching*, 152.

64. A brief note captures Alexander's approach: "In the making of sermons I have never so well succeeded as when I have forgotten all models, and consented to be myself. Every man has his own way, in which he is better than in all others. Those sermons have turned out the best in which I have turned the matter over in my mind several times, and then written without predetermined skeleton." Alexander, *Thoughts on Preaching*, 27–28.

Abundance of matter begets abundance of words; and if the things spoken of possess nobleness, there will be derived from that nobleness, a certain splendor of diction. Only let the man who is to speak or write be liberally trained by the education and instruction of his boyish days; let him burn with desire of proficiency; let him have natural advantages, and be exercised in innumerable discussions of every kind, and let him be familiar with the finest writers and speakers, so as to comprehend and imitate them; and (*nae ille haud sane* [then surely of that one you will not]) need give yourself no trouble about such a one's needing masters to tell him how he shall arrange or beautify his words![65]

It is arguable that Alexander's approach to preaching and pastoral ministry matured over the course of his lifetime. While Alexander never deplored the value of formal education, a number of his remarks suggest a more measured approach to its acquisition, no doubt reflecting the realities and exigencies of the "real-time" pastoral ministry in which he was involved throughout the majority of his life. Alexander understood that time is limited and talents differ, and he was therefore careful not to prescribe an identical course of preparation for men whose ages, background, and life experiences all varied.

As we have seen, Alexander's published writings on the calling and obligations of the Christian ministry focus more on a pastoral theology of identity than they do on the mechanics of sermon composition. His approach is to focus first on a theology of pastoral ministry and only secondarily on technique and methodology in sermon composition and delivery. The piety of the man takes precedence over his preaching style, adaptable as it will be based upon his gifts and the circumstances in which he exercises his ministerial calling.

While we may never know the exact nature of the book on homiletics that Alexander hoped one day to write, the present volume contains the rich crème of his thoughts on preaching and pastoral ministry and would likely have formed the substance of that work. Although some readers may demure the book's organization and random selection from Alexander's more obscure fugitive pieces that make up nearly a third of the volume's content, *Thoughts on Preaching* remains one of the finest treatments of its subject ever published. Readers seeking a text on sermon

---

65. Alexander, *Thoughts on Preaching*, 161.

composition will be disappointed, but for those in search of a biblically grounded theology of pastoral ministry, Alexander's collected writings remain a timeless classic.

These Eyes New Faith Receiving
A number of additional factors were influential in forming Alexander into the author, churchman, and pastor for which he gained renown. Grace was at work, both privately and publicly, in shaping Alexander into the likeness of his Savior. The likeness of Christ was being formed in both disposition and deed through the various exigencies of life that God's providence had orderd Alexander's path to pass through.

Suffering that Sanctifies
It is appropriate to note the way in which Alexander's lifelong struggle with melancholy was used by God to both humble and strengthen His servant. Whether neurological, physiological, or spiritual in origin (or some combination of the three), Alexander's battle with the disease was real and often affected his outlook on life. The trials of pastoral ministry, tragedies of premature family bereavement, and occasional separation from his wife and children likely exasperated his condition. But as with other areas of his life, grace ultimately proved victorious in the end, providing strength to perform the responsibilities of the pastoral office as well as to prepare him to die in the full confidence of Christ's completed work on his behalf.[66]

In his funeral oration on Alexander's behalf, Hall addressed the way in which God used suffering in the life of Alexander to cultivate his pastoral sensitivity for the hurting and helpless:

> Yes, my brethren, it is a somewhat painful, yet in all respect an impressive and interesting reflection for those who have obtained so much relief, so much sympathy, so much instruction from the tenderness of your late pastor, from the heart-reaching power of his discourse, his conversations, his whole intercourse, to know that

---

66. Hodge comments: "Dr. Alexander was a man of sorrows. Frequent family bereavements, repeated attacks of illness, some of them attended by great bodily agony, a shattered nervous constitution, caused him a degree of suffering protracted through many years, known fully only to God and his own heart. As he entered heaven, a voice might be heard saying: 'This is one who has come out of great tribulation, and has washed his robes and made them white in the blood of the Lamb.'" Hall, *Sermons*, 20–21.

to qualify him for this service, the wise and gracious foresight of Almighty God saw it necessary to lead his disciple, from his earliest Christian walk, in the path of some of the most poignant and overwhelming distresses that can oppress the human soul. Ascribe it to what immediate cause we may, to delicate or disordered nerves, to morbid sensibilities, whether physical or moral, to excessive intellectual excitement, to preternatural susceptibility to the extremes of enjoyment and suffering, we know from the result, that this part of experience, familiar to him in a greater or less measure from his youth to his last days, was the means sanctified to the production and maintenance of that depth, fullness, and richness of his spiritual traits, which laid the foundation of and gave the predominant characteristics and direction to his piety and his influence. For you—for us all—he thus suffered; through these sufferings he was borne by the same grace which meted them out, so that I do not believe that the Apostle Paul could say with more grateful consciousness than could your pastor: "Blessed be God, even the Father of our Lord Jesus Christ, the Father of mercies and the God of all comfort; who comforteth us in all our tribulation, that we may be able to comfort them which are in any trouble, by the comfort wherewith we ourselves are comforted of God. For as the suffering of Christ abound in us, so our consolation also aboundeth by Christ. And whether we be afflicted, it is for your consolation and salvation, which is effectual in the enduring of the same sufferings which we also suffer; or whether we be comforted, it is for your consolation and salvation." (2 Cor. 1:3–6).[67]

Purposeful Piety
The experience in suffering to which Hall refers was also accompanied by a life of deepening piety. Throughout Alexander's correspondence, a spirit of piety is evident. It comes to expression in every letter in some form or another. Whether implicit in the analysis he provides of contemporary events, response to a troublesome circumstance, or direct instruction on Christian living, a disposition of piety surfaces in relation to every area of life upon which Alexander comments.[68]

---

67. Hall, *Sermons*, 35–36.
68. "None could know him without believing that he was eminently and habitually pious; and that the cultivation of piety in himself, and its promotion in all whom he could reach, infinitely transcended in his estimation and pursuit every other object of human existence." "James Waddell Alexander," 80.

The piety that was nurtured in the innermost recesses of his soul found expression in Alexander's public deportment, leadership in worship, prayers, inspiring messages, publications, and encouraging conversations.[69]

> His personal piety had such prominent features that no observer could do otherwise than take knowledge of its depth and uniformity. What habitual reverence! what engagedness in worship! what hearty intentness in every public exercise! Making every one feel that he was acting not with the perfunctory solemnity of a sacred office, but with the personal sincerity of one who felt himself to be a sinner, yet a rejoicing believer and a happy worshipper. How the words of Scripture seemed to take the tone of his own experience! How the pathos of his prayers showed that it was his own experience! How the pathos of his prayers showed that it was his own soul, as well as yours, he was lifting up to God in confession, praise, and supplication! And who that has heard him, especially in more social assemblies or in the worship at his own fireside, or in the room of sickness and the house of affliction, does not remember how his deep absorption in devotion and the filial, affectionate nearness of his access to the Father of mercies and God of all comfort, caused him to forget what may be called the conventionalities of prayer, and to pour out his soul, indeed with the most abased humility and profound adoration, yet with a directness, familiarity, minuteness, freedom of expression, which was like the interviews of the patriarchs with the Lord God, "face to face, as a man speaketh unto his friend," (Exod. 33:11,) or like those of the apostle who leaned on his Lord's bosom at the holy table.
>
> In fact, this was the secret of the confidence he inspired, the affection he won, namely, the assurance which all felt that he was what he seemed, that he experienced what he declared, that he exemplified what he taught. It was his personal piety and its abundant fruits that wrought conviction upon every mind that observed him, that his "rejoicing" might be that of the apostle. "The testimony of his

---

69. "Most grave and devout in the pulpit, he often relaxed by the fireside into a sportive humor, which had the delicate flavor of Charles Lamb's. Never shall I forget a most fertilizing afternoon talk I enjoyed with him in yonder parlor of his father's house. His flow of merriment was wonderful. As he was then studying hymnology, I showed him a queer old Methodist camp-meeting hymn-book which contained this remarkable couplet—'When I was blind, and could not see,/The Calvinists deceived me!' Dr. Alexander laughed till the tears ran down his face, and he begged the loan of the book, which proved to be permanent." Cuyler, "James Waddell Alexander D. D. Address," 24–25.

conscience that in simplicity and godly sincerity, not with fleshly wisdom, but by the grace of God, he had had his conversation in the world, and more abundantly toward *you*" (2 Cor. 1:12).[70]

Practical Penmanship

In his lifelong work as an author, Alexander's writings display the spirit of charity and compassion for the needs of his generation that also comes to expression in his pastoral labors and churchmanship. As many of his contemporaries note, Alexander's writings were always "practical" in focus. The needs of the common man were uppermost in his mind.[71] Even his contributions to the *Biblical Repertory* were marked by this interest. As one writer observed, "It will be found that his prevailing object, from first to last, was to be useful, and useful in the highest and best of human concerns." His personal satisfaction in writing had given way following his conversion to the larger concerns of God's kingdom in how he used his pen to bring spiritual blessing to those around him:

> Gifted as he was with a capacity to enjoy and create the pleasures of imagination, his whole aim was to be practical. Though wit and humour had their place in his nature, they had their time too, and it was short and infrequent, compared with what passed in seriousness, and often in deep sadness. It was the soul—in its Divine and immortal relations—that was the chief object of his care, both as he considered himself and the world at large. For these concerns he watched, prayed, labored, and lived.[72]

Consecrated Churchman

As a churchman, a disposition of piety is evident in the manner in which Alexander conducted himself in relation to his fellow ministers and matters of dispute which erupted with precipitous force in the 1830s and whose continued influence would be of ongoing concern for Alexander

---

70. Hall, *Sermons*, 59–60.
71. One of numerous obituary reflections captures the extent of Alexander's literary influence: "Dr. James W. Alexander, soon after the establishment of the American Messenger, in 1842, commenced writing for it valuable but anonymous articles, which were continued, from time to time, to the number of thirty or forty articles, all on great and momentous themes pertaining to the common salvation. In this way alone, addressing each month not far from two hundred thousand families, he conveyed messages of Christian love to millions of men quite beyond the reach of his preaching or other written works." Hall, *Letters*, 2:236–37.
72. "James Waddell Alexander," 79–80.

in all the places he ministered until his death in 1859. While Alexander's participation in the affairs of his denomination in later years was somewhat diminished, whether due to ill health or frustration with its bureaucracy, the spirit in which he approached his fellow ministers was marked by a Christlike disposition that won the respect and affection of those with whom he disagreed, even if, in the end, it did not carry their conscience to the modification of the positions that they held.[73]

Respectful but principled in his motives and actions, Alexander embodied the ripened spiritual maturity to which every minister should aspire during times of doctrinal contention when the church's orthodoxy and very identity are at stake.[74] He was a friend to all in whom he discerned the Spirit of Christ at work—even among those outside the orbit of his own denominational heritage.[75] His catholicity of spirit served him well during times of doctrinal duress, even as it prepared him to minister with effectiveness amidst New York City's diverse denominational groupings in the 1840s and 1850s.

> It is more to my purpose to remark, that if he learned more than ever before of the spiritual evil of prejudice, uncharitableness, bigotry—more of the weakness of good men under the excitement of the best motives—more of the evils of strife and contention—more of the importance of the mind's being well grounded in sound doctrine as to all essential truth, and the heart at the same time moulded to the love

---

73. New School Presbyterian minister Albert Barnes eulogized Alexander's charitable interaction with his fellow clergy: "Though enrolled with the Old School branch of the Presbyterian Church, he had no bitterness of spirit towards his brethren of the other branch, or towards any Christians of any denomination. He was not indifferent to truth, or those views of truth by which the Presbyterian body is separated from other denominations of Christians; but my apprehension is, that he regarded those distinctions as of much less importance than the great doctrines of Christianity, in which all are united. I regard him as a man who was eminently qualified to commend religion, pure, simple, spiritual, kind, charitable, heavenly, as we find it in the New Testament, to his fellow men." Cited in Calhoun, *Faith and Learning*, 1:380.

74. Alexander's catholicity of spirit is evident in a letter in March 1848: "I believe I make less of [ecclesiastical] differences than I did. Though a reunion with the New School body, just as it is, would be unedifying, and a signal for unprecedented squabbles and disciplines, I think there are many among them with whom we ought to maintain the most brotherly correspondence." Hall, *Letters*, 2:81–82.

75. "The Christian grace of love or charity seldom has a more consistent and constant exemplification than was shown in him; nor is one often found, who, with such firm opinions, unites such freedom from bigotry, and such a disposition to approve and enjoy whatever has the appearance of good, and can be used for good, wherever it is found. His heart could not make an enemy or lose a friend." "James Waddell Alexander," 80.

and charity of the gospel, then his own painful exercises during that crisis were parts of his discipline for the defence and exemplification of that meekness and forbearance towards all who love the Lord Jesus Christ in sincerity, which marked his intercourse, in the large field of this city, with evangelical ministers and Christians of every name, and his sympathy with every project which his judgment approved, where co-workers of all such denominations were combined. How truly catholic was his spirit was shown, not in the declamations of the public platform, nor perhaps in making what is called the union principle a point of zeal as always the best system of doing good, so much as in his freedom as an ecclesiastic from prejudice and envy, and more especially in his love of holding fellowship with, and deriving instruction from, the unlimited host of good men and practical and devotional writers of all ages and connections. Wherever there was warmth, earnestness, simplicity—wherever there was the spirit of Christ, there was his heart and hand, and I may emphatically add, his voice; singing with Wesley, or Luther, or Gerhardt, or even from the breviary, as frequently as with Toplady or Watts; and literally praying "with all prayer and supplication," wherever, in old time or in late, in written form or in the gush of the rudest unpremeditation, he found disciples whom Jesus had taught how to pray.[76]

Hall's statement about Alexander's catholicity of spirit serves to further explain the widespread influence that he attained in the communities where he ministered.

> It was the fruit of this enlarged and comprehensive spirit of charity that we are called upon to have in remembrance now, after his decease, for our own following, as he in it so followed Christ. You have seen how this spirit won his way among all Christian people, gained their confidence, disarmed sectarian mistrust in hearing or reading him, and thus multiplied the number of those who will ever bless God for such a minister and author. In his practice he gave great weight to the axiom: "The servant of the Lord must not strive, but be gentle to all men...patient: in meekness instructing those that would oppose themselves" (2 Tim. 2).[77]

---

76. Hall, *Sermons*, 48–49.
77. Hall, *Sermons*, 49–50.

Debtor to All

In his funeral oration for Alexander, Hall took time to review Alexander's pastoral devotion to his congregation and the needs of the city's population. Alexander lived a life of self-sacrificing service on behalf of others. The spiritual needs and physical burdens of the community in which he lived were constantly before him, and his passion for both remained undiminished. Not a day passed that Alexander was not seeking some means of addressing these concerns. His heart was bent upon alleviating the troubles that confronted them. Although tasked with the pastoral care of a large and growing congregation, his focus never turned inward but always remained directed to the respective needs of both church and community, even at the cost of great personal sacrifice. As Hall summarized:

> I deliberately pronounce it a great work, and great not only in the scheme of it, but in its accomplishment. For when we take into consideration what it was to form a new congregation here; to fill this spacious edifice; to gather a band of seven hundred communicants; to form and maintain a successful Mission church; to attract and keep a large body of young men; to not merely win the acceptance, but engage the co-operation of so many, of every age, in his enterprises of doing good; to enlist so much zeal, and to draw out so much liberality; to satisfy such a miscellaneous multitude of hearers; to establish a name and influence outside of his own people, and acknowledged by the community of all classes and denominations— I say, this, that by the favour of God he accomplished, was a great work, in a little time. These walls, this registry of communicants and pew-holders, would not define the limits of your pastor's zeal, or of his success. His soul suffered at the sight of the destitutions, bodily, social, and spiritual, of the large population of this city, and was always praying to know what he should do for them, and sighing that so little seemed possible. Willingly would he have thrown open all these seats for the poor. He longed to see the day when churches should be as free as the parks of the streets to all who would come in. Never was he more animated than when originating or assisting some method of reaching the ignorant, degraded, neglected. His philanthropy was more than a lament, a prayer, a whine, a pulpit theory, an anniversary oration, a newspaper rhapsody. He not only talked, but acted, and not only acted, but loved to act; was not only skillful in directing the benevolence of others, but was himself benevolent, and often did the part of benevolence which is far more laborious and self-denying than that which is accomplished

by mere giving—though it is not too much to say that his own personal unpublished charities were fully equal, according to the scale of means, to what his influence obtained from others.[78]

For the Rising Generation
Alexander's personal commitment to a life of principled piety also finds public expression in the manner in which he exercised his pastoral ministry among the children of his congregation. He loved the children of his charge and those of the surrounding community. He was burdened with their spiritual needs and sought to communicate with them on their level of understanding.[79] While speaking of Alexander's labors on behalf of the Duane Street Church and later that of the Fifth Avenue Presbyterian Church, Hall reminded his hearers of Alexander's efforts in the writing of children's books and outreach to the youth of the city. Alexander's enthusiasm for the children and youth of his congregation and community began to find expression during his pastorate at Trenton and in the numerous publications he provided for the American Sunday-School Union over the course of his lifetime.

> He was then also employed in that series of writings for the young and for the plans which specially contemplate their benefit, which gave him, for the rest of his life, an intimate connection with the American Sunday School Union. This predisposition and its cultivation by him, deserve to be remembered among the means of his pastoral efficiency. You know how he loved your children; how he sought to do them good; what anxieties he showed for the youth of his congregation, with all their privileges, and for the youth of this city, with all their exposures and destitutions. You know how he worked and pleaded for the promotion of religious instruction and early piety here, and for the excitement of every patriotic, philanthropic, and religious motive to provide for the universal extension of Christian education. None know better than the children and the young men here, how he loved the souls of youth, yearned for their salvation and trembled for their perils. This object always gave a direction to his labours, caused

---

78. Hall, *Sermons*, 56–57.
79. Alexander recognized that the strength of the church and the moral fiber of the nation both depended on a pious citizenry. Early inculcation of biblical instruction was deemed essential for nurture of personal piety and its subsequent expression in the public sector.

him to simplify his presentation of truth, and increased the tenderness of his spirit towards his people as families.[80]

Preaching

Of the many qualities for which Alexander was renowned, it may be his instruction on preaching and published sermons for which he is most remembered. Although as a young man Alexander doubted his competency for preaching, his gifts for ministry matured with the passing of the years such that by the time of his death in 1859 he was recognized as one of the greatest preachers of his day.[81]

A number of factors contributed to Alexander's theology of preaching. First, and perhaps foremost, is the example that his father provided in his formative years and throughout the remainder of his adult life. Archibald Alexander was honored by many of his contemporaries as one of the most powerful preachers of the early nineteenth century. Appreciative of the experiential preaching heritage embodied in such men as George Whitefield, William Tennent, the Blairs, and Samuel Davies, Archibald Alexander's extemporaneous style of preaching won great acclaim among both Southern and Northern audiences alike.

From his earliest days throughout his teenage years, J. W. Alexander had the privilege of sitting under his father's pulpit ministry, learning through observation as well as by experience the felt realities of Spirit-anointed preaching. While he may not have been able to appreciate all that took place during these moments until his conversion at age seventeen, a foundation had been laid in his understanding of the beauties of the Reformed experiential preaching heritage.

---

80. Hall, *Sermons*, 40–41.
81. Words spoken at a memorial dedication summarize Alexander's widespread acceptance as a preacher: "The pulpit of New York has had more thrilling orators, and more brilliant pyrotechnists; but it never held a more symmetric, scholarly, spiritual, and satisfying minister of Jesus Christ than James W. Alexander. The word to describe him is—*satisfying*. He satisfied the intellect; he satisfied the purest taste; he satisfied the conscience; he fed the innermost soul of the devout believer; and it is no ordinary achievement to have equally satisfied the culture of Fifth Avenue, and the company of humble negroes who clung to him in the Witherspoon Street Chapel. If to-day both those surviving congregations could come to pay their homage before this tablet, I am sure that my departed friend would value more the 'two mites' of poor old 'Aunt Flora,' the negro woman, than all the costlier tributes of Murray Hill millionaires." Cuyler, "James Waddell Alexander D. D. Address," 21–22.

Alexander's study of rhetoric as a student and later as a professor also served to further his understanding of the principles and practice of public and persuasive speech through the written page, public oratory, and the pulpit ministry of the Christian church. Having taught the subject of composition, Alexander was familiar with ancient and modern treatments in the field of rhetoric. Similar in approach to his father and that of Samuel Miller—both of whom delivered lectures on preaching and pastoral care to the students at Princeton Theological Seminary in its early years—Alexander adapted the thinking of the best writers on rhetoric while suffusing their instruction on the mechanics of written composition and public oratory with a theology of public speaking that was all rooted in the Bible's teaching on the distinctive qualities and characteristics of the divine-human activity of Spirit-anointed gospel preaching.

In addition to his exposure to great preaching and formal study of the principles of effective speech, Alexander's impact as a preacher was rooted in an intimacy of fellowship with Christ and its influence upon the life of piety to which he was committed. For all the benefits that accompany formal instruction in sermon composition and delivery, something more is necessary for powerful preaching that cannot be found apart from a lively, growing, experiential piety in union with Christ. Hodge understood this factor, and drew attention to it in an extended statement found in his funeral oration on behalf of Alexander:

> But how was he so eminently fitted thus to preach? His first and most important, and, indeed, indispensable qualification for this work was, that he himself knew Christ. He had not only that knowledge which is attained by the study of the Scriptures, and learning what is therein revealed concerning the person and work of Christ, but that knowledge which is due to the inward revelation by the Spirit. Paul says that it pleased God to reveal his Son in him, that he might preach him among the Gentiles. He does not refer here to the outward manifestation of Christ which arrested him on his journey to Damascus, but to an inward revelation therewith connected. It was a spiritual illumination by which he was enabled to see the glory of God in the face of Jesus Christ. One glimpse of that glory transformed the blaspheming persecutor into the humble, adoring, devoted servant of the Lord Jesus. It was such a revelation that made your pastor what he was. Without this, all his other gifts had been of no account.

It is, however, an instructive fact, that the apostle who labored, suffered, and accomplished more than all the others, was the one most richly endowed with natural abilities and acquired knowledge. When these gifts are relied upon, and especially when they are made the ground of self-glorification, they are like the fire of thorns, brilliant and noisy, but which soon goes out in darkness, leaving nothing but ashes to be scattered by the wind. But when their possessor feels as Paul felt, that he is nothing, and can do nothing; when he relies, not on his powers of persuasion, but solely upon the demonstration of the Spirit, then God condescends to use them for his own glory and for the edification of the church.[82]

Effective preaching, as Hodge properly notes, is directly related to the character of the man. While extraordinary gifts of public speech may augment a minister's effectiveness in preaching, the more important matter is the underlying issue of a man's piety, or spirituality. Pious men embody the fragrance of Christ in their personal lives and public ministry. Their pulpit ministrations share this quality, and their preaching is often accompanied by a supernatural power in a sermon's delivery and reception by one's hearers. Natural gifts notwithstanding, pulpit proclamation of this kind has less to do with natural talent than of a Spirit-wrought empowerment that comes from outside the man upon his preaching and the commensurate experience of the same in the hearts and minds of the hearers as the Word of God comes with quickening and convicting power upon their souls.

This Spirit-wrought anointing was what gave life and power to Alexander's pulpit ministrations in the experiential and applicatory manner in which he preached "Christ and him crucified." Hodge's remarks provide an inspiring summary of why Alexander's preaching was so well received in the many places in which he ministered and at the Fifth Avenue Presbyterian Church in particular:

The pulpit was his appropriate sphere. There all his gifts and graces, all his acquirements and experiences, found full scope. Hence the remarkable variety which characterized his preaching; which was sometimes descriptive or graphic, bringing scriptural scenes and incidents as things present before the mind; often exegetical, unfolding the meaning of the word of God in its own divine form.

---

82. Hall, *Sermons*, 11–12.

Hence, too, the vivacity of thought, the felicity of style, and fertility of illustration which were displayed in all his sermons. He could adapt himself to any kind of audience. When a Professor in the College, he acted as voluntary pastor of an African church in Princeton, and we have heard him say that he regarded the sermons which he preached to that congregation the best he ever delivered. As we remarked in the commencement of this discourse, he preached Christ in a manner which seemed to many altogether peculiar. He endeavoured to turn the minds of men away from themselves, and to lead them to look only unto Jesus. He strove to convince his hearers that the work of salvation had been accomplished for them, and was not to be done by them; that their duty was simply to acquiesce in the work of Christ, assured that the subjective work of sanctification is due to the objective work of Christ, as appropriated by faith and applied by the Holy Ghost. He thus endeavoured to cut off the delays, anxieties, and misgiving which arise from watching the exercises of our own minds, seeking in what we inwardly experience a warrant for accepting what is outwardly offered to the chief of sinners, without money and without price. He was eminently successful in his ministry, not only in the conversion of sinners, but in comforting and edifying believers. The great charm of his preaching, that to which more than to anything else its efficiency is to be referred, was his power over the religious affections. He not only instructed, encouraged, and strengthened his hearers, but he had, to a remarkable degree, the gift of calling their devotional feelings into exercise. In his prayers there were those peculiar intonations to which the Spirit of God alone can attune the human voice, and at the sound of which the gates of heaven seem to unfold and the worshippers above and the worshippers on earth mingle together, in prostrate adoration. Your religious services under his ministry, were truly seasons of devotion, the highest form of enjoyment vouchsafed to men on earth. The man who can give us this enjoyment, who can thus raise our hearts to God, and bring us into communion with our Saviour, we reverence and love. This is a power which no one envies, from which no one wishes to detract, which surrounds its possessor with a sacred halo, attracting all eyes and offending none.[83]

Perhaps more than anyone else, Hodge summarized the defining characteristics of Alexander's legacy in a way true to his attainments and

---

83. Hall, *Sermons*, 18–20.

the spiritual priorities that shaped his life and flowed forth in his public ministry. Hodge writes:

> Dr. Alexander's pre-eminence, therefore, was due not to any one gift alone; not to his natural abilities, to his varied scholarship, to his extensive theological knowledge and religious experience; not to his divine unction, or to his graces of elocution. It was the combination of all these which made him, not the first of orators to hear on rare occasions, but the first of preachers to sit under, month after month and year after year.[84]

****

The life and ministry of James W. Alexander remains as a standing testimony to the grace of God in the manner by which he was prepared, shaped, and sustained in the work to which he had been appointed on Christ's behalf. The narrative of Alexander's life bears witness to the way in which God can overcome the natural impediments in a man's character and use him mightily in His service to the untold blessing of thousands, if not tens of thousands, of lives.

If there is a lesson to learn from Alexander's life for those who may be called to the work of the Christian ministry today, it surely is to be found in the personal devotional commitment to Christ that Alexander first made as a young man and continued to honor throughout the remainder of his lifetime. Although one of the most learned men of his generation, Alexander's intellect was early put to the service of Christ's church and the needs of the communities in which he served. Alexander knew that his life was not his own to do with as he pleased. He recognized the hand of God upon him and sought to use the natural talents and spiritual gifts with which he had been entrusted in the ministerial calling to which he had been set apart.[85]

While men of lesser talents may be envious of Alexander's multifarious gifts, the same effectiveness in ministry is available to anyone who devotes their heart to the living out of Christ's claims upon their life. As

---

84. Hall, *Sermons*, 20.
85. "Oh! at how many points my honored friend touched human life! Touched its rich and varied scholarship—touched the sympathies of sorrow's home—touched the highest reach of society and its lowliest—and touched every key of devout emotion! All his splendid attainments, all his many-sided and multiform life-work, he laid as an humble offering before the Throne." Cuyler, "James Waddell Alexander D. D. Address," 25–26.

with all Christian growth, the principled practice of personal piety lies at the heart of spiritual maturation and effectiveness in ministerial service. The disposition of devotion that underlays all that Alexander was committed to in his private life, home environment, and public ministry gives explanation for the profound influence of his pastoral labors in the churches and communities in which he labored.

Personal Bible study, prayer, and a worshipful orientation kept Alexander's spiritual vision clear and set on the kingdom horizons to which all Christ's people are to set their gaze. Likewise, his strong commitment to the Reformed confessional heritage in which he grew up, embraced as a Christian, and took formal vows to uphold as a minister all grounded his work in the orthodox theological heritage of his Presbyterian forefathers and the rich experiential preaching and pastoral emphases which it represented. Alexander viewed all his labors through a doctrinal lens. His theology of preaching and practice of pastoral ministry were rooted in the doctrinal affirmations that found expression in the Westminster Confession of Faith and its Larger and Shorter Catechisms.

For Alexander, the proper understanding of theology comes to expression in its experiential and practical application to the lives of God's people. Suffused with love for Christ, the church, and the needs of the lost, Alexander's pastoral leadership was merely the natural outflow of Christ's resurrection life pulsating through His servant's willingness to be used in his Master's service in whatever way would bring Christ the most glory.

The example of such a man is sure to have a profound effect upon those around him. Alexander's childlike faith, unaffected simplicity of devotion, pastoral transparency, deepening humility in the life of piety, and willingness to have his life spent in the service of others won the affection of his congregations, students, and communities where he labored. Alexander not only loved *as* Christ loved, but he also loved *that* which Christ loved. The fragrance of Christ's presence in his life was experienced by those who were the recipients of his pastoral attention. It drew them to entrust themselves to Alexander's ministry, and, even more importantly, the Savior of whom he preached and invited men to embrace as their own.

Men such as Alexander live on in the hearts and memories of their peers and remain an example of pastoral fortitude and devotion long after their earthly bodies have turned to dust. The rich pastoral legacy of

Alexander's personal life and public ministry found in his published and unpublished writings will still prove valuable for every man desirous of learning more of how Christ takes the brokenness of this present world and transforms it in the commissioning of men to be his representatives in the high calling of Christian ministry.

Charles Hodge's closing remarks, delivered at the commemorative services held on behalf of Alexander in October 1859, remind us of the Christ-centered focus that characterized Alexander's personal devotion, pulpit proclamation, and pastoral practice—a focus which he also invited his congregants to pursue, and one which those called to the office of the Christian ministry are bidden to follow in today if they would see God's blessing poured forth upon their pastoral labors as it was in the life of Alexander:

> The death of such a man is an irreparable loss. God indeed will raise up other instruments to carry on his work, but no one can ever supply his place to his immediate relatives, to his life-long friends, and to his children in the faith. They all must carry with them to the grave a wound which knows no healing. Such sorrow, however, is not like the sorrow of the world, which worketh death. It is the tribute which we willingly pay to those we love. It is not inconsistent with joy and gratitude in the remembrance of all that he was to us and to the church. He was one of the blessed of the Lord. Blessed in his parentage, in his early conversion, in his abundant gifts, in his long-continued and eminent usefulness, in the admiration, love, and confidence of the people of God. He has finished his course, he kept the faith, and henceforth there is laid up for him a crown of righteousness which the Lord the righteous Judge will give him at that day.
>
> In view of such a life and such a destiny, earthly distinctions sink into nothing. No man is so hardened, that he would not a thousand times prefer to be what your beloved pastor was and is, than to possess all of wealth and power the world has to give.
>
> As this discourse began with the name of Christ, so let it end. The worship of Christ is our religion; the service of Christ our loyal duty; and the enjoyment of Christ is our heaven. The sum and substance of the preaching ever heard within these walls, is, that Christ is the only source of truth, of righteousness, of holiness, and of eternal life, so that we are complete in him. To him, therefore, be honour and glory, might, majesty, and dominion, world without end. Amen.[86]

---

86. Hall, *Sermons*, 21–22.

Appendix 1

Presbyterial Charge: 1841

Invested as you have just been with the most sacred office known among men, you feel it, I doubt not, to be the most solemn hour of life, one to which you will look back with profound interest during all your pilgrimage—perhaps in your dying moments—and certainly from the eternal world. And whether the retrospect be one of joy or grief will depend on the manner in which you shall have fulfilled these vows. If you perform the duties of a gospel-minister with faithfulness, to the end of your course, you will shine as a star in the firmament of glory; but if you turn aside, seduced by sloth, fear, pleasure, literary or professional fame, ambition or lucre, your account will be as dreadful as your privilege is great.

Consider what it is that you have vowed. To be zealous and faithful in maintaining the truths of the gospel, and the purity and peace of the church, whatever persecution or opposition may arise to you on that account;—to be faithful and diligent in the exercise of all personal and private duties which become you as a Christian, and a minister of the gospel; as well as in all relative duties, and the public duties of your office; endeavouring to adorn the profession of the gospel by your conversation; and walking with exemplary piety before the flock over which God hath made you a bishop. And, finally, and specially, to discharge the duties of a pastor to this congregation.

These, my brother, are the duties which you have just now recognized as yours; and I am appointed to charge you, yea in God's name, solemnly to charge you to persevere in them. But why need I enlarge upon them? It is not the knowledge of our duties which is most needed, but the heart to perform them. We all know more than we do, and little would be gained if I were to rehearse to you the contents of all the volumes on the pastoral care. These you might know, and yet be a cast-away. But to *do* them is what only the Spirit of God in your heart will ever ensure. There is only one thing which will make you, and keep you a faithful pastor, and that is the new nature in vigorous life; evincing itself in love to Christ, and love to souls. Take heed, therefore, to *thyself,* as well as to all the flock over which the Holy Ghost hath made thee bishop, to feed the church of God, which he hath purchased with his own blood. Take heed unto *thyself,* and unto the doctrine; continue in them; for in doing this thou shalt both *save thyself,* and them that hear thee. Though you are a minister, it does not follow that you are a member of Christ. I am sure I speak your own convictions when I say, that all ministerial activity and success is hollow and deceptive, which does not flow from inward experience of the divine life. Without this, vanity is stamped alike on the tongues of men and of angels—on prophecy, mysteries, and all knowledge, on self-impoverishing alms and martyrdom itself. If you ever really preach Christ Jesus the Lord, it will be because God who commanded the light to shine out of darkness, shall have shined into your heart, to give you the light of the knowledge of the glory of God in the face of Jesus Christ. Have you, my dear brother, beheld that glory? Having the same spirit of faith with Paul, can you say I believed and therefore have I spoken? Does the love of Christ constrain you? Beware of preaching an unknown Saviour. It is He who is to be the theme of all your ministrations. Make sure of an interest in his death; and not only this, but strive to keep the fountain full, rather than to multiply the streams; cultivate the graces of the closet, in order that you may come forth in public and private, fresh from divine communications.

It is, after all, personal piety which makes the able minister. It is a mournful fact that the holiest services may degenerate into a routine, and we may preach and pray with hearts as dead as those of our hearers. Even the measures supposed to indicate the extremest zeal may be conducted in utter coldness and hypocrisy; and the preacher may come reeking from the heats of fanatical parades, to show in the domestic circle a frivolity and asperity, a sensuality, or a cupidity, at which even his unconverted hearers blush. O watch the fire within doors!

My brother, this is a true saying, If a man desire the office of a bishop, he desireth a good work. A bishop, then, must be blameless, the husband of one wife, vigilant, sober, of good behavior, given to hospitality, apt to teach, not given to wine, not covetous, one that ruleth well his own house, having his children in subjection with all gravity. Be thou an example of the believers, in word, in conversation, in charity, in spirit, in faith, in purity. Meditate upon these things; GIVE THYSELF WHOLLY TO THEM.

If these precepts be observed, you will the less need rules as to the details of duty. Love is wiser than rules. Love is wisdom, nay love is power. The particular measures to be adopted as to the communication of divine truth, I leave to your own Christian discretion. Love is inventive and will find out ways. Live in the Word of God; be mighty in the Scriptures; turn what you read into experience; and you will save the souls of those who hear you.

And now—May the blessing of God rest upon you, and the Spirit of Christ fill your heart! *Amen.*[1]

---

1. Hall, *Letters*, 2:305–7.

Appendix 2

"O Haupt boll Blut und Wunden"
A Passion Hymn by Paul Gerhardt

1 O Sacred head! Now wounded,
   With grief and shame weighed down,
   Now scornfully surrounded
   With thorns, thy only crown;
   O sacred Head! What glory,
   What bliss, till now was thine!
   Yet, though despised and gory,
   I joy to call thee mine.

2 O noblest brow, and dearest!
   In other days the world
   All feared, when thou appeared'st,
   What shame on thee is hurled!
   How art thou pale with anguish,
   With sore abuse and scorn;
   How does that visage languish,
   Which once was bright as morn.

3 The blushes late residing
   Upon that holy cheek,
   The roses once abiding
   Upon those lips so meek,
   Alas! they have departed;
   Wan Death has rifled all!
   For weak and broken-hearted,
   I see thy body fall.

4 What thou, my Lord, hast suffered,
   Was all for sinners' gain:
   Mine, mine was the transgression,
   But thine the deadly pain.
   Lo! Here I fall, my Saviour,
   'Tis I deserve thy place;
   Look on me with thy favor,
   Vouchsafe to me thy grace.

5 Receive me, my Redeemer,
   My Shepherd, make me thine;
   Of every good the fountain,
   Thou art the spring of mine.
   Thy lips with love distilling,
   And milk of truth sincere,
   With heaven's bliss are filling
   The soul that trembles here.

6 Beside thee, Lord, I've taken
   My place—forbid me not!
   Hence will I ne'er be shaken,
   Though thou to death be brought.
   If pain's last paleness hold thee,
   In agony opprest,
   Then, then will I enfold thee
   Within this arm and breast!

7 The joy can ne'er be spoken,
   Above all joys beside,
   When in thy body broken
   I thus with safety hide.
   My Lord of life, desiring
   Thy glory now to see,
   Beside the cross expiring,
   I'd breathe my soul to thee.

8 What language shall I borrow
   To thank thee, dearest Friend,
   For this, thy dying sorrow,
   Thy pity without end?
   Oh! make me thine forever,
   And should I fainting be,
   Lord let me never, never
   Outlive my love to thee.

9 And when I am departing,
   Oh! part not thou from me;
   When mortal pangs are darting,
   Come, Lord, and set me free;
   And when my heart must languish
   Amidst the final throe,
   Release me from mine anguish
   By thine own pain and wo!

10 Be near me when I am dying,
   Oh! show thy cross to me;
   And for my succor flying,
   Come, Lord, and set me free!
   These eyes new faith receiving,
   From Jesus shall not move,
   For he who dies believing,
   Dies safely through thy love.[1]

---

1. Alexander, *Breaking Crucible*, 7–10.

Index

abolitionism, 91n22, 150, 158–59, 304n73, 314
academic learning, 32, 106–8, 257–58
Academy of Music, 349
accountability, 13
actual preparation, 382–83
affections, 24, 29, 313, 404
affliction, 2, 27, 76, 93–94, 123n111, 127, 168, 198, 358
African Americans, 109–10, 149, 158–59, 160, 162–63, 184, 186–89, 229–33
alcohol, 170, 174–75
Alexander, Archibald (father), vii, 1, 7, 15, 20–21, 69, 97, 100, 126n115, 141, 161, 182, 205n1, 212, 258n49, 262, 279–81, 284, 340n22, 366, 367, 401
Alexander, Archibald (son), 110n81, 146–47
Alexander, Archibald George (son), 110–11, 122, 129, 168–69
Alexander, Elizabeth (wife), 93, 122, 129
Alexander, Henry Carrington (son), 110n81, 253–54, 351, 364n6
Alexander, Janetta Waddell (mother), 7, 291, 318–19n110, 366
Alexander, James Waddell
   as a churchman, 396–98
   conversion of, 11–12
   daily schedule of, 19, 26, 75, 87n11, 128–29, 205–6
   death of, 356–60
   legacy of, 3, 406–7
   marriage of, 93
   plans for the future, 33–36
   as seminary professor, 243–64
   sore throat of, 196, 322, 333, 334
   weekly schedule of, 19, 139–40, 151
Alexander, Jessie (daughter), 279
Alexander, John (son), 226
Alexander, Joseph Addison (brother), 100, 110n81, 211–12, 350–51, 364–65, 366
Alexander, Samuel (brother), 350
Alleine, Joseph, 185
American Board of Commissioners for Foreign Missions, 103
American Mechanic, The (Alexander), 101–2, 169
American Quarterly Review, 42
American Sunday-School and Its Adjuncts, The (Alexander), 266, 320–21
American Sunday School Union, 95–96, 99, 133, 135, 169n96, 173, 400
ancient languages, 69
angst, 77
antebellum culture, 11n13, 79n20, 229–30
antinomianism, 190
antitemperance movement, 174–75
anxiety, 199, 220, 221–22, 364–65
anxious meetings, 117, 118, 121
anxious seat, 84, 111–12n85, 121
apologetics, 41–42, 169–70
apostolic preaching, 100n54, 310, 390n57
Arminianism, 52

atonement, viii, 31, 113, 218, 337
Augustine, 252, 322, 374

bachelorhood, 77, 153
Bacon, Francis, 56, 211, 283
Baltimore, MD, 64–65
banking industry, 345–46
Baptists, 157, 363
Barnes, Albert, 99, 112–16, 397n73
Barrow, Isaac, 144, 145
Baxter, Richard, 56, 144, 172, 185, 193
Beecher, Lyman, 304n73
Beeke, Joel, 20n13
belief, 24, 53
bereavement, 153, 197–98, 371
Bernard of Clairvaux, viii
Bible. *See* Scripture
Biblical Repertory, 69, 89, 92, 100, 106, 115n90, 147–48, 150–51, 216, 257, 371–72, 396
bile secretions, 88
biography, 42–43, 252, 259, 281, 296
birthday reflections, 73–74
Blair, Hugh, 140–41, 215n38
body, and soul, 46
books, 85–86, 222–24
Bowdoin Street Church, 200–201
Boyce, James P., 260n54
Brainerd, David, 118, 132
Breaking Crucible and Other Translations of German Hymns, The (Alexander), 102
Breckinridge, John, 160
brevity of life, 33–36, 87
Brown, C. J., 273
Brown, John, 304n73
Brown, Thomas, 31
Bruce, John, 329, 330
budget, 234–35, 322n120
burial, 363
Burke, Edmund, 76
Butler, Charles, 81n28
Butler, Joseph, 42

Cabell, James L., 354, 355, 356–59
calling, 12, 58, 59, 60, 181–82, 365, 374–75, 392
Calvin, John, 20n13, 21, 97, 165, 178, 180, 270–71, 295, 384n42

Calvinism, 52, 156
Cambridge University, 49
Campbell, George, 141
Candor, James Montgomery, 248–49
Carnahan, James, 9
catechisms, 3, 31–32, 206, 227, 236n97, 273–74, 285–86, 289, 366, 385, 406
cathedrals, 269–70
catholicity, 284, 397–98
Cedar Street church, 63
Chalmers, Thomas, 30n29, 57, 60, 296
Charlotte County, VA, 68–70, 186
Charlotte Court-House Church, 73–82, 162–63, 176
Charnock, Stephen, 156, 167
childlike faith, 30, 124, 278, 406
children, 110–11, 146–47, 174, 225–28, 310–11, 312, 400
children's literature, 129–30, 150
choirs, 238, 293, 299, 311, 330
cholera, 238, 275, 284n16, 298
Christendom, 91
Christian biography, 42–43, 252, 296
Christian growth, 155–56, 214, 405–6
Christianity, divine origin of, 260–61
Christian literature, 222–24
church government, 320
church growth, 121, 122–23, 237, 287, 315–18, 342
church history, 21, 191–92, 245, 246–47, 250–53
church polity, 151–52
Cicero, 74–75, 140, 177, 391–92
city missions, 296–97
Clarke, Samuel, 31
Clarkson, Thomas, 91n22
classics, 14–15, 369, 386
"class meetings," 118–19
Coleridge, Samuel Taylor, 143, 208, 211
College of New Jersey, 1, 6, 9, 24, 27, 40–43, 136, 139, 342n28, 366, 369–70
Cologne, 272
Comfort, Daniel, 9
communion, 220–21
confessional statements, 100n54, 112–13, 385, 406
conflict, 148, 218, 378
Congregationalism, 201, 363

Consolation: In Discourses on Select Topics, Addressed to the Suffering People of God (Alexander), 293–94
construction, 311
consumption, 86
conversion, 11–12, 22–24
corruption, 165
cotton, 68n14, 79
covenant of grace, 153–54
Cowper, William, 2, 47–48, 81, 194–95
Crawford, George W., 10
creation, 271–72, 355n78
criticism, 173, 257–58
cultural differences, 79
"culture of the heart," 212–13
Cunningham, William, 195–96
Cuyler, Theodore L., ix, 141n10, 395n69, 401n81, 405n85

Dabney, R. L., 343
Danville College, 95
D'Aubigne, J. H. Merle, 191–92
Davies, Samuel, 21, 56, 57, 401
death, 28–29, 33, 72, 76, 80, 86–87, 221
   of Archibald Alexander, 280–81, 284
   of Archibald George, 146–47
   of Hall's wife, 91–93
   of Janetta Waddell Alexander, 291
   of J. W. Alexander, 356–60
   of Samuel Miller, 254–55
debate societies, 21
demon possession, 352
denominations, 397
depression, 26, 351, 354
despair, 76–77, 87–88
devotion, 375–76
dialect, 64
didactic style of preaching, 145, 161
didactic theology, 370
discipleship, 50, 104–5, 146–47
Discourses on Common Topics of Christian Faith and Practice, 324, 344–45
disillusionment, 88, 89
Disruption of 1843, 195
Divine monition, 352
division, 135, 158–59, 247
doctrinal error, 337–38
doctrine, 161–62, 214, 317

Dod, A. B., 164
Doddridge, Phillip, 98, 374
drunkenness, 175
Duane Street Church (New York City), 198–203, 245–46, 261–64, 281n8, 400
Dutch Reformed, 273, 363

eccentricity, 16, 18, 177
ecclesiology, 201
editor, 133–36, 368
Edwards, Jonathan, 21, 41, 49, 56, 117–18, 121
elderly, 170
elders, 206n10, 320
Elizabeth, Charlotte, 194
eloquence, 12–13, 141, 215n38, 292
emancipation, 187–89, 231–32
Emerson, Ralph Waldo, 208, 211
emotions, 79, 80, 182–83, 226, 227n71, 340
employment, 302–3
England, 268, 275–76, 325
entertainment, 210, 315
Episcopalians, 363
Erasmus, Desiderius, 178
eternity, 34, 87, 123, 313
European trips, 267–76, 325–31, 333
evangelism, 236
exegesis, 383
exercise, 26
experience, 20–21, 222
experimental piety, 305
expository preaching, 384
extemporaneous prayer, 159–60
extemporaneous preaching, 20–21, 66–67, 75, 141, 211–12, 388–90

faith, 12, 30, 120, 126, 127, 146, 278
family, 366
family worship, 226–28
fatherhood, 224–28
fatigue, 181n135, 248, 291, 343, 351, 378
Fifth Avenue Presbyterian Church (New York City), 281–323, 333–44, 400, 403–4
financial crisis, 345–46
financial security, 59
financial support, 307–8

Finney, Charles, 111, 116, 166, 208, 210, 214, 258–59, 341
First Presbyterian Church of Colour of Princeton, 149, 159, 176, 184, 370
First Presbyterian Church of Trenton, 85–136
Flavel, John, 156, 193
foreign languages, 69
foreign policy, 308
formal attire, 235
France, 268–70
Free Church of Scotland, 195, 216, 301–2
friendship, 18, 25, 28, 36, 45, 82
Fugitive Slave Law, 304
Fuller, Andrew, 43, 54–55
Fyler, Jared D., 9

General Assembly (1837), 158
General Assembly (1842), 189
Geneva, 270–72, 328
Gerhardt, Paul, 102, viii, 179–80, 413–15
German hymnology, 238
German immigrants, 289
German metaphysics, 163–65
German Protestants, 179–80
Germany, 272
gifts, 12, 391, 392, 403
God
    grace of, 405
    mercy of, 25, 36, 52, 76–77, 126
    providence of, 176, 243, 250
godliness, 19, 29, 51
gospel ministry, 12
    calling to, 58, 60
    and missions, 105
    and slavery, 232–33
gospel overtures, 52–57
Great Awakening, 231n83
Green, Ashbel, 9–10, 112, 115, 116n92, 194
grief, 226
Griffin, Edward Dorr, 145n30
Grotius, Hugo, 81n28
growth, 19, 119, 155–56, 173, 210, 220, 224, 300, 406
Guthrie, Thomas, 329–30

habitual preparation, 382–83, 389
Haldane, Robert, 191
Hall, John, 3, 10–12, 17, 138, 364
    conversion of, 22–24, 36, 52–57, 94–95
    death of daughter, 167–68
    death of wife, 91–93
    friendship with, 45, 82
    and legal profession, 34, 35–36, 75–76
    and pastoral ministry, 108
    preaching style of, 182–83
Hall, Robert, 144
Halsted, James M., 354
Hamilton, James, 9
Hampden Sidney College, 8
happiness, 17n3, 25, 81, 373, 378–79, 381
Hart, Joseph, 180
health, 193–94, 244, 248, 262, 333–34, 352–57
helplessness, 47
Hengstenberg, Ernst W., 103, 104
Henry, Matthew, 114n88
heresy, 148–49, 337
Hodge, A. A., 140
Hodge, Charles, vii, 14–15, 17, 19, 69, 89, 97, 140, 182, 193, 196–97, 314n100, 364, 369, 393n66, 402–5, 407
holiness, 312, 377, 378
Holland, 272–73
"Holy Flock, The" (Alexander), 336, 338
Holy Spirit
    agency of, 337–38
    illumination of, 52, 54
    Owen on, 98
    power of, 215, 380
    transformation of, 335
    work of, 116–18, 348–49
Home, Henry, 140
Homer, 14, 194
honesty, 218
hopelessness, 76–77
hospitality, 65–66
housing, 202–3, 238
Howe, John, 98, 144n26, 239
human reason, 54

Hume, David, 31
humility, 262
hymns, 47, 51n35, 102, 170–71, 179–80, 224, 238, 249, 395n69
hypocrisy, 377

idleness, 16, 78
idolatry, 269
ignorance, 34, 68, 337, 340n22, 371
illness, 33, 43, 76, 86, 122–30, 185, 193–94, 196, 221–22, 305–7, 352–57
immaturity, 34, 40, 45, 48, 366
indifference, 35, 61, 210, 282
ingratitude, 48
inheritance, 125
integration, 158–59, 232
Islam, 50

Jesus Christ
  character of, 147–48, 260–61
  communion with, 119
  death of, 217–18
  face of, 402, 410
  resurrection of, 358, 406
  suffering of, 124–25, 394
jokes, 212
Jones, Charles Colcock, 232n85
joy, 29, 147
justice, viii, 52, 231

kingdom of God, xi–xii, 23, 30n29, 33, 104, 275–76, 283, 406
knowledge, 23

labor, 302–3
Lamb, Charles, 213, 395n69
Lanphier, Jeremiah, 346
Law, William, 55–56
laypeople, 348, 385
learning, 385–87
legal profession, 34, 35–36, 75–76
Leibniz, Gottfried Wilhelm, 31
Leighton, Robert, 97–98, 374
Letters to a Younger Brother (Alexander), 142
levity, 16
liberal arts program, 106–8
Liberia, 68
library, 85
licentiate, 63–70

life, brevity of, 33–36, 87
Life of Archibald Alexander, D. D., The (Alexander), 301
Life of David Brainerd, The (Edwards), 49
lifestyle, 19, 50, 65, 79, 232
literary culture, 32
Literary Register, 42
liturgy, 308
Livingston, John, 280
Locke, John, 14
London, 326–28
loneliness, 77, 94, 334
Lord's Day, 364n5. *See also* Sabbath keeping
love, 411
Luther, Martin, 21, 98, 99n44, 179, 190, 192, 256, 260, 384n42

manipulation, 117–18, 184, 298, 316
"man-stealing," 230–31
marriage, 93–94, 133–34
Martyn, Henry, 49–50, 132
Mason, Lowell, 299
M'Cheyne, Robert Murray, 210n27, 211, 228n75
McIvor, Colin, 189
means of grace, 121
melancholy, 2, 26–27, 45–49, 393–94
Melanchthon, Philip, 178
memorial services, 363–64
Methodists, 56, 118, 134, 157, 176, 207, 363
Mexico, 233–34
millennial optimism, 102–3
Miller, Samuel, 15, 20–21, 141, 196, 239–40, 249–50, 253–55, 367, 402
ministerial office, glory of, 376
misanthropy, 26n21
missions, 102–5, 233–38
Moderatism, 208–9, 236
Monod, Adolphe, 268
Monroe doctrine, 308
mood swings, 89–90
morality, 188
Moravians, 51
Murray, Iain H., 121n104, 209n20
Muslims, 50

National Gazette, The, 42
nature, 127–28
Nettleton, Asahel, 80
New England, 305, 330
New Haven theology, 210
New Measures, 90n20, 111, 118, 120–21, 149, 165–66, 216, 298, 316–18, 335
New School, 112, 113, 135, 148, 158, 207, 214
newspapers, 177–78
Newton, John, 81
New York City, 90, 198–203, 234–35, 335–49, 371

occult spirituality, 288
old age, 88, 170
Old School, 112, 119–20, 133, 135, 138, 158, 397n73
Onesimus, 231
optimism, 275–76, 284–85, 313
ordinary means of grace, 121
ordination, 69–70
organ, 311
original sin, 113
orthodoxy, 113–14, 121n104, 164, 170, 337–38, 397
"O Sacred Head Now Wounded" (Gerhardt), 102, 413–15
overwork, 365
Ovid, 177
Owen, John, 97–98

pageantry, 270
pain, 283–84, 306–7
parenting, 174, 224–28
pastoral ministry
  cost of, 305–8
  obstacles to, 208–11
  office of, 39–40
  preparation for, 57–61, 382–83
  reflections on, 217–22
pastoral visitation, 65, 66, 110, 183
pastor's study, 388
pathetic style of preaching, 145
patience, 283n13
Payson, Edward, 118
Pearce, Samuel, 43
Pelagianism, 337

perfectionism, 258
perseverance, 409
personality, 2, 40n5, 312
personality conflicts, 218
personal piety, 410
Petersburg, VA, 65–67
pews, 234–35, 289–90, 294, 295, 316, 344, 368
Philadelphia, 8–9
Phillips, William W., 249
philosophy, 30–31, 164–65
piety, 4, 19, 22, 51
  and church history, 251
  exhortations to, 27–33
  as genuine, 126, 377–78
  life of, 192
  purpose of, 394–96
  sweetness of, 67
Plan of Union, 111–12, 158
plantation subculture, 69
Plato, 164, 211, 259, 298
Plumer, William S., 93, 249
polity, 151–52, 201, 320
population growth, 237, 350
poverty, 3, 207, 282, 296, 368
power, 31, 141, 145, 215, 326, 403
Power of the Pulpit, The (Spring), 257
practicality, 396
practical theology, 223, 370, 406
pranks, 41
prayer, 152
  as extemporaneous, 159–60
  and revival, 346–47
prayer-meetings, 335, 342, 349–50
preaching
  beauty of, 379–80
  effectiveness of, 403
  as entertainment, 210
  importance of, 201n187
  observations on, 258–60
  purpose of, 172, 367
  reflections on, 211–17
  style of, 161–62, 182–83, 192–93, 196, 300, 392
  theology of, 20–21, 401
  whole counsel of God, 214, 384
premature death, 221
Presbyterian, 130, 133, 136, 368, 373

Presbyterian Church in the U. S. A., 8, 111–16, 135–36, 208, 297–98
pride, 23, 49–52, 182
Prince Edward, VA, 176
Princeton Theological Seminary, 1, 4, 367, 371, 402
   criticism toward, 257–58
   founding of, 8
   missionary societies in, 104
   nomination to faculty, 240–41
   resignation from, 262–64
   student life at, 13–15, 17–22
prison ministry, 109
private meetings, 317
privileges, 67n13
profession of faith, 6, 27
Professor of Rhetoric and Belles Lettres, 139–203, 369–70
propitiation, viii
providence, 176, 243, 250
psalms, 170–71, 179, 224
pseudonym, 101n56
public education, 143–44
public speech, 141–42
public transit, 294–95
Puritans, 21, 156, 193, 213

qualifications, 12, 34, 243–44, 402–3
Quill, Charles, 101n56
Quintilian, 140

Raikes, Robert, 95
reason, 54
recuperation, 76, 189, 194, 267, 323, 357
Red Sweet Springs (Virginia), 356
Reformation, 98–99, 178–81, 191, 227, 384n42
regeneration, 92–93, 117, 121n104, 149, 317, 338
religious affections, 29
remorse, 86
repentance, 11–12, 54–55
resurrection, 358, 406
Revival and Its Lessons, The (Alexander), 345
revivals, 80, 134
   at College of New Jersey, 256
   influence of, 90n20, 116–21, 156–58
   manipulation of, 316–18
   methodology of, 165–66
   in New York City, 333–34, 335–49
   in Princeton, 183–84
   vs. Scottish preaching, 216
   rewards, 84
rhetoric, 141–42, 215–16, 292–93, 383, 391, 402
Rice, Benjamin H., 73
Rice, John R., 63–64
Richmond, VA, 64–65, 68n14, 353
Robertson, Noel, 80–81
Roman Catholic Church, 154, 268–69, 284
Romans, 128
Russell, David, 143

Sabbath keeping, 87, 294–95, 326, 330
Sachs, Hans, 179
salary, 154, 307–8
salvation, 22, 29–30, 35, 52–57, 338
sanctification, 393–94
satisfaction, 84, 379
Schaff, Philip, 247n17
scholarship, 382
Scotland, 273–75, 329–31
Scottish preaching, 216
Scottish Presbyterianism, 384
Scougal, Henry, 56
Scripture, 31
   memorization of, 128
   reading of, 53, 155–56, 224
   on slavery, 230–32
   study of, 31, 186, 386–87
Scripture Guide: A Familiar Introduction to the Study of the Bible, The, 99
self-denial, 154, 174
self-importance, 210
self-sacrifice, 399–400
seminary housing, 18
semi-Pelagianism, 258
Seneca, 177
Serious Call to a Devout and Holy Life (Law), A, 55–56
sermon composition, 57, 142, 144–45, 171–72, 216–17, 392, 402
sermon notes, 390
Servetus, Michael, 151
sexuality, 286
Shepard, Thomas, 167

Simeon, Charles, 49
simplicity, 292, 370
sin, 25, 301
singing, 311
skepticism, 164–65
slavery
    abolition of, 91n22, 177, 304, 314
    and evangelism, 162–63, 186–89
    opposition to, 64n3, 90n20, 149–50
    Scripture on, 229–33
    and Southern culture, 67–68, 77, 79, 368
"slough of despond," 78
small groups, 118–19
Smith, Samuel Stanhope, 9
social activism, 229
social awareness, 90–91
social development, 39n3
social intercourse, 62
solitary walks, 80
sorrow, 48
soul, and body, 46
Southern culture, 65–66, 74–82
"spirit of the age," 211
spiritual growth, 19, 119, 155–56, 173, 210, 220, 224, 300, 406
spiritualism, 351–52
spirituality, 146–47
"spirituality of the church," 229
"spiritual-knocking," 288
spiritual warfare, 2, 74, 130, 378
Sprague, William B., 321
Spring, Gardiner, 165, 257–58
Spurgeon, C. H., 326–28, 339
Stowe, Harriet Beecher, 304n73
street cars, 294–95
student days, 24
submission, 52
suffering, 91, 111, 124–25, 283, 393–94
summer vacation, 292, 298, 304–5
Sunday schools, 95–96, 99, 144, 320–21, 325
Sweeney, Douglas A., 229n79, 231n83
Switzerland, 270–72
sympathy, 380
Synod of Dort, 97
systematic theology, 100–101

Talmage, Samuel K., 40n5

Taylor, Jeremy, 168
Taylor, Nathaniel, 112, 113, 144, 210
technology, 294–95
Tennent, William, 21, 401
theology, 14, 97–98, 170, 385n45, 406
Third Presbyterian Church (Philadelphia), 8
Tholuck, August, 260
Thomas, Edward, 28
Thoughts on Preaching (Alexander), 371, 372, 392–93
throat issues, 196, 322, 333, 334
time, 313
tobacco, 68n14, 79
transcendentalism, 163–65, 211
translation, 102
Trench, Richard, 307, 328
Trenton, NJ, 78–79, 81, 135
trials, 146–47, 220
tribulation, 378
Turretin, Francis, 97
tutoring, 39–45, 59n50, 367–68

unbelief, 29, 164, 285
underprivileged, 109–10, 217
Unitarianism, 211, 305
University of Virginia, 260–61, 353–54

vacation, 292, 298, 304–5
Valentine's Day, 286
Virginia, 64–65
virtue, 28
visitation, 65, 66, 110, 183

Waddel, James, vii
Warm Springs (Virginia), 355
Waterbury, Jared B., 18n5
Watson, Richard, 42, 101
Watts, Isaac, 180
Way of Life, The (Hodge), 196–97
wealth, 69, 209–10, 235, 282
Wesley, Charles, 179
Wesley, John, 21, 98–99, 118, 190, 196
Westminster Confession of Faith, 112, 385, 406
Wetmore, A. R., 298
Whately, Richard, 141
Whitefield, George, 21, 56, 190, 196, 401

White Sulphur Springs (West Virginia), 356–57
whole counsel of God, 214, 384
Wilberforce, William, 91n22, 162n79
Witherspoon Street Presbyterian Church, 159
working class, 101, 169
Working Man, The (Alexander), 101–2
worship, 19, 298–99, 308, 315, 330

writing, art of, 44–45

Yale College, 112
young ministers, 373–74

zeal, 208, 234, 236, 373–74, 399
Zinzendorf, Nicolaus, 51n35
Zwingli, Ulrich, 178, 192